FIELDS OF FRIENDLY STRIFE

THE DOUGHBOYS AND SAILORS OF THE WWI
ROSE BOWLS

TIMOTHY P. BROWN

BROWN HOUSE PUBLISHING

ISBN: 978-0-9995723-0-6 (eBook edition)

ISBN: 978-0-9995723-1-3 (Paperback edition)

ISBN: 978-0-9995723-2-0 (Hardcover edition)

Brown House Publishing: West Bloomfield, MI

❀ Created with Vellum

John W. Richmond

WWII-era paratrooper with the 82nd Airborne and head football coach at Wauwatosa East High School from 1969 to 1995 who, like many high school coaches, was an inspiration to thousands of young men and women

CONTENTS

ACKNOWLEDGEMENTS

Researching *Fields of Friendly Strife* required assistance from various colleges, universities, museums, and other organizations in locating information about the players, teams, and military units described in the book. Almost everyone I contacted proved eager and willing to help me understand the people and events of one-hundred years ago.

Annette Amerman, Branch Head and Historian, Historical Reference Branch, Marine Corps History Division, provided useful background materials on the history of Marine football on the West Coast, as well as detailed biographies of the five Mare Island Marines that became U.S.M.C. generals.

Brian Williams, Lead Bi-Centennial Archivist at the University of Michigan, helped with background information on the three Michigan alums included in this story.

Malinda Triller-Doran, Special Collections Librarian at Dickinson College provided information on two students named John Quincy Adams that attended Conway Hall, a prep school formerly associated with Dickinson College. As best as I can tell, neither is the John Quincy Adams that played for the Mare Island Marines, but the assistance was appreciated nonetheless.

Lynn Armstrong of Blackburn College's Lumpkin Learning Commons also provided assistance with background information on the unique experiences of Joseph 'Jack' Foley during his days at Blackburn.

Martin Tuhey, Archivist at the National Museum of the American Sailor located at Great Lakes Naval Training Station, also provided useful comments regarding research sources for naval personnel stationed at Great Lakes during WWI.

Marlea D. Leljedal, Operations Clerk at the U.S. Army Heritage and Education Center in Carlisle, PA, was particularly helpful and gracious in helping me gather images and many documents used in this research. Her assistance was provided before, during, and after my visit to the center.

Barbara Davis and Joyce Giles were welcoming hosts during my visit to the Mare Island Museum and provided access to the Museum's collection of items related to the Mare Island Marines. Barbara also volunteered a driving tour of the island that gave me a better understanding of the physical environment the Marines experienced during their training days.

Special thanks go to Duane Denfeld, Ph.D., Architectural Historian at Joint Base Lewis-McChord in Washington, who has published articles on the 1917 Camp Lewis team. Duane provided newspapers articles from a 1917 base newspaper available only at the Lewis Army Museum as well as other articles, background information, and perspective.

I also benefitted from the insights of two fellow authors. Scott Ellsworth, author of *The Secret Game: A Wartime Story of Courage, Change, and Basketball's Lost Triumph,* provided advice on the editing process and the publishing world in general. I also spent an enjoyable afternoon and evening with Tom Benjey, author of *Keep A-Goin': The Life of Lone Star Dietz.* Tom provided additional perspective on the publishing process and, since Lone Star Dietz coached the 1918 Mare Island Marines, he acted as a sounding board for some of my interpretations of the football world of 100 years ago.

As part of the research I also attempted to contact descendants and extended family members of the men portrayed in this book. Despite some favorable responses, technical issues precluded me from continuing the dialogue. Nevertheless, I want to thank those who responded and particularly those who provided me with additional information or directed me to other resources. The latter group includes family members of A. L. Christensen / Christy, Earnest Leapart Damkroger, Bandini Dear, Harry Melvin Green, William Forest Holden, Walter Parks Hollywood, Emzy Harvey Lynch, William Alexander Russell, and Edward Granville Sewell.

Those mentioned above helped me gather the information behind the story, while another group helped me create the story. A handful of friends and family read early versions of this book and kindly informed me I had a good story in need of extensive trimming. Those readers, listed in chronological order of their enduring the painful review process, included Phillip Brown, MJ Brown, Carolyn Brown, Pat Brown, David Pagnucco, James Mulcrone, and Lisa Reid. Eric Hane provided much-needed professional editorial assistance to help make the book worthy of publishing. His assistance in helping me separate the core story from the extraneous was critical.

Robin Locke Monda helped this first-time writer understand the complexities of book cover design and produced a cover that clearly communicates the core of the story: the intersection of football and war.

On a personal level, my family and friends were patient and encouraging as this book moved from a pipe dream to reality. I cannot thank each of you enough for your support. Thanks once again to Dave Pagnucco for the morning pep talks over coffee. A tip of the hat to Phillip and MJ Brown who created illustrations for the book and willingly offered their perspective on a variety of style and content issues. Conor Brown has been and will be my primary technical support for fieldsoffriendlystrife.com, the companion blog that supports and extends this book, so I offer you my virtual thanks. My children have been incredibly supportive throughout this process and I am so proud to be their father.

Finally, my lovely wife, Carolyn, allowed me to find and tell this story while otherwise being severely underemployed. Your support and encouragement made this work possible and I owe you my deepest thanks for so many elements of my life beyond this book.

Finally, to my parents, who taught their children that the only stupid questions are those that never get asked.

OVER THERE

GEORGE M. COHEN

Johnnie get your gun, get your gun.
Take it on the run, on the run, on the run.
Hear them calling, you and me,
Every Son of Liberty.
Hurry right away, no delay, go today
Make your Daddy glad to have had such a lad.
Tell your sweetheart not to pine,
To be proud her boy's in line.

Over there, over there,
Send the word, send the word over there
That the Yanks are coming, the Yanks are coming
The drums rum-tumming everywhere
So prepare, say a prayer,
Send the word, send the word to beware–
We'll be over, we're coming over,
And we won't come back till it's over, over there.

Johnnie, get your gun, get your gun, get your gun.
Johnnie show the Hun, you're a son of a gun.
Hoist the flag and let her fly
Yankee Doodle do or die.

Pack your little kit, show your grit, do your bit.
Yankee to the ranks from the towns and the tanks.
Make your Mother proud of you
And the old red-white-and-blue.

Over there, over there,
Send the word, send the word over there
That the Yanks are coming, the Yanks are coming
The drums rum-tumming everywhere.
So prepare, say a prayer,
Send the word, send the word to beware—
We'll be over, we're coming over,
And we won't come back till it's over, over there.

PREFACE

The journey that led to my telling this story began when I was a kid in Wisconsin watching the New Year's Day bowl games, the best of which was the "Granddaddy of the Them All." Each year, the Rose Bowl kicked off in the Southern California sunshine while the ground outside at home was covered in snow. As the game progressed and the sun set on Pasadena, the game came to be played under the lights in a stadium filled with fans wearing short-sleeved outfits. The Big Ten of the Middle West was pitted against a Pac-8 team each year that threw the ball too often and too well. Despite many Big Ten losses, the Rose Bowl remained one of winter's highlights.

A few decades later I had become a collector of college football memorabilia, focusing on items related to the Rose Bowl. Having read a number of books and articles on the Rose Bowl's history, I knew more about its history than the average bear (or Badger) and was aware that service teams from the WWI military training camps had played in the 1918 and 1919 Rose Bowls, but I had not given much thought to how service teams had been selected for those games. That changed when I purchased a program for a game between two service teams participating in a playoff series to advance to the 1919 Rose Bowl.

Previously unaware of these playoffs, the interplay between the Rose Bowl and military teams was intriguing, so I began researching the 1918 and 1919 Rose Bowls and soon found an article written by John Beckett in December 1967 on the fiftieth anniversary of his captaining the Mare Island Marines in the 1918 Rose Bowl. In his reflections on the game played by men preparing for war, Beckett noted that nearly half the men who played in the 1918 game later died in action in WWI or WWII. The loss of life among the men who played in this game was surprising, but more surprising was the fact the story of these men had never been told.

I continued researching the 1918 and 1919 service Rose Bowl teams to understand what happened to the men before, during, and after their time in Pasadena. This book tells the story of those men, but in doing so reveals a bigger, broader, and better story about a time in America that is largely ignored today. It involves the history and evolution of American football. Few football fans are aware of how the game and its rules developed, how the game wrestled with broader concepts of amateurism and the role of sports in our colleges, and how the game's institutions, such as the Rose Bowl, originated. The men played the game when football was still transitioning from its early, brutish form to a more open style of play that came with the introduction of the forward pass and other rule changes. Much of the game that was played 100 years ago feels familiar today; other elements seem quite strange to today's eyes.

Similarly, most of us today have a limited understanding of WWI and the American experience during the war. The several years that are the focus of this book witnessed two of the greatest killing events in human history. World War I left sixteen million dead and the influenza pandemic, popularly known as the Spanish Flu, was the deadliest in human history other than the Black Plague, accounting for the loss of fifty to one-hundred million lives. Each represents a staggering loss of life, but the toll is more shocking because World War I and the influenza pandemic overlapped.

This book does not attempt to provide a comprehensive understanding of either the war or the pandemic, but those events are integral to the story of a unique set of men who played football during those times. As these men trained for war and played the game of football, they were aware of the slaughter occurring in Europe's great battles. They knew that 500,000 men like them died in the First Battle of the Marne. They knew the Battle of the Somme doubled that figure. Still, every soldier, sailor and Marine, every volunteer and draftee, knew the uniform they wore off the football field would put their lives at risk in the coming months. Despite that knowledge, they trained for war while they played a young man's game knowing their football glory would count for little once they entered the battle zone.

Telling the story of these times through the lens of several football teams provides an appreciation for their experiences, life in America one hundred years ago, and its impact on us today.

INTRODUCTION

John Beckett woke on New Year's morning, rising from his comfortable bed in Pasadena's Hotel Maryland, looking forward to a good fight, just as he had the previous New Year's Day. On New Year's Day 1917, Beckett captained Oregon's football team to a Rose Bowl victory over Pennsylvania. He was in Pasadena again on New Year's Day 1918, rested and ready to play in his second Rose Bowl game.

Pasadena had opened its arms the last several days, entertaining the teams playing in the big Tournament of Roses game, but Beckett's job as team captain was to keep the team focused on the game, not the young women and other fans seeking their attention in the hotel lobby. Beckett knew he could count on his fullback Hollis Huntington and end Cliff Mitchell, who were teammates from Oregon on last year's victorious team. He also could rely on Hugo Bedzek, Oregon's coach, who would be on the sidelines again that day. Beckett's concern was the rest of the team, who were playing in the Rose Bowl for the first time. His opponent was in the same boat. They also had three players with Rose Bowl experience, men Beckett knew well.

Beckett and the rest of the team spent the morning at the hotel, breakfasting and relaxing before heading to Tournament Park, the site of the game. Once at the stadium, the teams went through their normal routine. Ankles were taped, men quietly slipped into their uniforms, and then sat anxiously thinking about the coming game. In time, they made their way to the field for pregame warmups, readying their bodies for the battle ahead. Shortly before the game began, the referee called Beckett to midfield for the coin flip to determine which team would kick and which end of the field would host the game's early plays.

As his team lined up to receive the kick, Beckett looked downfield at his opponents in their khaki-colored jerseys, seeing three teammates from Oregon's 1917 Rose Bowl team who now played on the opposing side. So much of life had changed in the last year. The nation was at war and Beckett's former teammates now played for the Army's Camp Lewis team, while Beckett, clad in Navy blue, represented the Mare Island Marines. Unlike previous Rose Bowls that featured college teams, this game would be played by service teams from the training camps preparing the nation's men for the battlefield. Both team rosters were dominated by former college stars now in the military. Some of Beckett's Oregon teammates were now his opponents and some of his old college opponents were now his teammates.

Beckett's thoughts returned to the playing field as he watched Doug MacKay, the diminutive Camp Lewis quarterback, build a dirt tee on the field, plant the football against the tee, and step back, readying himself to kick to Mare Island to start the 1918 Rose Bowl game.

Flash forward fifty years and America was at war again; young men were dying in Vietnam, but the mood of the country was different than earlier wars. By then, Beckett was a retired Marine Corps Brigadier General. While he and his friends had been cheered by crowds when they paraded through the streets in 1917, there were few parades in 1967. As a man who spent his life in the Marine Corps and had good friends and many others he knew give their lives in service to the country, the lack of support for the men in the armed forces during Vietnam was difficult to accept.

January 1, 1968 was the fiftieth anniversary of Beckett's playing in the 1918 Rose Bowl with the Mare Island Marines. To mark the anniversary, Beckett was asked to share his memories of the time by writing an article to be syndicated in newspapers across the country. In collecting his thoughts, Beckett thought back to the Mare Island training camp in 1917, the men who transferred from Mare Island to units that were soon sent to Europe, and to his own path that led to France. Beyond his experiences in the WWI era, he surely thought of the 1930s when he commanded the Marine legation in Beijing, as well as the 1940s and Iwo Jima, when Japanese bullets flew in his direction. Like any man with similar experiences, Beckett could only find the meaning of playing in the Rose Bowl at the beginning of his Marine career in the context of what had come afterward. So, Beckett brought his mind into focus to remember the first day of 1918 when he led the Marine Island Marines to victory. After reflecting on his time, Beckett penned his article, *The Game That Saved The Rose Bowl*, in which he tells us:

> "Time has eroded my subsequent and perhaps more important milestones in my life, but somehow I can recall everything I saw, smelled, touched, tasted and heard on New Year's Day in 1918 from the time I awoke in Room 109 of the old Maryland Hotel on Colorado Boulevard in Pasadena, till nightfall, when I had captained the Mare Island Marines team to victory in the Rose Bowl.
>
> .... Most of us on both teams that day knew we were scheduled to go overseas within a matter of weeks (nearly half the 32 players were to die in action in World Wars I and II); so this was the last battle we would fight in the name of sport."[1]

The death toll among Beckett's teammates and opponents in the game is difficult to comprehend, but WWI was the first war in the country's history in which American troops marched into battle and died in large numbers on foreign soil. It was the first industrial war during which the killing capacity of new weapons outdistanced the battlefield tactics and the production capacities of the belligerent nations became the keys to victory. Only WWII superseded WWI's number of fatalities, but regardless of the war, the percentage of deaths in a limited group of men such as two football teams is difficult to grasp, as is the impact of the deaths on those who survived.

But the real difficulty with Beckett's story of the high number of Mare Island and Camp Lewis players that died in action is that the story is simply not true. Some Mare Island and Camp Lewis players died in action during WWI, and others died in the service after the war, but they did not die in the numbers claimed by Beckett, though his story continues to be cited in various articles and books to this day.

Of course, the truth was not apparent when I began the research for this story, but in the course of trying to verify and ultimately discrediting Beckett's story, I found a larger truth. Though they are largely forgotten today, each of the men on the 1918 and 1919 Rose Bowl teams entered the services knowing their primary job was to prepare for battle, and they did so willingly; most did so voluntarily. The real story is not about Beckett and the tale he told fifty years later. The real story is about the teams and their men. Collectively and individually, they provide a window through which those of us living one hundred years on can gain insight into a formative period in the world of football, the U.S. military, and American society as the nation first stepped onto the world stage as a global power.

1

FROM THE TOWNS AND THE TANKS

The 1918 Rose Bowl featured the Mare Island Marines against the Army's 91st Division of Camp Lewis, while the 1919 Rose Bowl saw Mare Island return to the Tournament of Roses with an entirely new cast of players in a clash with the Great Lakes Naval Training Station. These teams played just prior to college football's Golden Age of the 1920s when the game exploded in popularity as college enrollments expanded, massive stadiums were built, and games were broadcast on the radio. Some of the explosion in popularity of college football and the emergence of professional football occurred because of the service football teams and the exposure these teams achieved within the armed forces and the country more broadly.

Much of what we love and hate about the game today also happened during the 1917 and 1918 seasons. Coaches were fired and players switched teams during through the season, concerns about professionalism abounded, fans bickered about which part of the country played the best football, and which teams deserved a spot in the big postseason game. But there was a key difference: the nation was at war, brothers and friends were dying in battle, and so many elements of the games played during the Tournament of Roses festivities in 1918 and 1919 differed from other years.

The World They Lived In

One hundred years provides three or four or five generations of separation between us and the men who played in these games. Depending on your age, the service Rose Bowl players grew up during the same period as your parents, grandparents, great grandparents, or even great, great grandparents and led lives like those pictured in dusty family albums. The oldest player on these teams was born when Rutherford B. Hayes was President and three others were born in 1886 during Grover Cleveland's first term in the White House. Only two were born in the twentieth century. The majority were children of the 1890s who grew up in world much different than ours.

All but two of the players was born before Henry Ford stopped working for Thomas Edison and began building his third automobile. All were born into a world without aeroplanes and a country without plug-in appliances. Perhaps 5 percent of households had electricity and those that did used it only for lighting. There simply was not much else you could do with electricity since all electrical devices had to be hard wired into the household grid, eliminating the portability and ability to swap plug-in devices we take for granted today.

The older men on these teams were born into a nation that united only thirty-eight states with North and South Dakota, Montana, and Washington joining in 1889; Idaho and Wyoming came along in 1890. Most of the players entered the world in a nation of forty-four states. Utah attained statehood in 1896, Oklahoma in 1907, and Arizona and New Mexico in 1912. For those that lived long enough, Alaska and Hawaii also became states during their lifetimes.

The background of the players is also emblematic of America's immigrant past. While only three of the players were born outside the U.S.—two in Canada and one in Mexico (of American parents) —19 percent were from families in which both parents were immigrants and another 17 percent had one immigrant parent. Canada and Northern Europe were the previous home for all but three of the immigrant families.

Regardless of their origins, Americans were moving west and we see that movement reflected in their family histories as well. Among the players on the Mare Island and Camp Lewis teams, both of which were located on the West Coast, 23 percent were born east of the Mississippi, as were 55 percent of their native-born parents. How they got out west is lost to time for most, but the story goes that Emzy Lynch, a Camp Lewis halfback, moved as a child from Texas to the Arizona Territory in a covered wagon. That is definitely old school.

America was a predominantly rural nation. It wasn't until 1920 that our urban population exceeded the rural population. Forty percent of the players lived at least part of their childhood on a farm, orchard, or ranch. A few grew up on farms that sat inside the city boundaries of Los Angeles or Palo Alto, though neither of those towns has much land under the plow today. The small-town influence was greater still because the percentage that grew up on a farm, orchard, or ranch does not include those who grew up in small towns whose fathers were lawyers, merchants, ministers, or blacksmiths. Of course, profiling the employment status of the families is all about the fathers since only a handful of mothers worked outside the home and, in almost all cases in which they did, the mother was widowed or otherwise without a live-in spouse.

In 1898, the tallest habitable building in the Western Hemisphere was Milwaukee's City Hall—the Washington Monument was the only taller man-made structure. And not to go all beer chest on Milwaukee, but it had a larger population than the quaint coastal burg of Los Angeles.

The scientific revolution that impacted life in the twentieth century was still early in its development. Darwin published *Origin of Species* in 1870 and it took time for the importance of his argument to evolve into one of the most influential in the world. Most physicians completed medical school and entered practice without ever dissecting a cadaver, conducting a laboratory experiment, or seeing a patient during their training. Most saw their first patient only after they hung up their shingles. Similarly, only a limited number of lawyers attended law school.

Many of the political and social revolutions that shaped our world had yet to occur. Germany was ruled by the Kaiser, Russia by the

Tsar, and the Austro-Hungarian Empire by an Emperor. Britain ruled nearly a quarter of the world's people. When American troops sailed to Europe in 1917, women had the right to vote in fewer than twenty states and some troops were still in Europe when Congress passed the 19th Amendment. These men sailed to France, fought and won a war, and then waited two years before the first baseball game was broadcast over radio and another five years before the first talkies came to the silver screen.

The difference in their world to ours is also reflected in the names their parents gave them at birth. Parents whose sons grew up to play for Great Lakes were perfectly comfortable bestowing them with monikers such as Auben, Hyrle, Merrill, and Verne, while a few of their future opponents at Mare Island went through life named Millard, Amor, and Elmer. Similarly, the teams had players that grew up knowing life ain't easy for a boy named Cloy or Aurelius or Rhodolph or Zenas.

And, of course, all the men profiled in this book were white, assuming the Caucasian category includes those of Irish ancestry. African-Americans were oppressed by a wide range of practices as civilians and in the military. They were draft-eligible in WWI and were drafted at a higher percentage than whites, in part because they had less access to the skilled jobs for which they might have earned exemptions. Conversely, black physicians were less likely to be accepted into the Army's Medical Corps than their white colleagues. The Army was also reluctant to have African-Americans fight in battle under the American flag, so almost all black soldiers that saw action did so in segregated units led by white field officers under French command. Genl. John J. Pershing, the commander of the American Expeditionary Forces (AEF) in WWI, was nicknamed "Black Jack" because he once commanded the 10th Cavalry Regiment comprised of Buffalo Soldiers. When bestowed, the nickname was not meant as a compliment.

Native Americans were accepted as volunteers and draftees into regular units, but it was still a time when the Bureau of Indian Affairs forced Native Americans to become equal by educating and assimilating them at Indian schools outside their reservations. Football and other sports at these schools were viewed as a means of immersing Native Americans into the dominant culture; Carlisle in Pennsylvania and Haskell in Kansas are among the better known Indian schools largely due to their success on the football field.

The service Rose Bowl players lived in a different time, but we should not think of their time as simpler, just different. They had skills few of us possess today. They could manage a team of horses, milk a cow, and dress a chicken. They knew how to till a field behind a horse or mule, manage a crop, and dig an outhouse. Any tractor they might have used was steam powered, but they knew how to stoke its fire and operate it. The city boys dealt with the same or more ethnic diversity than exists in our metropolitan areas today. They got around town on trains and trolleys and studied the classics in school. As football players, they gave their all for Ol' Alma Mater and Old Glory. They sweated through grueling practices and afterwards chased their campus sweethearts. They used the latest innovation, postcards, to keep up with friends, and they were among the early adopters of new technologies such as automobiles, aeroplanes and radios. It was a different time and yet their thrills and tragedies resonate today.

The Rules of the Game

Just as the world and society have changed dramatically since these men came of age, so has the game of football. Like many aspects of history, it is easy to think that football followed an inevitable progression that led to the game we have today, as if the football gods guided its path. Instead, the game's rules, like all laws and rules, were modified over time to eliminate negative aspects of the game, enhance positive elements, and fix the unanticipated consequences of previous rule changes. Today's rules are the rules because past rule makers tried some of this and some of that and we ended up where we are today. Nothing in the game's rules was inevitable and nothing in the current rules is inviolable.

To compare college football in 1917 with the game played today, it helps to separate the discussion into three parts. The first concerns the origins of the game. The second involves the game as played on the field, specifically the evolution of its rules and strategies up to 1917. The third addresses the environment outside the lines including issues of player eligibility, coaching, scheduling, facilities, and other issues that provided the context in which the game was played.

Origins of American Football

Games in which one team attempts to kick or carry a ball across a goal defended by another team go back to ancient times, but the American and Canadian game of football has its origins in the games of soccer and rugby played in nineteenth century England. A variety of kicking games were played in England with the rules at each playing ground, the "ground rules," varying from place to place, until the London Football Association codified a set of rules in 1863 that outlawed carrying the ball. The "association rules" formalized the game Americans call soccer. Others in England preferred a style of kicking game originating at The Rugby School, a prep school in Warwickshire, England. Their rules allowed players to both kick and carry the ball. Adherents of the rugby game formed the Rugby Football Union in 1871 and this great secession has separated rugby from soccer ever since.

Americans visiting England and vice versa led to the association rules crossing the water and the soccer version of the kicking game became dominant at East Coast colleges. Harvard was the exception, playing a game unique to Boston that had similarities with rugby. The Princeton-Rutgers game of 1869, which is universally considered the first intercollegiate football game, was played under association rules. That means, embarrassingly enough, the first college football game was a soccer match, so Princeton and Rutgers might want to reconsider their chest thumping about that contest.

In 1874, Harvard played a few games with McGill University of Montreal, where rugby was king, with the teams alternately using the Boston and rugby rules in their games. The Harvard boys enjoyed the rugby game played by McGill and began playing by rugby rules in Boston. As the various colleges started to play one another, the need arose for a consistent set of rules for the intercollegiate games. Students from Columbia, Harvard, Princeton, and Yale met in 1876 to define those rules and formed the Intercollegiate Football Association (IFA). A key decision for the 1876 meeting was whether to adopt the association or rugby rules. Harvard and the rugby rules won the day and that decision set the course for a combined rushing and kicking game that evolved into American and Canadian football. The IFA formed by these select schools remained the de facto arbiter of football rules until the football crisis of 1905.

The next football rules meeting was held in 1878 and is notable for the fact that one of Yale's representatives was a player named Walter Camp, who is regarded as the father of American football. Camp was a dominant force in nearly every rule-making meeting of the IFA and its successors until his attendance at the 1925 meeting, during which, he died. During Camp's tenure, he pushed for the 'scientific' approach to the game that reduced the role of chance in favor of effective planning and team play. The most important rule change reflecting the scientific approach was the elimination of the scrummage in 1890. Like rugby, after a runner was downed, the two teams formed a scrummage or scrum in which the ball was put in play by tossing it between the two teams. Both teams attempted to kick the ball behind the scrum line to a teammate who picked up the ball and ran with it or kicked it to advance the ball. The scrummage gave both teams equal opportunity to gain possession of the ball, so it was considered bad form by the supporters of the scientific approach.

With the elimination of the scrummage, the team with the ball retained possession and aligned on the line of scrimmage and one player, the 'snapper-back' started play by snapping the ball backward *with his feet* to his teammate, the quarterback. The snapper-back, later known as the center, had teammates on either side protecting him during the snap and they became known as guards. The players outside the guards frequently made tackles while on defense and became known as tackles. And, of course, those at the outermost positions on the line were called ends. In the backfield, the player farthest back from the center became known as the fullback, other players set half as deep as the fullback were called halfbacks, and the player who received the snap from center was aligned midway between the halfbacks and the center, so he became known as the quarterback.

The introduction of the "scrimmage" was critical to football's development as a distinct game because starting play with a controlled scrimmage allowed the development of structured alignments and plays different in kind from the free-flowing plays of soccer and rugby.

Point values were established for football's various scoring methods in 1883. The values differ from today's and, since football evolved from a kicking game, scoring via kicking earned more points than scoring via rushing:

- Safety: 1 point versus current 2 points
- Touchdown: 2 points versus current 6 points
- Goal after touchdown (extra point): 4 points versus 1 or 2 today
- Goal from field (field goal): 5 versus 3 today

The Football Crisis

Football came under heavy criticism near the turn of the century due to the high number of injuries and deaths, and the general brutality of the game. Football was dominated by mass plays in which multiple players on the offensive side went in motion prior to the snap and ran *en masse* at one of the defenders. To reduce mass plays, an evolving set of rules ultimately allowed only one player in motion at the snap and required seven men on the line of scrimmage. Despite these changes, mass plays took other forms so football remained a brutal game. The issue came to a head in 1905 when Teddy Roosevelt, a football proponent, met with the rule makers and told them he would abolish the game if they did not reduce its violence. Due to the obstinacy of the IFA, a rival rule making body, the Intercollegiate Athletic Association of the United States (IAAUS), was formed and the IAAUS eventually absorbed the IFS. The IAAUS was renamed the National Collegiate Athletic Association (NCAA) in 1910.

The IAAUS considered a range of approaches to create a more open game and announced a set of new rules in April 1906 with the most well-known change being the approval of the forward pass. The rule allowed an offensive player to throw a pass forward provided the passer was more than five yards to the right or left of the center. To help the lone referee judge whether the passer was five yards from the center, stripes were painted perpendicular to the goal lines such that the field resembled a gridiron; hence, one of the football field's nicknames.

Although the new rules allowed forward passes, incomplete passes that did not touch an offensive or defensive player before hitting the ground resulted in a loss of possession with the ball given to the defensive team at the spot the pass was thrown. The severity of the penalty left many coaches leery of the forward pass and gave early adopters extra motivation to determine the best technique to throw the ball accurately.

You might think it would have been obvious to players and coaches in 1906 that the best way to throw a forward pass is the overhand spiral pass we use today. It's even hard for us to think of reasonable alternatives to the overhand spiral. But the best throwing technique was not obvious to them since no one had ever thrown a legal forward pass. Coming from the rugby tradition, passing in football had been limited to the backwards, underhand laterals still in use in rugby, so the football innovators tried a number of passing techniques. Some held the ball in the flat of their hand and tossed it with a straight arm like one might toss a grenade. Others gripped the ball at one end and flung it end over end toward the receiver. The basketball set shot technique was tried by some as well.

These seemingly odd techniques made more sense due to the shape of the football in 1906, which was slightly longer than today's and shaped like a watermelon. The ball's shape and size made the overhand spiral throw difficult for almost anyone that did not have large hands, but the overhand pass proved the most successful. The ball was reduced in size in 1912 and the less bulbous ball made it easier for many to throw the overhand pass effectively. The dimensions of the football went unchanged until 1972, when the ball was made slightly slimmer again.

Anticipating the 1906 season, St. Louis University's coach, Eddie Cochems, took his football team to a training camp in Wisconsin to escape the heat and humidity of St. Louis. Cochems spent the summer thinking of ways to take advantage of the new forward-pass rule and the St. Louis team worked on his new plays in camp. Prior to returning to St. Louis, Cochems scheduled a game in Wisconsin with Carroll University on September 5, 1906. St. Louis threw the first forward passes in that game and won, 22-0. While St. Louis and Cochems are widely credited with throwing the first forward pass in a college game, as a Carroll alum, I believe too little credit is sent Carroll's way for its invention of pass defense. After all, the first legal forward pass was an incompletion.

Cochems and Carlisle's Pop Warner were innovators in the passing game and forward passes provided the winning plays in several high-profile games over the next few years, but it took further rule changes to make its use widespread. Later changes reduced the penalty for an incomplete/untouched pass to fifteen yards rather than loss of possession, allowed the ball to be thrown from any location in the backfield provided the passer was at least five yards behind the center, and allowed passes to be thrown into and legally caught in the end zone. Previously, a ball thrown into the end zone resulted in a touchback. Since forward passes had to be thrown from five yards behind the line of scrimmage, many of the top passers of the day were halfbacks rather than quarterbacks.

The 1906 rule makers also allowed the so-called 'onside kick', which was essentially the same as the forward pass, but players kicked the ball to their teammate rather than passed it. While some used this approach, it didn't catch on like the thrown pass and was removed from the rule book a few years later.

Another 1906 rule change to enhance player safety came with the definition of forward progress. Today we know that forward progress ends when the ball carrier stops moving toward the opponent's goal line under his own power, with the ball being marked at the player's farthest progress toward the goal. Prior to 1906, the play ended only when the offensive player placed the ball on the ground and yelled, "Down." Under that rule, defenders simply held the runner upright, preventing him from "touching down," and pushed him backwards. The runner's teammates, of course, joined the fray pushing the runner toward the goal line, thereby making a dangerous situation worse. Instituting the forward progress rule eliminated these melees and reduced injuries.

The last major rule change to enhance safety and open the game was the shift from the offensive team having three possessions to gain five yards for a first down to their having three possessions to gain ten yards. While it may seem counterintuitive, the intention was to force teams away from mass plays that often gained only one or two yards per play. Doubling the number of yards needed for a first down meant teams had to find new formations and plays to gain more than one or two yards each play. The change proved onerous and the rule was changed again in 1912 to give teams four plays to gain ten yards.

The 'proper' quarterback positioning as shown in a training pamphlet of the time.

One of the archaic elements of the game in the 1910s was the quarterback's positioning. Although quarterbacks commonly align in the shotgun formation today, we think of the "traditional" formation as one in which the quarterback aligns directly behind the center, places his hands between the center's legs, and takes the snap directly from the center. Back then, the quarterback squatted behind the center (much like a baseball catcher), caught a short toss from the center, and then handed off or lateraled to one of the running backs before becoming another blocker. The squatting quarterback seems silly now, but the alignment made sense when the quarterback's original job was to pick up the tumbling ball after the center snapped it with his feet. Although centers had snapped the ball using their hands since 1898, no one thought to implement the direct center-quarterback exchange until the Chicago Bears did so in 1930 with the introduction of their famous T formation.

Another longstanding rule prohibited the first player receiving the ball from the center, typically the quarterback, from running with the ball toward the line of scrimmage until at least one teammate touched the ball. The rule allowing the first player receiving the ball to run forward was added in 1910, changing the quarterback's role from that of a blocking back to one that could now run with or pass the ball. With the ball getting into the hands of a legal runner more quickly, the rule change enabled more effective options and sweeps. The standard offensive formation and sweep play in use in 1912 is shown in the following diagram.

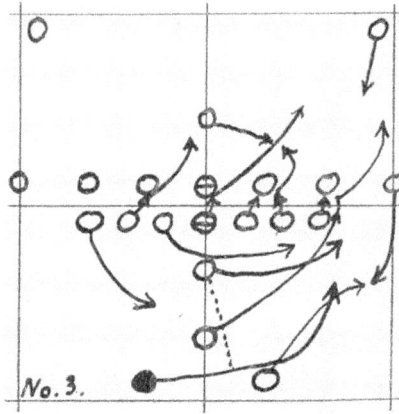

Pop Warner's 1912 illustration of a short end run from the traditional formation. The center snaps the ball to the quarterback, who pitches the ball to the left halfback and joins the other backs blocking to the right.

In 1912, Pop Warner took advantage of the new rule by creating the Single Wing offense. The Single Wing included a direct snap from the center to the halfback which further enhanced the speed of sweeps and enabled reverses to the new Wing Back position. Warner designed the Single Wing with his star, Jim Thorpe, in mind and it proved effective since Thorpe was a triple threat—effective at running, passing, and punting the ball. The Single Wing became widely used, though many teams continued to employ the traditional formation or used combinations of the two. The Single Wing formation and short end run is shown in the following diagram.

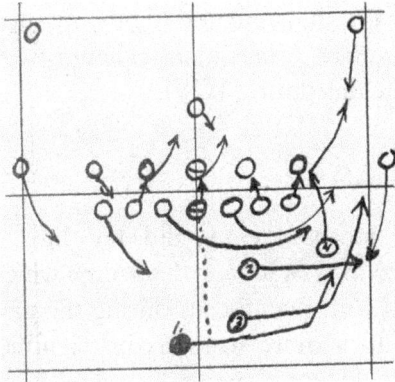

*Pop Warner's 1912 illustration of a short end run from the Single Wing.
The center snaps the ball directly to the deep halfback, leading him as he
begins his motion to the right.*

The playing field dimensions were set in 1875 at 130 yards in length
and 53 1/3 yards wide, giving the field a 55-yard line and two ten-
yard end zones. The 1912 rules reduced the field length to 120
yards, eliminating the 55-yard line. So, when Americans wonder
how those goofy Canadians came up a version of football with three
downs and a 55-yard line, we have to acknowledge that they simply
stayed true to an earlier set of rules.

Each of these rule changes were opposed by various coaches and
rule makers, but coaches and players adapted to the new rules, and
the game persevered to the point it is hard to conceive that some
former rules were ever part of the game. There is a lesson here for
the proponents and opponents of rule changes aimed at addressing
football's current ills.

Football in Context

While the game of football itself was evolving, so was the context in
which teams played. Football evolved from little more than a sport
played by pickup teams to one formally organized by the colleges
and universities with professional coaches, increasingly larger stadiums, and players subject to stricter eligibility requirements. At the
same time, the college game became increasingly commercialized,
the advent of the Rose Bowl being just one example. Some of the

same tensions between informal and highly organized teams, as well as player-coaches versus professional coaches, would emerge with the training camp teams during WWI.

Coaches and Officials

Early on, college football teams did not have coaches. Teams selected a captain to lead practices, determine which players entered the game, and deal with the officials during the games. However, as the game evolved to a more structured, 'scientific' game, coaches played a larger role in team success.

Some coaches became nationally known figures and were highly paid, but for every highly experienced coach like Fielding Yost, Amos Alonzo Stagg, or Pop Warner, many other college coaches were only a few seasons removed from their college playing days. For example, Knute Rockne became Notre Dame's head coach four years after graduating in 1914. Shy Huntington was captain and quarterback of the Oregon team that won the 1917 Rose Bowl and became Oregon's coach the next season, later leading them to the 1920 Rose Bowl. Down in Texas in 1916, St. Mary's College hired as its head coach a young lieutenant who had played football at West Point and was stationed at nearby Fort Sam Houston. Dwight Eisenhower promptly landed St. Mary's a winning campaign.

Most full-time football coaches were the only paid coaches at the school, so they often skippered the basketball, baseball, and other teams as well. Despite the emergence of full-time coaches, their role during games was limited because coaching from the sideline was considered poor sportsmanship and subject to a ten-yard penalty. The prohibition of coaching from the sideline is the reason why quarterbacks called the plays until that rule was eliminated in 1967. Even the few substitutes that entered the game were not allowed to communicate with their teammates for one full play lest they bring coaching instructions from the sideline, though a 1917 rule change allowed a player substituting at quarterback to call the signals upon entering the game.

Other rules limited the number of people that could stand on the sideline during games. The number varied over the years, but starting in 1914 everyone on the sideline had to be seated and that rule remained in place for decades. This rule explains why almost everyone seen on the sideline in pre-1960s pictures of football games is seated on the bench.

The game officials of the day were untrained. Most were former players and coaches who had reputations as honorable men and opposing teams negotiated the acceptability of officials on a game-by-game basis. Even the separation of the press from the games they covered was permeable. Walter Eckersall, a former All-American at Chicago and well-known sportswriter for the *Chicago Tribune*, traveled to Pasadena to cover the 1916, 1918 and 1919 Rose Bowls. He had a unique view of each contest for a sportswriter, since he was on the field refereeing the games. This happened despite Eckersall's having been a backfield mate at the University of Chicago with Hugo Bedzek, Mare Island's coach in the 1918 game. Another of the 1918 game officials was W. S. Kienholz, the head of the Tournament of Roses Football Committee. He was also the uncle of one of the assistant coaches involved in the game.

Schedules and Opponents

Today's college football season starts around Labor Day and ends in January. In the 1910s, college classes and the football season started the first week of October and the season ended by Thanksgiving with teams playing seven to nine games per year. Team schedules and game contracts were handled by student managers who were undergrads or recent graduates. Season schedules were finalized over the summer and adapted as needed to drop or insert a game or two, particularly the games with local amateur athletic clubs that dotted college schedules. The nationally prominent teams regularly played schools that no longer play football or play at lower levels today. Schools like Willamette, Occidental, Gonzaga, Centre, Kalamazoo, and DePauw had regular nonconference games and occasional victories over their respective state schools.

One of the reasons the big schools played small schools back then was the fact that the big schools weren't all that big. Colleges and universities were elite institutions serving a narrower swath of the population than today. In the 1910s, less than 20 percent of the school-age population graduated from high school and less than 10 percent of high school graduates attended college. (Nearly one-third of American soldiers during WWI were illiterate.) The nation had only seven colleges and universities in 1916 with enrollments over 5,000 students: Cal, Columbia, Cornell, Illinois, Michigan, Ohio State, Penn, and Wisconsin. Penn was the largest with just over 8,000 students. Washington State had less than 1,800 students when it won the 1916 Rose Bowl and Oregon's enrollment was less than 800 students when it won the 1917 Rose Bowl. Little Washington & Jefferson played California to a scoreless tie in the 1922 Rose Bowl with an enrollment of 600 students.

The Stadiums

Archeologists study the buildings left behind by civilizations to gain a sense of their sophistication and values. The commitment made by the Greeks in constructing the Panathenaic Stadium or the Romans building the Coliseum tells us something about those societies. The same is true when we look at the stadiums used by college teams early in the century. Their capacity, the materials used to construct the stadiums, and their overall design tell us about the place of college football in the grander scheme.

We will talk more about the stadiums in a minute, but let's first talk about postcards. Stadiums and postcards are connected, as you will soon see. Postcards were introduced to the U.S. in the 1870s with the U.S. Postal Service being the only authorized printer of the documents and they printed all of them in a beautiful shade of white without other images.

The situation changed on Christmas Eve 1901 when the postal service first allowed private companies to print postcards as long as certain rules were followed. Anyone who has sent or received a postcard knows the back side of the postcard is divided into a left and right side. You write your message on the left side and the addressee information on the right. However, when postcards were first allowed in the U.S., the sender was prohibited from writing anything on the back side of the postcard other than the addressee's name and address. It seems crazy now, but those were the rules, so the sender wrote short notes atop the image on the front side of the postcard. Some postcard printers left a half inch white strip on the front side for the sender to jot a quick note. The postal service approved the "divided back" postcard in 1907 and that is the format we know today.

These changes caused or coincided with an absolute craze of postcards being printed, mailed, read, and saved. Postcards were the e-mail or text message of their day because they provided an inexpensive way to send quick messages to distant friends or to simply instruct someone to pick them up at the train station next Saturday. Postcards were printed with every conceivable image on the front; one subset of images showcased local buildings demonstrating the progress occurring in whatever locale they originated. Some of those building images were college football stadiums. It just so happened that a few colleges opened new stadiums smack dab in the middle of America's postcard craze and a slew of postcards were festooned with images of the new stadiums. Postcards remained popular for decades and all manner of them were sent during WWI, examples of which are the primary illustrations used throughout this book. Collecting postcards was popular as well and many were saved in scrapbooks, so old postcards litter America's antique malls to this day.

The college football stadiums of the first two decades of the twentieth century were exceedingly modest by today's standards. Only a few sat more than 15,000 people and almost all had simple wooden bleachers with the fancier ones having a grandstand covering part of the home sideline. Most stadiums were multipurpose, accommodating a running track and/or a baseball field.

Wisconsin's Camp Randall had the old-school look of a race track grandstand.

The exceptions to the modest stadium model occurred in the Ivy League, which only became a league in 1954. The Ivies enjoyed a pre-war stadium building boom such that several of its stadiums dwarfed all others. Harvard and Princeton has stadiums seating 42,000, while the Yale Bowl's capacity reached nearly 71,000. The real building boom for college stadiums came post-war when a host of "memorial" stadiums were built.

Harvard Stadium pioneered the use of reinforced concrete in the construction of large buildings.

Football Outside the Colleges

For all intents and purposes, professional football did not exist before the war and athletes had few opportunities to play football after college. There was a smattering of professional teams along the Great Lakes, but all were low-budget enterprises of interest only to local fans. Many who played football after college did so for the amateur athletic clubs in various cities that were often the focal point of sporting life outside of professional baseball. Many clubs fielded football teams that played one another and area colleges, with some attracting thousands of fans and extensive newspaper coverage. Still, many of those playing for the club teams and the professional football teams had not played college football. There were essentially no teams in the country composed of former college stars until the arrival of the service teams of WWI.

The Development of the Rose Bowl

SEC. ROW SEAT
B 26 16
TUNNEL
Tournament of Roses Stadium
$1.65
Monday, January 1st, 1923
Retain This Check
BILLINGHAM PTG. CO., L. A.

A 1923 Rose Bowl ticket stub shows the newly built Rose Bowl was originally called Tournament of Roses Stadium.

Despite being historically inaccurate, this book uses the term "Rose Bowl" to refer to the early New Year's Day football games sponsored by the Pasadena Tournament of Roses. Just as the first Heisman Trophy was not called the Heisman Trophy and the first Super Bowl was not called the Super Bowl at the time, the first nine Rose Bowls were not called the "Rose Bowl" when they were played. *Tournament of Roses Stadium* was constructed in time for the 1923 game, and the "Rose Bowl" term was coined in the run-up to that game. The term became popular and ultimately became the official designation for the new stadium and the game itself.

Against this backdrop, we have our friends in Pasadena to thank for giving birth to the Granddaddy of Them All. The Tournament of Roses began in 1890 as a celebration of the citrus harvest. The Tournament become a tourist draw for Easterners and Midwesterners, in part due to the number of transplants from those regions that called Pasadena home. With a desire to continue growing as an attraction, the Tournament of Roses sought ways to attract more attention and larger crowds, but the Tournament elected a new board each year, so the annual event was shaped by the preferences of each year's board members. That and the desire to ensure the Tournament stayed within budget.

In 1901, the Tournament of Roses hit on the idea of fielding a football game between top Eastern and Western teams. It was an ambitious idea since intersectional games were rare at the time. Midwestern, Southern, and Eastern team seldom played one another and only twice before the 1902 Rose Bowl did teams from east of the Rockies cross the mountains to play West Coast teams.

The Tournament of Roses invited Michigan in the summer of 1901 and Michigan was agreeable, provided the Tournament made appropriate financial arrangements and found a suitable opponent. Although Cal defeated Stanford in the 1901 Big Game, Cal was reluctant to play Michigan. Stanford was not and the contract was finalized in early December. (It was not uncommon for schools to turn down the Rose Bowl's overture until well into the 1920s.) The Tournament of Roses quickly acquired an empty lot in Pasadena and built wooden bleachers for the game.

Since this was only the third time an Eastern team traveled to the West Coast for a game, the excitement was high. Tickets for the game sold quickly and a sellout of the grandstand and patron boxes was assured. Others among the 8,000 attendees watched the game from their buggies sitting along the sidelines. Michigan's team was led by Fielding Yost, who had coached Stanford the previous year. Michigan came into the game undefeated and unscored upon with its 21-0 victory over Ohio State being their closest contest. The Michigan eleven thrashed Stanford, 49-0. Though lopsided, the gate receipts well exceeded the cost of transporting and hosting the teams. However, the Tournament of Roses was in the red overall due to the one-time cost of acquiring the land and building the new stadium.

The next Rose Bowl was not played until 1916, and a legend has grown suggesting Michigan's dominance of Stanford was the reason for the gap in play. But the legend is largely untrue. The Tournament of Roses made multiple attempts to schedule other games, but they could not finalize the deals. It came closest in 1903, the year after Michigan's dominant win, when Wisconsin received and accepted an invitation to the 1903 Rose Bowl. Wisconsin's agent and the Tournament President went to Berkeley to negotiate the contract but could not convince California to play the Badgers, so Wisconsin fans waited another fifty years before their team played in its first Rose Bowl. Discussions for a game started in 1904 as well, but that year's Tournament President favored chariot races over football largely due to the $1,000 outlay needed to transport an Eastern team to Pasadena, and the fear that another lopsided game would prove a farce. Chariot races became part of the New Year tradition for nearly a decade.

The final nail in the football coffin came amid the 1905 football crisis when Stanford and Cal dropped American football in favor of rugby, leaving California without a college playing high-level American football. USC, whose program gained prominence in the 1920s, then played in a league with the likes of Pomona and Occidental, while UCLA was still the Los Angeles State Normal School. (Note: Many college and university names evolved over the last century. All are referred to in this book by their current names rather than their period names.) The lack of a California-based team meant the Tournament faced higher travel costs and reduced local enthusiasm for the potential matchups. Still looking for entertainment draws to interest tourists, the 1909 Tournament reached out to the Wright Brothers to stage a flying exhibition, but those plans never got off the ground. Attempts were made to schedule games in other years as well, but travel costs remained the primary barrier.

Support for hosting a football game gathered steam in 1915 and Tournament officials formed a Sports/Football Committee headed by W. S. Kienholz. Kienholz played for Minnesota in the 1890s and then had one-year coaching stints at half a dozen schools. After his coaching career, he worked for the Los Angeles school system and was the president of the high school sports association in Southern California. Kienholz had the insight to extend provisional offers to Oregon, Oregon State, Washington, and Washington State to assess their interest and provide them time to gain approval from their athletic and faculty boards. Ultimately, Washington State won the championship of the Pacific Northwest Conference and agreed to play the game.

The 1915 Washington State College team was paraded through Pullman after their victory over Oregon Agricultural College (Oregon State).

In the East, Michigan, Illinois, and Cornell were considered potential invitees, but Brown was invited and accepted the bid in mid-November, a few days after losing to Harvard. The Brown team travelled 3,000 miles for the first football game between colleges whose states bordered the Atlantic and Pacific Oceans. Washington State—coached by Lone Star Dietz—surprised the Eastern football world with a 14-0 win over Brown.

During the 1916 season Kienholz again asked the Western teams to commit to participating in the game if they were selected. Kienholz gained the University of Pennsylvania's commitment for the 1917 Rose Bowl and immediately invited Oregon, giving fans the only Quaker versus Quacker Rose Bowl. Oregon, coached by Hugo Bedzek, subsequently rang Pennsylvania's bell, 14-0.

The victories by Washington State and Oregon gave bragging rights to Western football fans at a time when the Rose Bowl was the only intersectional, postseason game in the country. It remained so until the Cotton, Orange, and Sugar Bowls arrived in the mid-1930s. With all of that, football fans in isolationist America entered 1917 hoping their favorite team might vie for an invitation to represent their region in Pasadena on New Year's Day 1918. But that all changed on April 6, 1917 with America's entry into the war.

With the nation on war footing, Kienholz would face greater challenges selecting and gaining commitments from prospective teams for the 1918 and 1919 Rose Bowls. Both games, of course, ended up featuring service rather than college teams due both to the patriotic fever that swept the nation and the service football teams proving to be among the nation's best.

THE YANKS ARE COMING

There is extensive literature on the military strategies and battles of WWI for those interested in understanding the war at a deeper level than is covered here. This book covers the war in broad strokes, and dives deeper only into those events in which members of the service Rose Bowl teams were involved. Since it turns out that service Rose Bowl players were involved in most of America's major engagements during the war, those events are covered, but the focus within those engagements is on the units that included service Rose Bowl players.

Most know the story of Gavrilo Princip's assassination of Archduke Franz Ferdinand in Sarajevo and the combination of tangled alliances and national pride that plunged the world into war in 1914. The shooting on the Western Front started when Germany executed its Schlieffen Plan, a strategy that called for a quick victory over France before Russia could mobilize its troops on the Eastern Front. Under the Schlieffen Plan, Germany invaded France through neutral Belgium to avoid battling through the Maginot Line, France's line of fortresses along its border with Germany.

Britain sent its troops to defend Belgium and parts of northern France, while French troops covered the rest of northern and eastern France. In their initial attack, the Germans made rapid progress coming within fifty miles of Paris, but were stopped in the First Battle of the Marne in September 1914. The first three months of the war saw open movements by both sides, after which the war settled into the defense of territory held by each side, and a multiyear battle of attrition began. Both sides created extensive networks of trenches and fortified positions stretching 475 miles from the North Sea in the northwest to Switzerland in the southeast. The Germans held better defensive positions in many areas and spent considerable resources building up their fortifications. The French, on the other hand, were less enthusiastic about fortifying their trenches since they saw them as temporary positions.

More than one million died on the Western Front in 1914 and many more in 1915, in part because the many advances in military technologies (e.g., advanced artillery, machine guns, grenades, poisonous gas, aeroplanes) were not met with a comparable evolution in tactics. Huge numbers died on the Eastern Front as well. In February 1916, Germany attacked near the city of Verdun along the Meuse River, hoping less to gain territory and more to drain France of fighting men. It worked. In 303 days of fighting, Germany suffered 430,000 casualties, while the French lost 550,000. The Battle of Verdun pulled French troops away from a planned British and French offensive along the Somme River in northern France, but the British moved forward with the attack resulting in 19,240 of their men being killed the first day. The British suffered one million casualties during the four-plus-month Somme Offensive and advanced all of seven miles.

In late July 1917, the British went on the offense in the Flanders region of Belgium where they held the Ypres Salient. In preparation for the Third Battle of Ypres, the British sent 4.25 million artillery shells into German positions over a ten-day period. The shelling inflicted little harm on the Germans, but it further damaged the drainage systems the Belgians had developed over the centuries in low-lying Flanders. Rain began to fall shortly after the attack launched and did not let up for weeks, resulting in fields of mud that prevented effective movement. Nonetheless, the British continued their attack, taking the Passchendaele heights in November before halting, having gained little advantage and losing 310,000 men versus 260,000 for the Germans. The horrendous loss of men for minimal gain remains burned into the British consciousness today.

America Enters the Great War

America was an isolationist nation before its entry into WWI, and many Americans viewed the country's lack of martial tradition and small military with a sense of pride. Wilson was reelected in November 1916 based on his promise to keep us out of the war, but after nearly three years of official neutrality, but clear support for the Allies, Germany's resumption of unlimited submarine warfare and the scheming behind the Zimmerman telegram brought America to declare war on April 6, 1917.

England and France quickly sent delegations to the U.S. to help plan America's roles in the war. Their primary message was the need for America to send troops to Europe as quickly as possible, even asking the U.S. to send untrained men to Europe, who the Allies would train and insert as replacements for existing English and French units. The U.S. demurred. This was the first of many instances during the war in which America would insist on its troops fighting as units under American command. The U.S. agreed to send a limited number of troops to Europe as soon as possible, but their numbers were limited and American troops had little military impact until the summer of 1918.

America was ill prepared to wage war in Europe. Prior to entering the war, the American people did not want and Congress did not fund an armed force capable of meeting the new requirements and there were few American men with experience in battle. Outside of a limited number of Marines who had seen combat in various overseas excursions and a smattering of Army and National Guard troops involved in the 1916 Punitive Expedition in Mexico, the only men with combat experience were those left over from the Spanish-American War. There were few of those men.

Americans had not fought in a major conflict since the Civil War and had never fought a major war outside North America. Building an armed force for the Great War was a material, logistical, and administrative challenge unlike any the U.S. or any other country had faced.

Preparing the Army

The Allies' primary manpower request of the U.S. was for ground or infantry troops, so the American Army faced a massive recruiting and training effort. Despite some pre-war build up, the U.S. had only 133,000 soldiers in the Regular Army and 173,000 National Guard troops. By war's end, the Army had nearly 4,100,000 soldiers with over 2,000,000 in France. Across all services, nearly 4,735,000 men were under arms by war's end.

The Army went to war with three types of divisions: Regular Army divisions, National Guard divisions, and National Army divisions. The Regular Army divisions were comprised of soldiers from the permanent army, supplemented by draftees, and these were the first to go overseas. The 1st Division was the first American fighting force sent to France, sailing from New York on June 14, 1917, just over two months after war was declared. Their arrival in France marked the beginning of the American Expeditionary Forces (AEF), as the American military organization in Europe was called.

First American Troops in France

The 1st Division was the first of the two million men to arrive in France as part of the American Expeditionary Forces.

Many National Guard units were called up in 1916 to patrol the Mexican border, where they remained intact as distinct units. During WWI, the National Guard divisions were typically formed from units of neighboring states merged into single divisions. The National Guard divisions were also supplemented by draftees pulled from the National Army divisions still in training.

Although nearly two million volunteered during the war, their numbers were limited initially and volunteers were also problematic from a manpower-planning perspective; keeping skilled tradesmen and chemistry students in their current roles provided greater long-term value to the overall war effort than having them man trenches in Europe. To obtain the necessary number of troops, the Selective Service Act authorizing the draft was passed on May 18, 1917. All men between the age of 21 and 31 registered at locations around the country on June 5, 1917. Those who registered were reviewed and drafted as needed to meet the quotas set for each of 4,648 local draft boards.

While some training camps were in place in April 1917, they were limited in capacity. Building the training camp facilities was the easiest challenge because the country had plenty of masons, carpenters, and plumbers along with the contractors willing and able to complete this work. Across the country, training camps capable of handling ten to forty thousand men were constructed on previously open land. However, there were severe shortages of uniforms and equipment, as well as the officers and non-coms to properly train the troops.

Camp Lewis during its construction in 1917.

Shortly after the U.S. entered the war, the Army selected volunteers into sixteen three-month-long Reserve Officer Training Camps (ROTC) at locations across the country. Several thousand men from the western states were selected for the first officer training camp that opened in May at the Presidio in San Francisco. With few exceptions, the men assigned as officers to the 91st Division at Camp Lewis were from the first officer training class at the Presidio. Most were college graduates with limited military experience. Some were members of National Guard units and others had experience in the corps of cadets at their universities. They were patriotic, enthusiastic, and very green, so men with limited military experience trained those with no experience, all while the training camps were constructed around them, and the uniforms and weapons they needed trickled out of the factories.

Recruits arriving at Camp Lewis in October 1917.

Preparing the Marines

The historical mission of the U.S. Marine Corps was to provide shipboard security on U.S. Navy vessels, act in combat roles in boarding actions on the old sailing ships, and provide security at naval bases. They also had an infantry role projecting American force in overseas locations during the Boxer Rebellion in China, the Banana Wars in Central America, and in defending Guantanamo Bay, Guam, and other American possessions in outpost locations.

The Marines entered the war with less than 14,000 men; forty percent of them were stationed outside the continental United States or served aboard Navy ships. To keep Wilson's promise of getting troops to France as quickly as possible, the Marines cobbled together the new 5th Infantry Regiment (aka 5th Marines) with just over 3,000 men and they sailed from New York in June with the Army's 1st Division.

At the same time, control of the Marine Corps transferred from the Navy to the Army for the duration of the war. The Marines continued to meet their naval obligations, but the Marines on the ground in France served under Army command. Although the Marines grew to approximately 75,000 men by war's end, much of the Corps remained in domestic and overseas locations other than Europe. Only the 5th, 6th, 11th, and 13th Marines went to France.

Life in training at Quantico and in France with the 13th Marines.

Marine recruits who volunteered in locations east of the Mississippi went to Quantico, Virginia or Parris Island, South Carolina, a new facility that was under construction when America entered the war. Those enlisting at locations west of the Mississippi River were trained at Mare Island Naval Yard, a large naval base and shipyard in San Pablo Bay, the northern extension of San Francisco Bay. The west side of Mare Island had the Marine barracks and training facilities.

Looking north from atop a hill at the western shore of Mare Island. The Marine Barracks, completed in 1917, is at center right. The parade grounds, which acted as the football field, is to the left and in front of the barracks. (Courtesy: Mare Island Museum)

Marine recruits entered an eight-to-ten week period of basic training with emphasis on marksmanship. Upon completing basic training, the former recruit was considered a competent Marine capable of handling all basic duties. Some new Marines at Mare Island stayed there to assist in training the next batch of recruits, performed other duties on base, or were transferred to naval bases on the West Coast, in the Pacific, or in Asia. Most new Marines from Mare Island were sent to the Marine Barracks in Quantico, Virginia for specialized training (e.g., non-commissioned officer training, machine gun training) or to gain additional infantry training in preparation for shipment overseas.

Preparing the Navy

The strength of the American armed forces entering the war was the Navy's dreadnoughts or battleships, but by the time the U.S. entered the war, Britain had the German surface fleet bottled up in the Baltic, so the U.S. battleships had little strategic impact on the war. Instead, the U.S. Navy's focus during the war was convoy protection and troop transport. Prior to America's entry into WWI, a nation had never attempted to move troops and supplies across an ocean on the scale of America's effort. (Canada, Australia, New Zealand and other Allied dominions did the same, but not at America's scale.) The Allies supported the U.S. Navy in this effort by providing troopships, but the U.S. Navy managed the process and used its own escort ships for this logistical challenge.

At the start of the war, the U.S. Navy had only one aging troop transport ship and another in the final stages of construction, the *U.S.S. Henderson,* at the Philadelphia Naval Yard. The *Henderson's* maiden voyage, or at least the timing of its voyage, illustrates America's lack of readiness to fight. Ordinarily, new ships undergo a shakedown cruise during which the ship is tested and returned to port, where adjustments are made as needed. The *Henderson* did not have a shakedown cruise. Instead, her boilers were fired for the first time on June 8, 1917, and after sailing from Philadelphia to New York, she left on her maiden voyage a few days later with 1,500 of the 2,600 5th Marines heading to France. While doing so upheld the Marines' claim to be the "First to Fight," it came with risks. Several times during the voyage the *Henderson* experienced problems and dropped back from the convoy or the convoy slowed to allow her to keep pace.

The U.S.S. Henderson sporting a "dazzle" camouflage pattern. Dazzle was not meant to conceal ships, but to make it difficult for German submarines to determine their size, type, and bearing.

Much of the solution to America's shortage of transport ships came from a collection of seventeen German ocean liners interned in American ports in 1914. These ships had not sailed in three years and their German crews sabotaged the engines and other machinery, but the ships were taken to U.S. naval yards, fixed, and fitted to carry U.S. troops to Europe. Using the seized German ships, the U.S. Navy transported nearly half the American troops that went to Europe. British troopships moved slightly more than the American ships, and ships flying under Italian, French, and Brazilian flags moved the remainder. In total, the Navy's Transport Service moved nearly 2.1 million men and women across the Atlantic during the war with almost 1.4 million transported between May and September 1918.

Naval Training

Historically, naval training occurred on ship, not in classrooms. Raw recruits boarded a vessel and learned their craft on the job. This approach to training became less effective as ships and their weapons systems became more technologically advanced. Coal and oil powered turbine engines replaced the wind-powered ships of the past. Cannons aimed by eye, if aimed at all, gave way to sophisticated gun systems with central fire control that required groups of sailors to perform complex calculations to determine the range and direction of fire needed to hit moving enemy targets. The advent of other weapons, such as torpedoes, required increased technological training as well.

During Teddy Roosevelt's time in office the Navy recognized that many recruits hailed from the Midwest, so they built the Great Lakes Naval Training Station north of Chicago, along Lake Michigan, which opened in July 1911. Most Navy recruits from the Midwest had never seen the ocean and many of those that grew up far from the Great Lakes had never seen a proper lake. Before the war, Great Lakes NTS trained 2,000 sailors per year. The war required a change of plans and by war's end, Great Lakes trained 125,000 men with up to 45,000 in training at one time.

Great Lakes Naval Training Station as it appeared in 1918 with the parade yard on the right.

Specialized naval training occurred at other locations and these facilities expanded greatly during the war as well. For example, the only naval aviation station at the start of the war was in Pensacola, Florida and it served both training and operations missions. By war's end, the Navy had fifteen aviation training locations and naval aviators trained at another dozen locations in conjunction with the Canadian, British, and French forces, or directly with aircraft manufacturers.

BEFORE DIVING into the role of athletics and football in America's military training camps during WWI, it is worth stepping back to explore why there was any role for athletics and football in the camps the first place. Although it may seem an odd fit, the justification for football in the training camps had its roots in the same thinking that led to football's role in the nation's colleges. Just as the formal role of athletics in schools is a uniquely American phenomenon, the formalization and extent of the athletic programs in the military was also solely American.

Athletics in America

Although athletic teams represent schools in selected sports in other nations, nowhere is the system as pervasive as in America. It began in the second half of the 1800s as increased urbanization and the expansion of sedentary office jobs led to concerns that men lacked the physical robustness that came with the more traditional life of days gone by. Equally important was the perceived impact on their spirit and morality. While there were many and differing reactions to this situation which do not roll up into a tight ball, one reaction was the Muscular Christianity Movement that justified athletics for philosophical and moral reasons.

Muscular Christianity sought to counteract these conditions by encouraging physical exercise and competitive games. It had its origins in England, but took hold in America among the upper classes and the elite schools on the East Coast. While football was recognized as a violent sport, the violence, if contained properly, was thought to offer the opportunity to build character by forcing players to face physical danger and become toughened. Football also provided the opportunity to operate in a team environment, give or take orders, and play your part in a larger enterprise. This line of thinking justified the value of football for school participants at the end of the eighteenth century and has never left the game. As football grew in popularity as a spectator sport, successful teams were also recognized for their ability to unite a school or local community and enhance their identity in comparison to outside groups.

While some focused on the value of athletics in building the elites, others saw the value of sport for all. The most prominent proponent of the latter view was the Young Men's Christian Association (YMCA), originally a social-outreach organization focused on improving the lot of the lower classes. The YMCA came to embrace Muscular Christianity, promoting 'Fitness for All.' The Muscular Christianity theme remains embodied in the YMCA's triangle logo today, reflecting the need to improve the Body, Mind and Spirit.

Many sports fans are familiar with the story of James Naismith inventing basketball at Springfield College in Massachusetts. During

Naismith's time, Springfield College was still known as the International Young Men's Christian Association Training School, whose purpose was to train physical directors for the YMCA locations popping up around the country. William G. Morgan, who studied under Naismith and graduated from the school, was the Physical Director at a YMCA when he invented volleyball (he called it Mintonette) as a game to be played by those who could not handle the rigorous running required in basketball.

Athletics in the Training Camps

The seeds of athletics and football were planted in the military prior to WWI, but they came into full flower in the training camps during the war years. Prior to WWI, recreational athletics were encouraged for fitness and stress relief, but the process was informal and depended on the personal preferences of local commanding officers. Naval ships had a history of boxing matches on deck and some capital ships in port played football games against club and college teams. In addition, football games were played among the National Guard regiments stationed along the Mexican border in 1916 and 1917. Camp Lewis' Charlie Turner was one of the stars of the 2nd Texas Infantry team during that time.

Of course, there was great prewar interest in varsity athletics at West Point and Annapolis, and their teams competed at the highest level against other college teams. But the academy experience mirrored that of other elite academic institutions on the East Coast and did not carry on with the graduates when they entered regular service.

The role of athletics in the training camps was representative of an inflection point in the role of athletics in America: the tug between the YMCA's view of "Fitness for All" and the desire for athletics at a premier level. One called for athletics for the masses; the other called for athletics to be watched by the masses. Neither excluded the other, but each pushed for dominance.

Athletics for the masses had three primary justifications in the camps: physical readiness, moral benefits, and the direct applicability of athletics to soldiering. The physical readiness justification was apparent. Prewar estimates showed that thirty percent of draft-age men in the U.S. were physically incapable of serving in the military and the evaluation of early draftees confirmed that estimate. The camps were expected to prepare men for the physical demands of combat and physical conditioning was a fundamental component of their training process. Calisthenics, drilling, long marches, and similar activities whipped the troops into shape in preparation for combat. Athletics for the masses was a complementary means to achieve a military end.

Significant athletic facilities for the average soldier were built at the camps. Camp Lewis was the largest Army cantonment of the war and the scope of the athletic facilities built for the average soldier was substantial. Their facilities included twelve football fields with goal posts and seating; six YMCA fields with volleyball, basketball, and other courts with all equipment provided by the YMCA; and sixteen baseball fields. Camp Lewis also built a stadium seating 18,000 for football and baseball that included a quarter-mile track and a 220-yard straightaway.

Camp Lewis and other camps had a range of inter-regimental athletic contests, including this track and field meet.

The YMCA alone spent $4 million (about $80 million today) for bats, balls, gloves, uniforms, and other sports equipment used at the camps and in Europe. Other groups such as the Knights of Columbus and the Jewish Welfare Board did their part, and other monies were raised for athletic funds at the training camps through admissions and fees generated by the camp all-star teams.

The athletics for the masses approach was also thought to bring moral benefits, by helping avoid sins of the flesh. Sports kept the men busy and gave them a healthy alternative use for their idle hands. Some also believed it helped reduce the incidence of sexually transmitted diseases, whose impact on military readiness proved a significant concern when 11.4 percent of 1917 draftees and 15 percent of 1918 draftees were found to have venereal diseases.

Finally, many inside and outside the military saw sports and football as a surrogate for combat training. The title of this book is drawn from Genl. Douglas MacArthur's famous quote, which encapsulates the thinking that lessons learned on athletic fields apply to the battlefield:

> *"Upon the fields of friendly strife*
> *Are sown the seeds*
> *That, upon other days, on other fields*
> *Will bear the fruits of victory."*

Though MacArthur wrote these lines in the 1920s, when he was West Point's Superintendent and had the lines engraved at the entrance to West Point's gymnasium, others expressed similar thoughts before and during the war.

William "Big Bill" Edwards, a College Football Hall of Famer from his Princeton days at the end of the previous century, published an article in the *New York Sun* that was syndicated across the country, arguing that athletics and football helped the average man become a soldier:

> "War, like football, has to have good generalship. ...Every scrimmage represents a battle, the offence and defence (sic) winning and losing ground. Ten miles and ten yards are synonymous gains. ...I have no doubts that the record shows that the athletic contests at the training camps have transformed many a youth who was inclined to be afraid into a real thoroughbred and fearless fighter. ...The need of physical recreation and athletics has clearly been proved by this war. One of the first to recognize it was Genl. Pershing. Now all the allied commanders recognize it. Governments have seen its value. And the men are loud in their praise of it. A good athlete makes a good soldier and a good soldier always is a good athlete."[2]

Similarly, Walter Camp argued as early as 1890 that football provided opportunities to develop leadership, virility, and pluck, and further, that football resembled war:

> "...there is no sport known that in its very nature so mimics that art of war as the game of football. The tactics, the formations, the attack and defense, all belong equally to the military commander and the football captain."[3]

Walter Camp might be dismissed as just another old varsity footballer, but Camp was named the head of the athletic division of the Navy Commission on Training Activities, while Joseph Fosdick of Princeton received a similar assignment with the Army. In his role, Camp was the Athletic Director for naval bases nationwide. He oversaw the appointment of a network of athletic officers assigned to each base that oversaw their physical conditioning and recreational activities. Camp's view mattered and many of his appointments were football coaches or former players who held similar views. "By" Dickson, the Lehigh and Bucknell football coach, headed athletic training in the Fourth District, which included League Island in Philadelphia. Bo Olcott, the Kansas football coach, became the coach at the Great Lakes Naval Training Station, while Andy Smith, the Cal football coach, was charged with athletic training for the sailors at Mare Island. Similar men took on these roles at camps across the country.

While athletics and football for the masses had their proponents in the Navy, it had a more strident proponent in the Secretary of War, Newton Baker. (Today's presidential cabinet has a Secretary of Defense that oversees all branches of the military. During WWI, there were separate Secretaries of the Navy and War [Army]). Baker clearly stood on the side of athletics geared toward the common man rather than elite athletics when he sent a letter to the December 1917 meeting of the NCAA, telling them, "A large number of sound bodies is the primary purpose rather than a small number of specialists."[4] The NCAA, which then was an advisory body comprised of 164 of the academic and athletic elite colleges and universities, took his words under advisement and published a statement saying:

"Resolved we recommend to all institutions, collegiate and secondary:

First, that athletic sports be subservient to the work of military preparation and be made therefore an essential factor in military training.

Second, that intercollegiate and interscholastic schedules be arranged for so long a time and so far as national and local conditions permit that possible encouragement be given to developments of promoting intramural sports with a view to promoting the participation of all students.

Third, that professional coaching and the expenditures incidental thereof be reduced to a minimum.

Fourth, that there be no pre-season coaching or practice, no scouting and no training table.

Fifth, that the number of officials at intercollegiate games and their fees be kept as low as possible.

And, further, be it resolved this association reaffirms its belief in the eligibility rules which it has already indorsed, including the freshman rule, and therefore recommends that there be no lowering of standards during the present crisis."[4]

Despite the well-meaning commitment, the nation's colleges and universities had no intention of following those principles. The university presidents, then and now, understood they were captive to the beauty and the beast that is intercollegiate athletics and few had the power or will to shut down varsity athletics.

The training camp commanders had never been subject to the beast of elite athletics and could see only its beauty. They saw elite competitive athletics as a tool to stimulate pride in their camps, generate positive publicity, and provide an entertainment diversion for their men. The large crowds and press coverage that ensued simply confirmed this view.

As a result, virtually every military location of note, and many that were not of note, formed a camp or base-sponsored football team that played nearby colleges, clubs, or other service teams during the

1917 and 1918 seasons. Many had basketball, baseball, boxing, and track and field teams as well. The large camps also formed inter-regimental leagues that played spirited games among themselves and, occasionally, played teams outside the base. The service athletic teams were viewed as a continuation of the best elements of college athletics and provided exposure to that experience to the 98 percent of servicemen that had not attended college.

EVERY SON OF LIBERTY

The training camps provided an athletic meritocracy that allowed players from colleges large and small to compete for positions, and a few players contributed that had not attended college or played college football. On average, the men on the service Rose Bowl teams were 24 years old and were experienced, high-level athletes. Almost all had played college football or rugby and most of the others were high school stars or proven athletes in other sports. They commonly lettered in multiple college sports and remained active in sports following their college and service days. A few played professional sports before the war and number did so after, while others coached high school and college sports or became college referees.

Some performed at the highest levels in sports other than football. The Great Lakes team alone had four team members who played major league baseball: Paddy Driscoll, George Halas, Bert Griffith, and Dick Reichle. Camp Lewis had Louis Guisto, who played four years of football and baseball at St. Mary's, and was playing first base for the Cleveland Indians in 1917 when he was drafted. Two Camp Lewis players went to the Olympics after the war. Ken Bartlett placed fifth in the discus at the 1920 Antwerp Olympics, while Charles Austin coached the U.S. rugby team to a gold medal at the 1924 Paris Olympics, albeit France and Romania were the only other countries competing in the event that year.

Despite being top athletes, they were physically smaller than today's college and professional football players. Part of the difference in size results from improved nutrition and disease control that has made today's average American taller and heavier than their 1917 counterpart; the strength and conditioning regimens we take for granted today also make a difference. However, most of the difference in player size results from differences in football's substitution rules and the pace of play of one hundred years ago. Like soccer today, early football players could not return to the game after being replaced by a substitute, though a 1917 rule change allowed substituted players to return to the game at the start of the next quarter. Since players in "one-platoon" football played both offense and defense, they needed the stamina to play a sixty-minute game and the pace of play made that more challenging. Back then, the clock kept running on incomplete passes or when the ball went out of bounds and, equally important, teams seldom huddled. After completing a play, the teams lined up quickly, the quarterback called his signals to indicate the play to be run (like audibles in today's game), and the ball was snapped within ten to fifteen seconds of completing the previous play. The pace of play remained close to football's rugby roots and you seldom see rugby players the size of today's football linemen; the biggest are the size of linebackers. The combination of these factors resulted in college running backs commonly weighing 140 to 170 pounds with the largest tipping the scales at 185 pounds; most linemen were only slightly bigger than the backs. Linemen who stood over six feet tall or weighed more than two hundred pounds were regularly noted in the press for being of exceptional size.

Ninety-five percent of the players attended college before they played service football; one was a practicing physician and there were a handful of lawyers. At the time, many lawyers served a law 'apprenticeship' before taking the bar exam rather than study law in school. Those that attended law school earned law degrees as undergraduates and began practicing law immediately after their undergraduate days, assuming they passed the bar exam. A similar system of undergraduate education applied in dentistry and several players were dental students or dental graduates prior to joining the service.

The 1917 Mare Island Team

Since Mare Island trained Marine recruits who enlisted west of the Mississippi, many Mare Island players were from the far West. Some were from Minnesota, Illinois, Texas, or Nebraska, and there was one transplanted Floridian who had played football at North Carolina.

Similarly, just as there were far fewer Marines than there were soldiers in the Army, Mare Island had far fewer men than their future opponent, Camp Lewis. Camp Lewis held thirty thousand men, while Mare Island never had more than 2,700 Marines at any point during the war and had less than 500 when the 1917 Mare Island team was formed. The limited number of men at Mare Island led to problems with team depth, but the football team made up for it by making a concerted effort to recruit top football players to enlist in the Marines.

John Beckett, who captained Oregon to victory in the 1917 Rose Bowl was Mare Island's team captain and coach. For his efforts with Oregon during the 1916 season, Beckett was the first Westerner recognized by Walter Camp on his All-American teams. Beckett enlisted shortly after the war started, arrived at Mare Island in May 1917, and was ordered to form the Mare Island Marines football team. (Mare Island had a separate navy team known as the Mare Island Sailors.) Beckett received permission to spend two weeks in the Northwest scheduling games and recruiting future Marines, all of whom happened to be top college football players. He returned to Mare Island having scheduled two games and gained several commitments to enlist. The core of the 1917 Mare Island Marine team was a group of players from the University of Oregon. Besides Beckett, Oregon contributed starting right end Cliff "Brick" Mitchell and starting fullback Hollis Huntington from the 1917 Rose Bowl team, as well as starting right tackle Ed Bailey, starting right guard Elmer Hall, and substitute back John Coshow from earlier Oregon teams.

Mare Island scheduled seven regular season games, with the early games against teams from the college-laden, San Francisco area, before traveling to the Northwest and Los Angeles later in the season. The Mare Island schedule for the 1917 season is shown below.

1917 Mare Island Regular Season Schedule

Sept. 15	California	California Field, Berkeley
Sept. 29	California	California Field, Berkeley
Oct. 10	San Francisco Olympic Club	Mare Island
Oct. 21	St. Mary's	Oakland
Nov. 3	Oregon	Multnomah Field, Portland
Nov. 10	Camp Lewis	Tacoma Stadium
Nov. 24	21st Division	Washington Park, LA

Mare Island opened its season on September 15, by traveling twenty miles south to Berkeley for a test with the University of California eleven. Cal was still getting back to playing football after dropping the sport in favor of rugby from 1906 to 1914. California was coached by Andy Smith, one of college football's all-time great coaches, who would lead Cal's Wonder Teams to several Rose Bowls in the early 1920s. But they were not there yet. The Cal team of 1917 was respectable, but no match for the Mare Island Marines.

The star of the game was Mare Island's quarterback, Walter Brown, who started his career at Wisconsin, before returning to the Northwest to play at Washington State. He opened the scoring in the first quarter with a 30-yard run up the middle and then connected with right end Cloy Hobson for a 40-yard touchdown pass in the second quarter. After the half, Brown scampered around the left end for an 85-yard touchdown run. In the fourth, he connected with Hobson again for a 40-yard gain to the 3-yard line. Fullback Hollis Huntington earned the final touchdown with the game ending at 27-0.

While California was held scoreless, the Marines substituted at every position other than for Stan Ridderhof at center. Robert Wilson, who attended Michigan but did not play varsity football, subbed at right tackle for John Beckett. That proved to be Wilson's only appearance in a game that season since he was transferred to Quantico in early November. Wilson will appear again in the story when the Marines fight battles of far greater consequence in the summer of 1918. Including Wilson, eight of the twenty-eight Marines on the Mare Island Marines team were transferred to other locations during the 1917 season.

The Marines returned to California for a second game two weeks later. The Cal Bears limited Mare Island to one first half touchdown, that coming on a 20-yard run by Darrell Gardner. In the second half, Brown connected with Cliff "Brick" Mitchell for a 30-yard completion and followed it with several runs before getting into the end zone himself. Fred Molthen added two touchdown runs resulting in a 26-0 final score. The Marines run-pass combination along with another strong defensive effort gave them a second dominant victory.

The 1917 Mare Island football team on the parade grounds at Mare Island in September 1917.

Mare Island's third game of the season came against the San Francisco Olympic Club (SFOC) on October 10. The SFOC was founded before the Civil War and is the oldest athletic club still operating in the United States. Like many athletic clubs around the country, SFOC was as much about social functions and business connections as it was about athletics, but its athletic teams were the club's core and were very successful. They fielded their first football team in 1890, the same year the SFOC was accused of recruiting players by offering them jobs with local businesses. The American Athletic Union (AAU) investigated and determined that while some SFOC players were offered jobs, doing so did not violate amateur rules and constituted only "semi-professionalism." Although that incident is often cited as the origin of the term "semipro," the term was used in the press to describe baseball teams at least eight years earlier.

After two easy victories over Cal, Mare Island played an uninspired, sloppy game against the Olympics, accumulating more than 130 penalty yards. Mare Island scored first half touchdowns after an SFOC fumble, and via Stan Ridderhof's punt block and recovery in the end zone. The second half saw Brown connect on touchdown passes to Hobson and Mitchell, but the most notable play came in the last few minutes when SFOC kicked a field goal to score the first points against Mare Island in the 1917 season.

Mare Island's fourth game came against another local team, St. Mary's, then located in Oakland. St. Mary's football had moments in the sun several decades later when they played in the 1938 Cotton Bowl and the 1945 Sugar Bowl, but their teams of the 1910s were not at that level. Walter Brown dominated offensively with three touchdown runs and a punt return during which he broke six tackles. Although St. Mary's moved the ball successfully through much of the game, they were unable to score and lost 27-0.

The soldiers of the sea headed north two weeks later for a November 3 game with Oregon, the alma mater of six Mare Island players. As a big game having the potential for a large crowd, the tilt was played at Multnomah Field in Portland rather than at Oregon's smaller stadium in Eugene.

Oregon was coached by Hugo Bedzek who, if nothing else, did not take kindly to B.S. Like many coaches in 1917, the loss of key players to the armed forces put him in a foul mood. Entering the season with zero, nada, zilch returning starters, the less-than-optimistic Bedzek had this to say at the end of a preseason practice:

> "No chance. No chance. Don't try to kid yourself into thinking that we may turn out a winning team this year – it can't be done.

There is no issue talking, I cannot do the impossible – develop a team from among that bunch. (Nodding toward players heading to the locker room.) I don't mean we won't have a team. We will have that, but not one we can expect much from. Why, half of these fellows are just out here because of their loyalty to the school. They are green; they have no experience. It looks as though one year I was to have my greatest team and the next year my poorest. We will do the best we can, however, and before the end of the season we will have some kind of a team." (Author's note: Oregon ended the season with a 4-3 record.)"[5]

The Marines entered the game knowing they outweighed the Webfoots by ten pounds per man. Ed Bailey, the former Oregon man, was the heaviest Marine tipping the scales at a monstrous 220 pounds. Beckett was the second heaviest at 195. Oregon likely held its only advantage in the punting department via the foot of Bill Steers, their stud running back. Perhaps the Marines made an impression that day, since Steers later enlisted and played for Mare Island during the 1918 season.

Oregon's 1917 zero, nada, zilch team practicing at their home stadium, Kincaid Field.

Confident the Marines were and they had their eyes on a bigger prize than bagging a few ducks. Beckett, in the lead up to the game, said:

"We are ready for a grueling game, and we will be out there to give old Oregon and the fans the best we have in our football vocabulary. We want that Pasadena game and want it bad. If we can hold Oregon scoreless and do the same to the All Officers' eleven at Tacoma next week I think the Pasadena people will give our eleven consideration when making their decision as to the Western team for the big New Year's game during the Tournament of Roses."[6]

Patriotism was on display during the pregame ceremonies with the local police band and the Navy's 44th Regimental Band playing the "The Star-Spangled Banner." For those of us attending sporting events today, the "The Star-Spangled Banner" has always preceded sporting events, but even that tradition started at some point and it did so during WWI. It arrived on the national scene in Chicago when the Cubbies faced the Boston Red Sox in the 1917 World Series, but they played it during the seventh-inning stretch. The Mare Island-Oregon game is the earliest instance your author found at which "The Star-Spangled Banner" was played before a football game. Still, we're not saying the pregame tradition started here; let's just say the folks in Portland were early adopters.

The Marines scored early against Oregon on a drive that featured a 15-yard tackle-around by Beckett. Following the Marines' touchdown, Oregon elected to kick off to the Marines rather than receive the kick. After a series of short gains and a fifteen-yard sweep by Brown, Darrell Gardner ran it in for the score, but the punt-out by Huntington went over Gardner's head and sea soldiers lost their chance at the extra point attempt. Neither team moved the ball successfully the remainder of the half, so the score stood at 13-0 Marines at half.

Since it is halftime, we'll take a break from the game to note that Oregon kicked off to the Marines following each of the Mare Island touchdowns. This another instance in which the game's rules differ from today since the team that had been scored on had the choice to kick or receive the ball. Since many games were low-scoring affairs and field position was vital, coaches sometimes kicked the ball after being scored on in the hope that the opponent would turn over the ball or have a poor punt, either one leading to a field-position advantage. The rule and strategy is hard to fathom today, but that's just the way it was.

Another oddity of the time was the punt-out. On the point after play following a touchdown, the scoring team was given the ball at the spot the ball crossed the goal line on the touchdown play. From there, they had two options. The first option was for the kicker to walk at a 90-degree angle from the goal line until he reached a spot on the field that gave him a favorable angle to kick the extra point. This worked well if the scoring play occurred near the goal posts, but less so if the touchdown was scored near a sideline, since the scoring team could only achieve a reasonable kicking angle after walking thirty to forty yards down the sideline, making for a long kick.

The scoring team's second option was the punt-out. On a punt-out, the scoring team took the ball at the point it crossed the goal line and punted it to a teammate located on the playing field, normally positioned between the uprights, who could fair catch the ball and attempt a kick from the spot of the catch. If a teammate did not catch the punted ball, the scoring team lost its opportunity to attempt the extra point. The punt-out was often the best option, but involved risk, and its failure had significant implications in close games.

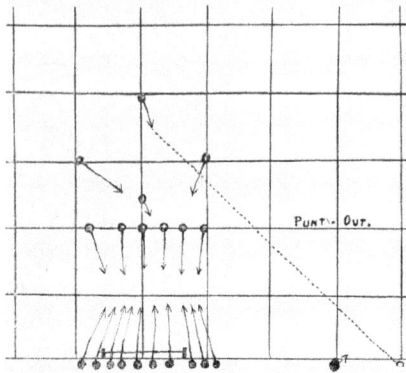

Pop Warner's 1912 illustration of the proper formation for a punt-out. The defense is behind the goal line and the offense is aligned at the ten-yard line between the goal posts. The punt is intended for the offensive player standing on the 20-yard line, but anyone on the offensive side was eligible to catch the punt-out.

Mare Island dominated Oregon the rest of the game. In the second half, Brown dodged and sprinted his way to an 80-yard punt return for a touchdown (contributing to his 170 punt return yards that day). One reporter, describing Brown's performance in the ethnic-ity-laced language of the times, wrote, "Brown was here and there and everywhere. He ate up the ground like an Irishman eats corn beef and cabbage."[7] Being of predominantly Irish ancestry, allow me to add that Walter Brown was so good that any number of Irish, cabbage-eating rooters in the stands took notice, stood on their hind legs, and clapped their forelegs in appreciation. The Marines' final scoring drive had several big gains by Ed Bailey on tackle-arounds, but it was another Oregon man, Hollis Huntington, who took it in for the final score and another 27-0 shutout.

The victory over Oregon gave Mare Island a 5-0 record with four wins over college teams, including two against California. No team on the West Coast could boast a more impressive record to that point in the season. Mare Island's next game came against Camp Lewis which, like Mare Island, was loaded with college stars. Surviving that game would position Mare Island as the best team on the West Coast.

The Camp Lewis Team

Frederick Hunter while playing for Washington State in 1909. Note the one-piece uniform with laces up the front and leather shoulder pads sewn into the uniform.

Let's turn our attention to the boys of the 91st Division at Camp Lewis, located outside Tacoma, Washington. Camp Lewis was the largest Army training camp of WWI with more than 66,000 recruits passing through its gates. Besides the 91st Divisions, the 13th Division was formed and trained at Camp Lewis after the 91st Division was sent to France in 1918.

The core of the 91st Division (approximately 25,500 men) was four infantry regiments—the 361st, the 362nd, the 363rd, and the 364th Infantry—each of which was further divided into thirteen companies named by the letters A through M (e.g., A Co., B Co.), plus a regimental Headquarters Company, Supply Company, and a Machine Gun Company. The division also had artillery, machine gun, medical, and other support units. The 91st was four to five times larger than the largest universities of the day (and the university enrollment figures included female students). The sheer number of men gave Camp Lewis a large pool of candidates for their football team and an even larger number of trainees to keep entertained.

The 91st drew its trainees from eight western states: Arizona, California, Idaho, Montana, Nevada, Oregon, Utah, Washington, and Wyoming and the football team reflected the larger camp. All but one of the men who played for Camp Lewis lived in a Rocky Mountain or West Coast state and the exception, Douglas McKay, was from North Dakota.

Camp Lewis' team included officers and enlisted men and many of the officers were a bit older than the typical service player. Fred "Jumbo" Hunter was 31 years old, having lettered at Washington

State from 1908 to 1910 before becoming a miner. (It was not uncommon for college men to take time off from their studies or graduate and become miners in the hope of striking it rich.)

Camp Lewis was coached by William "Fox" Stanton, who led Pomona and Occidental to five conference titles in the nine years through 1916. A veteran of the Spanish-American War, Stanton was a 1st Lt. with the 91st Division's 316th Supply Train and served with the unit in France in 1918. He was assisted by Eddie Kienholz, a former Washington State player and assistant coach with their 1916 Rose Bowl team.

The Camp Lewis schedule included an eclectic mix of opponents of varying quality with only a handful of opponents we recognize today. Whereas Mare Island started its season on September 15, Camp Lewis got a late start because its draftees did not begin arriving at Camp Lewis until September 8.

1917 Camp Lewis Regular Season Schedule

Oct. 13	Washington State	Tacoma Stadium
Oct. 27	316th Sanitary Train	Tacoma Stadium
Nov. 3	Oregon State Frosh	Multnomah Field, Portland
Nov. 10	Mare Island	Tacoma Stadium
Nov. 17	Multnomah AAC	Multnomah Field, Portland
Nov. 23	Chemawa Indian School	Camp Lewis
Nov. 29	U. Washington NTS	Tacoma Stadium
Dec. 8	Fort Stevens	Camp Lewis

The first game of the season played by soldiers from Camp Lewis was a fundraising game in Tacoma on October 13, between the 362nd Infantry Regiment Officers and Washington State. The 362nd Officers team preceded the development of the Camp Lewis all-star team which represented Camp Lewis for most of the season. The first coaches meeting for the Camp Lewis all-star team occurred on October 11, two days before the Washington State game, and the all-star team held tryouts through at least October 17, four days after the 362nd Officers team met Washington State. Although only four players on the 362nd team appeared in games with the Camp

Lewis team once the latter team was fully organized, the 362nd Officers team was a precursor to the Camp Lewis all-star team. So, we will track the 362nd Officers team separately and still consider its players to be part of the service Rose Bowl teams.

The 362nd Officers team is also worth tracking because the 362nd Infantry went to Europe in 1918 and was involved in heavy fighting in the Meuse-Argonne Offensive in France and the Lys-Scheldt Offensive in Belgium. The 362nd Officers team members are an example of a concentrated group of men who took heavy casualties based on where, when, and how they fought and provides an opportunity to illustrate the doughboys' experience in the war.

So, the team that played Washington State consisted solely of officers from the 362nd Infantry Regiment, a pool of approximately 100 officers. Despite the low number of candidates for a football team, it was a very talented group. Eleven of the twenty-two played college football or rugby and three were college team captains. Others played college football after the war and almost all were high school or college athletes in football or other sports.

Though the 362nd Officers team included one man directly out of high school—and he had served on the Mexican border with the California National Guard while in high school—and a few that graduated from college in 1917, the bulk of the officers were several years out of college and had started their careers when America entered the war. These were men that did not need the Army; they believed the Army and nation needed them. They were the model of the men America admired then and many admire now: physically strong, educated men who left their careers behind to serve their country in a time of need. They arrived at Camp Lewis before the draftees and began bringing the training camp into order.

The team had some interesting players. One was Captain James R. Montgomery who, at 38, was the oldest player on the 362nd Officers team, having been a newspaper reporter in El Paso, at the time he volunteered for the ROTC. Montgomery served with the 1st Texas Volunteers during the Spanish-American War and was wounded in 1899 while with the 33rd U.S. Volunteers in the Philippines. Promoted to corporal, he also served in China during the Boxer Rebellion before leaving the Army in 1906. His commissioning as a

Captain was due, in part, to his being one of the exceedingly rare ROTC men with combat experience.

Another 362nd officer was Elijah 'Lige' Worsham, a native of Evansville, Indiana where he was a high school football star. He continued his football career as a running back at Purdue, lettering in 1904 before venturing off to the Yukon Territory. He made his way to Oregon where he became a salesman for a macaroni brand and a member of the Oregon National Guard's machine gun unit. His National Guard experience qualified him for the ROTC at the Presidio and his performance there resulted in him being commissioned a Captain. Along the way, likely while stationed at the Presidio, Worsham met and became engaged to Corona Ghirardelli of San Francisco, whose grandfather ran a confectionary shop that grew into the chocolate manufacturer of the same name.

SOUVENIR
FOOTBALL PROGRAM

Officers, 362nd Inf., vs.
Washington State College
Benefit Enlisted Men's Athletic Fund
362 nf. Infantry
Tacoma Stadium   Saturday, October 13, 1917

Game program cover for the 362nd Officers versus Washington State game. (Courtesy: Manuscripts, Archives, and Special Collections, Washington State University)

THE GAME between the 362nd Officers and Washington State was a major event in Tacoma given that Camp Lewis had more than 30,000 men in the camp less than 15 miles from downtown Tacoma. At a time when few, if any, American soldiers were actively fighting in France, a fundraising football game involving men preparing to fight for Uncle Sam was cause for celebration and ceremony. The game was a benefit for the 362nd Infantry's Enlisted Men's Athletic Fund, but it was a complete production. During an era when many football game programs had only a few pages of simple typeface, the program for this game was twenty-eight pages long with team pictures, lineups, profiles, and many pages of advertising.

Camp Lewis brought five-thousand soldiers and the 362nd regimental band to the game, and the various units paraded through the streets of Tacoma on their way to the stadium. The 15,000 spectators were the largest crowd for a football game in Tacoma's history.

The starters for the 362nd Officers against Washington State and all other players on the roster during their three-game season are shown in the following table.

Player	Rank	Position	College
Frank 'Deke' Gard	1st Lt.	LE	Stanford
Elijah 'Lige' Worsham	Capt.	LT	Purdue
Wellslake Morse	2nd Lt.	LG	Cincinnati
Bill Russell	2nd Lt.	C	California
Samuel 'Jack' Hayes	2nd Lt.	G	Idaho
Charles Thorpe	Capt.	RT	Stanford
Arthur Duerr	2nd Lt.	RE	Culver Military (HS), USC*
Dixon 'Dick' Kapple	1st Lt.	QB	Utah State
Ben Dorris	2nd Lt.	LHB	Oregon*
William Bell	2nd Lt.	FB	Redlands HS (CA)
Everett May	2nd Lt.	RH	Oregon State
Substitutes			
Howard Angus	2nd Lt.	RHB	Occidental
John Burgard	1st Lt.	LG	Oregon*
Frederick Campbell	2nd Lt.	RHB	None
George Crary	2nd Lt.	G	Stanford
Rhodolph Esmay	2nd Lt.	HB	None
Harry Evans	1st Lt.	QB	Harvard*
Vernon Heilig	2nd Lt.	E	None
Ralph 'Spec' Hurlburt	2nd Lt.	FB	Michigan
William Hutchinson	2nd Lt.	LH	Stanford
John McLean	1st Lt.	FB	McGill
Carl Middlestate	2nd Lt.	E	None
James Montgomery	Capt.	T	None
Thomas O'Brien	2nd Lt.	B	Unknown
Walter Tuller	Maj.	T	California

*did not play football

On the first play from scrimmage, Everett May, the former Oregon State captain and the Officer's team captain, dislocated his knee, so the team's leadership transferred to Lige Worsham. Washington State moved the ball effectively, but their quarterback, Dick Hanley, lost a fumble in the red zone and missed two first quarter field goals. The Officers were bigger and heavier than Washington State, with a tackle-to-tackle weight averaging 191 pounds. Despite the size advantage, the 362nd Officers could not run the ball effectively.

HERE'S THE OFFICERS' TEAM ITSELF

Reading from left to right the players are: Top row—Lieutenant May, captain and tackle; Lieutenant Evans, quarterback; Lieutenant Gard, end; Lieutenant Burgard, guard; Lieutenant Hutchinson, halfback; Captain Thorpe, guard. Middle row—Lieutenant Campbell, guard; Lieutenant Bell, halfback. Bottom row—Lieutenant McLean, fullback; Lieutenant Kupple, quarterback; Lieutenant Russell, center; Captain Montgomery, tackle; Lieutenant Doris, end; Lieutenant Esmay, halfback; Lieutenant Middlestate, end.

A motley looking crew in the 362nd Officers team picture from the Washington State game program. (Courtesy: Manuscripts, Archives, and Special Collections, Washington State University)

The second half was more of the same with both teams playing a ragged game with exciting plays interspersing longer periods of short gains and fumbles. Frank 'Deke' Gard, playing left end for the Officers, gained twenty yards on an end around and caught a 25–yard pass to bring some excitement to the game. Throughout, Washington State moved the ball well on the ground, but failed to complete a pass all game and turned the ball over several times. The game ended in a 0-0 tie.

Washington State finished the 1917 season without allowing a touchdown and five of their starters went on to play for Mare

Island's 1919 Rose Bowl team. All this means the 362nd Officers were a pretty fair team having played a top college team to a draw.

The first game for the Camp Lewis all-star team came against the 316th Sanitary Train. (Sanitary Trains were the ambulance and medical units of the day.) Earlier in 1917, a group of University of Oregon students, including several top football players, joined the Oregon Medical Corps, a volunteer ambulance unit later absorbed into the 316th Sanitary Train, which itself became part of the 91st Division at Camp Lewis. Just as the 362nd Officers formed their own regimental team, so did the boys in the 316th Sanitary Train. It's fair to say the 316th Sanitary Train had as much talent as the Camp Lewis all-star team since the Camp Lewis-316th Sanitary Train game ended in a scoreless tie.

Substituting at quarterback for Camp Lewis against the 316th Sanitary Train was H. B. "Pete" Lenz, Occidental's star quarterback a few years earlier. The 316th game was the only game in which Lenz appeared since he and five hundred other draftees were soon transferred to Camp Green in North Carolina to fill out the ranks of the 116th Engineers of the 41st Division. Lenz and the 41st Division shipped to France at the end of November, making Lenz the first member of a service Rose Bowl team to join the fight over there.

More important than the outcome of the Camp Lewis-316th Sanitary Train game was the fact that seven players from the 316th Sanitary Train team joined the Camp Lewis all-star team over the next few days. Three of the seven started for Camp Lewis in their next game and six of the seven players were on Camp Lewis' Rose Bowl travel roster at season's end. With the addition of four players from the 362nd Officers team and seven players from the 316th Sanitary Train, the Camp Lewis team gained a great deal of talent. Their talent pool continued to increase over the season as draftees arrived at Camp Lewis. Despite increasing their talent, Camp Lewis faced the challenge of integrating the new talent and playing as a team. That proved to be a season long challenge.

After failing to score in the first two games of the season, Camp Lewis was hoping to change things around in the rain against the Oregon State freshmen on November 3, a game in which Camp Lewis held advantages in speed, size, and experience. Camp Lewis' first touchdown of the game and season came via an off-tackle run by Dick Romney, the 145-pounder who had starred at Utah State. Romney's surname is familiar to anyone with a pulse, but unless you live in Utah, and even if you do, it's not likely due to Dick Romney's storied career as a player and coach at Utah State. Most people know the name due to the accomplishments of his second cousin, George W. Romney, former Governor of Michigan, 1968 Republican presidential nominee wannabe, and Secretary of Housing and Urban Development. However, even George W. Romney's fame is fleeting and he is now best known for having fathered Mitt Romney, former Governor of Massachusetts and 2012 Republican candidate for President. (And for those trying to keep score genealogically, Dick and Mitt Romney are second cousins once removed.)

Despite the muddy field, Camp Lewis' lightest player, the 140-pound Doug McKay, spent much of the day sweeping around Oregon State's end for long gains, including two touchdown runs, making him the star of the 20-0 victory.

An action shot from an unknown game or scrimmage at Camp Lewis. The linebacker (identified by the arrow on left) is Walter Hollywood, a backup player for Camp Lewis. (Courtesy: Walter P. Hollywood Family)

Next up for Camp Lewis and Mare Island was a midseason game against one another, a game that proved to be the toughest challenge for either team during the regular season.

THE OLD RED-WHITE-AND-BLUE

Following their 27-0 victory over Oregon in Portland on November 3, the Mare Island Marines left Portland and headed to Eugene, Oregon. They arrived on Sunday evening for four days of practice under Oregon's coach, Hugo Bedzek. The players stayed at fraternity houses on the Oregon campus while the coaches and other officers stayed in a Eugene hotel.

It might seem a bit odd that a coach would spend large portions of a week tutoring a team that stomped his own team a few days earlier, but that was Hugo Bedzek's nature. It helped that five of the seventeen Mare Island players making the trip were Oregon football alums and three had played for him the previous year. Beckett knew his team needed fine-tuning. He sought it out, and he received it from Coach Bedzek.

It also helped that Bedzek was bit of a mercenary. Born near Prague, Bohemia (now the Czech Republic), he emigrated to America at age six and grew up on the south side of Chicago, playing at the University of Chicago under Amos Alonzo Stagg.

After graduating, he became the coach at Oregon for one year, before returning to Chicago as an assistant, and then became head coach at Arkansas. Bedzek returned to Oregon in 1913 to coach football, basketball, and baseball. That might seem like a full schedule to some, but no one ever accused Bedzek of being lazy. To fill in the open spots in his schedule he scouted for the Pittsburgh Pirates and in the middle of the Pirates' 1917 season, they hired him as their manager, and he kept that job through the 1919 season, all the while coaching multiple sports at Oregon.

Bedzek put the Marines through two three-hour sessions on Monday as well as morning sessions on Tuesday, Wednesday and Thursday. The latter three morning sessions were followed by afternoon scrimmages with the Oregon varsity whose next game was a week away.

Based largely on Mare Island's reputation, the local scribes considered Mare Island the favorite in the matchup with Camp Lewis and the sentiment was echoed by Everett May, the 362nd Officers team captain who injured his knee against Washington State. Unable to play, Everett May scouted the Mare Island-Oregon game and came away impressed with Mare Island. He also was concerned that the Marines had the full week to concentrate solely on football, while the Camp Lewis team members maintained their regular Army duties. Since Camp Lewis' players were spread across the division's many units, each of which maintained their own schedules, the football team had difficulty finding practice times when the full team could be available. Having access to many potential players spread across distinct units at the large camp was not always the advantage it was cracked up to be.

If Tacoma had been excited about the 362nd Officers-Washington State game, there was a new level of excitement for the Camp Lewis-Mare Island game. Special trains brought 10,000 soldiers from Camp Lewis to Tacoma who again paraded through the streets to Tacoma Stadium accompanied by four regimental bands. Twenty-five thousand people witnessed the contest, which was preceded by a special moment courtesy of the 362nd Regimental Band. To honor their French comrades, including four French officers who were instructors at Camp Lewis and attendees at the game, the band played "Marseillaise" and "The Star-Spangled Banner."

The game opened conservatively with neither team moving the ball. The Marines came within field goal range once in the first quarter, but Walter Brown missed the placed kick. In the second quarter, Brown popped several 10-to-20 yard runs and moved the ball to the 2-yard line before Huntington powered across the line for the score. Molthen converted the extra point to make it 7-0 Marines.

Scene on the field at Tacoma Stadium, presumably in the pregame ceremony.

Like others, Molthen was a multi-sport star. He was a high school track star in Butte, Montana, winning several state titles in the middle-distance events. Lest you think winning a title in Montana is unimpressive, he competed in a national high school track meet in Chicago in 1916, placing first in the mile run. As a high school fullback, he literally powered his team to the intermountain championship in a win over a Salt Lake City team. One of his football teammates at Butte High was Skimmett Dee of the Camp Lewis squad.

Camp Lewis dominated the second quarter with four first downs versus the Marines' one, and drove to the Marines' fifteen-yard line, but could not take it across for a score.

At halftime, Bill Hayward, Oregon's long-time trainer and track coach, for whom Oregon's famous Hayward Field facility is named, ripped into the Marines in shades of blue they hadn't known were in the spectrum. It seemed to motivate them at the start of the second half as they drove to the Army seven before turning the ball over on downs. Camp Lewis substituted in a series of players to gain an advantage, but it was for naught. The Marines drove down the field on their first possession of the fourth quarter. The key play came on an inadvertent quick snap that surprised Camp Lewis' defense as much as it did Walter Brown, but Brown carried the oval for a 27-yard gain to the Army six. Four plays later, Brown took it the last foot into the end zone for the game's final touchdown and score, leaving it a 13-0 Marines' advantage.

It was a clean, well-played game during which neither team was penalized and each team completed only one forward pass.

Although the Marines outgained Camp Lewis 259 to 179, Camp Lewis managed to hold Mare Island to their lowest score of the season.

Finishing the Regular Season

Camp Lewis played the Multnomah Athletic Club of Portland the next week on November 17. Multnomah was the visitor and traditionally one of the stronger club teams on the West Coast; seven service Rose Bowl players were members of the Multnomah team before or after the war. Like the college teams, however, the Multnomah roster was depleted by men entering the services.

Multnomah was nursing injuries following their recent games with Oregon State and the Chemawa Indians, and entered the game missing some key players. The soldiers were also missing several linemen who had started at least one game, including E. L. Damkroger, Harry Green, Bill Holden, and Emzy Lynch. The game opened with Romney taking the ball 40 yards from scrimmage and his 15-yard off tackle run a bit later put the ball on the 4-yard line. Following a 15-yard penalty, McKay kicked a 20-yard field goal four minutes into the game. Late in the first period, Multnomah drove into Camp Lewis territory and tied the game on a 45-yard field goal.

In the second half, Bill Russell, Raymond MacRae, and Charles "Truck" Lane led the Camp Lewis blocking on a 75-yard drive that ended in a McKay run for a touchdown and a 10-3 lead. The Multnomah game was Lane's first playing for Camp Lewis. He was in the midst of preseason practice at Cal when he received his draft notice and assumed he would be called shortly, so he left the Cal team and did not play in Cal's two early games against the Mare Island Marines. After a delay in being called to report, Lane returned to school and the football field. Lane was then ordered to report a few days before Cal's game with Washington, but he negotiated with the local draft board to allow him to report a few days after the game. He did so after Cal beat Washington and started for Camp Lewis against Multnomah later that week. It's a good thing he played, since his contribution as a lineman allowed Camp Lewis to eke out a 10-3 victory in a game that should not have been close.

Next up for Camp Lewis was the Chemawa Indian School of Salem, Oregon. Chemawa had a long tradition of playing top club and college teams throughout the Northwest and down to the Bay Area. They were not a pushover, having previously defeated the 4th Engineers team at Vancouver Barracks and tied the same Multnomah Athletic Club eleven that Camp Lewis had beaten 10-3. Chemawa was coached by a former Cornell footballer and lawyer, Bill Warner, whose previous experience included coaching for one-or-two-year stints at Cornell, North Carolina, Colgate, St. Louis, and Oregon.

Bill's older brother, Glen, better known by his nickname, "Pop," had taken Carlisle to national prominence and was now the coach of the reigning back-to-back national champions at Pitt. Pop won his third national championship at Pitt in 1918 and his fourth at Stanford in 1928, but Bill Warner wasn't Pop and Chemawa wasn't Carlisle and Camp Lewis proceeded to pound Chemawa, 49-0. Camp Lewis had a number of long runs against Chemawa with Doug McKay accounting for 25 of the team's 49 points.

It was an impressive win, made more impressive by the fact that fifteen miles away in Tacoma, the 362nd Officers team was playing and beating Fort Flagler, 13-6. Among those playing for the 362nd Officers team was Camp Lewis' captain and starting center Bill Russell, starting quarterback Dick Kapple, backup tackle Edward Sewell, and backup end Deke Gard. How the decision was made to allow two starters to play for their regimental team rather than the division team is unclear, but that's what happened.

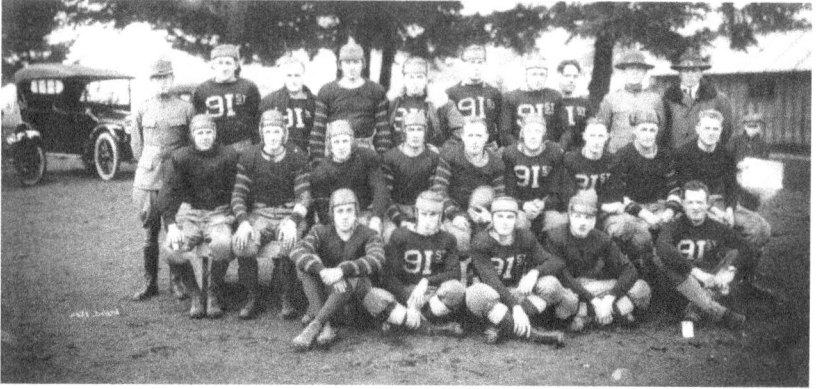

1917 Camp Lewis / 91st Division football team. Back row: Col. Jordan, MacRae, Patterson, Christiansen, Sewell, Hunter, Lane, Lt. Stanton, Capt. Cook. Middle row: Gard, Bartlett, Snyder, Kapple, Russell (Capt.), Craig, Hollywood, Monteith, Rowland. Front row: Romney, Bynon, Maguire, McKay, Gougar. (Courtesy: U.S. Army, Lewis Army Museum, Joint Base Lewis-McChord)

The following day, November 24, Mare Island played USC in its last regular-season contest. Mare Island was originally scheduled to play the 21st Infantry Regiment based at Camp Kearny, in San Diego County. (Camp Kearny changed hands a few times over the next several decades and is now Marine Corps Air Station Mirimar.) However, the situation on the Mexican border flared up again and the 21st Infantry was ordered to deploy along the border. Their football coach appealed to the camp commandant to allow the football team to stay behind and play its scheduled game with Mare Island, but the appeal was denied and the 21st Infantry's football players left camp with the rest of the division.

Despite the cancellation by the 21st Division, the game's promoter and Mare Island wanted a game in Los Angeles and they looked for any available opponent. USC was open on November 24th, but had a big Thanksgiving Day game scheduled with Cal five days later. USC's coach, Dean Cromwell, took the challenge but was up front that he would use second and third stringers liberally to ensure his team was ready for what he viewed as their more important contest with Cal. While that strategy can be respected, it did not bode well for the men of Troy against the Mare Island Marines.

The game was played at Washington Park, one of several locations

USC used for home games prior to the Coliseum opening in 1924. USC was 4-1 entering the game having won handily over Arizona, lost a close game to St. Mary's, beaten the 21st Infantry 3-0, and crushed Fort MacArthur and Utah.

The Marines, who traveled to Los Angeles aboard the *S.S. Yale* with their 67-piece band, scored on their second possession. The Trojans mounted their white horse and a series of runs got them to the Marine 14-yard line, but an interception ended their gallop. They were shut down thereafter and by the end of the game, a chorus of Mare Island passes and runs gave them a 34-0 advantage and their sixth shutout of the year, having surrendered only one field goal to the San Francisco Olympic Club.

The Marines were pleased with the easy victory over USC, but were elated when news arrived that evening that the Tournament of Roses Football Committee officially invited the Mare Island Marines to represent the West in the Rose Bowl game on New Year's Day. The Marines deserved the honor; no team on the West Coast could argue with the selection. The Marines had faced and beaten the best college teams on the coast and had beaten their only service challenger, Camp Lewis, by a 13-0 score.

The victory over USC left Mare Island with a 7-0 regular season record.

1917 Mare Island Regular Season Results

Sept. 15	California	27-0	California Field, Berkeley
Sept. 29	California	26-0	California Field, Berkeley
Oct. 10	San Francisco Olympic Club	27-3	Mare Island
Oct. 21	St. Mary's	27-0	Oakland
Nov. 3	Oregon	27-0	Multnomah Field, Portland
Nov. 10	Camp Lewis	13-0	Tacoma Stadium
Nov. 24	USC	34-0	Washington Park, LA

With west coast teams having won the last two Rose Bowls, the Marines were confident in their ability to match up with any of the five or six eastern teams worthy of consideration. The only unanswered question for Mare Island was which eastern team they would meet in the Rose Bowl.

The 1918 Rose Bowl Selection Process

As the 1917 season began, the Tournament of Roses Football Committee planned to invite college football teams to participate in the 1918 Rose Bowl, but service teams proved to be among the best in the nation as the season progressed. This was particularly true among for service teams that organized early and were stocked with former college talent.

Another factor at work, however, was the wartime focus of the country and a desire to honor those in uniform. West Point and the Naval Academy did not play one another during the 1917 regular season and some suggested they should play in the Rose Bowl. The matchup would have satisfied both the college and military crowd, but the issue was put to rest in early November when the Assistant Secretary of War, William Ingraham, announced the service academies would not play in the Rose Bowl. In his view, the academies had more pressing issues at hand and would not benefit from taking time away from their studies to prepare for a football game.

In fact, it wasn't a foregone conclusion that a football game would even be part of the 1918 Tournament of Roses. The Committee considered cancelling the 1918 game and, to help make the decision, they sought President Wilson's opinion. As an undergraduate at Princeton in the 1870s, Wilson was the secretary of Princeton's Football Association, meaning he scheduled the team's game and handled its finances. When Teddy Roosevelt convened his investigation into the game of football in 1905, Wilson was President of Princeton and supported efforts to modify rather than abolish the game.

Wilson convened a Cabinet meeting to review the Rose Bowl issue and subsequently telegraphed the Committee saying, "I can't see how a celebration like this could hurt the government's war activities... I think the normal life of the country should continue in every possible way."[8] With Wilson's support, the Rose Bowl game moved forward; they only needed to find two teams able and willing to play. Nowadays, teams are contractually obligated to participate in their assigned bowls based on conference contracts, but in those days some schools displayed no interest in ever playing in the Rose Bowl and others turned down the invitation for reasons unique to a specific season. As a result, there was no guarantee that the teams the Committee desired would reciprocate that interest.

As had been the tradition in the first three Rose Bowls, the Committee wanted eastern and western representatives, and Mare Island was the obvious western choice based on its performance. A few eastern college teams stood out as potential invitees, specifically Pittsburgh and Georgia Tech. Pitt was 8-0 and widely considered the best college team in the East. However, Pitt's faculty committee did not support postseason play and they were eliminated from consideration.

Georgia Tech, which famously or infamously beat Cumberland 222-0 in 1916, was an independent southern team at a time when southern football was not highly thought of outside its region. They dominated their opponents in the previous four seasons, besting their 1916 foes by a combined score of 421-20, including that 222-0 victory. Their combined score in 1917 was even better at 491-17. Georgia Tech's coach was John Heisman, whose namesake trophy keeps him famous today, but Georgia Tech's faculty vetoed post-season games as well, removing them from consideration.

With the top college teams out of the running, several service teams could argue for being the best team in the East. Three service teams stood apart from the others: the United States Army Ambulance Service (USAAS) team of Allentown, Pennsylvania; the 2nd District team from the Newport Naval Base in Rhode Island; and the Camp Custer's All-Officers team in Michigan. Since there were several candidates, the slate of games on Thanksgiving Day (November 29) and Thanksgiving Saturday (December 1) was likely to winnow the list of candidates.

USAAS recruits included future writers e.e. cummings, John Dos Passos, and Ernest Hemingway, though none played football, and the camp nearly went without a football team as well. However, the camp higher ups wanted a team and their first practice was called on September 26, three days before their first game with Penn State, which the ambulance drivers lost 10-0. A 19-7 loss to Fordham followed the next week. USAAS then went on a tear, winning their next eight games, including two victories over the tough League Island team from the Philadelphia Naval Yard, led by Harvard All-American, Eddie Mahan.

There was talk of a playoff game between USAAS and Newport Naval Base, but Newport was upset by Syracuse in their final game, putting Newport Naval Base' candidacy out out to sea. USAAS' season finale was scheduled for Thanksgiving Day against George-town at Griffith Stadium in Washington, D.C., while Camp Custer was scheduled to play Camp Grant two days later.

The Football Committee surprised everyone the day before Thanksgiving by inviting USAAS to be the eastern representative for the Rose Bowl. It was a bad decision. The next day, USAAS and Georgetown played on a cold, wet field, with the sleety snow making a bad field worse in the second half. Georgetown outplayed the stretcher bearers in the first half and led 6-0 at the break. To add insult to injury, Georgetown converted three second-half USAAS turnovers into touchdowns for a 27-0 trouncing. Now standing 8-3 with an embarrassing season-ending loss, USAAS had one thing the other candidates lacked: a Rose Bowl invitation.

Camp Lewis also played on Thanksgiving Day against the University of Washington's Naval Training Station (UWNTS). Like a handful of colleges and universities around the country, Washington hosted training classes that included an aviation ground school and training for Yeomanettes, women who entered the Navy to handle administrative tasks, thereby releasing men for other roles.

Coach Stanton believed the UWNTS team would provide a greater challenge than Mare Island, and he was nearly right. The game started quickly for Camp Lewis when Harry Craig returned an interception for a touchdown and Camp Lewis converted the extra point. The UWNTS team scored in the second and fourth quarters, missing one of its extra-point attempts for a 13-7 lead, but McKay then led Camp Lewis on an eighty-yard drive for the score and converted the extra point to take a 14-13 lead. On the last drive of the game, the UWNTS boys attempted a last-second field goal that missed by a few inches, allowing Camp Lewis to escape with a one-point victory.

Following USAAS' loss, some in the press argued that USAAS should decline the invitation in deference to a better team, but only Camp Custer, playing their finale two days later, could make the last stand as a possible eastern replacement for USAAS.

Camp Custer, located near Battle Creek, housed the 85th Division, a National Army division with recruits from Michigan and Wisconsin. Like Camp Lewis, Camp Custer's officers arrived at the camp earlier than the enlisted men and formed a football team. Unlike Camp Lewis, Camp Custer's All-Officer team remained the camp's primary team facing outside competition.

Camp Custer's roster was chock full of former college players and they had beaten the Great Lakes Naval Training Station twice, had victories over Camp Funston, the semipro Detroit Heralds and the professional Fort Wayne Friars. They were undefeated with their final game against Camp Grant scheduled at the University of Chicago's Stagg Field. Amos Alonzo Stagg agreed to assist Camp Grant for the game while Michigan's Fielding Yost worked with Camp Custer. Stagg and Yost had not faced one another since Michigan's 1905 win over Chicago, which had inspired the writing of Michigan's fight song, "The Victors."

Soldiers by the thousands traveled to Chicago for the party and some attended the game. Before a crowd of 15,000, the largest in Chicago that year, the soldiers of Camp Custer and Camp Grant played a back-and-forth game. Each team scored a pair of touchdowns, but Camp Custer missed the first of its extra-point attempts. Down 14-13 late in the game, Camp Custer reached the thirty-yard line before time ran out, dashing their Rose Bowl hopes.

As the following week progressed, many in the press argued that USAAS should decline the Rose Bowl invitation, but no other eastern team provided a clear alternative. Behind the scenes, Camp Lewis' Athletic Director, Capt. Trevanion G. Cook, lobbied the Committee, arguing that USAAS' season-ending loss should disqualify them, while Camp Lewis was qualified, willing, and able to play. One also suspects that Camp Lewis worked the back channel and had insights into the Committee's thinking since W. S. Kienholz, the Committee chair, was the uncle of Eddie Kienholz, Camp Lewis' assistant coach. Despite the family relationship, the Committee clearly wanted an eastern representative, so the family connection might have opened communication channels, but it did not drive the Committee's decision.

On December 7, the day before Camp Lewis' season-ending game with Fort Stevens, USAAS informed the Committee they would decline the Rose Bowl invitation with regrets. USAAS offered no further explanation, but their failure to secure the War Department's permission to travel to California was the clear culprit. That left the Committee in a pickle and they could only hope for a Camp Lewis win the following day.

Fort Stevens sits at the northwestern tip of Oregon at the mouth of the Columbia River. Since we live in a time in which guided missiles keep unfriendly ships from approaching U.S. waters, it is easy to forget the defensive role once played by coastal artillery. Forts with artillery batteries were long built at the mouths of harbors and at chokepoints on navigable rivers. West Point, Fort McHenry, and Fort Sumter being examples of American forts that served that purpose.

Coastal artillery was still a thing during WWI and many coastal states, including Oregon, had state militia units manning their coastal batteries. Fort Stevens was one of those locations. (Coastal artillery remained a thing in WWII and Fort Stevens was shelled in June 1942 from the deck gun of a Japanese submarine, making Fort Stevens the only military installation in the continental U.S. to come under enemy fire during WWII.)

A view of Fort Stevens from a 1906 postcard with the half-inch white border.

The Fort Stevens team was largely filled by former high school players, but a few had college experience. They were not optimistic about their chances entering the game, but were willing to give it the old service try. Try as they might, Camp Lewis dominated the game from start to finish, allowing Fort Stevens only two first downs. McKay set the tone by reeling off an eighty-yard touchdown run on the team's first possession. McKay had a second touchdown, but was injured shortly thereafter and Roy Sharp, the former California halfback, replaced him and proved every bit as successful with two touchdowns of his own. With a halftime score of 34-0, Coach Stanton substituted freely in the second half and the scoreboard showed a final tally of 53-0, leaving Camp Lewis with a 5-1-2 record for the season, with the caveat that one of the ties came from the 362nd Officers-Washington State game and the other came against the 316th Sanitary Train. The best players on the 362nd Officers and 316th Sanitary Train teams now played for Camp Lewis.

Later that day, the Committee extended an invitation to Camp Lewis for the 1918 Rose Bowl game. Camp Lewis immediately accepted and began planning the trip. The regular season schedule and scores for Camp Lewis are shown in the following table.

1917 Camp Lewis Regular Season Results

Oct. 13	Washington State	0-0	Tacoma Stadium
Oct. 27	316th Sanitary Train	0-0	Tacoma Stadium
Nov. 3	Oregon State Frosh	20-0	Multnomah Field, Portland
Nov. 10	Mare Island	0-13	Tacoma Stadium
Nov. 17	Multnomah AAC	10-3	Multnomah Field, Portland
Nov. 23	Chemawa Indian School	49-0	Camp Lewis
Nov. 29	U. Washington NTS	14-13	Tacoma Stadium
Dec. 8	Fort Stevens	53-0	Camp Lewis

Camp Lewis' invitation to the Rose Bowl set up a game featuring two service teams, a matchup symbolic of the changes sweeping the country. Millions of lives had changed as fathers, sons, and husbands were uprooted from their civilian lives and left for training camps to prepare for war. The war in Europe was no longer an Old World problem; it was now America's problem as well, and one the country was gearing up to address. Still, while the European countries experienced fighting on their lands and millions of lives had been lost, America was experiencing the war from thousands of miles away and its battle deaths numbered less than one hundred as 1917 came to a close. Although the war had disrupted American lives, the destruction of life and property, the reality of war, remained distant to America.

For most Americans, the most tangible evidence of the war remained the recruiting posters, fundraisers, and overtime hours in munitions factories and on farms. In the absence of true battles, football became symbolic of the war and articles written during the season reminded fans of the comparison. The games were substitutes for battle and an opportunity to display the spirit and physical ruggedness that would play an important role in the coming months in Europe. As the Rose Bowl approached, the *Los Angeles Times* echoed the notion that the action in the Rose Bowl was a prelude to what the Germans would soon face on the battlefield:

> *"Sailors (sic) from Mare Island and soldiers from Camp Lewis will engage in a gridiron contest that veteran football men are looking forward to with expectancy. The players are mighty, modern gladiators that have enlisted to fight*

against Germany. Any of the Kaiser's adherents who chance to see tomorrow's game will get small comfort in watching them.[9]

The 1918 Rose Bowl also gave many more Americans a connection to the game than existed for Rose Bowls past. The games between Washington State and Brown in 1916 and the Oregon-Penn game in 1917 were important to sports fans and those associated with the four schools, but a game between Army and Marine teams provided a connection for tens of millions of Americans with friends and family in the services. The service teams playing in the Rose Bowl symbolized the greatness of a nation that entered the war to make the world safe for democracy. A simple football game played on a grand stage would provide evidence of the vitality and commitment of America's fighting men.

TAKE IT ON THE RUN

The Tournament of Roses celebration and parade had a theme each year, and with the nation at war, the Patriots' Day theme selected for the 1918 Tournament of Roses must have been the only option given serious consideration. All the military camps in Southern California were invited to join the parade, along with any Pasadena-area servicemen home for the holidays. The service participants were the first people to march, rather than ride on a float, in the history of the Tournament of Roses Parade. Beyond the marching men and bands playing patriotic music, the parade included floats decorated as a British tank, artillery pieces, and others adorned by the Red Cross insignia and American flags. The Tournament of Roses' decision to donate all monies raised to the Red Cross reinforced the patriotic theme.

Preparing for the Game

Then, as now, the teams did all they could to get themselves ready for the game. Recognizing they needed their best performance, John Beckett asked his former Oregon mentor, Hugo Bedzek, to coach Mare Island in the Rose Bowl, and Bedzek agreed, with $1,000 reportedly changing hands. Mare Island's seventeen players took a steamer from San Francisco to San Pedro, arriving on Christmas Eve. Bedzek joined the team in Pasadena on Christmas Day.

Coach Stanton at Camp Lewis did the same by asking Oregon State's coach, Joseph Pipal, to assist in preparing Camp Lewis for the Rose Bowl. Stanton and Pipal were well acquainted from competing against one another for five years when Pipal coached Occidental and Stanton coached Pomona. Pipal was an experienced football man, but he was Oregon State's basketball coach as well and their season was approaching, so he could devote only one week to working with the team at Camp Lewis. After that, Stanton was on his own.

Following their Rose Bowl invitation, Camp Lewis' camp commander excused the players from all military duties, allowing them to focus of football until after the Rose Bowl. Camp Lewis originally announced that thirty-three players would travel to Pasadena, but later cut the list to twenty-four. One of those missing from the second list was Allan Bynon, who substituted at left end against Fort Stevens. Following the Fort Stevens game, Bynon received orders to immediately ship to France with the Quarter-master Corps, sailing on Christmas Eve. His arrival in France made him the second service Rose Bowl team member to go over there, though he did not stay long. Bynon returned after a short stay and shipped to France a second time in late March 1918.

Camp Lewis left for Pasadena by train the evening of the 21st with plans to arrive on Christmas Day. Each team had two-a-day practices in the week leading up to the game, with Camp Lewis laying plans to use its speed and passing game to neutralize Mare Island's size advantage. Two days before the game, Camp Lewis lost substitute end, C. J. Quill, due to a "wrenched shoulder," while Mare Island's Cliff Mitchell injured his ankle, but was available to play. Mare Island was favored going into the game, having beaten Camp Lewis earlier in the season and given up only three points all season. Camp Lewis' supporters argued that Camp Lewis had played Mare Island shortly after merging the best of the 91st Division and 316th Sanitary Train teams and the combined team had practiced together for only eight days prior to the teams' regular-season meeting. In the end, the argument would be settled on the field at Tournament Park on New Year's Day.

The Game

An estimated 25,000 people overflowed the stands and sidelines at Tournament Park. Among those in the crowd was Charles W. Fairbanks. Not to keep pounding on the "fame is fleeting" theme, but for most readers, Fairbank's name likely conjures up thoughts of Douglas Fairbanks or even Fairbanks, Alaska, which is, in fact, named after our Rose Bowl attendee. With that little hint, you surely now recall that Charles W. Fairbanks was the 26th Vice President of the United States serving under Teddy Roosevelt, even though they didn't like one another, which is why Fairbanks was Roosevelt's Vice President for only the first of Teddy's two terms. Fairbanks was also Charles Evans Hughes's running mate in 1916 when Woodrow Wilson defeated Hughes, still thinking he could keep America out of the war. Wilson was unable to keep that promise, which is ultimately why there were two service teams, rather than two college teams, playing in the 1918 Rose Bowl.

Today, millions of dollars are spent to increase the production value of the pregame and halftime ceremonies at premier bowl games— as if the games themselves lack sufficient value—but this is now, and that was then. For the pregame ceremony in 1918, they thought it sufficient to have a young woman costumed as the Goddess of Liberty escorted to a small stand on the field. The stand was three steps high and of such simple construction that scouts on a weekend jamboree might have slapped it together in an hour. Once on stage, the Goddess of Liberty was handed one American flag by an Army officer and a second by a Marine officer. Following the flag presentation, the combined Army and Marine bands played "The Star-Spangled Banner," with the moment being captured by moving picture camera operators.

Camp Lewis wore khaki-colored jerseys with *Camp Lewis 91st* emblazoned across their chests, while Mare Island wore dark blue jerseys. Both teams had numbers on the backs of their jerseys with all of them displaying a jersey number below 30. (Numbers started appearing on football jerseys a few years earlier and the mandatory numbering of college offensive lineman with numbers between 50 and 79 did not arrive until 1966.)

Nine of Mare Island's Rose Bowl starters had started in the teams' earlier meeting. Keith Ambrose started the Rose Bowl in place of the injured Mitchell and Lawson Sanderson started at left halfback, as he had two of the last three games. Mare Island dressed seventeen players. The Mare Island roster for the game follows.

Player	No.	Position	Weight	College
Keith Ambrose	13	LE	190	Montana
John Beckett	1	LT	195	Oregon
Stanley Ridderhof	3	LG	180	Occidental
Lawrence Teberg	11	C	200	Minnesota
Elmer Hall	4	RG	183	Oregon
Ed Bailey	5	RT	220	Oregon
Cloy Hobson	6	RE	165	Nebraska
Walter Brown	7	QB	155	Washington State
Lawson Sanderson	9	LH	180	Montana
Hollis Huntington	10	FB	181	Oregon
Darrell Gardner	8	RH	170	Utah
Substitutes				
Thomas Cushman	16	C	178	Washington
Clinton Gardner	14	E	170	Utah
Cliff Mitchell	2	E	180	Oregon
Frederick Molthen	15	B	170	Montana
Irving Purdy	12	G/T	185	Minnesota
John 'Mel' Parker	17	B	175	North Carolina

Camp Lewis started eight players who started against Mare Island earlier in the season. After playing well in a substitute role against Fort Flagler, Roy Sharp started at quarterback for the first time, while Doug McKay shifted to halfback. The combination gave Camp Lewis more backfield speed for their planned sweeping around the Marines' ends. Raymond MacRae started at right end, as he had the last three games. A. L. Christensen started most of the season at right guard, but had been a substitute in the first Mare

Island game, and Harry Craig started at fullback. Camp Lewis dressed twenty-three players. The Camp Lewis roster is shown in the following table.

Player	No.	Position	Weight	College
Charlie Turner	5	LE	170	Texas
Sam Cook	25	LT	185	Oregon
Bill Snyder	16	LG	197	Oregon
Bill Russell	4	C	193	California
Anker 'A.L.' Christensen	6	RG	210	Montana State
William 'Ken' Bartlett	8	RT	180	Oregon
Raymond MacRae	21	RE	215	Willamette
LeRoy Sharp	10	QB	156	California
Doug McKay	9	LH	148	North Dakota
Harry Craig	3	FB	190	Wyoming
Ernest 'Dick' Romney	17	RH	149	Utah State
Substitutes				
Emmet 'Skimmett' Dee	22	E	155	Butte HS (MT)
A.T. Frolich	19	C/G	UNK	Unknown
Frank Gard	UNK	F	170	Stanford
Harry Green	12	C/G	185	Utah State
(Unknown) Hastings	23	T	185	Fresno HS
Walter Hollywood	UNK	C	175	USC
Frederick Hunter	14	T	190	Washington State
Charles 'Truck' Lane	11	C/G	190	California
Emzy Lynch	6	T	190	Arizona
Charles 'Dick' Kapple	2	QB	156	Utah State
Ward McKinney	15	HB	170	Oregon
Thomas 'T.O.' Monteith	18	FB	175	Oregon

Raymond MacRae's start at right end is worth noting since he is unique in Rose Bowl history and will likely remain so. MacRae was a football, basketball, and baseball star at Willamette University, captaining the Willamette football team in 1912. Upon graduating from Willamette, he entered medical school and graduated with an interest in the still new field of radiology.

As a young radiologist in the Tacoma area, Dr. Raymond became involved with the medical staff at Camp Lewis and was attached to the 91st Division. He spent his days using his radiological skills examining incoming recruits for tuberculosis, while his free time was spent on the football field. Best as I can tell, Raymond MacRae is the only practicing physician to start a Rose Bowl game or play in one. A year after his Rose Bowl appearance he coauthored a paper about his work at Camp Lewis that appeared in the January 1919 issue of the *Journal of the American Medical Association*. But let's not forget what's important here: Raymond MacRae was one hell of a football player.

The game officials were attired in white shirts and pants and included W. S. Kienholz, Rose Bowl Committee chairman; Dean Cromwell, USC Head Coach; Graham Moody, former coach at Hollywood High School; and Jack Wells, a former Occidental player. The latter two were regular officials for games in Southern California.

The Marines won the toss, elected to receive, and returned Dougl McKay's kick to the twenty-seven. Cloy Hobson, Mare Island's right end, was injured on the second play from scrimmage, so Brick Mitchell, who was injured two days earlier, hobbled onto the field and played the remainder of the game. Mitchell proved to be Mare Island's only substitute in the game. The first quarter witnessed Mare Island trying to pound the ball and Camp Lewis attempting to outflank the Marines, but each team earned only one first down. After Beckett punted for the third time for the Marines, Camp Lewis had the ball on their own 40-yard line and chose to punt on first down, giving the ball back to the Marines on their own twenty.

An action shot during the shows Camp Lewis punting to Mare Island. Both teams had uniform numbers on white squares sewn onto the back of their jerseys. #2 Mitchell is on the far right for Mare Island, #21 MacRae of Camp Lewis can be seen blocking a man to the left of Mitchell, and #25 Cook is seen in the middle running downfield to cover the punt. (Credit: Tournament of Roses)

HUNTINGTON OPENED their drive with a 23-yard run over the right guard and the Marines earned another first down before Ambrose attempted and missed a 40-yard field goal. The soldiers of Camp Lewis started moving the ball as the second quarter began and earned two first downs, but a Romney 5-yard run ended in a fumble. With the Marines back in possession of the ball, Brown and Huntington had back-to-back 15-yard runs before the drive stalled, but Ambrose made a 25-yard field goal to give the Marines a 3-0 lead.

Following the kick, Camp Lewis had a three-and-out and punted with the Marines starting their possession on their own 43-yard line, but Walter Brown fumbled on the first play and Cook recovered for the soldiers. Now it was Camp Lewis' turn, though it didn't start well. McKay lost five yards and then completed a pass to Craig two plays later for a first down. With fourth and one on the next series, McKay scampered around right end for a nine-yard gain, giving Camp Lewis first and goal at the four. McKay again lost a few yards on first down, but Romney followed that play by taking it around left end for a touchdown. Having scored on a sweep, the soldiers opted to punt out and McKay sent a clean boot to Sharp, who then kicked goal, giving Camp Lewis a 7-3 lead. The Marines were an unhappy lot. Not only had they lost a fumble in their own territory, they had given up their first touchdown and were losing for the first time that season.

On the ensuing kick, McKay booted the ball to Brown, whose 39-yard return brought the Marines to their own 44-yard line. The Marines then had two short runs before connecting on a 14-yard pass to Beckett, the left tackle, followed immediately by Brown throwing a 35-yard pass to Sanderson who took the oval another 10 yards to the 5-yard line. The next play saw Brown sweep right for a touchdown. After the missed point after, the Marines led 9-7 with little time left on the clock. The Marines had answered the Camp Lewis challenge and, unexpectedly, had gained most of their yardage through the air. Mare Island then kicked to Camp Lewis, but the soldiers could muster only five yards before the first half ended.

The tradition of marching bands performing during halftime at football games did not begin until the 1920s, so the Rose Bowl's decision to entertain the crowd by having two military teams play a game of pushball at half was a delight. The game of pushball involves two teams pushing a large ball (six feet in diameter and weighing fifty pounds) over or under goals like those on a football or soccer field. It's not played much anymore, but was a common game in military training camps.

Turn-of-the-century British sailors having a go at pushball.

Following the splendid halftime entertainment, the Marines kicked off and Camp Lewis began moving the ball again, gaining a first down, but they lost twelve yards on a fake punt play and then opted for a real punt. With the ball on their own twenty-nine, the Marines gained a first down before Sanderson fumbled and Camp Lewis' Snyder recovered the ball on the Marines' 47-yard line. This was the break Camp Lewis needed to defeat Mare Island, but they could not move the ball. A coffin corner punt left the Marines at their own 5-yard line, so the Marines punted the ball back on first down and Roy Sharp returned the punt and to the Marine's 40-yard line and the Marines were penalized for roughness, moving the ball to the Marines' 27.

Inside and outside runs brought the ball to the 18-yard line and facing fourth and one, the soldiers handed the ball to their fullback, Monteith, but he fumbled and the Marines recovered at the twenty, ending the Camp Lewis threat. Following another exchange of punts, the Marines began a back-breaking drive that extended into the fourth quarter. They ran eighteen straight plays between the tackles, and other than a 22-yard run by Darrell Gardner, each play went for only a handful of yards, but the combination brought the ball to Camp Lewis' 1-yard line. On the nineteenth run, Huntington cross the goal line to give the Marines a 16-7 lead after Ambrose' extra point conversion.

After receiving the kickoff, Camp Lewis failed to move the ball and lost 15 yards on an incomplete forward pass. McKay's punt was returned 29 yards by Brown to the Camp Lewis 27, but the Army defense and Marine penalties stopped the Marines' drive, so Ambrose attempted and converted a 33-yard field goal to give the Marines a commanding 19-7 lead.

Each team had two more possessions, but neither did much and time ran out with the Marines in possession of the ball. In the end, Mare Island turnovers had given Camp Lewis opportunities to win the game, but the Marines dominated Camp Lewis in the game's deciding second half drive, despite ten men playing the full game and the eleventh playing fifty-nine minutes for the Marines.

It had been a hard-fought game and it showed as the players left the field. As James J. Richardson of *The Oregonian* wrote:

> "...when players of both teams went to the showers after today's game a number of them were bleeding freely.
>
> Examination disclosed that Turner had three broken ribs, Christensen one rib broken, Lynch a dislocated shoulder, and

MacRae a badly strained back. Hobson, of the Marines, is in the hospital with ligaments in one of his legs torn."[10]

Another report indicated Camp Lewis' Harry Green had an injured leg, and Hastings had a bad ankle, though Hastings' injury is a bit of a mystery since the game reports indicate he did not play in the game.

After caring for those injured in the game, the day's festivities ended with the Tournament of Roses Grand Ball attended by Pasadena and Los Angeles society's finest. The soldiers and Marines put on their dress uniforms and attended the ball where they were celebrated long into the night. Some players were accompanied by their wives or dates, while the bachelors found no shortage of dance partners. Surely the Marines enjoyed the affair more than their interservice rivals, but all the evening's celebrants recognized the game's end also signaled an important turning point for the football-playing trainees. All the fanfare and celebration over the patriotic tournament could not hide the fact that the game was over and the clock was ticking on the new year. Each passing hour reduced the time until those in uniform would face their destiny.

6

WE'RE COMING OVER

Following the Rose Bowl and their return to the camps, some players continued their involvement in sports playing for the camp rugby, basketball, or baseball teams. Deke Gard and Charles Austin played rugby for Camp Lewis; Dick Romney, Roy Sharp, and Eddie Kienholz were Camp Lewis cagers; and Louis Guisto and Douglas McKay played with the Camp Lewis nine. Regardless of their sports adventures, the men became reabsorbed into military training knowing they could well be in France in the coming months.

At the beginning of the war, the Army and Marines filled their officer training camps with civilian volunteers, but both services now had a large pool of officer candidates in their enlisted ranks and they encouraged enlisted men to take the officer candidate exams. Since most of the service Rose Bowl players were college students or graduates when they joined the services, they had the mathematical and other qualifications for specialty training ranging from the quartermaster corps (supplies and logistics) to artillery and aviation.

Many of the service Rose Bowl players applied and qualified for officer or other advanced training. Some quickly moved into those training programs. Others, who otherwise would have entered the queue to be sent to France as enlisted infantry men, instead spent months waiting for an open training slot and then spent several more months in the training courses themselves. Based on the timing and type of training, some completed their training and were sent to France by summer, while others remained in training through the end of the war. Twenty of the twenty-eight Mare Island players from the 1917 team entered an officer training or aviation training program that qualified them for their lieutenancy. Eighteen earned their bars.

Of the twenty-eight players on the 1917 Mare Island team, eight had been transferred from Mare Island before the football season ended and several were in Europe by spring 1918. Robert Wilson, who played in the first game of the season against California, was the third member of a service Rose Bowl team to reach France when he arrived in February 1918. William Buss was the fourth, arriving in April 1918. Twelve of the twenty-eight Marines that played for Mare Island in 1917 ultimately became part of the AEF.

For Camp Lewis, only a handful of players were sent for officer or other specialized training, but that is partially explained by the fact that a number of Camp Lewis players were commissioned officers when they arrived at Camp Lewis. Fifteen Camp Lewis players went to France with the 91st Division and seven who transferred to other locations went to France with other units. Twenty-one of the twenty-six men on the 362nd Officers team shipped to France and all twenty-one went there with the 91st Division. (The numbers above double count four officers from the 362nd Officers team that also played on the Camp Lewis team.)

The numbers for the 362nd Officers illustrate that the National Army divisions largely trained together, shipped out together, and fought together over there. The same did not occur with the Marines, particularly for Marines trained at Mare Island. Mare Island was smaller than Quantico, on the opposite coast from the war, and it did not offer advanced training. Marines trained at Mare Island were assigned to posts on the West Coast or in the Pacific, but most were sent east for additional training or assignment to new units.

Before discussing how the players on the 1917 service football teams got over there, let's step back and review how the war progressed prior to the arrival of large numbers of American troops.

American Troops Over There

The Fifth Marine Regiment, or 5th Marines, sailed for France on June 14, with the Army's 1st Division. The 6th Marines followed them starting in September 1917. The first wave of American fighting men in France was more a ripple than a wave, having been sent for public relations and solidarity purposes rather than for their ability to influence the tide of battle. The U.S. had only 175,000 troops in France through January 1918 and less than 400,000 troops in France at the end of March. However, a tsunami rolled into France between May and September 1918 when nearly 1.4 million American soldiers arrived.

To provide insight into the experience of those arriving before the tsunami, we'll focus on the Sixth Marine Regiment, or 6th Marines for two reasons. First, the 6th Marines' process of acclimating to France and preparing for battle was similar to many of the Army units that followed them. Second, Robert Wilson joined the 6th Marines as a replacement in France and, since the purpose of this book is to tell the story of the service Rose Bowl players, focusing on the 6th Marines allows us to follow his unit and provide insight into his experience.

6th Marines in the mess line while on a training march.

As the elements of the 6th Marines arrived in France, they underwent additional training that included instruction from Allied officers with battle experience and greater focus on coordination with artillery units and large-scale maneuvers. By mid-March, they were ready for initial frontline duty and were transferred to a quiet sector near Verdun. They stayed for two months receiving a taste of combat by conducting nightly patrols, but most of their experience with war came from the Germans lobbing a few shells over the lines each day and occasionally sending more intense bombardments, one of which accounted for most of the 230 Marines who were killed or wounded during their time near Verdun.

German Spring Offensive

With the war entering its fourth year, Germany's economy and people were becoming drained from fighting a two-front war. The situation changed substantially with the revolution in Russia and the signing of the Treaty of Brest-Litovsk on March 3, 1918, which removed Russia from the war. Russia's exit emboldened Germany and while they remained skeptical of America's ability to successfully transport and support the large numbers of men that ultimately arrived in Europe, the Germans chose not to take any chances and planned a Spring Offensive. Fifty German divisions transferred from the Eastern Front to the West and made ready to attack.

The German Spring Offensive launched in March with successful attacks against the British in Flanders and along the Somme. The Germans then attacked the French along the Aisne River in northeastern France in early May. They made rapid progress against the French troops, breaking through the lines on May 30, and coming within fifty miles of Paris, causing the French government to prepare to flee. The broad battle in the Aisne sector is known to historians as the Second Battle of the Marne. Americans know it by four words: "Château-Thierry" and "Belleau Wood."

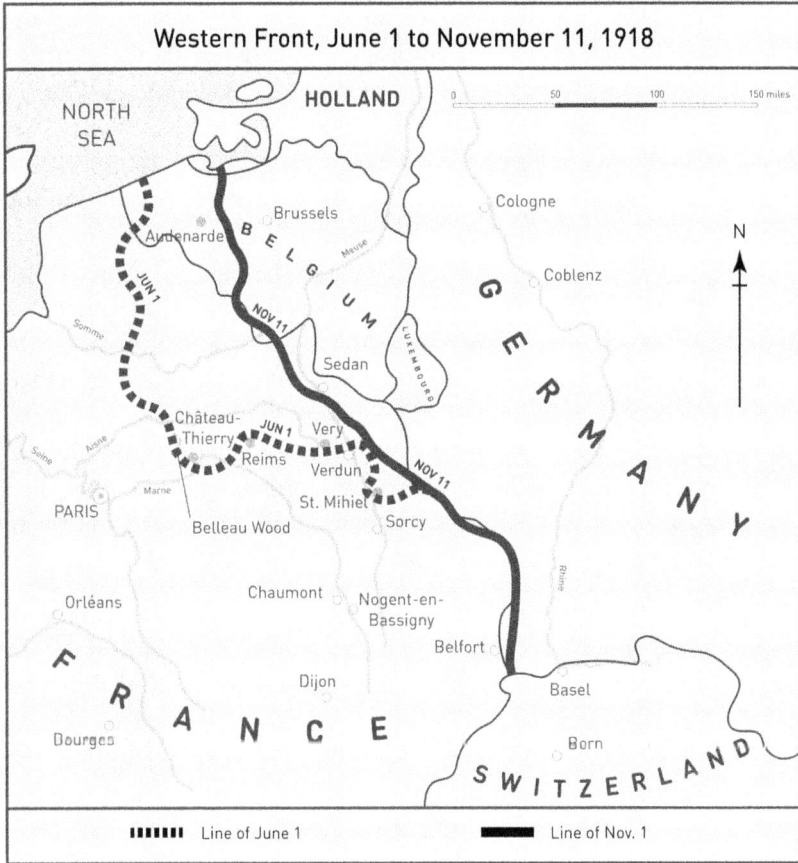

Western Front, June 1 to November 11, 1918

Line of June 1   Line of Nov. 1

Map showing battle lines at the height of the Spring Offensive versus the ground retaken by the Allies by the end of the war.

Château-Thierry and Belleau Wood

Despite reservations that his troops were not ready for battle, Pershing had little choice other than to commit all available American forces to the Aisne sector. Pershing ordered the 3rd Division to the front and positioned it in and around Château-Thierry (west of the city of Reims) which had several bridges crossing the Marne River. The 3rd Division took up defensive positions and held, stopping the German attack. Their defense at Château-Thierry in June and July earned the division its nickname, "The Rock of the Marne."

The 2nd Division, which included the 5th and 6th Marines, and the Marines' 6th Machine Gun Battalion, was ordered to the front as well. The Marines established positions west of Château-Thierry near Lucy-le-Bocage. They were subjected to German shelling as they watched long columns of French troops retreating through their lines. Lucy-le-Bocage was close to an ancient royal hunting forest called Bois de Belleau or Belleau Wood which, at three hundred acres, was less than 40 percent the size of New York's Central Park. Belleau Wood had not been logged or otherwise cleared like other forests the Marines had seen in France and was thick with tangled trees. It also had rocky outcrops which provided excellent defensive positions for the Germans who by then occupied the woods. The surrounding farm fields, much of it planted in wheat, provided little protection for those attacking the woods. The combination made Belleau Wood a wonderful defensive position to hold and a terrible position to attack.

The 5th and 6th Marines received orders to attack the village of Bouresches through Belleau Wood the morning of June 6. They attacked in waves across the open fields and were mowed down by machine gun fire. Rallying his men, 1st Sgt. Dan Daly cried, "Come on you sons of bitches! Do you want to live forever?"[10] Inspired, the Marines entered the woods that morning and spent the next twenty-four days fighting for its control. It was arduous fighting with positions changing hands repeatedly.

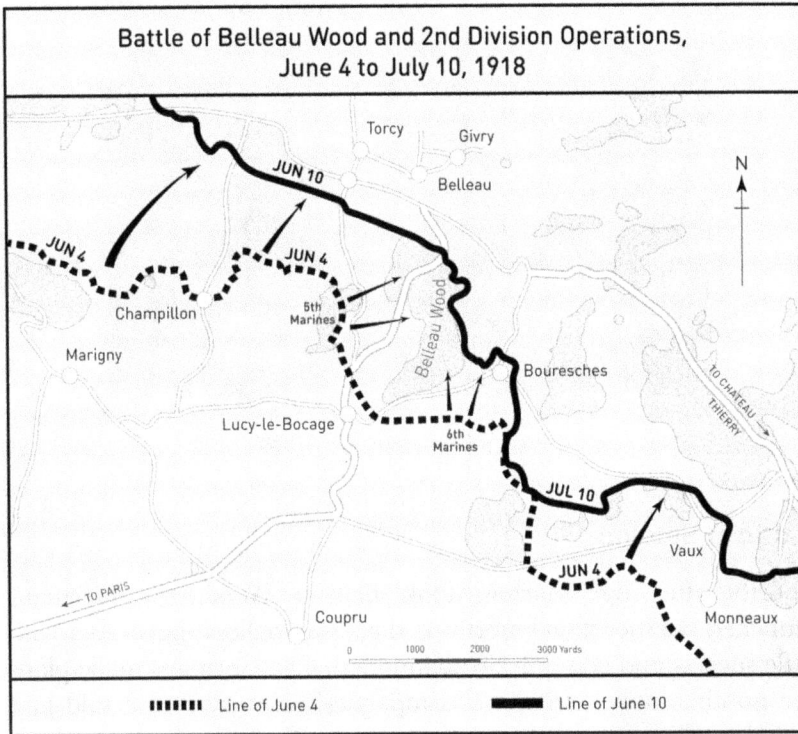

Battle of Belleau Wood and 2nd Division Operations, June 4 to July 10, 1918

The 5th and 6th Marines attacked Belleau Wood from the east and south, while also taking the town of Bouresches. (Adapted from American Armies and Battlefields in Europe, A History, Guide, and Reference Book.)

The Marines received replacements on June 13. One of those replacements was Robert Wilson, the Mare Island tackle, who was assigned to the 84th Company, 6th Marines.

The Battle of Belleau Wood continued until June 26th, at which point all of Belleau Wood came under American control. By then, 1,062 Marines had been killed and 3,615 wounded; the combination represented nearly one-third of all Marines in France at the time. Since Belleau Wood was the first significant offensive action by American troops, and the Marines had proved both fearless and capable, it helped shape perceptions of the Americans' fighting abilities among their German adversaries, the Allies, and American troops themselves.

Belleau Wood as it appeared after the battle.

Battle of Soissons

Shortly after the Marines took Belleau Wood, the Germans launched another attack north of the Aisne Salient, but it met with little success and was quickly abandoned. The Germans made plans for another attack in the Champagne-Marne area for mid-July. Allied intelligence gained advanced warning of the German plans, so troops were shifted appropriately and French Genl. Ferdinand Foch, who commanded all Allied troops at the time, developed plans for a counterattack.

The Germans attacked on schedule on both sides of the city of Reims on July 15. The 6th Marines were shifted to the area and held in reserve until the morning of July 19th when they moved through the frontlines to lead the day's attack east of the village of Vierzy.

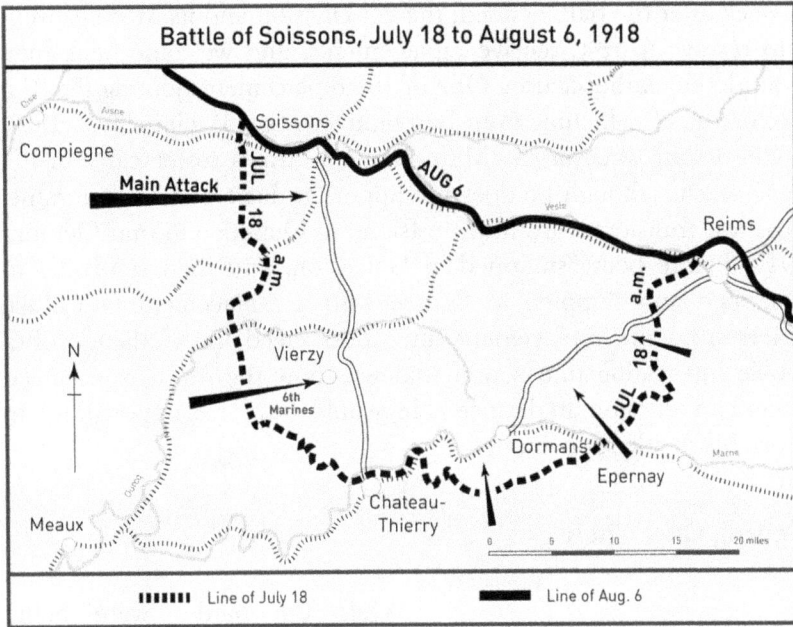

The 6th Marines, including the 84th Company attacked Vierzy from the east. (Adapted from American Armies and Battlefields in Europe, A History, Guide, and Reference Book.)

The 1st and 2nd Battalions of the 6th Marines led the attack with the 3rd Battalion in reserve less than a mile behind. The first wave was met by hellacious machine gun fire and a gap opened between the 1st and 2nd Battalions. The 3rd Battalion was ordered forward to fill the gap, so the 3rd Battalion's 83rd and 84th Companies moved forward, including Robert Wilson. Facing intense fire and losing large numbers of men, the attack ground to a halt and the troops were ordered to dig in before being relieved that evening. The 3rd Battalion had 2,450 men involved in the attack and 1,300 or 53 percent were killed or wounded that day, including every officer in the 84th Company. Others were missing in action; among them was Cpl. Robert Wilson. No one that survived the day knew whether Robert Wilson had been killed, captured, wounded, or buried by shellfire. He was simply missing in action and would be listed as such on the 84th Company's muster roll until February 1919 when his body was found and identified by a burial detail. Though it was not recognized at the time, Cpl. Harold Wilson was the first of the service Rose Bowl players to die in action. Others would follow.

A week after the battle ended, the 2nd Division and its Marines went into reserve to rest, receive replacements, and welcome back men wounded in earlier action. One of the replacements joining the 81st Co. of the 6th Machine Gun Battalion was Sgt. William Buss. Buss, a Nebraskan, was on the Mare Island Marines roster early in the 1917 season, though he does not appear to have played in a game. Buss was transferred from Mare Island to Quantico in mid-October 1917, before being stationed in Galveston, and then returning to Quantico and shipping to France with a replacement unit. Like others from the replacement unit, Buss faced the challenge of a rookie integrating into a unit that was now the most experienced American division in France. He would have his opportunity to prove his mettle soon enough.

Getting Over There

YMCA postcard given to 91st Division soldiers upon leaving Camp Lewis. The back of this card was inscribed by a soldier from D Company, 361st Infantry on June 23, 1918. He survived the war.

While the battles were being fought along the Marne and Aisne Rivers, other American divisions were stateside preparing to ship to France, a movement that took a full month for the 91st Division.

The 91st Division headquarters and advance party left Camp Lewis on June 19th and the rest of the division shipped out over the following days. The first leg of the trip was a six-day cross-country journey on the Great Northern Railroad to the East Coast. Some elements went to Camp Merritt in Bergen County, New Jersey; others to Camp Mills on Long Island. The 363rd traveled on the Canadian Pacific Railway on a public relations tour and were celebrated in a number of Canadian cities before shipping from Philadelphia. It is safe to assume that most of the men on the trains heading to the ports saw the lands east of the Rockies for the first time in their lives. For many, the trip was the last time they would see those sights.

The 91st spent a week in the processing camps prior to sailing for Europe. New uniforms were issued, paperwork was checked, and medical exams were administered for each man. Given the size of the division, its units were allocated across several ships. Parts of the 361st boarded the *S.S. Karao* in Brooklyn, with others sailing on the *S.S. Scotian* from Hoboken. The 362nd boarded the *R.M.S. Empress of Russia* in Brooklyn. The 363rd sailed on the *S.S. City of Cairo* from Philadelphia and the 364th boarded the *R.M.S. Olympic* in New York. Some attached units found space with the infantry regiments and others, particularly artillery units, sailed up to a week later.

Unit histories written after the war indicate that two notables joined the 364th aboard the *S.S. Olympic*: the Under Secretary of the Navy, Franklin D. Roosevelt, and the head of the U.S. Food Administration, Herbert Hoover. The *Olympic's* passenger list shows Hoover was aboard and he gave a speech to the men during their ocean passage, while FDR actually crossed the Atlantic on the *U.S.S. Dyer*, a Navy destroyer. Nevertheless, both men were in the convoy as it headed east, zigzagging throughout the twelve-day journey to Liverpool. From Liverpool, the 91st traveled by rail to Southampton and then by channel boat to Le Havre, France, arriving on July 23.

American troops disembarking their troopship in France.

The division rested from their month-long journey for a day in Le Havre, and then entrained for the French interior on the infamous 40:8 railroad cars. The French box cars were half the size of a U.S. train car and were marked "40 Hommes—8 Chevaux," indicating the car could handle 40 men or 8 horses. The troops appreciated a train car that transported men rather than horses on its previous journey.

The first train left Le Havre the afternoon of July 25, and made a stop that evening in the village of Bonnieres with the troop train sitting on the main line. Shortly before midnight, a passenger train barreled into the station at full speed, crashing into the rear of the troop train. Seven of the troop train's cars were demolished and others were thrown from the track. Men from the remaining cars as well as villagers, and doctors and nurses from a local French hospital, did what they could for the injured and dying. Twenty-nine men perished in the train wreck and seventy others were injured, most of whom were from Captain Worsham's Machine Gun Company. The troops that were not injured boarded another train that night to continue on to the training camp, but a contingent of officers and enlisted men were left behind to see to the burial.

One of the men left behind in Bonnieres was Pvt. Alvin O. Monson. Prior to the war, Monson and his brother started a grocery store in Seattle that leveraged the new self-service grocery store concept. Self-service stores allowed customers to pick items directly from open shelves in the store rather than having a clerk pick items from shelves behind the counter. The concept reduced labor costs and those savings were passed on to customers in the form of lower prices. Like the also new concept of self-service cafeterias, their *Grocerteria* store grew to a chain of thirty stores by 1917, when Monson was drafted and sent to Camp Lewis. We will meet Private Monson again during the coming battles.

The two-and-a-half-day journey brought the 91st to the French Department of Haute-Marne (an administrative unit akin to a U.S. state) on August 1. Once there, they began a ten-week infantry training program under French instructors.

American artillery units in WWI primarily used French weapons and since the French guns were not available in the U.S.-based training camps, the artillery units needed additional training time in France to become familiar with the French weapons. Machine gun units also used French-made weapons, but their training was accomplished more quickly since the weapons and coordination issues were simpler.

St. Mihiel Offensive

As the summer passed, Genl. Foch began planning a continuous Allied attack on the Germans at a range of locations across the front, an effort that has become known as the 100 Days Offensive. Under Foch's plan, each attack had limited objectives to ensure that successful penetrations did not become overextended and, by hitting the Germans in multiple locations along the front, the strategy reduced Germany's ability to shift troops to defend a given attack. The British and French pressed again for American troops to serve under their command during these attacks, but Pershing resisted once more, particularly because the number of American troops in Europe had reached critical mass, allowing the formation of the First American Field Army, with twenty-four American divisions, that operated independently moving forward.

The First Army's initial test came with the St. Mihiel Offensive. The Germans had taken the St. Mihiel Salient in 1914 and, despite repeated French attempts to reduce the salient over the next four years, the Germans had not budged. The plan called for the American forces to eliminate the salient and then shift the bulk of those troops sixty miles to the north over a two-week period to spearhead the Meuse-Argonne Offensive. The detailed plans for both offensives and the transfer of personnel and materiel were developed by Pershing's Operations Officer, Col. George C. Marshall, who served as Chief of Staff of the U.S. Army during WWII and become more famous for a different plan as the Secretary of State in 1947.

Despite completing only five of the expected ten weeks of in-country training, the 91st Division was ordered to the front and began marching toward St. Mihiel on September 7. Since the 91st Division's field artillery units were not sufficiently trained on their French weapons, they remained behind for additional training.

The St. Mihiel Offensive launched on September 12, with eleven American divisions and one French division involved. By coincidence, the Germans, wanting to even up their lines, began withdrawing from the St. Mihiel Salient just as the offensive began. This resulted in German troops being scattered outside their fortifications and their artillery heading east, and they were unable to effectively defend the attack. The salient was eliminated in four days with 7,000 American casualties while the Germans lost 22,500 men, 15,000 of whom were taken prisoner. Among the American divisions participating in the offensive was the 2nd Division, with William Buss of the 6th Machine Gun Battalion getting his first taste of action.

The 91st Division was held in reserve five miles behind the front and were exposed to German artillery fire during their time there, but were not otherwise involved in action. After the First Army achieved the battle objectives without using reserve troops, the 91st Division left the area on September 16, and headed to the Meuse-Argonne where it had orders to go over the top the morning of September 26. Like all the divisions shifting to the Meuse-Argonne, the 91st moved only at night, hiding in the woods during the day to stay out of sight of German pilots so as to avoid tipping off the Germans to the troop movements and plans.

The coming Meuse-Argonne Offensive was the largest battle ever fought by American forces, involving more than 1.2 million troops. No battle before or since had as many American troops involved and it remains the deadliest battle in American history. The American First Army achieved a limited objective in the St. Mihiel Offensive. It was now time for a full test in the Meuse-Argonne Offensive and the 91st Division would be at the point of the spear during the attack.

7

SEND THE WORD TO BEWARE

W hile many of the men who entered the military in 1917 were in Europe, new men entered the training camps in 1918 and the camp athletic programs carried on. However, two factors impacted the 1918 college and service football season in ways never seen before or since. One was the Students' Army Training Corps and the other, the influenza pandemic, which caused substantially more deaths than were caused by four years of war. The influenza pandemic of 1918 and 1919 was second only to The Black Plague of the Late Medieval period as the deadliest pandemic in human history.

College Enrollments and the Students' Army Training Corps

As September 1918 approached, the nation had been at war for seventeen months. During the 1917-1918 academic year, college enrollments dropped by 20 percent from the previous year. Beyond those entering the service, other college men believed they could best serve themselves, their families, and their country by returning to their farms or working in industries vital to the war effort. The combination of these factors, and the prospect of additional men volunteering, left the nation's colleges and universities with increasingly fewer male students.

The nation's college football teams faced the coming season with an abnormally low number of experienced players. The Big Ten and Missouri Valley Conferences, both of which prohibited freshman from playing varsity sports, partially addressed the problem by allowing freshmen to compete in football in 1918, giving them four years of varsity eligibility. Schools such as Alabama, Cornell, Missouri, and Yale canceled their football seasons before the season started or based on factors that played out during the season.

However, the impact of dropping enrollments on college football paled in comparison to the Students' Army Training Corps (SATC). The SATC was the brainchild of the War Department's Committee on Special Education and Training (CSET), which anticipated the need to identify and train 6,000 commissioned and noncommissioned officers per month moving forward. College graduates comprised 90 percent of the officer corps at the time and with the fighting increasingly dependent on technology, the War Department wanted the nation's colleges to continue training men on advanced skills while enabling the War Department to control the timing and selection of the men siphoned from the universities.

The CSET announced the formation of the SATC in May with operations to begin October 1. More than five hundred schools opted into the program and they comprised virtually every major university and significant college in the land. School administrators were trained during the summer on the program requirements and how to prepare for the coming year. Among program requirements was the need to adapt college dormitories and other buildings to create separate SATC barracks and mess halls, sequestering the SATC students from others in the student body. Coursework for SATC members was modified as well and required the student-soldiers to receive 11 hours of military instruction (i.e., drill, military theory) and 42 hours of academic instruction per week. (The 42 hours of instruction per week included 14 hours of classes or labs and 28 hours of supervised study). Three of the fourteen hours of academic instruction were devoted to a war issues class.

Army officers were assigned to each participating school to run the military side of the program. Most of these officers were recent graduates of the officer training camps and had all of three months of military experience themselves. Their inexperience was a major criticism of the SATC after the war, but that was a few months down the road. For now, the colleges and their faculties supported the program despite some misgivings about academic integrity and independence.

Although the SATC was conceived as a voluntary program, Congress changed the minimum draft age to eighteen in August 1918. To ensure their target college students would not be drafted by the local boards, the CSET made SATC participation mandatory for all able-bodied male students, effectively federalizing male higher education in America. Across the nation, colleges held mass swearing in ceremonies at noon Eastern Time on October 1. Over 150,000 students were sworn in that day and 30,000 more joined shortly thereafter.

Students taking their oath to enter the Students' Army Activity Corps on October 1, 1918.

Once enrolled, the SATC men wore Army private uniforms, were subject to military law and discipline, awoke to reveille each morning, and could be ordered to report for active duty at any time, but were not draft eligible. In return, the SATC gave students a sense of pride in serving their country by remaining in school—a pride reinforced by a national adverting campaign—and the government paid the students' tuition and room and board, along with $30 pay per month, the same amount paid Army privates.

The prescribed daily schedule for the SATC clearly showed they were in the Army now:

- 6:45 a.m.: Reveille
- 7:00 a.m.: Mess
- 7:30 – 9:30 a.m.: Drill
- 9:30 a.m. – 12:00 p.m.: Recitation and study
- 12:15 p.m.: Mess
- 1:00 – 4:30 p.m.: Recitation and study
- 4:30 – 5:30 p.m.: Athletics and recreation
- 5:30 p.m.: Mess
- Mess – 7:30 p.m.: At student's disposal
- 8:30 – 9:30 p.m.: Study under supervision
- 10:00 p.m.: Taps

SATC men marching through Sather Gate at the University of California.

The last-minute change to mandatory participation led to confusion about many issues. The SATC schedule allowed only one hour per day for athletics and recreation, so questions arose regarding its impact on intercollegiate athletics. University presidents and athletic officials sought clarification on whether their teams would have the time available to practice and play. Most assumed the season would go forward as usual since the military had promoted the value of sports and football for preparing men to become soldiers.

In mid-September, Col. R. I. Rees, chairman of the CSET, issued the following bombshell:

> "Athletic sports as formerly pursued, involving extended trips and specialized training, are inconsistent with the soldiers' program of drill and study. Athletic directors and professors of physical education who are already in the employ of the students' army training camp institutions can be used in connection with intramural sports and for the assistance of the officers in charge of military physical training. The commanding officer at each institution will be in charge of the physical condition and training of the men under his command, and will be responsible for co-ordinating the military training and discipline with athletic sports."[12]

Col. Rees' statement brought howls of protest; university presidents appealed to their Senators and anyone else who might listen. Their protests had an effect because Col. Rees issued an amended statement on October 4, though it confirmed that the needs of the Army superseded those of the nation's colleges and universities, particularly as related to niceties such as college football. The new rules allowed intercollegiate football under the following conditions:

> "1. SATC members are eligible to participate if they maintain satisfactory standards in military and academic work.
>
> 2. Teams are allowed ninety minutes of football practice per day, including the time to dress and bathe.
>
> 3. No games are allowed in October that require absence from the institution for a longer period than noon to taps on Saturday. Two trips will be allowed in November provided they do not require longer absences than from retreat on Friday to taps on Sunday. The time spent on these trips will be considered furlough.
>
> 4. Team member selection should be made on November 1 based on the result of intercompany play.
>
> 5. Spectacular contests for soldiers of the SATC involving large gate receipts are not appropriate."[13]

Though the revised ruling gave teams the time needed to travel to more distant contests in November, the rules for October gave teams only ten hours to travel to, play, and return home from an away game, amounting to a virtual travel ban and wreaking havoc on team schedules. Every school scrambled to find nearby teams to play in October and schedules were rejiggered across the country. The ruling had a more dramatic impact on teams outside the East Coast where travel distances between schools was greater. The Missouri Valley Conference cancelled all conference games scheduled for October and later dropped the conference schedule altogether.

Ironically, these restrictions were not placed on the athletic teams representing the training camps. The play of student-soldiers was restricted, while the play of honest-to-goodness soldiers, sailors, and Marines was not. In fact, the travel ban had the unintended effect of encouraging the real service teams to schedule away games against the college and university teams that had travel restrictions.

If the SATC ruling did not cause enough issues for schedule makers, a far more devastating problem was in the offing that made the deaths caused by the war seem limited in comparison. Moreover, whereas the SATC requirements could be adapted to once known, the influenza pandemic was out of man's control and its impact was far less predictable than the SATC ruling.

The Influenza Pandemic

The medical community in the U.S. and other countries was little more than a band of faith healers through much of the nineteenth century, but advancements in the scientific approach to medicine took hold and tremendous progress was made in the forty years leading up to WWI. Research in Germany, France, the United Kingdom, and the United States developed an understanding of infectious diseases and vaccines which, along with public health measures, substantially addressed many of the world's worst scourges including smallpox, cholera, typhoid, yellow fever, and diphtheria. The medical community better understood infectious disease prevention, but was less able to treat diseases once they developed. Among infectious diseases, the understanding and ability to address influenza was less developed. Influenza viruses mutate rapidly and present a moving target for which it was difficult for medical science to develop vaccines. Even today, medical science cannot prevent influenza. All we can do is monitor its path and offer vaccines targeted to the version most likely to occur in the coming months.

Armies and civilian populations in their vicinity have historically lost more people to disease than to combat. Although medical advances had reduced the impact of several diseases during the Spanish-American War and other conflicts, they remained a problem for all armies in WWI. From September 1917 through March 1918, more than 5,700 U.S. servicemen died of pneumonia resulting from complications from a measles epidemic. Measles, like many infectious diseases, is a relatively stable virus, in that it does not readily change its form. The constancy of its form means that an individual who survives the measles is effectively inoculated against catching the measles a second time. Such is not the case with influenza which constantly mutates. Influenza is also a highly contagious, airborne virus that often occurs in waves as it travels through the host population before burning itself out when there are no new individuals to infect. That is, until it mutates again and in 1918, it mutated into the first known version of the H1N1 strain.

The training camps of the armed forces were virtual soup kitchens for the spread of infectious diseases. Men from disparate communities living in ill-prepared, crowded quarters allowed diseases to spread quickly once they took hold. Inadequate camp medical facilities and staffing exacerbated these conditions, despite the U.S. military drawing many of the best and brightest medical researchers and practitioners away from the civilian community. The field of medicine in 1918 simply did not have the bench strength and resources it has today.

Though epidemiologists have since identified likely precursors, the first documented case of influenza occurred at Camp Dunston in Kansas when a cook was admitted to the base hospital with influenza symptoms on March 4, 1918. The crowded conditions of Camp Dunston and the regular movement of troops between Camp Dunston, soldiers' homes, or other military locations provided an excellent transportation system for the virus.

The first influenza wave moved faster and farther than the measles epidemic. It spread across the United States and landed in Brest, France within one month of being reported at Camp Dunston. It spread to Allied troops such that during the spring of 1918, 10 percent of British troops in France were sick and unable to report for duty on any given day. The flu reached across No Man's Land as well and roared through the German army. Genl. Ludendorff, who headed Germany's Spring Offensive that nearly broke the Allies, ultimately blamed the influenza for bogging down the German offensive. (There were other reasons, of course, but he blamed influenza.) The rest of Europe and the world fell prey to the virus as well. Whereas press controls in the warring countries limited newspaper coverage of the influenza, neutral Spain openly reported on the epidemic, including the fact that its King was sick with the influenza, so the epidemic became popularly known as the Spanish Flu. Although the first wave of influenza was strong and widespread, it affected the typical patient for only a few days and was limited in its killing power. By August 1918, it had exhausted itself.

As the first wave of influenza waned, the second wave was already underway. Among the first reported cases in the U.S. were those at Commonwealth Pier in Boston and Camp Deven, another overcrowded army base forty miles outside of Boston. Beginning in late August, cases of pneumonia popped up at the same time among Navy personnel that had transferred by train from Boston to the Great Lakes Naval Training Station north of Chicago. Any number of other military personnel and civilians who had been in the Boston area were moving about locally and in more distant locations.

The typical influenza virus, including that of the first wave, primarily claims the lives of those with the weakest immune systems: the youngest, the oldest, and pregnant women. The second wave was different in that it ferociously struck the healthiest members of society: those between 20 and 40 years of age whose immune systems were at the height of effectiveness and, in many cases, the immune system reacted so strongly that its overresponse resulted in death.

The variation and intensity of the symptoms were unlike those normally associated with influenza and contributed to its misdiagnosis. Victims bled from their ears, eyes, and nose; were sensitive to the touch and wracked with pain; became delusional; and most frightening to many, suffered from cyanosis, a condition in which their bodies turned blue or purple from oxygen deprivation. Some hospital workers became infected, collapsed at their stations, and were dead within twelve hours. Other patients lasted weeks before dying or recovering. Regardless of the misdiagnoses, there was little the medical community could do other than provide basic care and comfort. They simply did not have the tools to combat influenza.

There were, however, steps available to public health authorities to limit the spread of the disease, including the imposition of quarantines. The inability of public health officials to understand the epidemic, along with outright incompetence or worse, led to the early failure to ban public gatherings and enforce quarantines, contributing to the epidemic's spread. Moreover, the clamp down on media coverage of anything suggesting a chink in the military's armor contributed to the lack of early publicity regarding the deadliness of the epidemic. Newspaper reports initially showed indifference, then a stage of daily reports citing exceedingly low numbers of men dying in the camps, and finally a stage of fright when the influenza hit their city; all the while blaming the victims for not preventing their own infection. Despite early missteps, quarantines and bans on public gatherings became commonplace as the epidemic coursed through cities, states, and regions nationwide. Even then, most quarantines and bans were imposed too late to address the problem.

In the end, the second wave of influenza took the lives of one in every sixty-seven soldiers in the U.S. Army and it did so in a ten-week period. Fifteen times as many civilians died as did soldiers. The influenza accounted for the death of 675,000 Americans at a time when the U.S. population was approximately 105 million, less than one third its current size. Due to the number of deaths and the high number of younger people who died, the influenza epidemic depressed the average American life expectancy by more than ten years.

The second wave of the influenza epidemic started just as the nation's football teams were beginning their season. The epidemic impacted virtually every football team and their schedules nationwide, including the Great Lakes Bluejackets and Mare Island Marines

The Great Lakes Team

The Great Lakes Naval Training Station fielded an all-station team in 1917 that lost its first two games to Marquette and Camp Custer, and then won five of their last six, including a victory over Iowa. The coach in 1917 and 1918 was Herman P. "Bo" Olcott. Olcott played for Yale in 1901 and 1902 before coaching at North Carolina and New York University. He was coaching at Kansas when Walter Camp, a fellow Yalie, appointed him the coach at Great Lakes.

Even the most ardent football fan today is likely unfamiliar with Bo Olcott, but you could marshal a sizable group of folks who are familiar with the Great Lakes band leader, Lt. John Philip Sousa. Sousa, of course, was the former head of the Marine Corps band and composed the National March of the United States, "Stars and Stripes Forever"; the official March of the United States Marine Corps, "Semper Fidelis"; and modified another march, which in its present form is the U.S. Army's official song, "The Army Goes Marching Along." The Great Lakes Band served a public relations function headlining many Liberty Bond events, while touring the country for parades and rallies associated with the bond effort.

Olcott had Jimmy Conzelman of Washington University, Hugh Blacklock of Michigan State, Hal Erickson of St. Olaf, and Kent McCauley of Geneva College returning from the 1917 team and held practice with select players in early August. Open tryouts in mid-August yielded more than 150 participants. That group was winnowed as new players continued to arrive.

Great Lakes had so much talent they began the season carrying sixty men on the football squad and ultimately divided the squad into the Starboard or first team, and the Port or second team. When the Starboard team played away games as part of Great Lakes' main schedule, the Port team played and won home games against a handful of other camps and local colleges. The second team also provided a solid scout team during practices and acted as a farm team as injuries occurred or players developed. Seven of the twenty-three players that suited up for Great Lakes in the 1919 Rose Bowl came from the Port team. Great Lakes also had a fourteen-team regimental league that provided further depth.

Coach Olcott's biggest challenges early in the season were to sort through the talent, fit the players to their best positions within his style of play, and gain buy-in from the all-star players accustomed to other systems and coaching styles. Olcott proved only moderately successful in meeting those challenges.

In mid-August, Great Lakes announced a tough slate of games in which it planned to travel to six colleges, including three Big Ten teams and Notre Dame, with games against service opponents still being negotiated. Great Lakes also looked to play one of the stronger eastern colleges with Syracuse considered the likely target. Their initial seven-game schedule is shown below.

1918 Great Lakes Naval Training Station Initial Schedule

Sept. 29	Iowa	Iowa City
Oct. 12	Illinois	Campaign-Urbana
Oct. 26	Western Michigan	Kalamazoo
Nov. 2	St. Louis U	St. Louis
Nov. 9	Notre Dame	South Bend
Nov. 26	Purdue	West Lafayette
Nov. 30	Camp Grant	Great Lakes

In negotiation: Syracuse, Camps Dodge, Taylor, Custer, and Funston

The 1918 Mare Island Team

It is a cliché to say that elite college football teams do not rebuild, they reload, but this cliché was especially apt for the 1918 Mare Island team. None of the players on the 1917 team were left at Mare Island when the 1918 season kicked off. Most had transferred for further training and six were in France. The 1918 Mare Island roster had an entirely new cast with most men having enlisted in the late spring and summer of 1918.

West Coast players dominated the 1917 Mare Island roster, with its core coming from the University of Oregon. The same was true in 1918, but this time its core players came from Washington State, including fullback Lloyd Gillis, halfback Fred Glover, quarterback Dick Hanley, right end LeRoy "Pat" Hanley, left end Clarence Zimmerman, right guard Mike Moran, tackle Leo Shannon, and substitute lineman John McGregor. The similarity to the 1917 team extended to Mare Island's lack of depth. Its top eighteen players were solid, but many of the remainder were young—including several straight out of high school. Like John Beckett the year before, quarterback Dick Hanley, took furlough and spent time in the Northwest recruiting players, adding several men to the roster, including his brother Pat. Others wanted to join as well, but the Marines suspended additional enlistments on August 8, 1918, with the exception of those enlistments in process before the suspension took hold. Clarence Zimmerman, Hanley's teammate at Washington State, was working on the family farm awaiting his Army call up, when he received a telegram from Hanley informing him: "Secured permission from Washington for your enlistment on grounds you applied to me for enlistment before August eighth. Lt. Potter will aid in securing your release. Got permission for Bangs…"[14] (Bangs was another Washington State teammate.) Zimmerman formally enlisted at Mare Island on September 3, and joined the football team. Other, more creative, approaches supplemented the roster late in the season as injuries took their toll.

Mare Island did not formally release a schedule in 1918, largely due to their desire to have open dates during the second half of the season to schedule games against the best teams that emerged in the first half of the season. Their initial schedule can be pieced together based on announcements made by their opponents. Half of those games had tentative locations and dates, including both games scheduled with California.

1918 Mare Island Marines Initial Schedule

Sept. 21	Goat Island/Yerba Buena Sailors	Grove Street Grounds, Oakland
Sept. 28	Camp Fremont 8th Ammo Train	Stanford Field, Palo Alto
Oct. 5	St. Mary's	Ewing Field, Oakland
Oct. TBD	California	TBD
Oct. TBD	Spruce Production Division	Multnomah Field, Portland
Nov. 2	Oregon	Home
TBD	California	TBD
TBD	Washington	Seattle

In negotiation: Multnomah Athletic Club

During the preseason, Dick Hanley and Jake Risley (of Oregon) acted as player-coaches for Mare Island. However, a few days before their first game, the Marines named William "Lone Star" Dietz as coach of the 1918 team.

Dietz grew up in Rice Lake, Wisconsin, as a dark-skinned son of white parents, who after learning his biological mother was Sioux, embraced his Native American heritage. He enrolled at Carlisle Indian School and played tackle, blocking for Jim Thorpe. Dietz was also an artist and married Angela DeCorsa, a Carlisle faculty member and top Native American artist of the time. After assisting Warner at Carlisle, Dietz was hired to coach Washington State, installed the Carlisle system or Single Wing at Washington State, and led his first team to an undefeated season and a victory in the 1916 Rose Bowl. His 1917 went undefeated, but he ran afoul of the new university president who did not care for Dietz' celebrity or the color of his skin. Dietz' contract was not renewed for 1918 and the fledgling film career he pursued in the meantime was, let's say, underdeveloped.

As the fall of 1918 rolled around, Dietz was available and a natural fit for a Mare Island team whose core players were Washington State men. A solid tactician, Dietz was a master of communication and motivation, rather than intimidation. He was also a dandy, with a wardrobe ranging from the finest New York fashions to a host of Sioux regalia, which he proudly wore when the situation called for it or didn't. By almost any measure, he was unlike any other football coach in the land.

Mare Island's season opened on September 21, with a game against the sailors stationed at Goat Island, also known as Yerba Buena Island, in San Francisco Bay. As the opening football game of the 1918 season in the Bay Area, the game was heavily promoted by the local press, and the money raised from the game was donated to the two bases and a local provider of services to military personnel. Oakland was in a festive mood that Saturday morning when the teams met at city hall to hear a greeting from Oakland's mayor, followed by a parade of bands and thousands of supporters to the Grove Street Grounds, a minor-league baseball park expected to fill to its capacity of 8,000.

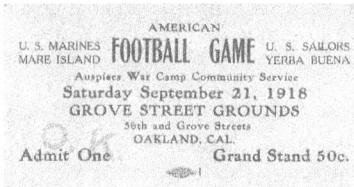

> AMERICAN
> U. S. MARINES **FOOTBALL GAME** U. S. SAILORS
> MARE ISLAND YERBA BUENA
> Auspices War Camp Community Service
> Saturday September 21, 1918
> GROVE STREET GROUNDS
> 56th and Grove Streets
> OAKLAND, CAL.
> Admit One   Grand Stand 50c.

The ticket for Mare Island Marines vs. Goat Island / Yerba Buena Sailors game indicates the teams played American football, not rugby football, as was still popular in the Bay Area at the time.

Goat Island was coached by Andy and Pete Smith, the coaches at California and St. Mary's respectively, and its roster was cluttered with former college players. Local sportswriters anticipated a competitive game. They were almost half right.

Mare Island brought thirty-two players to the game, perhaps anticipating the opportunity to play a few subs that afternoon. The game opened with Goat Island kicking off to Mare Island with the coverage stopping Mare Island short of the twenty. On the first play from scrimmage, quarterback Dick Hanley gave the ball to his right halfback Fred Glover who took it up the middle for a short gain. The Goat Island team celebrated the stop since it confirmed they could play with the vaunted Mare Island Marines, but they had only taken the bait. As Goat Island's players puffed their chests, Mare Island quickly lined up. Glover, who had just run the ball from the halfback position, lined up at center, while Jake Risley, the center, aligned at left half. Glover snapped the ball to Hanley and the surprised Sailors watched Hanley scoot around left end for an 80-yard touchdown. Mare Island converted and was up, 7-0. Other than Mare Island gaining field position through Bill Steers' punting, neither team did much until the last play of the first half when Hanley hit Clarence Zimmerman on a 35-yard touchdown pass as time expired. Dick Hanley missed the conversion, so the Marines held a 13-0 lead at a half.

The second half saw the Marines employ a power running game that led to two rushing touchdowns by Oregon's Bill Steers and another by Cal's Jim Blewett for a 31-0 victory. Although Mare Island finished with a convincing win, they showed they could play sloppy football. Fumbles and missed extra points marred an otherwise strong game. Lone Star Dietz had some work to do.

The Friday after the Goat Island game, Mare Island traveled south to the campus of Stanford University to play the 8th Ammunition Train from Camp Fremont. Like most WWI training camps, Camp Fremont did not exist prior to the war and was built on 6,200 acres of Stanford land and bordering properties. All forms of army divisional training occurred there, including live artillery fire; unexploded artillery shells still pop up occasionally on Stanford property and in the surrounding area.

We do know that Lone Star Dietz was apprehensive coming into the game because his quarterback, Dick Hanley, and fullback, Bill Steers, did not play and both had been critical to their win over Goat Island six days earlier. Hanley was replaced by Amor Galloway, who was Jim Blewett's teammate on the dominant Los Angeles Manual Arts High School teams prewar. Steers was replaced by Lloyd Gillis, a Washington State player under Lone Star Dietz, who was voted All-Pacific Coast Conference twice after the war.

Mare Island on offense during the Camp Fremont game at Stanford Field. Dick Hanley appears to have the ball as he and others kick up dust as they run across the unwatered field. (Wasco County Pioneer Association and Columbia Gorge Discovery Center & Museum)

Dietz, who liked trick plays, had his team prepared to pull another one on Camp Fremont. With the score tied 0-0 in the first quarter, fullback Lloyd Gillis took a handoff from Galloway up the middle. After being tackled, Gillis did not get to his feet, but his teammates lined up in formation around him and, while lying on the ground, Gillis snapped the ball to Galloway, who handed it to Blewett, and Blewett took off for the first touchdown of the game. That may have been the end of the trickeration, but it was only the beginning of the domination. The Marines ended the half with a 33-0 advantage and after substituting freely, repeated the effort in the second half for a 66-0 final score.

Unfortunately for our purposes, games between apparently mismatched services teams were not covered well by the press. Less newspaper coverage also meant less comprehensive box scores, so we often do not know which players substituted into those games in which substitutes were most likely to play. Camp Fremont was one such game.

Following the game, the team returned to Mare Island. Unbeknownst to them, it would be several weeks before they left the base again. Earlier in the week, the senior medical officer at Mare Island received a letter from his counterpart at Great Lakes detailing Great

Lakes' experience with the second wave of influenza. The letter gave Mare Island a heads up on the ravages they could expect if they did not take appropriate action. Mare Island's medical corps immediately implemented a plan to isolate the symptomatic. Its 200-bed hospital was reserved for those with pneumonia, and a city of tent hospitals was set up to care for those with less severe influenza symptoms. In combination, the hospital and tents were sufficient to handle the predicted volume of patients— both for the Marines and sailors on Mare Island.

Two days after receiving the letter from Great Lakes, a Navy corpsman who had returned from leave in Oklahoma was diagnosed with influenza. Influenza also broke out among civilians across the river in Vallejo. On Saturday, the day after the football team returned from Camp Fremont, all liberty was cancelled, large group gatherings were banned, and the Mare Island Naval Base was quarantined. (Civilian workers in the shipyard who were building or refitting naval ships continued to come to work and go home throughout the quarantine.) The football team joined all other military personnel in being confined to the base. Mare Island's games with St. Mary's and California were now threatened.

Establishing quarantines and isolating the patients with pneumonia reduced the number of deaths at Mare Island.

Accountings of the influenza epidemic within the military differ in the details, but the core story remains the same. Great Lakes had 40,000 sailors stationed there in September and October of 1918 and more than 9,600 were diagnosed with influenza within 30 days of its first diagnosis at Great Lakes. Of those, 10 percent developed pneumonia.

While the truth about the influenza epidemic was shared within the naval medical community, the epidemic was downplayed to the public. Capt. William A. Moffett, a Congressional Medal of Honor winner and the Great Lakes commander, gave the press accurate numbers regarding the number of infected men, but dramatically underplayed the death rate by sharing a total number of deaths to date that was lower than the number that died the previous day. The following chart shows the number of deaths by day from influenza and/or respiratory disease at Great Lakes and Mare Island from September 15 to October 31, 1918. The chart illustrates the intensity and rapidity in which the influenza epidemic struck Great Lakes, after which it made a gradual decline and returned to single-digit levels before all but disappearing. The ten days starting on September 21 claimed 692 lives or seventy percent of the deaths during the influenza's reign at Great Lakes.

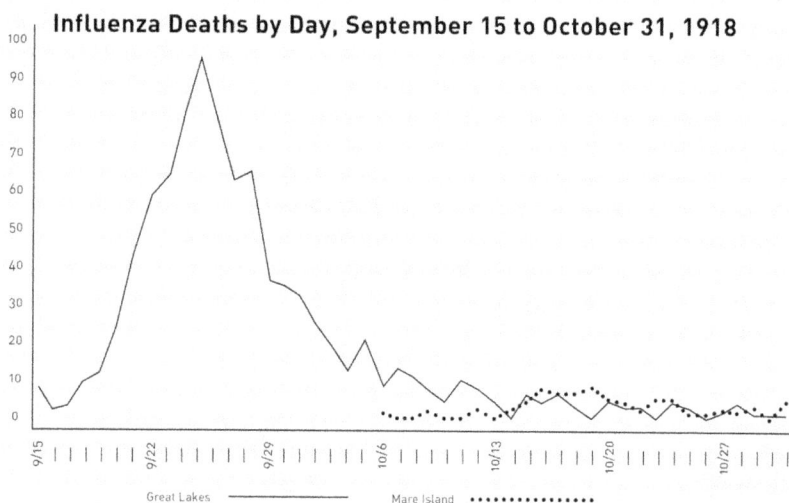

Influenza Deaths by Day, September 15 to October 31, 1918

Influenza deaths by day at the two locations show the benefit of advance warning for Mare Island. Data sourced from: Officers and Enlisted Men of the United States Naval Service Who Died During the World War. Washington, D. C.: Bureau of Navigation of the Navy Department, 1920.

The influenza epidemic hit Mare Island one month later and while Mare Island's absolute number of deaths is lower than Great Lakes, it also had far fewer personnel than Great Lakes. Moreover, with the advanced warning it received, Mare Island's medical and military authorities implemented a quarantine and took other preventive measures available to them. Mare Island did not experience the spike in deaths that occurred at Great Lakes, but like Great Lakes, 70 percent of the men that died during this period did so in a ten-day stretch.

LITTLE WAS WRITTEN at the time or since on how the football teams reacted to fellow sailors dying around them. We do know that Great Lakes assured outsiders that the football team had been isolated and symptom free for three weeks prior to traveling to their first game against Iowa. (Note: These assurances came within days of the team moving into their newly-built, separate barracks.) Nevertheless, the Great Lakes team left its highly infectious base in Waukegan on September 27, presumably transferring through Chicago's busy Union Station, for their 250-mile train ride to Iowa City and its opening game with the University of Iowa.

Great Lakes traveled with twenty-two players including starting halfback, Leland "L. L." Mendenhall, who started at halfback for Iowa in 1916. Mendenhall played in one more game before testing into a pilot training program and transferring to the Dunwoody Institute in Minneapolis.

The game at Iowa City attracted a crowd of 4,000, the largest-ever crowd for an opening game at Iowa. In the first quarter, the Great Lakes quarterback, Bill McClellan, aligned the team in a passing formation, but could not find an open receiver as he rolled left, so he took off running, dodged two Hawkeyes, and ran into the corner of the end zone. Following the touchdown, McClellan punted out to Eielson, who converted the kick. Paddy Driscoll substituted for Eielson at halfback in the third quarter and gave Great Lakes the field position advantage with a long first-down punt and several runs that preceded his drop kicked 30-yard field goal to give the Bluejackets a 10-0 lead. Iowa drove inside the Great Lakes twenty late in the fourth quarter, but could not convert, so the game ended with a 10-0 Bluejackets advantage.

WHILE THE FOOTBALL season was now underway and the influenza was roaring across the country, the situation for American troops in France had changed dramatically. Following its success in the St. Mihiel Offensive, most of the U.S. First Army shifted north in preparation for the Meuse-Argonne Offensive in northwestern

France, which launched on September 26, two days before Mare Island's game with Camp Fremont and three days before Great Lakes played Iowa.

We'll turn back the clock a few days to follow those units in which the men of the 1918 service Rose Bowl teams were fighting.

AND WE WON'T COME BACK

By late September 1918, the Allies' 100-Day Offensive was underway, and after seventeen months of preparation, America's most significant battle of the war was at hand. Of the nearly 1.2 million soldiers that participated in the Meuse-Argonne Offensive, 26,277 men lost their lives, accounting for nearly half of all American battle deaths during the war. Another 92,250 Americans were wounded in the forty-seven days of fighting.

During the same period, the second wave of influenza reached across the ocean and decimated troops on both sides of the conflict. Although seldom mentioned in unit reports and other histories after the war, various diseases caused approximately half the number of deaths in the AEF as did battle, and most of the deaths from disease occurred during the time of the Meuse-Argonne Offensive. The timing of the influenza outbreak further reduced the military effectiveness on both sides and added to the burden placed on their medical corps.

The Meuse-Argonne Offensive

When we last discussed the 91st Division, they had crossed the ocean and partially completed in-country training, before being ordered into the St. Mihiel Offensive, where they were held in reserve. At the end of the St. Mihiel Offensive, the 91st Division took to the road on the evening of September 17, marching to a destination unknown to the men. Over the next few days, the 91st moved sixty miles to the north and arrived at Foret de Hesse, where they were positioned for the Meuse-Argonne Offensive. Among them were thirty-seven men who, less than a year ago, spent much their free time playing football on the Camp Lewis or 362nd Officers teams. Many of these players would experience the most severe test of their lives and the lives of several would end during the next week.

Foret de Hesse was two miles behind the front in an area that had witnessed month upon month of artillery fire during the Battle of Verdun in 1916. Some areas were virtual moonscapes, while others remained wooded. Though the men of the 91st could not yet see it, the land on the German side of the front looked similar with a mix of woods and open farmland.

Strategically, the objective of the Meuse-Argonne Offensive was to penetrate the German defensive positions and seize the heights in the area, after which there was open country all the way to Sedan, a major railroad center through which half of Germany's supplies to the Western Front flowed. Seizing Sedan would cripple Germany's ability to fight the war. Like St. Mihiel, the American attack at Meuse-Argonne had its underpinnings in Genl. Pershing's philosophy of open warfare. His approach rested on the ability of individual soldiers and smaller units to adapt and display initiative while working within their assigned area. His order to the American Army in Europe on September 5, 1918, stated:

> "From a tactical point of view, the method of combat in trench warfare presents a marked contrast to that employed in open warfare, and the attempt by assaulting infantry to use trench warfare methods in an open warfare combat will be successful only at great cost. Trench warfare is marked by uniform formations, the regulations of space and time by higher commands down to the smallest details: 1) fixed distances and intervals between units and individuals, 2) little initiative.
>
> Open warfare is marked by: 1) irregularity of formations,

comparatively little regulation of space and time by higher commanders, the greatest possible use of the infantry's own fire power to enable it to get forward, variable distances and intervals between units and individuals, 2) brief orders and the greatest possible use of individual initiative by all troop engaged in the action, 3) the infantry commander must oppose machine guns by fire from rifles, his automatics and his rifle grenades and must close with their crews under cover of this fire and of grounds beyond their flanks, and 4) the success of every unit from the platoon to the division must be exploited to the fullest extent.

Where strong resistance is encountered, reinforcements must not be thrown in to make a frontal attack at this point, but must be pushed through gaps created by successful units, to attack these points in the flank or rear."[15]

Despite the logic of Pershing's strategy, it has received its share of criticism in that the initial stages of the battle still required American troops to charge into hails of machine gun fire coming from the well-entrenched Germans, much like the British and French soldiers had done earlier in the war. Moreover, the division assignments and orders themselves precluded the flanking approach beyond the company level since each division along the eighteen-mile Meuse-Argonne front was assigned an alley or zone of responsibility from which they were not to deviate. Thus, when one division or another gained penetration, their neighboring divisions could not move troops through their neighboring division's alley to attack German strongpoints from the flank or rear.

Moreover, inadequate communication within and between divisions largely eliminated the possibility of such flank or rear attacks. The use of radio communication on the battlefield was in its infancy during WWI, so the front lines tried to coordinate with their supporting artillery via telephone wires running on the ground or strong on trees. However, one of the primary effects of the German artillery fire was to destroy the American telephone lines. As a result, communication often depended on signal flares and runners; that is, men who literally ran back and forth carrying hand-written messages between the front lines, headquarters, and artillery units. Timely and effective communication between the frontlines and those behind the lines was problematic and communicating across frontline divisions was nearly impossible.

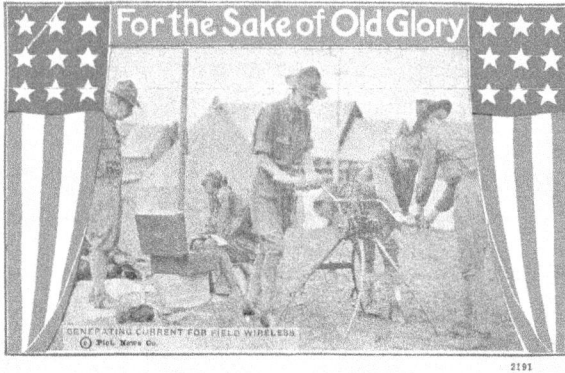

"Wireless" referred to radio communication at the time. The wireless sets were ungainly, as were their portable generators.

Going over the top was difficult enough in WWI, but doing so underequipped made it more problematic. The men of the 91st Division had plenty of rifle and machine gun ammunition, but little or none of the heavier weapons that were supposed to be carried within each regiment. The 362nd Regiment, for example, was short on the rifle grenades needed to take out machine gun nests. They also had a full company of men who had trained over the past year on the three-inch Stokes mortar, but none of those weapons had arrived. The regiment also had half the horses needed to move its heavy weapons, supplies, rolling kitchens, and ambulances. Finally, by cutting short their training in France, they also were insufficiently trained in coordinating fire with their supporting artillery units.

Opposite the Americans were a series of trenches and fortifications stretching across the front. The 91st Division's sector included four sets of trenches, including an initial trench line just beyond No Man's Land, the *Hagen Stellung* situated two miles back, and the *Volker Stellung*, positioned another three miles back on a ridge that protected the villages of Eclisfontaine and Epinonville, giving the Germans a clear field of fire across the open meadows leading up to the villages. The fourth trench, known as the *Kriemhilde Stellung*, sat seven to eight miles behind the front and ran through the village of Gesnes. Interspersed throughout the area were connecting trenches and machine gun nests positioned to guard one another and the trenches. The sector had a limited number of roads, particularly those running between the American rear positions and the 91st Division's assigned alley, which created difficulties maintaining supplies and evacuating the wounded over the next few days. An unseasonably cold rain fell during the first days of the offensive and with the roads subjected to American and German artillery fire, they were muddied in the best case and impassible when the supporting engineering units were unable to patch the shell holes.

Late in the afternoon of July 25, the 91st Division received orders to go over the top the following morning on "D" Day at "H" Hour along with the rest of the divisions lined up for the offensive. The 91st was the fourth of the nine American divisions on the left along with three French divisions to the right. Within the 91st Division, the 364th, 363rd, 361st and 362nd regiments were aligned left to right. The 35th Division was to the left of the 364th and the 37th Division was to the right of the 362nd.

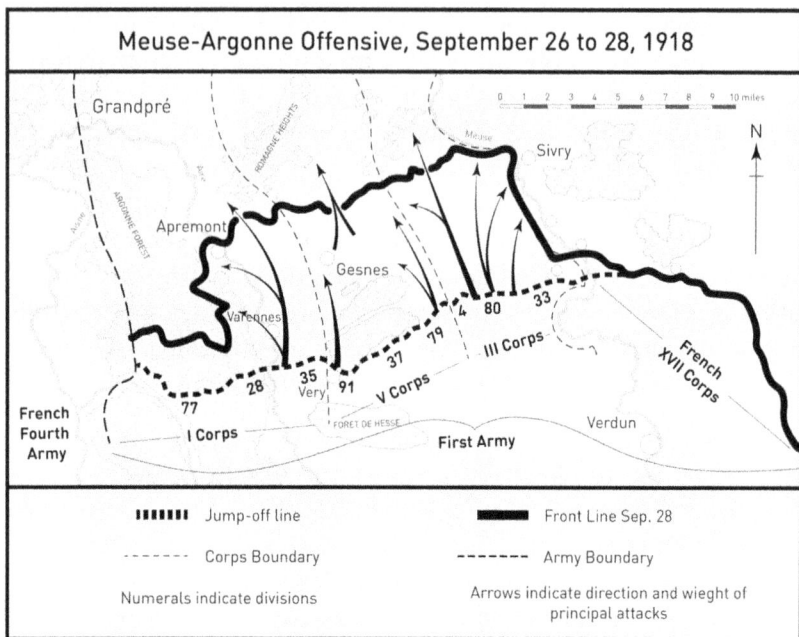

The 91st Division held the fourth position from the left and were flanked by the 35th Division on their right and the 37th Division on their right. (Adapted from American Armies and Battlefields in Europe, A History, Guide, and Reference Book.)

At 3:30 a.m. on September 26, the Meuse-Argonne erupted in a continuous chorus of artillery fire coming from behind the Allied lines, landing miles behind the German front line. The chorus ended after 90 minutes. Thirty minutes later, the chorus began again, with the shells now landing on the German front lines.

Among the soldiers manning the big guns firing on the Germans was Lt. Doug McKay, the Camp Lewis quarterback. McKay had completed officer training at Camp Lewis and shipped to France in May for artillery training. He was assigned to the 59th Coastal Artillery Corps, which provided heavy artillery support at St. Mihiel and was positioned on the far left of the Meuse-Argonne Offensive supporting the 77th and 28th Divisions. To his right, and immediately left of the 91st Division was the 35th Division, which included Captain Harry S. Truman of Missouri, who commanded Battery D of the 129th Field Artillery.

At 5:55 a.m. on September 26, whistles blew and the men of the

362nd climbed from the trenches and moved forward. They walked

View of World War I No Man's Land typical of that faced by the 91st Division in the Meuse-Argonne.

carefully through the fog shrouding No Man's Land, crossing it without a shot being fired by either side. They marched through the first line of abandoned German trenches, continuing forward for ninety minutes before facing their first bursts from German machine guns. The machine guns killed their first man and Capt. Charles Thorpe of I Company, a lineman for the 362nd Officers team, was severely wounded with four bullets in his leg. He was out of the war in the first two hours of action, and never fully recovered from his wounds.

The 362nd encountered and eliminated machine gun nests and snipers one after another, regularly stepping over bodies of German soldiers killed by the morning's artillery fire. In the late afternoon, they approached Epinonville, situated on the *Volker Stellung* trench-line, five miles back from the front. Captain Lige Worsham, who commanded the 362nd Machine Gun Company, moved forward to reconnoiter the town's defenses to determine where best to locate his machine guns for the coming attack. In short order, the one-pound mortars and machine guns went to work eliminating the enemy and the 362nd took the town. They started digging in to defend the town, but were soon ordered to withdraw because they had taken more ground than the 35th Division on their right, exposing them to a flanking attack. The regiment moved back to their afternoon location facing Epinonville. This was but one instance of the American command's concern about a German flanking attack, while failing to use the same tactic themselves.

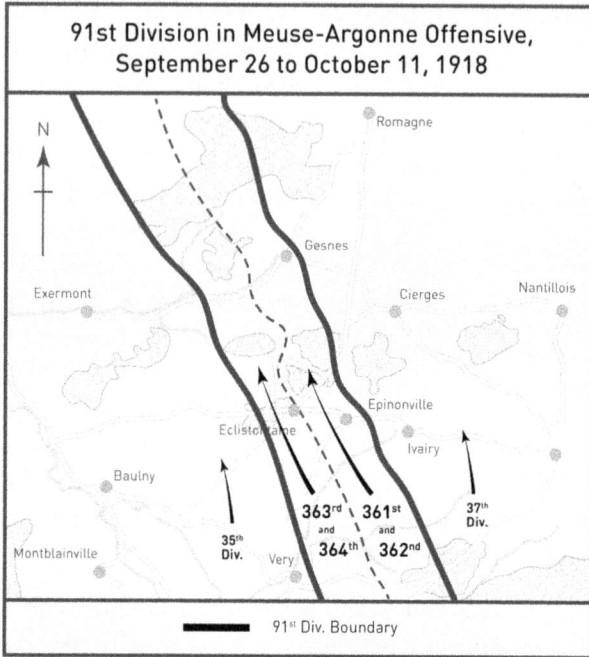

Plan of attack for the 91st Division in the Meuse-Argonne showing key locations such as Eclisfontaine, Epinonville, and Gesnes. (Adapted from Zone of Action, 91st Division, Meuse-Argonne, produced by Topo Section, G-2, 1937)

The Germans reinforced Epinonville overnight. Early on the morning of the 27th, Lt. John Burgard, a left guard for the 362nd Officers team, was organizing the battalion headquarters location when he spotted Germans on the right flank setting up machine gun positions to pour fire on his men. Burgard fired his rifle at the Germans to sound the alarm and charged forward, leading his Headquarters Company in an attack on the German positions. His men succeeded in the attack, killing seven of the enemy, capturing twenty-one Germans and three machine guns. Burgard was awarded the Distinguished Service Cross for his gallantry that morning.

Allowing the Germans to reinforce Epinonville made the effort to retake the town on the 27th deadlier than the previous day. The regiment was pinned down crossing the open meadow when American artillery shells fell short of Epinonville and landed among the Americans in the meadow. Signal flares finally brought the friendly fire to a stop, but the 362nd remained exposed. Colonel John "Gatling Gun" Parker, whose machine gun support had been critical twenty years earlier covering the American troops charging up San Juan Hill, rejoined the regiment and personally led the charge up the hill as the regiment took Epinonville for the second day in a row.

Shortly after taking Epinonville, a double column of one hundred German soldiers was spotted marching through a nearby clearing, unaware the Americans now controlled Epinonville. Three of Capt. Lige Worsham's machine guns waited until the entire German column was exposed in the clearing before opening fire and wiping them out. Later that afternoon the 362nd was attacked by German planes using the new strafing technique in which they flew low over the American positions machine guns ablaze. The German planes were unopposed by their American counterparts and made repeated attacks in the vicinity. The German pilots also communicated the 362nd's positions to their colleagues in the artillery and shells soon fell on the men of the 362nd. Through the evening, German high explosive and gas shells rained into Epinonville, leading to another sleepless night.

By the third day of the offensive, September 28th, the Germans recognized the seriousness of the American and French action and brought in reinforcements. Word arrived that the 361st, which was to the immediate left of the 362nd, had lost most of its officers in the fighting. While the 362nd was limping itself, it was ordered to take over positions held by the 361st and the move was accomplished overnight.

Late in the evening of the 28th, orders were received to attack again the following morning indicating, "the attack would be resumed not later than 7 a.m., September 29, and that the divisions would advance independently of each other, with utmost vigor, and regardless of loss."[16]

The Attack on Gesnes

While preparing to attack the morning of the 29th, Captain Worsham was coordinating the efforts of his men when he encountered Pvt. William J. Lake of Montana, an ammunition runner. Lake had arrived at the front that morning after being held back in England due to influenza. Now healthy and ready to do his bit, Lake met Worsham and started to salute his Captain when Worsham caught his arm, warning him not to salute an officer on the frontline since that officer then became a sniper's target. After their greeting, the two set off to their work.

The 362nd moved forward fighting under heavy artillery fire through the Bois de Cierge, a wooded area straddling the right side of their alley and the left side of the 37th Division's area of responsibility, capturing a number of German dugouts, some of which were well-appointed officers' quarters that had been decorated like hunting lodges during the German's four-year stay. They soon reached the reverse slope of a ridge two miles outside the village of Gesnes. Between the 362nd and Gesnes was a shallow, open valley with three softly rolling ridges running parallel to their lines. The ridges in the open fields afforded little coverage given the Germans machine guns and light artillery positioned to the sides and on several hills just beyond Gesnes. Other machine gun nests were hidden in the fields and around the town. All had clear lines of fire on the open field.

Lt. William Hutchinson, who started at left halfback for the 362nd Officers against Washington State, was with the A Company of the 362nd, and was assigned to liaise with the 37th Division on the right. Hutchinson encountered several 37th Division officers during the fight and was told the 37th was more than two miles ahead of the 91st, though his eyes and all other information told him otherwise. Hutchinson knew the 362nd was ahead of the units on either side, but the 37th Division's claimed advances had been reported back to headquarters, making the 362nd Infantry and the 91st Division appear to be laggards. The error held terrible consequences for the 362nd.

At 3:10 p.m., the company commanders within the 362nd gathered and were told an American artillery barrage would hit Gesnes shortly and they were to attack Gesnes immediately after the barrage lifted. Everyone in the 362nd recognized that crossing the open fields to take Gesnes would result in horrible losses. Col.

Parker, who had been wounded earlier, asked permission to delay the attack until he had time to join his men in the attack and ensure all were positioned correctly. Captain Worsham set out in advance of his machine gunners to survey the field and identify the best positions for his guns. Shortly after Parker arrived and the barrage lifted, the 362nd launched the attack.

The companies advanced in waves across the fields, with Worsham's machine gun company repositioning itself as the other companies advanced past the first of the rolling ridges. Worsham continued to lead from the front and at one point, took over a captured German machine gun, turning it on the fleeing enemy. The attack continued across the two miles of open field with the men charging to points in which the smallest roll of the land might afford protection, but terrible numbers of dead and wounded were strewn across the meadow.

After reaching the third rolling ridge seven hundred yards from Gesnes, a final push was ordered. Worsham laid unprotected atop the ridge looking through his field glasses. Eight of his company's machine guns were with him, positioned in shell holes for protection. Worsham's second-in-command, Lt. Ray Hays was beside him as their guns laid covering fire for the American soldiers rushing into Gesnes. As the town was taken, the machine guns were silenced to avoid hitting their own troops.

Keeping the machine guns on the ridge in the event of a German counterattack and still under heavy fire from the Germans atop the nearby hills, Lt. Hays moved into one of the shellholes that held a machine gun. Fifteen minutes later an officer from headquarters came up from behind and asked Hays why they had not moved forward. Hays pointed toward Worsham, saying, "The Captain's right there." The officer approached Worsham, touched his back, and realized he was dead from a rifle bullet that had struck him in the face.

Meanwhile, Lt. Hutchinson saw wave after wave of men mown down by machine gun fire and artillery shells. Viewing speed as his best option, he rushed forward with a handful of men, reaching a small clump of bushes to the right and just outside of Gesnes. One hundred yards ahead was a crossroads with a disabled tank in the middle and a dead German lying alongside. Hutchinson and his men moved forward and saw A Company's Captain Bradbury coming up the road with another group of men. Together they rushed to a hill just past Gesnes on the right and took over a shallow trench. They spent an hour there while indirect machine gun fire from Germans over the next hill penetrated the trench, killing one man and wounding another. The same machine gun burst hit Hutchinson's eyeglass case and destroyed the gas mask he carried in his satchel. The men began digging in for the night and were relieved to see two hundred reinforcements come up the hill, adding to the men already in Gesnes.

Nearby, 2nd Lt. Howard Angus, the former *Los Angeles Times* sportswriter and 362nd Officers halfback, led his men in capturing several German cannons. They immediately turned the cannons around and used them to fire on the fleeing Germans. Angus and his men reached Gesnes and found troops from various companies intermixed. Angus took charge and directed its defense by organizing the men and placing them in defensible positions. For his leadership in the attack and defense of Gesnes, Angus was promoted to 1st Lt. the following day.

Lacking radio and telephone communications, messages were sent on slips of paper via runner. Shown is the carbon copy from Lt. Farley E. Granger's (codenamed 'Murphy') message book indicating that he and Lt. Angus were holding a hill beyond Gesnes with men from a mixture of 362nd companies. (Farley E. Granger File, 91st Division, World War I Veterans Survey, U.S. Army Heritage and Education Center, Carlisle, PA)

Private Alvin O. Monson, who was one of the men left behind in Bonnieres two months earlier to coordinate the funeral of the men killed in the train wreck, was with Worsham's Machine Gun Company during its attack on Gesnes. Due to his business background, Monson spent most of his time in France working as a company clerk, but with so many men killed in the first few days of the battle, Monson was ordered forward as an ammunition runner.

Twenty years later, Monson, who clearly suffered from PTSD, testified about the charge into Gesnes. He witnessed one lieutenant have his leg blown off and die before Worsham had ordered Monson to return to the starting point to get an ambulance for the wounded. During a court case seeking a veteran's pension that had been denied, Monson described his experience at Gesnes, saying:

"And we keep on advancing, about five miles and those big shells just whistled. It was cross fire in the air, and machine guns too. Then later we gets up and starts to go down the ravine, a low place there. I was still a runner going after ammunition, two boxes or one box for machine guns, and the Captain (Worsham) came beside me and said "Monson, how are you?" and I said "Fine, Captain." We started advancing some more. We started to the top of the hill. He was maybe fifty feet from me and the Top Sergeant right close to him and off to the left fellows with machine guns already set up, not set up and going, sat on top of the hill. As we advanced we all got on top of the hill. I got in a shell hole and how those shells, the big guns, 77's, went in all around; around and among the men. All over this hill. I was still in this shell hole. The Sergeant said, "Come on Monson, let's go," and the others started to advance and as soon as I got out of the big shell-hole and got where the Sergeant was, a big shell came in and blew up the hole I had just been in. The Sergeant said, "I guess I saved your life" and I said "Gee, Sergeant, I will buy you the finest dinner you ever had when we get back to New York; the finest feed you ever had." I was still clear and not frightened all that time. Then he told me my Captain was killed. He told me right after that. Captain Worsham will killed right on this hill. That left Sergeant in command. Both lieutenants were killed and the new Captain."

"...I went and lay alongside a tree; a willow tree, I would think, two or three feet the other side of the bank, and then I went and lay down there, and there were six or seven or eight fellows lying right along there, -maybe five or six. I lay down there, and there were five of six others lying right beside me like this. To the right there was not anybody until about half a block and then a big shell hit. When I came to and raised up all these fellows were torn to pieces. I could not tell you know they looked."[17]

Besides Monson's testimony, Worsham's actions that day were detailed in a letter written by Ray Hays to Roy Heilman, a friend of Worsham's back in Evansville. Hays, who was promoted to Captain and succeeded Worsham as the leader of the 362nd Machine Gun Company, wrote the letter several weeks later from Oostveleteren, Belgium, after the 91st was transferred there.

Dear Sir:

Your letter to the commanding officer, 362nd Infantry, concerning Captain Worsham, has been referred to me.

While Captain Worsham was in command of the machine gun company, I was one if his officers. Since his death I have had the honor of commanding his company, and it is his company, known universally as Captain Worsham's company, and not the machine gun company. Inspired by his ideals and teaching, I am trying to run the company as he did, but no one can take his place.

We first went over the top at Rendevous de Chasse and the first day advanced about ten kilometers. We met with stiff resistance at Ejononville (sic) the next morning, and it was largely due to the Captain's courage, tactics and machine gun company that our division held out, while divisions on our flank were forced back.

During the two days of fierce fighting we advanced some eight kilometers, until, on the 29th, we were held up. A small town, by the name of Gesnes, seemed to be the point of resistance, and about 3 o'clock in the afternoon of September 29th the battalion to which we were attached was ordered to take the town. The magnificent manner in which it was charged and taken will never be forgotten by the surviving participants. Led by our Captain, we followed the assault wave and, under his direction, mounted our guns on a ridge commanding the town, were we could use direct fire over the head of our own troops.

We had some wonderful targets, but were subject to direct observed artillery fire, front and flank, the flank organizations having failed to obtain their objectives.

After getting my guns in action, I found the Captain firing a machine gun, the crew of which had become casualties. Under the cover of the gun he was firing and three others from my platoon, I removed the remainder of the guns forward to escape the heavy barrage.

Then I rejoined the Captain. Shortly he gave the order to cease firing, our troops having advanced so far that is was dangerous to continue firing over their heads.

We continued to observe, waiting for dusk to advance. I left the Captain to give orders to one of my gun crews. When I found him a few moments later he was dead, shot with a rifle bullet. He had started forward, field glass in one hand, rifle with fixed bayonet in the other.

We advanced with heavy hearts and heavy feet to help reorganize and consolidate the line for the night, because that is what he would have us do. It was two or three days before the body was recovered and laid to rest in a grassy meadow in the Forest of Argonne, beside that of one of his Lieutenants, who gave his life the same day.

He was your dear friend, you say. To us he was more – peerless leader, boon companion, comrade, instructor and friend. We mourn his loss in a way words cannot express. His men and his officers loved him as he in his whole-hearted way loved them. The fateful German bullet cost the army a valiant leader and officer, a true soldier in very sense; robbed the government of a valuable citizen, and deprived all who were privileged to know him in the future society of a beloved friend and always cheerful companion.

Pardon me, sir, for so much detail about an action that I was in, but I loved and admired the 'Old Skipper,' as he will always be to us, that it is a relief to talk to one who, likewise, knew and loved him. I dream of him by night and think of him by day, and always in my plans for his company, I wonder if he would approve of my actions were he here. Most of my military education, all my machine gun experience, was received from him, and perhaps his invisible hand is still guiding me in my effort to take his company home as he would have taken it.

Even your high regard for Lige Worsham, the citizen, would have been increased had you known the Captain E. W. Worsham that I knew and served under. He understood men and by his own high ideals brought out the best in them. I truly sympathize with you in the loss of a friend,

Sincerely yours,

Captain Ray W. Hays

M.G. Co., 362 Inf., AEF"[18]

Back home in Evansville, Worsham's father, who had been suffering from pneumonia and a heart ailment, also died on September 29th, likely within hours of his son.

Such are the vagaries of life and war that Capt. Elijah Worsham, an exceptional leader, was killed that day rather than any other soldier, including Pvt. William Lake, whom Worsham talked with briefly the morning of the attack. Some readers may recognize Lake from Robert Rubin's book, *Last of the Doughboys*, which is based on interviews with the last surviving Americans of WWI. William Lake proved to be exceptional in his own right by carrying on with life for another eighty-four years, passing away in 2004 at the age of 108. That made Lake the longest surviving American veteran of the Meuse–Argonne Offensive, and likely, the longest surviving soldier that fought on either side of the battle.

1st Lt. Frank Gard, who many considered the best rugby player in America during his Stanford days, was in the attack with M Company and also fell during the final rush into Gesnes. Following his death, Frank Gard's commanding officer wrote the following letter to Gard's parents.

> My Dear Mr. and Mrs. Gard: -
>
> I realize how little can be said at a time like this when both your hearts are heavy with sorrow, but think what little I can say about the manner in which Frank died, may be of some comfort to you.
>
> We were ordered to attack the town of Gesnes, France, at 3:40 in the afternoon of September 29th. I had been put in charge of the battalion that a.m., so Frank was a member of my staff.
>
> Frank and I started together and for the first half hour of the fight I remember seeing him several times, always cool, and setting a wonderful example of courage to all the men.
>
> The attack was in reality an assault upon the town and the high ridge just beyond it. Both the town and ridge were strongly occupied by the enemy, and all the ground between us and them was thoroughly covered by their artillery and machine gun fire.
>
> Frank's keen knowledge of terrain enabled him to spot where the

enemy machine guns were located and with his knowledge we were able to knock them out. I believe his work in this line saved us many lives. It was while so engaged that he was hit by a rifle or machine-gun bullet and died instantly, just before our infantry made its final rush, capturing the German position.

Frank had always said if his turn should come he hoped it would come just as it did. He died doing his duty, and with his face to the enemy.

Some of Frank's own staff went out that night under heavy shell fire and brought his body in. I know of no tribute which could be paid to him greater than that those men whom he had trained should risk their lives to bring him in.

Next day he was buried beside a hedge at Ex Moriel Farm, near Eclisfontaine, in the Argonne, and a cross erected. His own men performed the ceremony. There was no better loved or respected officer in the regiment than Frank. His fearlessness under fire, his ability and his wonderful personality all combined to make him intensely popular among his brother officers, and an idol to his men.

I think his loss is felt more than that of any other officer who has gone, and they are many.

The fight in which he gave his all to his country will some day be written in history, and it will go down to future generations along with Pickett's Charge at Gettysburg, and the charge of the 600.

It was on that field that American manhood proved itself and Frank set an example which men had to follow.

To you at home who have lost a son, I can simply say that Frank's name will always be at the top of the Roll of Honor of the regiment."[19]

2nd Lt. Ralph Hurlburt of K Company, who played at Michigan in 1909 and 1910 and practiced with the 362nd team early in the season, was last seen alive on the final ridge leading into Gesnes. As he led his men rushing forward, his men saw Hurlburt fall face down on the ridge, but his men continued the attack into Gesnes without him. Later, his men found him in the same location, face down, having been struck and killed by a German bullet.

Lt. John R. McLean, who started in the backfield for the 362nd Officers team, was severely wounded at Gesnes, though the details and specific nature of his wounds are unknown.

By taking Gesnes, the 362nd was the first regiment in the Meuse-Argonne to penetrate *Kriemhilde Stellung*, the last of the Germans' four main trench systems. While taking Gesnes speaks to the valor of its men, doing so put the 362nd in an exposed position. They were two miles in front of the units on either side. Had the other units kept up, the 91st would have had to protect only the two miles of the line to their front. Without support from the units on either side, the 362nd was forced to protect the two miles to their front and two miles on either side. Holding that ground was untenable given the losses suffered over the last four days, so they were ordered to withdraw from Gesnes under cover of darkness. Having twice achieved their objective at heavy cost, only to be ordered to return to an earlier position, the 362nd performed a slow withdrawal, carrying the wounded back to safer territory and bringing back many of the dead, a task that took all night while the ongoing rain turned to sleet.

The 362nd lost over 500 men in the attack on Gesnes. Lt. Everett May, who took command of I Company after Capt. Charles Thorpe was wounded in the first hours of the offensive, led his company over its first four days at Meuse-Argonne. His company started the attack on Gesnes with 178 men and ended the day with 74. May was the only officer left and he had suffered an eye wound. Another company started with 179 men; all but 19 were killed or wounded in the same four days. In four days of battle, the 91st Division lost 8 field officers (majors and above), 125 company officers (captains and lieutenants), and 3,000 enlisted men.

The men of the 362nd later learned that the officer behind the lines that ordered the attack on Gesnes had tried to rescind the order, but was unable to reach the 362nd in time to stop the attack.

The following day, most of the 362nd was sent into reserve to consolidate and another unit took their place on the line. Dysentery was rampant among the men of the 362nd, but they received hot meals for the first time in five days and rested. While they were resting, the 363rd and 364th stayed in position and the divisions on either side of the 91st were replaced. The new divisions (the 32nd and 1st) quickly made advances despite severe shelling occurring throughout the area. By October 2nd, the 91st had another 15 officers and 1,000 enlisted men killed or wounded, largely from enemy shellfire. The division was relieved the evening of October 3 through the morning of October 4 and rested until October 6, when they received orders to move to reserve deep behind the lines. However, the orders were changed such that the 363rd and 364th were sent into deep reserve while the 361st and 362nd were ordered back into the line to fill a gap between the 1st and 32nd Divisions. Over the next six days, the 361st and 362nd were variously under the command of the 1st or 32nd Divisions, participating in several attacks that took key hills in the area and wiped up other enemy resistance.

For his courage and calmness under fire during October, 1st Lt. Howard Angus was promoted to Captain and put in command of D Company of the 362nd on October 12. Angus was wounded and gassed that day, prior to the 361st and 362nd being relieved from frontline action.

The 361st and 362nd then marched for three days to Nettancourt, forty miles behind the front. Having entered the Meuse-Argonne Offensive with slightly less than 20,000 men, the 91st had 1,019 men killed and 3,916 wounded for 4,935 total casualties or over 25 percent of the men that entered the fight fourteen days earlier. During that period, the Germans captured 11 men from the 91st Division, while the 91st captured 11 German officers and 2,360 enlisted men. The difference in rates in which men surrendered was a clear indicator of the state of the German army relative to the fresh American troops during the final months of the war.

The men of the 91st had fought hard in the Meuse-Argonne, and many displayed extraordinary acts of bravery. But like other inexperienced American troops, they had reverted to the same tactics for which British and French commanders had been so roundly criticized. Men in combat for the first time rushed boldly into machine gun and artillery fire. Their own artillery support was sporadic and coordination with neighboring divisions was virtually nonexistent. Supply shortages were common, particularly the field kitchens needed for warm food, and the limited number and poor conditions of the roads made the evacuation of the wounded problematic.

But most American troops had shown themselves willing to fight in difficult terrain. Despite many shortcomings that could be addressed by experience, they proved themselves a capable fighting force that put additional pressure on an increasingly ineffective German army.

The Battle of Blanc Mont Ridge

With the Allies executing the 100 Days Offensive at locations across the front, the Meuse-Argonne was not the only place American troops were fighting in France. The French Fourth Army planned an attack in the Champagne region immediately east of the American positions in the Meuse-Argonne on September 26—the same day the Meuse-Argonne Offensive launched—and they asked Genl. Pershing for American units to help gain the desired breakthrough. Pershing responded by offering the untested 36th Division and the well-tested 2nd Division, which had previously fought at Château-Thierry, Belleau Wood, the Aisne-Marne, and St. Mihiel. The 2nd Division, which included the 4th Marine Brigade, comprised of the 5th and 6th Marine Regiments and the 6th Machine Gun Battalion, had moved into reserve after fighting at St. Mihiel and was awaiting assignment in the Meuse-Argonne Offensive, but their new orders sent them ten miles further northwest.

The French plans called for a pincer attack on either side of a set of hills known as Blanc Mont Ridge, highlighted by Blanc Mont itself, a heavily fortified, chalky white promontory that dominated the surrounding land. The Germans took Blanc Mont in 1914 and had defended numerous efforts by the French to take it back over the last four years. Taking or surrounding Blanc Mont Ridge and seizing the town of St. Etienne that sat behind the ridge would force the Germans to retreat more than thirty miles to the Aisne River, the next defensible position in the sector.

After learning the French planned to use the two Marine regiments separately, Genl. Lejeune met with French Genl. Gouraud and negotiated a revised plan calling for the full 4th Brigade to directly attack the well-defended German positions atop the ridgeline. On the evening of October 1, the Marines took over a 2.5-mile section of the front across from Blanc Mont Ridge with the 6th Marines on the left and the 5th Marines on the right. The French 21st Division was to the left of the Marines.

A limited attack by the 6th Marines began in the late afternoon of October 2, and successfully cleaned up a trench works to the left and below Blanc Mont Ridge. The attack was supported by the 81st Machine Gun Company, which included Ken Buss. The main attack started at 5:50 A.M. on October 3. The Marines made solid progress but the attack by the French 21st on the left stalled, exposing the left flank of the 6th Marines. Throughout the day, the Marines continued to advance, increasing the exposure of their left flank, so small units were pulled from the attack and positioned to protect the left flank. The Germans on the left and on the heights above poured fire into the 6th Marines' position throughout the day as its reserve battalions passed through the original attacking battalion to maintain the attack. By late in the day, the Marine succeeded in taking part of Blanc Mont.

The following day the 5th Marines passed through the positions taken by the 6th Marines and continued pressing the Germans. Harassment by machine gun fire and shelling from the heights on their left continued with the Marines suffering more than 1,100 casualties that day. Continuing the leapfrog approach, the 6th Marines passed through the 5th Marines the morning of October 6, and succeeded in taking the rest of Blanc Mont Ridge. Though exhausted and undermanned, the Marines received further orders to take the nearby town of St. Etienne, which they succeeded in doing on October 8. Taking St. Etienne sent the Germans into the predicted retreat and opened the way for the 36th Division, which relieved much of the 2nd Division and the 4th Marine Brigade on October 10. The Marines counted their remaining men after retiring from the battlefield. In nine days of fighting, the 4th Marine Brigade had seen 494 killed and 1,864 wounded, roughly half the number killed and wounded at Belleau Wood.

One of the missing Marines was William Buss, the substitute end for Mare Island in 1917. Like Robert Wilson who had gone missing during the Battle of Soissons, Buss went missing on the first full day of battle on October 3, and continued to be listed as missing in action until after the Armistice. While the 6th Marines could not account for Buss, he was found safe, but not sound. Sometime during the battle Buss had been taken to an evacuation hospital and diagnosed with psychoneurosis or shell shock. His hospital records do not mention physical injuries, but he was clearly wounded in a different sense during the Battle of Blanc Mont Ridge. Buss returned to the lines in the final days of the war.

Camp Lewis Players Elsewhere in France

Roy Sharp who transferred from Camp Lewis for Field Artillery training, arrived in France in June 1918, completed his officer training there, and was promoted to 2nd Lt. He then volunteered for a balloon squadron and received additional training to prepare him to direct artillery fire from an observation balloon basket. He was transferred to the 13th Balloon Squadron, which arrived at the Meuse-Argonne in the last days of the war.

Right guard and Lt. Anker "A. L." Christensen arrived in France in April with a Quartermaster Corps Repair Shop unit and was promoted to Captain in the Motor Transport Corps while in France. Other information on his service in France has not been found.

2nd Lt. Emzy Lynch (tackle) and 2nd Lt. Charlie Turner (end) were with the 347th Field Artillery which, while officially part of the 91st Division was still in training in France when the 91st was engaged in the Meuse-Argonne. Lynch had been with the unit since Camp Lewis, while Turner shipped to France in August as part of a replacement group from Camp Jackson, before joining the 347th. Their unit arrived in the Meuse-Argonne sector in early November.

The Mare Island Marines in the War

Eleven of the twenty-eight players on Mare Island's 1917 team were in France with the AEF before the Meuse-Argonne Offensive started. Three players—Clinton 'Mark' Gardner, Darrell Gardner, and John Parker—transferred from Mare Island to the Marine Flying Field in Miami in April 1918 and were in France by July.

A squadron of de Havilland DH-4s bearing British roundrels.

In France, the three served with the First Marine Aviation Force, which acted as the Day Wing of the Navy's Northern Bomber Group along the coast, near Dunkirk. The Day Wing's intended mission was to search for German submarines stationed at the Belgian ports, but the Marine planes arrived too late to be of use, so the Marine pilots were loaned to British aviation units in Belgium and flew with them while waiting for their own planes to arrive. Most of their missions were high level bombing runs over Belgium flying in de Havilland DH-4s, a two-seater with the pilot in front and machine gunner sitting behind him. As the war progressed, the Marines aviators moved forward with the British taking over air fields abandoned by the retreating Germans.

The Gardner brothers were promoted to Sergeant and John Parker was promoted to Gunnery Sergeant while in training, but their duties in France are not entirely clear. Both Gardners are listed in the muster rolls as Police Sergeants, while Parker appears to have manned a machine gun in DH-4s for several months with the British. (Darrell Gardner's obituary indicates he was a pilot during the war, but that is unlikely since he spent only three months in aviation training before shipping to France.)

Beyond those engaged in action, other American troops continued to arrive in France. John Beckett, Gerald Craig, Elmer Hall, and Irving Purdy were among the highest scoring enlisted men that tested into the Marines' first officer training program. All four were sent to Quantico for the officer training camp. One of their classmates in the camp was John McGregor, who played for Mare Island early in the 1917 season before being transferred to Quantico and then spent December 1917 through May 1918 at Guantanamo Bay,

The 94th Co., 7th Marines on patrol in Bayamo, Cuba in 1918.

Cuba guarding Cuba's sugar cane fields. (Cuba joined the Allies shortly after the U.S. entered the war.) McGregor also tested into the officer training camp and was sent back to Quantico in May.

All five completed their officer training and received their commissions as 2nd Lieutenants in July 1918. By then, the Marines had formed the 5th Marine Brigade, which included the 11th and 13th Regiments. Beckett went to France in September with the 13th Regiment, while Craig, Hall, McGregor, and Purdy went with the 11th Regiment, though Hall transferred to the 13th Regiment soon after arriving in France. The 11th and 13th Marines spent their time guarding supply lines and the port cities on France's western coast and were not sent into action. Also with the 13th were Sgt. George McMillan, a substitute fullback at Mare Island, and Pvt. Wallace Enright, my paternal grandfather, who had enlisted and arrived at Quantico on the Fourth of July.

Another former Mare Island player, Henry Shields, was transferred to Quantico in November 1917 and completed officer training camp in July. By September 1918, he was in the Dominican Republic with the 3rd Marines and spend the next year in periodic skirmishes with local bandits.

The 13th Marines crossing the ocean in September 1918.

In July 1918, seven players from the 1917 Mare Island team—Walter Brown, Thomas Cushman, Cloy Hobson, Goodyear Kirkman, Clifford Mitchell, Fred Molthen, and Lawson Sanderson—entered the Naval Aviation School at MIT in Boston which hosted aviation classroom or ground training. All were promoted to Gunnery Sergeant at the time. After completing ground training in October, Cushman remained at MIT as the divisional officer and the others moved to the Marine Flying Field in Miami as student pilots. All six were there on Armistice Day and all but Mitchell subsequently earned their wings and lieutenancy at the Marine Flying Field in Miami in January 1919.

Other 1917 players remained at Mare Island until August or September 1918, before qualifying for the Marines' fourth officer training camp that started in September and ended in December 1918. These included Hollis Huntington, Stan Ridderhof, Keith Ambrose, Ed Bailey, and Lawrence Teberg. Meanwhile, John Coshow was transferred to Quantico in December 1917 and was stationed at naval bases in Rhode Island for the rest of the war.

Fifty-four of the eighty-six men who played for the Mare Island Marines, Camp Lewis, or the 362nd Officers team were in France by September 1918 and the overwhelming majority were in the front lines with their fellow citizen soldiers. In exchanging their leather football helmets for steel doughboy helmets, they did not ask for or receive special treatment. Their football glory counted for little when they were tested on the fields of unfriendly strife. Like other soldiers and Marines placed in battle, they had acquitted themselves well and expected to experience additional tests in the coming month as the war drew to a close.

SHOW YOUR GRIT

While many of the men from the 1918 Rose Bowl teams were fighting in France and others were in advanced training, the football season continued against the backdrop of the scheduling turmoil caused by the SATC restrictions and the ravages of the influenza epidemic. Every school in the country spent October rescheduling games based on the SATC directive only to have many of the rescheduled games wiped from the schedule as the influenza epidemic took hold. Some schools cancelled their season, but most slogged through the period scheduling games against any opponent they could find. Many games were played in empty stadiums as people outside the camp or campus were barred from attending for fear of spreading the virus.

Despite the hundreds of thousands dying from the influenza, a pattern quickly emerged that the influenza burned through a city for several weeks to a month with 20-25 percent of the population becoming ill, then the influenza subsided, finding new victims elsewhere. In each city it affected, the number of new cases dropped off in a tail that lasted several months; the later cases were generally milder than those at the peak.

THE NEWSPAPERS PROVIDED extensive coverage of the new SATC rules, but many schools received their official orders only in the first week of October. Pitt received theirs on October 2, three days before their season-opening matchup with Great Lakes. The orders forced Pitt to change the dates or opponents for five of the nine games on their schedule; this for a team in the East in reasonable proximity to its opponents.

With the travel restrictions making the likelihood of intersectional games slim, the Pitt-Great Lakes matchup was expected to be one of the few intersectional games played in 1918. The game also had high expectations due to Great Lakes' highly-touted roster and Pitt's status as the two-time returning national champions riding a 28-game winning streak. By season's end, Pitt would be named the collegiate national champions for the 1918 season, so they were an excellent ball club. Going into the game, Great Lakes clearly had the talent to sink Pitt and they continued adding talent with Jimmy Conzelman returning from injury and Hugh Blacklock, who played for Great Lakes in 1917, joining the team after being reassigned on the base. Nevertheless, questions remained about Great Lakes' ability to harness the talent and play effectively as a team.

The Great Lakes Jackies left Chicago and were in Pittsburgh Friday afternoon by the time Pitt officials learned that Pennsylvania's health commissioner had banned all public gatherings due to the influenza epidemic. Although the game was cancelled, Great Lakes and some combination of Pitt players scrimmaged one another on Saturday. A Washington Times article published nearly a month later tells us Great Lakes was trounced, struggling to move the ball, and allowing Pitt to score on six consecutive attempts from the 50-yard line. The Great Lakes base newspaper printed the Monday after the scrimmage indicated the teams were evenly matched with Great Lakes being more likely to win a real game. Either way, the Jackies was disappointed in not playing a game, making for a long train ride home to Chicago.

Next up for Great Lakes was the in-state battle with Illinois on October 12. Despite returning only two starters from the 1917 team, Illinois improved throughout the season and went on to claim the 1918 Big Ten title. Illinois was coached by Bob Zuppke, who led the Illini to four national titles during his twenty-eight years at Illinois.

Jimmy Conzelman started at quarterback for Great Lakes against Illinois, leading a march down the field on the opening series. The drive was capped by a 25-yard run by Hal Erickson, followed by a Conzelman pass to George Halas that gave the Jackies first and goal on the one. Fullback Paul Dobson then ran the oval the final yard for a touchdown. The extra point made it to a 7-0 lead. Beyond that score, however, the Great Lakes offense stalled and they were unable to get inside the Illinois 25-yard line. Olcott put Driscoll into the lineup at the start of the second half at left halfback and he promptly returned the kick sixty-five yards, but Great Lakes could not move the ball after that and Olcott resorted to replacing all eleven players at the start of the fourth quarter. The subs could do no better than the starters, and Great Lakes headed back north with a 7-0 victory. Following the Illinois game, Paul Dobson, who scored the only touchdown, received word he had qualified for the Navy's balloon training program. Dobson, who led Nebraska to the Missouri Valley championship in 1917 before joining the Navy, was sent to MIT for ground school training.

The next game on the schedule for Great Lakes was a tilt with the University of Chicago on October 19. Like Pittsburgh, Chicago entered the season with a legendary coach who could not make heads or tails of how the SATC program would impact his team. Amos Alonzo Stagg was in the twenty-sixth of his forty years at the helm at Chicago when the SATC announcements came out. As his team finished its last two-a-day practice on August 31, he reminded his players before sending them to the showers that they, and the rest of the male student body, would take oaths the next morning to enter the SATC program. Stagg told them that neither he nor anyone else in the athletic department could tell the players whether or when the SATC schedule would allow time for football practice. Such was the state of communications regarding the SATC program.

Like other colleges, Chicago lost veteran players to the services before the season, but the Big Ten's decision to allow freshmen to play varsity football increased the pool of players. One of the freshmen joining the team was a lad Stagg nicknamed "Fritz" after a concert violinist with a similar surname. Fritz Crisler started for three years at Chicago before becoming an assistant coach there and then becoming head coach at Minnesota and Princeton. At the latter, he gave his team their distinctive winged helmet before taking the silly design with him when he became Michigan's coach. At Michigan, he painted the helmets in the maize and blue colors college football fans have endured for eighty years. Admittedly, they are better looking than Princeton's orange and black version, but that is the definition of damning with faint praise.

The Chicago team lost their first game the week before their meeting with Great Lakes. The team was then staggered when they learned six team members would be transferred from Chicago's SATC program to an officer training camp in Texas, Crisler among them. Things were not looking good for the Maroons and they only got worse. It was October and bad humours were in the air, causing Chicago's Board of Health to cancel all high school and college football games in the city. Great Lakes offered to host the Maroons for Saturday's game, but since the local papers were still publishing obituaries for sailors dying of influenza at Great Lakes, Stagg politely declined the invitation. Having had the Pitt and Chicago games cancelled, Great Lakes could only look forward to their game with Western Michigan in Kalamazoo the following week.

Unfortunately, the influenza was roaring through Michigan as well and health authorities prohibited games for the next two weeks, so Great Lakes now had another open date. Great Lakes tried unsuccessfully to get Camp Funston of Kansas to travel to the Windy City, but those plans fell through. A few miles south of Waukegan, Northwestern had an open date that weekend and was scheduled to play at Michigan the following weekend, but the Michigan game was now cancelled by the same public health order that cancelled the Great Lakes-Western Michigan game. Northwestern contacted Great Lakes about a possible matchup and on the Thursday evening before the game, Great Lakes announced they would host Northwestern at Sailors' Field.

Beyond simply having a game to play, Great Lakes was excited to play their first home game in front of their fellow Jackies. Unfortunately for the 15,000 fans in attendance and the players on the field, several days of rain left the playing field a quagmire. Both teams struggled to move the ball in the mud. Forward passes and end runs were largely eliminated from the playbooks and the windy conditions affected the game's many punts. Both teams struggled to find their feet and move the ball in the first quarter, but in the second quarter a series of line plunges by Willaman, the fullback, and reverses to Paddy Driscoll brought the Jackies to the Northwestern 19-yard line. Great Lakes failed to move the ball further. On fourth down, Driscoll was in the process of preparing the ground in front of him for a drop-kicked field goal attempt when Marty Conrad, the center, snapped the ball early. Driscoll barely caught the ball and fell to the ground without attempting the kick.

In the third quarter, Great Lakes again moved the ball into scoring territory, reaching the Purple's 25-yard line, but erratic play calling left them dependent on another Driscoll field goal attempt. Although Driscoll kicked the ball this time, the ball travelled only 15 yards before dying in the mud. Nothing else of note happened the rest of the game and the contest ended in a 0-0 tie. Once again, despite its talented roster, Great Lakes was unable to get its offense moving.

While people across the country were hunkered down avoiding gatherings that might spread influenza, one more government-ordered change impacted the nation's beleaguered football coaches that weekend. President Wilson had signed the Standard Time Act in March 1918 and Daylight Saving Time sprang forward at 2:00 a.m. on March 31 and fell back at 2:00 a.m. on October 27. Since the nation's clocks had never fallen back until that weekend, the country's football coaches were surprised by how early in the day the sunlight disappeared. Since college players' daily schedules marched to the beat of the SATC drum, teams were left with limited daylight for their late afternoon practices. With few schools having lighted practice fields, the nation's football teams were left in the dark once again.

A November 2 game at St. Louis University was next on the docket for Great Lakes and while the influenza epidemic was easing in the St. Louis area, health officials continued to ban public gatherings.

St. Louis University suggested moving the game to a later date and Great Lakes countered by inviting St. Louis to play the game at Great Lakes, even sending a representative to negotiate with SLU's athletic director. The approach failed and the game was cancelled two days before it was to be played. While Great Lakes' first team did not play that week, Cornell College of Iowa visited Great Lakes and lost to the Jackies' second team, 33-3, after having lost to Iowa's first team 34-0 two weeks earlier.

With the schedule in turmoil, Great Lakes looked forward to their upcoming game at Notre Dame, where the influenza appeared to have a passed, but the big news that week was the announcement that Coach Bo Olcott had been demoted and replaced by Assistant Coach Lt. Clarence J. McReavy. Great Lakes' official explanation for the change was that Capt. Moffett wanted an officer in charge of the team rather than a civilian like Olcott. However, it was understood that Great Lakes officials were not happy with the team's performance to date. Though Olcott had a reputation as a disciplinarian, he was unable to relate to the players and his commands went unheeded.

McReavy was a Naval Academy graduate who played football at Navy from 1911 to 1913 and captained the 1913-1914 basketball team. McReavy was serving aboard a destroyer when America entered the war and went with the ship when it was sent to patrol the waters near the British Isles. He later returned to stateside and was assigned to Great Lakes to head its officer material (aka officer training) program. McReavy immediately changed the players' daily schedule to add more structure, and altered the lineup as well. Notre Dame's Charlie Bachman was shifted from left tackle to center and newly-arrived Con Eklund of Minnesota took Bachman's place at tackle. That gave the team an interior line with three Golden Domers: Emmett Keefe at left guard, Bachman at center, and Jerry Jones at right guard. McReavy also moved Paddy Driscoll from halfback to quarterback, a position he preferred not to play.

Notre Dame was led by rookie coach Knute Rockne, who played in South Bend from 1910 to 1913, before assisting there for four years while also playing semipro and pro football in Ohio. Notre Dame lost key players to the military, but opened the roster to freshmen before the SATC did so for all schools. The day before the tilt, local health authorities confirmed there was no longer any sign of influenza on Notre Dame's campus, so the game could go on. Revitalized by the coaching change, the Jackies sported a new optimism as they made the short trip to South Bend.

The game opened with Great Lakes kicking off to Notre Dame. End runs by Notre Dame's left halfback George Gipp, of "Win just one for the Gipper" fame, and runs up the middle by freshman fullback Curly Lambeau, of Lambeau Field in Green Bay fame, brought the ball within scoring range. Notre Dame took the ball over for the touchdown only five minutes into the game and Gipp converted the extra point to give Notre Dame a 7-0 lead. The game descended into a brutal test with neither team moving the ball effectively, while Great Lakes saw a stream of players leave the game with injuries. Frank Willaman, the starting fullback, broke his leg and was expected to be out for the rest of the season.

In the third quarter, Driscoll and Abrahamson put together a string of solid runs that brought the ball to Notre Dame's 35-yard line. Driscoll then took the ball around end and raced unstopped for the end zone before converting on the extra point. Through the remainder of the third quarter and all the fourth quarter, defense dominated and the game ended in a 7-7 tie, with Notre Dame feeling like the victors.

Although the impact of the coaching shakeup did not show itself on the field against the Irish, its impact was coming and a different Great Lakes Bluejackets team would emerge in the coming weeks.

DURING THE WEEKS in which Great Lakes team played Illinois, Northwestern, and Notre Dame, Mare Island was not so fortunate. After playing Camp Fremont on September 28, their slate of October games with St. Mary's, Mather Field, and Vancouver Barracks were cancelled due to the quarantine. The same was true of tentative contests with the Presidio and California.

Outside the base, the Oakland and San Francisco newspapers reported on influenza deaths across the country, showing figures we now know were undercounted. Despite schools, theaters, and other public gathering places being closed or banned in Los Angeles and other communities, the San Francisco and Oakland health authorities took a wait-and-see approach, ordering more substantive measures only after the epidemic took hold. For example, San Francisco waited until October 24 to institute fines against anyone not wearing a gauze mask in public. By then, eighty to ninety people were dying per day of influenza-related symptoms in the city. While it is easy to play the armchair health commissioner one-hundred years later, the local health authorities did not act swiftly, while those at Mare Island did so and likely saved many lives.

Around the country, twenty-five army camps were under quarantine and Great Lakes finally acknowledged that hundreds of deaths had occurred there. Although some locales were reporting a reduction in the rates of new infections and deaths, the end of the epidemic did not seem near.

With the cancellation of Mare Island's October schedule, Capt. Lynn Coovert, Mare Island's new Athletic Director, scrambled in late October and early November to arrange future contests. Mare Island, having won the 1918 Rose Bowl and shown themselves to be one of the best on the coast during their early games, remained an attractive opponent. On an almost daily basis, the newspapers reported that Mare Island had confirmed arrangements with a new team or had rescheduled a previously cancelled contest. Twenty-three different opponents or dates were cited in various newspaper reports and, of course, even Mare Island could not play them all. But potential opponents had little to lose by announcing a game with Mare Island and each team that announced such a game increased Mare Island's negotiating power with whomever they ultimately played.

Beyond finding a way to play any team, Coovert wanted to schedule and defeat quality opponents to demonstrate Mare Island's dominance, while also generating the money needed for Mare Island's self-funded football operations. In the end, Coovert proved too successful and he overscheduled his team, forcing them to play too many games in too few days. Their schedule would challenge the team's ability to finish the season in the manner they intended.

After last playing on September 28, Mare Island was finally able to play a game on November 2 against Fort Baker. Fort Baker was another coastal artillery installation that now sits below the northern end of the Golden Gate Bridge and is operated by the National Park Service. The Marines likely traveled to the game aboard ship, but any mode of transportation would have worked for Mare Island. The Marines kicked off to start the game and the ball rolled over the goal line. Thinking the situation called for a touchback, the Fort Baker players did not touch the ball, letting it sit in the end zone. Lloyd Glover thought otherwise and landed on the ball, scoring the first of his four touchdowns on the day. The crowd might have cheered the touchdown, but the game was closed to outside spectators and was played in relative silence. There was little other excitement in the game. The Marines scored three times in both the first and second quarters and twice in each quarter of the second half, winning 67-0, Fort Baker failed to earn a first down the entire game.

Having finally eluded the grasp of the influenza epidemic and played another game, the Marines were eager to take on the rest of their opponents, make some news, and solidify their reputation as the best team in the West. But it was early November 1918, and far more momentous news was only days away across the Atlantic.

SHOW THE HUN

The 361st and 362nd Regiments remained in the fighting in the Meuse-Argonne for ten days longer than their brethren in the 363rd and 364th Regiments, who rested in Nettancourt far behind the lines. While in Nettancourt, the division received 4,000 replacements from the 84th Division, which had trained at Camp Sherman in Ohio and was broken up in France with its men scattered as replacements for units that lost men in the fighting. Some 91st Division men who were hospitalized with minor wounds during the Meuse-Argonne Offensive also made their way to Nettancourt. The 363rd and 364th were issued winter clothing in Nettancourt and ordered to entrain for an unknown destination. As they were boarding, the 361st and 362nd Regiments marched into town and were instructed to quickly board the trains without receiving their winter clothing.

After thirty-six hours aboard the trains, the 91st Division pulled into Dunkirk, Belgium where the men learned that they and the 37th Division, the unit to the right of the 91st at Meuse-Argonne, were now assigned to the French Army serving under King Albert of Belgium. Their orders were to participate in the Lys-Scheldt Offensive, so called because its objectives were to drive the Germans across the Lys and Scheldt Rivers. The Scheldt is the westernmost of Belgium's two largest rivers (the other being the Meuse) and runs north through Antwerp before emptying into the North Sea in The Netherlands. From a strategic standpoint, the Allies intended to drive the Germans east of the Scheldt, freeing western Belgium or, at least, ensuring the German troops remaining in the area would be cut off from supplies.

From Dunkirk, the division marched east toward Ypres. Along the march, the 91st faced scenes of utter devastation as they marched through the Passchendaele and Ypres areas that had seen constant fighting and shelling between the British and Germans over the last four years. The landscape was cratered by shell hole upon shell hole. There were virtually no trees or buildings standing for long stretches of the march. Upon arriving in Ypres, they pitched their tents and bedded down for the night.

The remains of a village in Flanders with water-filled shell holes on the left.

The following morning, they learned that some support elements of the 91st Division had stayed in the Meuse-Argonne Offensive, while others were arriving in Belgium and detraining in helter-skelter fashion near Ypres. To organize themselves, all units marched on assigned roads to a nearby town where the replacements were allocated to the 361st and 362nd Regiments. It was there that Everett May, now Capt. May, received replacements for all his fellow officers in the company that had been lost at Meuse-Argonne.

After spending a week working with the replacements, the 91st was ordered to the front the evening of October 29, replacing the French 164th Division south of the Belgian village of Waeregham. They overlooked a wooded knoll called Spittals Bosschen, beyond which was the city of Audenarde. They were subjected to periodic shelling, but unlike their experience at Meuse-Argonne, the Allies controlled the air over this section of Belgium so the German shelling was ill targeted. The division was to go on the attack the next morning.

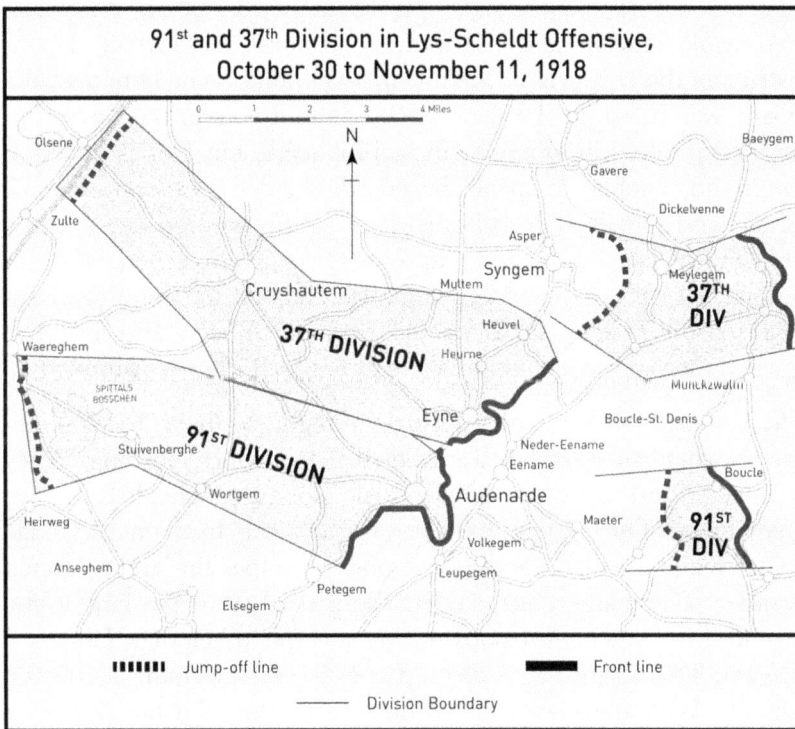

91st and 37th Division in Lys-Scheldt Offensive, October 30 to November 11, 1918

The 91st attacked east to west through Spittals Bosschen to Audenarde. After being relieved for a few days, they returned to the line shortly before the Armistice. (Adapted from American Armies and Battlefields in Europe, A History, Guide, and Reference Book.)

Moving west to east, the Division attacked Spittals Bosschen at 5:30 a.m. on October 30. Once again, the 91st Division charged through heavy machine gun fire coming from the German machine gun nests hidden in the woods. 1st Lt. John Burgard who, in the Meuse-

Argonne offensive, led an attack against German machine guns setting up to fire on the battalion command post, was now with H Company of the 362nd. Early in the attack, Burgard's company commander was wounded, so Burgard took command and was leading the fight when a high explosive shell landed nearby. The concussion fractured his back. As he tried to rise, Burgard was struck by shrapnel that hit the trench mirror he kept in his breast pocket, likely saving his life, but the injuries sent him to the hospital. Ben Dorris, an end on the 362nd Officers team, was nearby and took command of H Company. While continuing the attack on Spittals Bosschen a shell exploded fifty feet from Dorris, taking down two men while leaving a third man, a corporal, untouched. Dorris instructed the corporal to tend to the wounded men. Minutes later, Dorris was struck in the face by shrapnel, a wound that broke his jaw and resulted in Dorris losing all his teeth, but Dorris stayed in command. Unable to speak, he coordinated his company's attack using hand signals. The fighting went on through the day and the 91st finally enveloped and captured Spittals Bosschen. For his actions, Dorris was cited for valor by General Pershing and was awarded the Belgian Croix de Guerre. Four officers and forty-five enlisted men were killed that day and another 175 were wounded.

The Germans fled the area during the night, so the 91st was unopposed when they attacked again the following morning. They reached a crest overlooking Audenarde along the Scheldt River five miles away. They spent that evening and the next on the ridge before taking Audenarde opposed only by sniper fire and a limited number of machine guns. Audenarde proved to be the largest city captured by American troops during the war other than Château-Thierry. The capture of Audenarde pushed the Germans across the Scheldt. With the Germans in full retreat, they did not put up a credible fight over the next several days. More important for the men of the 91st, with the Germans now on the east side of the Scheldt, their mission was complete and they were withdrawn for a few days of rest on November 3.

The action in Flanders was only part of the broader 100 Days Offensive. The German Army was being pushed back across the front—from the North Sea down to the fighting that continued in the Meuse-Argonne. German lines that had seldom moved backwards since 1914 were now pushed back fifty or more miles in most locations. As shown in the following map, most of the advances were made by British, Commonwealth, and French troops, but the American troops made important contributions simply by being over there with fresh troops putting additional pressure on the German Army. The American forces in the Meuse-Argonne were approaching Sedan, their objective in the offensive, and they soon captured portions of the critical rail lines carrying supplies to the German troops west of Sedan.

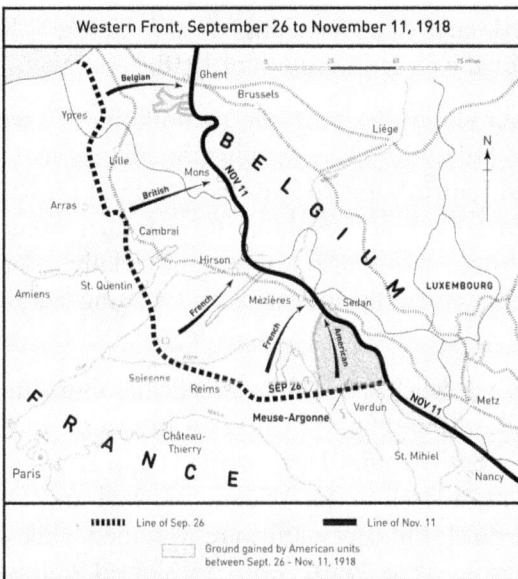

Although American troops fought at locations across the front, most American troops fought at St. Mihiel and the Meuse-Argonne (gray shaded area). The ground captured by the 91st and 37th Divisions in Belgium can be seen near the top of the map. (Adapted from American Armies and Battlefields in Europe, A History, Guide, and Reference Book.)

Beyond the battlefield in Belgium and northeastern France, the Central Powers were crumbling. The Ottoman Empire signed an armistice on October 30 and the Austro-Hungarian Empire followed suit on November 4. In Germany, sailors of the German fleet mutinied in late October and there was civilian unrest in a number of German cities. Finally, Kaiser Wilhelm II, who had ruled Germany for the last thirty years, fled for The Netherlands the night of November 9.

Earlier on November 9, the 91st Division marched toward Audenarde with orders to attack across the Scheldt on November 11 unless word was received that Germany had signed the Armistice. The division was in Audenarde at 8:00 a.m. on November 11 preparing to attack east across the Scheldt, but the attack never launched. Word came through that Germany had signed the Armistice in French General Foch's private railroad car in the Forest of Compiegne at 5:00 a.m. Paris time on November 11, 1918. The fighting ended later that morning at the eleventh hour of the eleventh day of the eleventh month of 1918.

As occurred all along the front, the men of the 91st were relieved, but celebrated little. Most were simply grateful they had survived the war and could return home to lives they had put on hold. Unfortunately for the 91st, nothing about their return home happened quickly and they endured six weeks of relative deprivation in Belgium before returning to France and waiting for their passage home.

With the fighting over, it should be noted that four other members of the Camp Lewis and 362nd Officers teams were wounded during the war. Stable Sgt. Bandini Dear of the Camp Lewis team and the 364th Regiment, as well as Lt. William M. Bell and Lt. Rhodolph Esmay of the 362nd Officers team were wounded while serving with the 91st Division. Pete Lenz, who transferred out following the game with the 316th Sanitary Train and became the first service Rose Bowl player sent to France, was also severely wounded during the war and was sent back to the States in October 1918. The details of where, when, and how these men were wounded are not known.

Armistice and Demobilization

The terms of the Armistice required Germany to surrender the bulk of its artillery, machine guns, planes, trucks, naval vessels, and a specified number of locomotives and rail cars. The Germany Army also had to quickly retreat from Belgium, Luxemburg, and France and surrender all German land west of the Rhine. The terms also gave the Allies authority to occupy three bridgeheads on the east side of the Rhine River at the cities of Mayence, Coblenz, and Cologne. Each bridgehead covered a semicircular area eighteen miles in diameter from the center of the city. Moreover, a six-mile wide neutral zone was established on the east side of the Rhine, bumping out around the three bridgeheads. The U.S. Army was responsible for the Coblenz bridgehead, with France later taking partial responsibility for the area. America's occupation force required eight divisions (about 200,000 men) and the force included Camp Lewis' Charlie Turner and Emzy Lynch. As part of the 347th Field Artillery, they arrived in the Meuse-Argonne area shortly before the Armistice and were sent to the Rhineland as part of the Army of Occupation on Thanksgiving Day.

A few days after the Armistice, the 91st Division was reassigned to the 7th French Corps and received orders to participate in the occupation of the Rhine as well. They began marching east on November 16 and continued for two days before receiving new orders cancelling their role in the occupation. The 91st Division turned around and marched west, ultimately encamping near Dunkirk.

The Army started planning for demobilization only one month before the hostilities ended, and the planning task was handled by one colonel with little staff. The resulting plan called for the AEF to demobilize by division with the task of determining the order in which divisions went home falling to Genl. Pershing and his staff. With over two million men in Europe and only 200,000 required for the Army of Occupation, 1.8 million men now had few responsibilities in Europe. They wanted only to go home. The prioritization could not make everyone happy given limits on the number of available transport ships, and the 91st received relatively low priority, so the 91st had a long wait before heading home.

Back in the States, the armed services quickly began discharging men back into civilian life. Men who were in the U.S. and were not in the middle of advanced training courses were the first to leave the services. Priority was given to men who had urgent business or family matters and those who intended to return to school for the spring semester. Paul Dobson, who started for Great Lakes early in the season, earned a quick release from his balloon training program and returned to Nebraska. His release proved so quick that he played for Nebraska in its game with Notre Dame on November 18 and against their Missouri Valley Conference foe, Washington University, on December 7. A handful of other men were released in 1918, but most were discharged in early 1919.

For the 91st Division, most of the six weeks following the Armistice was taken up marching from one Belgium location to another in a pattern with little apparent logic other than to keep the men busy. The areas they marched through and quartered in were desolate, being among the areas on the Western Front that suffered the greatest effects of the war. There had been little agricultural production in recent years, limited building stock for quarters, and even less wood or coal available for heat. Beyond that, the 91st was not well connected to the American supply lines in France so they were undersupplied with food, clothing, and blankets.

Despite the lack of supplies relative to most American troops, the 91st was far better provisioned than the local populace. While spending the Christmas season in Oostveleteren, Belgium, the men pooled their money to buy presents for local children and the money that went unspent was given to the neediest local families. Starting on New Year's Day, the 91st boarded trains to Le Mans, France, about fifty miles from the embarkation ports of St. Nazaire, Nantes, and Le Havre.

———

THE SIGNING of the Armistice coincided with the end of the second wave of influenza, so those playing college and service football in late 1918 were relieved of two terrible threats.

At the same time, most of the American battle deaths and wounds during WWI occurred during the six-week period between late September through the Armistice. Due both to the sheer confusion of battle and slower communication methods during WWI, families and others were not notified of the dead and wounded until weeks later. Well into December, newspapers around the country carried long Honor Rolls listing the names, ranks, and hometowns of those who had died in battle or of disease, those who were missing in action, and those who had been wounded. These lists and the knowledge of family, friends, and others on the Honor Rolls cast a pall on an otherwise celebratory country. As a result, post-Armistice service football came to symbolize the American willingness to fight, while also providing an opportunity to honor the sacrifices of the fallen, and to celebrate that it was all over.

IT'S OVER, OVER THERE

I t is difficult to capture the excitement in the sporting world that came with a November intersectional tour of the east coast by a Great Lakes team touted as the best the Midwest had to offer. Due to the travel restrictions, many top college teams had played inferior, but nearby, opponents leading to many lopsided games, whereas the Great Lakes-Rutgers game featured two top teams playing on the first weekend after the war ended. Every newspaper had one or more articles about the matchup; still, the eastern newspapers tended to underestimate the farmers of the midwest and the midwestern newspapers underestimated the fancy boys of the east coast.

Great Lakes was originally scheduled to play the Detroit Naval Station that day, but Detroit stepped aside to allow Great Lakes to play Rutgers at Ebbetts Field in Brooklyn, in a game in which all gate receipts went to the United War Work Fund. The United War Work Fund was major fundraising effort coordinated by seven religious and secular organizations that provided goods and services to the men in uniform. Among their many fundraising efforts were sporting events, particularly college and service football games. Ironically, the campaign launched on November 11, so the Fund organizers woke that morning to news of the Armistice. Nonetheless, the campaign moved forward and exceeded its $170 million goal by raising $203 million (more than $4 billion today).

Rutgers came into the game undefeated over a two-year period and had outscored Lehigh, Penn State, and three other opponents by a combined 178-3 score. Rutgers was clicking on all cylinders with its star running back Paul Robeson, a 1917 All-American and one of the premier black (or white) gridiron men of the day. Robeson would end his career at Rutgers as the class valedictorian before launching a long singing career.

The game was preceded by a stunt demonstration by Navy pilots above Ebbets Field that ended with a football being dropped from one of the planes into the arms of a waiting sailor. On the field, Robeson led an opening quarter drive for a score and when Great Lakes failed to move the ball on the next series, Rutgers leveraged its field position to take a 14-0 lead. Then things changed. Following the kickoff, Driscoll took the first snap for an 80-yard touchdown run and Great Lakes stymied Rutgers on the ensuing series. Driscoll returned the Rutgers punt 55 yards for a second touchdown. The missed extra point left the score at 14-13 Rutgers at half.

Great Lakes opened the second half with a quick score by Erickson, followed by a third Driscoll touchdown on the next possession. Driscoll scored three more touchdowns and then handed the scoring duties over to Dutch Lauer, who added one tally. The game ended as a Great Lakes romp and a 54-14 victory. Driscoll finished the game with six touchdowns, while converting five of six extra-point attempts, finishing with forty-one points on the day.

1918 Great Lakes Naval Training Station football team. (Top row, left to right): Combs, Ivy, Swanekamp, Foley, Andrews, Collins, Hellberg (Manager), Commander Kaufman (Athletic Officer), Lt. McReavy (Coach), Welsh, Richards, Bliss, Doherty, Griffith, Paulsen. (Second Row): Byers, Bachman, Driscoll, Eielson, Conzelman, Langenstein, Abrahamson, McClellan, Lauer, Erickson, Willaman, Williams. (Bottom Row): Reeves, Miller, Chester Barnard, Jones, Keefe, Halas, Reichle, Lester Barnard, Eklund, Knight.

Great Lakes' trouncing of Rutgers and Paddy Driscoll's performance created a sensation among eastern sportswriters who had previously not seen him in action. As the leader of a Great Lakes team that had struggled against midwestern competition before coming east and spanking one of the best teams in the region, comparisons were drawn between Driscoll and Jim Thorpe, which was the highest compliment to be paid at the time. The sports pages were filled with articles extolling the team and its coming matchup with the Naval Academy on November 23.

Besides Rutgers and Navy, the top college teams in the east were Pitt, riding a 30-game unbeaten streak and Georgia Tech, who possessed a 39-game unbeaten streak. Georgia Tech received permission to travel for another United War Work Fund charity game at Pitt on November 23, the same day Great Lakes played Navy. Although Pitt and Georgia Tech had the records to warrant a Rose Bowl invitation, their faculties continued to veto their participation and that left a handful of service teams as potential Eastern representatives: the League Island Marines, the Cleveland Naval Reserves, Camp Greenleaf in Georgia, and Great Lakes. A Great Lakes victory over Navy would position it well compared to its service competitors.

Gil Dobie was the Naval Academy coach. He went 8-0 in two years as the coach at North Dakota State and then had an eight-year run at Washington during which his teams went 58-0-3. He moved to Navy in 1917 and led them to a 7-1 record. The 1917 defeat to West Virginia marked the first loss of Dobie's then eleven-year coaching career. Their 1918 season started with three blowouts of naval training station teams and, the week before playing Great Lakes, they were a 127-0 pain in the Ursinus College schedule.

A record crowd was expected at the Academy's Farragut Field, with a train full of sailors, including John Philip Sousa's band, coming from Great Lakes. Everyone in attendance had high expectations for the game, but no one foresaw the play that decided the game and has defined it ever since.

The first half of the game was dominated by the defenses. Driscoll attempted three field goals in the first half, with one of them sailing wide by several feet. The other two were tossed by the wind and were not close.

At halftime, Coach McReavy was talking to the team when Capt. William Moffett, the Great Lakes commandant, entered the locker room holding a telegram he received earlier in the week. Moffett informed the team that the telegram came from the Tournament of Roses Football Committee and indicated they would offer Great Lakes the Rose Bowl invitation if they beat Navy that afternoon. Moffett's talk gave the team all the motivation they needed as they left the locker room for the second half.

Great Lakes kicked off to open the third quarter and following an exchange of punts, the Middies executed a series of runs, driving to the Great Lakes' 15-yard line. The next play was a double pass in which Navy threw the ball across the field for an easy touchdown near the sideline. Since the touchdown occurred near the sideline, the Middies attempted a punt-out, but it was a poor punt and Middies were unable catch the ball, losing their opportunity for the extra point. This left the Middies with a 6-0 lead and susceptible if Great Lakes could score a touchdown and convert the kick.

Through the remainder of the third quarter, the Middies outplayed Great Lakes except for a 34-yard gain by Driscoll, who left the game shortly thereafter due to injury, further threatening Great Lakes' chances. A few minutes into the fourth quarter, Conzelman dropped back to punt when a Navy guard broke through the line, blocking the punt. Navy recovered on the Great Lakes 10-yard line. The Great Lakes defense held on four straight runs, giving the Jackies the ball on their own 4-yard line. Playing the field position game, Conzelman punted on first down, but he shanked the kick and it rolled out of bounds at the Great Lakes 25-yard line with under seven minutes to play.

Navy then completed a 15-yard pass and followed it with an eight-yard run giving them second down at the Great Lakes 2-yard line with under five minutes left. Navy was threatening to put the game away and, with it, Great Lakes' opportunity for the Rose Bowl. The Jackies needed a miracle.

On second down, the Middies ran the ball up the middle. Hugh Blacklock blasted the runner as he neared the goal line and the ball popped several feet into the air. After a seeming eternity, Harry Eielson of Great Lakes caught the ball three yards into the end zone and started running toward the other goal line, more than a hundred yards away. Three key blocks by teammates sealed off the nearby Navy players and Eielson broke into the clear with three teammates trailing him down the sideline, each in position to block any Midshipmen approaching Eielson from behind. As Eielson raced past the Navy bench, Bill Saunders, a Navy substitute, was warming up to enter the game, and enter the game he did. Saunders came off the sideline onto the field and tackled Eielson. Seeing what had happened, Eielson's three trailing teammates began educating Saunders with their fists and a brief melee ensued.

After order was restored, the officials convened with the coaches to announce their call. No one had seen a play like this before and the football rules of 1918 did not specifically address the situation, allowing only a 15-yard penalty for unsportsmanlike conduct. One account of the aftermath was told in a newspaper interview with Harry Heneage, the referee, within days of the game. Heneage claimed he gave the ball to Emmett Keefe, the Great Lakes captain, and instructed him to walk the ball into the end zone and touch it down, after which the play was ruled a touchdown. Another account indicates the whistle never blew on Saunders' tackle, so Heneage allowed Eielson to get up and continue his run down the field for the touchdown. A third account tells us that Heneage initially indicated he would penalize Navy fifteen yards from the point of the infraction, per the rules, but Capt. E. W. Eberle, the Superintendent of the Naval Academy, overruled him and in a display of both proper sportsmanship and military authority, exclaimed, "I said it was a touchdown. I run this place and a touchdown it is."[20] Whichever scenario actually occurred, a touchdown it was, as one of the Great Lakes players took the ball downfield and scored by placing the ball down between the goal posts, thereby eliminating the need for a punt-out. With the score tied 6-6 and only minutes remaining, Hugh Blacklock, the Jackies' kicker, calmly put the ball straight through the uprights for a 7-6 Great Lakes lead. Navy failed to move the ball on their next possession and the clock wound down to a 7-6 Great Lakes victory.

Harry Eielson, whose fumble recovery and 103-yard run led Great Lakes to victory over the Naval Academy.

Some readers may think they have seen film clips of Eielson's run, but there are no known recordings of the 1918 play. If you can see the play in your mind's eye, it likely comes footage of a similar play in the 1954 Cotton Bowl when Tommy Lewis of Alabama came off the bench and tackled Dicky Maegle of Rice. Maegle was awarded a touchdown for his run as well. Of course, the game and Saunders' tackle went viral, in that every newspaper in the land gave it coverage, including the *Muncie Evening Press*, which ran with the headline, "Bonehead Play of Football is Made by Middy." Bonehead play or not, the Great Lakes Jackies were headed to the 1919 Rose Bowl.

Great Lakes practicing field goals while warming up for Purdue. The holders on field goal attempts commonly laid on their stomachs during the period.

The following Saturday, in a game played at Northwestern, the Jackies entered their game with Purdue hoping to minimize the number of snaps played by their first team. During much of the first half, Great Lakes' offense could not sustain a drive, but Purdue could not start one and a touchdown pass to Halas was the game's only score at half. The Great Lakes starters scored a second touchdown in the third quarter and then left the game, leaving the second stringers to finish the 27-0 victory. Doing so boosted the motivation of the subs as they headed into an additional month of training for the upcoming Rose Bowl game.

Great Lakes' regular season results are shown in the following table.

1918 Great Lakes Naval Training Station Regular Season Results

Date	Opponent	Score	Location
Sept. 29	Iowa	10-0	Iowa Field, Iowa City
Oct. 12	Illinois	7-0	Illinios Field, Campaign
Oct. 26	Northwestern	0-0	Sailors Field, Great Lakes
Nov. 8	Notre Dame	7-7	Cartier Field, South Bend
Nov. 16	Rutgers	54-14	Ebbets Field, Brooklyn
Nov. 23	Navy	7-6	Worden Field, Annapolis
Nov. 30	Purdue	27-0	Northwestern Field, Evanston

Great Lakes finished with a regular season record of 5-0-2. Despite a fitful start, Great Lakes ended the regular season as the best football team east of the Rockies, with every other team that might claim that title having suffered a late-season loss. The team had evolved from a collection of individual stars to a well-oiled machine under the direction of a new coach. Switching Paddy Driscoll to quarterback had expanded the team's play-calling repertoire and placed its finest athlete in a role that made him a threat on every offensive play. Although they were touted early in the season based on their talent, Great Lakes and Paddy Driscoll exploded on the national scene by dominating Rutgers and were fortunate to eke out a victory over Navy. Great Lakes had rightfully earned their place in Pasadena over all other eastern college and service teams.

Mare Island Returns to Action

Lest you think Great Lakes' narrow victory over Navy meant they had a tough path to reach the Rose Bowl, it was an absolute cakewalk compared to the challenges faced by Mare Island.

As the quarantine at Mare Island was approaching its end in late October, Benton "Biff" Bangs, a twenty-five-year-old county agricultural agent in Skagit County, Washington was busy conducting experiments for his master's degree. Bangs was recruited by Dick Hanley in August and tried to enlist in the Marines at the time, but his work for a government agency made him ineligible for the service. Later, Bangs received permission to enlist and he was at Mare Island by November 2.

Bangs starred at running back on Washington State's 1916 Rose Bowl team and was named to Walter Camp's list of the top 75 college players in 1917. He was a fast, solidly-built player who ran with his knees high, was difficult to tackle, and became the best passer on the team the moment he stepped on the field. Given his qualifications, he started at left halfback when Mare Island met St. Mary's on November 16 on California Field in Berkeley.

The Marines scored on their first offensive play on a Bill Steers run ball up the middle and the newly-arrived Benton Bangs scored on the Marines' second play from scrimmage. Though it appeared a rout was on, St. Mary's started executing on offense and moved the ball inside the Mare Island 10-yard line before fumbling. Dick Hanley scored at the end of a long second-quarter drive, effectively putting the game out of reach. In the second half, the California crowd called for Jim Blewett of their 1917 freshman team to enter the game, and Coach Dietz relented. Passing well with Blewett in the game, Mare Island scored two more times. As the game closed, St. Mary's scored the first touchdown against Mare Island that season on a 90-yard touchdown run for a final score of 34-7.

Benton Bangs during his Washington State days.

Following the win over St. Mary's, Mare Island began their multi-week swing through the northwest. Wanting to prove their quality and add to their athletic kitty, they had games scheduled on November 23 with the unbeaten Multnomah Athletic Club in Portland, a Thanksgiving Day game five days later at Camp Lewis, another game two days after that with Idaho, and a season finale with Camp Perry in Bremerton, Washington one week later. Given the length of the trip, Camp

Lewis travelled with a large contingent to ensure they had sufficient numbers to scrimmage in practice and as insurance against injuries or further influenza attacks. The expense of traveling with the large group brought pressure to ensure the contract terms and gate receipts funded the trip. Band members and Marine vocalists also joined the traveling party. They made appearances in the days leading up to the games to drum up interest and attendance.

Thirty-five football-playing Marines, coaches, and support staff left Mare Island with plans to arrive in Portland midweek and practice there before the game. Multnomah invited the governor, mayor, and city council to witness the top football game in the city that year. Thousands of soldiers stationed in Vancouver, Washington, which sits directly across the Columbia River from Portland, were expected to attend the event at half-price, with the local press expecting the soldiers to cheer for their service brethren. The Marines expressed concern about the challenge they faced in the Winged M team, citing Multnomah's 7-0 victory over Camp Lewis earlier in the season. Multnomah's offense, led by 124-pound quarterback Hughie McKenna, was considered a threat.

While the Marines practiced on Thursday, heated discussions occurred regarding the contract terms for the game. Multnomah expressed interest in playing Mare Island in late September, but the Marines wanted a $1,750 guarantee and scheduled a game with the University of Oregon instead. Given the turmoil with college schedules, Oregon found a way to schedule a game with conference foe California the same day, so Oregon dropped Mare Island from its schedule and suggested Multnomah as a substitute. The second round of negotiations for the Mare Island-Multnomah game were not finalized because Capt. Coovert was hospitalized for two weeks with influenza and he was bed ridden for two additional weeks. Worse, Coovert's wife and sister-in-law died of influenza while he was in the hospital.

The contractual sticking point was Multnomah's insistence on applying their standard terms, under which the Multnomah Club received 25 percent of the net gate receipts as a stadium rental fee before splitting the remainder with the visiting team, while the

Marines sought 50 percent of the gross receipts. Capt. Coovert was a former Multnomah Club member, so he was surely aware of these terms, but he was coming off a very difficult month. Given Mare Island's concern about funding the trip, and the power they held as an attractive opponent, the Marines held their stance. Unfortunately, so did Multnomah's board of directors, and the much-anticipated game in Portland was cancelled the Thursday afternoon before the game.

The Marines found a willing if not able, opponent in the soldiers at Vancouver Barracks. The Marines' previously scheduled game with Vancouver Barracks had been cancelled in October due to Mare Island's quarantine, so it was good fortune that both the Vancouver Barracks team and local Vaughn Street Grounds stadium were available for the Saturday game.

Vancouver Barracks was the first U.S. military facility in the Northwest when it was established in 1849. It served a variety of roles: protecting early settlers, warehousing supplies, recruiting and training soldiers, and coordinating military activities in the Northwest. Army officers stationed there during their careers included the likes of Ulysses S. Grant, George B. McClellan, George Pickett, and George C. Marshall, who commanded the Civilian Conservation Corps in the Northwest in the 1930s.

Vancouver Barracks was also the headquarters of the Spruce Production Division. Sitka spruce produces wood that is lightweight, strong, and, as it turns out, does not shatter when struck by anti-aircraft bullets, making it the ideal material for military airplane frames at the time. To enhance and ensure the production of spruce, the Army Signal Corps took over the Northwestern lumber industry until the end of the war and the Spruce Division lumberjacks hoped to log a victory over the Marines.

Before a rain-soaked crowd of 2,200, a smaller crowd than was expected against Multnomah, the first quarter ended in a scoreless tie, but the Marines led 19-0 at half, with a 55-yard punt return by Bangs highlighting the action. The Barracks boys finished the half with little or no yardage gained. Bangs scored again early in the second half and the score stood at 26-0. Mare Island substituted players through much of the second half and ended the game with a dominating 39-0 victory over a competitive team. The Marines were again showing themselves to be the best of the West.

The Monday *Oregonian* indicated that a decision had been reached to send Mare Island to the Rose Bowl if they won their remaining games, but the season had taught the Marines that schedules are open to change, and the promised Rose Bowl might be another mirage in the long line of unrealized expectations. Their intuition proved correct.

The game at Camp Lewis on November 28 was the third meeting of the teams in two years, Mare Island experienced 100 percent turnover from its 1917 team, and the same was nearly the case for Camp Lewis. The 91st Division left Camp Lewis in late June and had fought at the Meuse-Argonne and in Belgium by the time this game was played. The 13th Division began training at Camp Lewis in July with some men from the 91st Division remaining there to train the 13th. The only leftover from the 1917 Camp Lewis team was Fred "Jumbo" Hunter, who was thirty-one years old when he suited up for the 1918 Rose Bowl, likely the oldest player to ever do so. Hunter stayed at Camp Lewis for an officer training program, which he completed along with his classmate, Earl Warren, who later became the fourteenth Chief Justice of the United States Supreme Court.

Hunter had not played football for the 13th Division to that point in the season, but the lure of playing the Mare Island Marines in a third game, and beating them, was too much to ignore. At thirty-two years old, Hunter dragged his tired body out to the practice field that week and started at left tackle for Camp Lewis against Mare Island.

Composite of the 1918 Mare Island team created after the season. (Courtesy of Manuscripts, Archives, and Special Collections, Washington State University)

Meeting once again in Tacoma Stadium before 10,000 spectators, the first quarter was played in the middle of the field, with neither team able to move the ball. That changed in the second quarter when the Marines had the ball on the Camp Lewis 30-yard line. Bangs completed a pass to Dick Hanley, the quarterback, who made a difficult catch twenty yards downfield and ran another ten yards for the score. Later in the second quarter, the Marines had a series of runs up the middle before sending Bill Steers around the left end where he dragged two Camp Lewis players with him for the touchdown. With the missed extra point, the score stood 13-0 at half. Steers added a second-half field goal and the Marines left the field with a 16-0 victory.

Following their Thanksgiving Day victory over Camp Lewis, the Marines travelled across the state to Spokane to meet the University of Idaho two days later in a game at the Interstate Fairgrounds in

Spokane. The University of Idaho sits directly across the Washington-Idaho border from Spokane and a large contingent of their fans were among the nearly 4,000 spectators. Little information is available about the game itself. We do know that Mare Island was bigger, faster, and better than Idaho and allowed Idaho only two first downs while beating them 68-0. We can only assume that everyone in a Mare Island uniform played in the game.

Bremerton Navy Yard in the days of the Great White Fleet.

Mare Island's last game in the Northwest came a week later on December 6 against the Bremerton Naval Yard, now the Puget Sound Naval Shipyard, which sits across Puget Sound from Seattle. Bremerton provided the Marines a $2,000 guarantee, half of which came from subscriptions paid by local businessmen.

Bremerton, often referred to by sportswriters as Camp Perry, played Camp Lewis a month earlier and lost 13-0, so they were not expected to be a tough matchup for Mare Island. They more than met that expectation. As with the Idaho game, there was limited newspaper coverage of the contest, but the Marines dominated from the start, scoring twenty points in the first quarter and twenty-one in the second. The game got rough, and six Mare Island players left the field with injuries, including Dick Hanley and Hugh Stendal leaving with broken ribs. Nate Shanedling started at left tackle but reinjured a previously broken ankle, so Leo Shannon took his place and shortly thereafter broke his finger. Carl Lodell left with a wrenched back and Bill Steers came up lame as well. Perhaps due to the injuries, the Marines did not let up on Bremerton scoring fourteen points in the third quarter and a message-sending thirty-four points in the final stanza for an 89-0 victory.

The Marines notched four wins during their three-week campaign in the Northwest, but were heading home with a handful of injured players and needed to ready themselves for a game on Saturday with unbeaten Mather Field, easily the best team they would face to that point in the season. The Marines went to the Northwest expecting that an unblemished record and a final victory over Mather Field would propel them to the Rose Bowl. But life was not that simple and frustrations were ahead, despite the dominance they displayed on the field.

1919 Rose Bowl Selection Process

As it turned out, the earth shifted under Mare Island while on the northwestern trip, and their path to the Rose Bowl became more difficult and complicated. The Tournament of Roses Football Committee became reluctant to invite Mare Island to the Rose Bowl a second year in a row when there were other undefeated service teams on the West Coast, so they outlined a plan to determine the invitee via a playoff series. The plan was announced on November 26, two days before Mare Island played Camp Lewis on Thanksgiving Day. The Committee communicated with the teams as they developed the plan, and accounted for the previously scheduled games during the period in which the tournament was to occur. One is forced to give the Committee credit for working the scheduled games into the playoff format, but they failed to anticipate a few important issues, leading to some embarrassing moments as the playoffs transpired.

As outlined by the Committee, five service teams from California were included in the playoffs: Mare Island; Mather Field of Sacramento; Balboa Park Naval Training Station and Rockwell Field of San Diego; and the San Pedro Submarine Base in the Port of Los Angeles. Oddly, San Pedro had not yet played a game—which ensured they were undefeated—but they were included in the tournament because they had quality football players stationed there and, perhaps, there was interest in including a Los Angeles-area team in the playoffs.

There had been a handful of playoffs at the high school and club levels in the past, but this playoff series was the first in American football with such high stakes. The Committee outlined a series of four games as shown in the following chart.

December 7	December 14	December 21
	Northern Service Championship Mare Island vs. Mather Field	
		Western Service Championship Northern vs. Southern Champions
Preliminary Game Rockwell Field vs. San Pedro Submarine	Southern Service Championship Rockwell Field vs. Balboa Park	

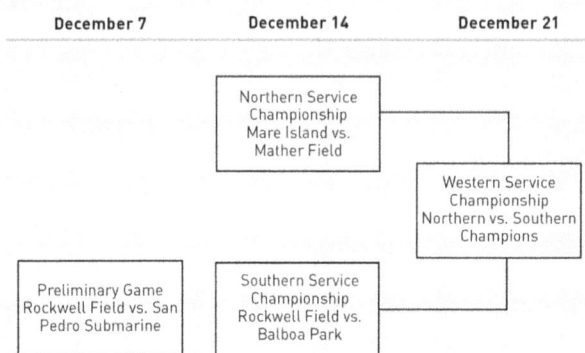

The top of the bracket made sense with Mare Island and Mather Field playing for the Northern Service Championship, but the bottom of the bracket did not provide a true single-elimination play-off, since the Committee called for Rockwell Field to meet Balboa Park on December 14, regardless of the outcome of Rockwell Field's game against San Pedro on December 7th. Nevertheless, the sequence of games was their best attempt to decide a champion on the field.

Rockwell Field, which sat at the northern end of the Coronado Peninsula across the bay from San Diego, was one of only three Army air fields that existed prior to the war. It served as a flight training school during WWI and is now part of Naval Air Station, North Island. One of the flight leaders and gunnery instructors at Rockwell Field during WWI was Jimmy Doolittle, who became a world-famous racing pilot after the war. He also led the "Doolittle Raid" in April 1942, when his flight of B-25 medium bombers took off from the *U.S.S. Hornet*, an aircraft carrier, for a one-way bombing run over Tokyo and other targets. From a football standpoint, Rockwell Field had played an all-service team schedule with the exception of a 7-7 tie with Pomona College.

San Pedro travelled from Los Angeles to Rockwell Field by submarine and submarine tender (surface ships that support submarines), which is likely the only time a football team has used that mode of transportation for an away game.

Earlier, we noted that new football rules were added as problems were identified or unanticipated events transpired. One of those occurred in the Rockwell Field-San Pedro game. Despite a spirited game, the teams ended their sixty minutes of play in a 3-3 tie. Although football games of the day often ended in ties, the Committee did not anticipate how a tie might impact their playoff brackets. (The NCAA created rules for overtime games when play-offs where introduced in the lower football divisions in the 1970s.)

The following week, Mare Island was set to meet Mather Field, an Army flight training school located southeast of Sacramento. Mather Field had one of the best weapons in the country in Jim DeHart, their player-coach, who quarterbacked Pitt to a national title in 1916. DeHart was the media darling, but Mather Field had a host of solid college players from all over the country surrounding him.

Mare Island and Mather Field tried to play one another twice earlier in the season, but neither game occurred, so their December 14th game was eagerly anticipated. One of the interesting sidelights to this game and others of the era is the frequency in which sports-writers mentioned players betting directly with their opponents or with opposing fans; players gambling on games was common and accepted. The day before the game, Ed R. Hughes of the *San Francisco Chronicle* closed his game preview by noting:

> "The Flyer want odds today, but the Marines think the betting should be at even money. It is hard to see how the Flyers figure they should be the short-enders. All along they have professed to be willing to bet the bank roll against any competitor, so they should make good today. There is nothing in the dope that makes one of these teams a two-to-one favorite over the other, yet the Flyers are asking those odds. Two teams good enough to play for the honor of representing the Pacific Coast in the big game at Pasadena on New Year's Day should be evenly enough matched to make the betting even money."[21]

Of course, nine months later the 1919 World Series was rocked by the Black Sox scandal and attitudes toward players betting on games in American sports changed forever.

It is not clear how the Mather Field team travelled to the game, we know they flew in their one-seaters or two-seaters to other games, so we'll assume they flew to Berkeley for this one. Flying to games was cool and allowed the student pilots to log more flight hours. In another instance of emerging technologies, Mather Field's transportation choice surely made them among the first sports team to fly to their game destination.

During much of the game. Mather Field's plays emphasized rugby-style laterals to DeHart on sweeps around end, an approach that was old school even then. Despite several nice runs, DeHart was tackled for losses on numerous plays. The scoring started in the first quarter with the Flyers deep in the own territory. A bad lateral resulted in a fumble that rolled into the end zone, where Roscoe Pike fell on the ball for Mare Island's first score. A missed extra point left the game at 6-0 at halftime.

The Marines started the second half with a Steers field goal. A bit later, Jake Risley penetrated the line and blocked the Flyer's punt. This was followed by Dick Hanley hitting Clarence Zimmerman downfield for the Marines' second touchdown. With another missed kick, the score stood at 16-0 as the third quarter ended.

Mather Field started the final quarter with a series of inside and outside runs along with a forward passing game that resulted in a score. The Marines responded with three completed passes and a 35-yard Glover run for the touchdown. With the kick, the Marines made it 23-6. After the Marine kick, the defense kept the Flyers grounded and for the second time in the game, a Flyers' punt was blocked, rolling into the end zone where Paul Mohr grabbed it for the touchdown. The extra point was good and Mare Island was up 30-6. Mather Field had the ball one last time and completed three forward passes, the last one going for a touchdown. With the extra point, the game ended with the Marines winning the wager, 30-13, and the right to the Western Service Championship Game.

Down in San Diego, Rockwell Field was playing Balboa Park for the Southern Service Championship. Balboa Park won the game 6-3 when a third quarter Rockwell Field punt was blocked and recovered by Balboa Park in the end zone. Due to Rockwell Field's tie

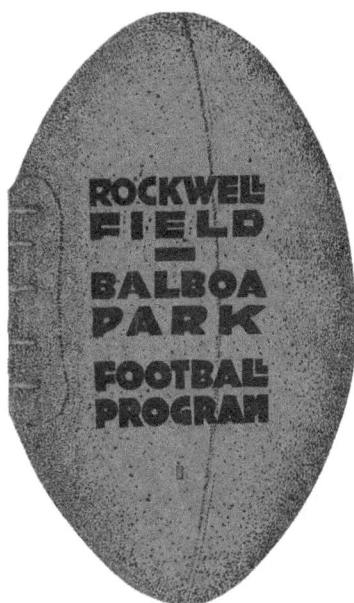

Cover of the Balboa Park-Rockwell Field game program from December 14, 1918. Original is 11" x 6.75."

with San Pedro the previous week, Southern California was left with two undefeated teams—Balboa Park and San Pedro—and the Committee in a bit of a quandary.

W. S. Kienholz, the Committee chairman, first called for Balboa Park and San Pedro to play one another in the next few days to determine the Southern Champion, but Balboa Park would have none of it. Kienholz called a meeting in Pasadena the next day to discuss the situation with Balboa Park and San Pedro. Balboa Park's coach argued that forcing the teams to play one another and then play Mare Island a few days later would disadvantage whichever team won. He preferred the Committee make a choice and Balboa Park would abide by it. He also argued that Balboa Park beat Rockwell Field, while San Pedro tied Rockwell Field the previous week, so by comparative scores, Balboa Park was the more qualified team. The Committee agreed with Balboa Park and unanimously named them the Southern Service Champion. Although the Football Committee was publicly embarrassed by this turmoil, the situation now seemed neatly tied and wrapped in a bow. But there was more trouble ahead.

It turned out that Mare Island objected to playing Balboa Park for several reasons. First, the Mare Island Sailors, not the Marines, had a game scheduled with Camp Lewis on December 21, in San Francisco. The game was being highly promoted and Mare Island did not want to dilute interest in or attendance for that game. The Marines offered to play Balboa Park on Christmas Day or not at all. Second, the Marines needed a few days more rest since they were coming off an arduous series of games and were weary and banged up. While this was true, each day of rest prior to the Balboa Park game was one less day of rest leading up to the Rose Bowl, should they beat Balboa Park.

Third, despite creating the playoff series, the Committee did not have a contract with Mare Island to play in the Rose Bowl, assuming they beat Balboa Park, and the Marines wanted a larger guarantee than the Committee had promised. Last, and this is informed speculation on my part, Mare Island was clearly displeased by the Committee's failure to directly select their team into the Rose Bowl, which would have avoided the need for a Western Service Championship Game. In keeping with the holiday spirit, Mare Island let the Committee's chestnuts roast for a few days while visions of a Great Lakes team traveling west with no one to play danced in the Committee's heads.

The situation was still unresolved on Saturday the 21st, when Camp Lewis beat the Mare Island Sailors, but a day or two later Mare Island signed its contract, and the game moved forward in Vallejo on Christmas Day.

———

WHILE THE CONTRACTUAL posturing was going on, the Marines' football team continued to practice. They also kept busy with roster management. With the war over, military necessity no longer ruled the day and interservice rivalries took on greater meaning. For the greater good of the Corps, several Marine commanders at other locations agreed to transfer selected Marines to Mare Island. The result was that several Marines—who had played the full season for other teams—arrived at Mare Island and joined the football team.

One was Millard Calhoun from Bremerton, who earned honorable-mention status as a running back on Walter Camp's All-Service team. He transferred to Mare Island the week after Mare Island beat Bremerton in Seattle. Calhoun arrived at Mare Island on December 13th, the day before the Mather Field game, but did not play for Mare Island in that game.

Back east, John Budd and Ed Crosetto started the year playing for the League Island Marines, representing the Marine Barracks at the Philadelphia Naval Yard. Midway through the season most of the Marine players were transferred elsewhere, so the remaining Marines formed a team with both Marine and Navy personnel. League Island finished the season undefeated and received some consideration as the eastern representative for the Rose Bowl prior to the bid going to Great Lakes. John Budd starred for League Island, earning first-team honors on Walter Camp's All-Service Team. He went on to star at Lafayette, and was an All Pro with the NFL's Frankfort Yellow Jackets in 1926. His League Island counterpart, Ed Crosetto, played fullback and guard for St. Bonaventure and the University of Dubuque before the war. The two comprised the starting guard tandem for League Island and both were transferred to Mare Island, arriving on Christmas Day when Mare Island was playing Balboa Park.

It was a good thing that new men were added to the battered Mare Island team. In the days leading up to the Balboa Park game it became clear that five starters would miss the game or play only as substitutes. Dick Hanley, the Marines' quarterback, was bedridden and then hospitalized with influenza. Starting backs Lloyd Gillis and Bill Steers, and starting left tackle Nate Shanedling were also nursing injuries, while starting right end Pat Hanley was stricken by influenza. None of those players were expected to play against Balboa Park. Other players were banged up as well. Missing five starters who played both ways is the equivalent of missing ten starters in the unlimited substitution game played today. In addition, Dick Hanley was the primary kicker and Bill Steers was the primary punter for Mare Island, so that put the team at further risk at a time when the kicking game was as important as the offense or defense. Despite the injuries, Mare Island remained confident they would win based on the star quality of Benton Bangs and the depth of their bench relative to Balboa Park.

Balboa Park, on the other hand, was equally confident. They had a strong backfield with all four backfield men having major college experience. None of them matched the star quality of Mare Island's players, but the Sailor backfield was touted as better than the sum of its parts; at least that is how their supporters rationalized their willingness to take all available bets.

The game was played at the Cycodrome, which despite being the Marines' home stadium in Vallejo, was hosting the Marines for the first time that season. If the Marines were overconfident, the action in the first quarter did nothing to shake their opinion. On their first possession, the Marines drove down the field with Bangs completing passes to Glover and Blewett. With the ball on the Balboa Park 5-yard line, Bangs ran it in for the score. Carl Lodell, the backup kicker, missed the conversion, so the score stood at 6-0.

Play stagnated in the second quarter. The game reports do not include player substitutions, but some reports indicate the Marines substituted freely during the game, seeking to rest as many key players as possible. It became a wide-open game in the third quarter with Balboa Park making many of the better plays.

In the fourth quarter the Marines started moving the ball and drove to the Balboa Park 40-yard line when disaster struck. Due to miscommunication among the Mare Island players, Jake Risley, the center, made an errant snap. The ball rolled well behind the running backs before Dean, a Balboa Park back from USC, picked up the ball at the 35-yard line, got some blocking from his teammates, and raced into the end zone. The Sailors made the extra point to give themselves a 7-6 lead. Mare Island's missed conversion in the first quarter now had potentially lethal consequences for the team. The Marines needed at least a field goal on their coming possession.

With only nine minutes left in the game, the Marines were under pressure to score on their next drive. Although having nine minutes left on the clock typically gives teams more than one possession in today's game, there were fewer clock stoppages in 1918. At that time, the clock stopped for kickoffs, touchbacks, and other long delays as determined by the referee. The clock did not stop for first downs, runners going out of bounds, incomplete passes, or most injuries.

Following the kickoff, the clock did not prove a problem for the

Marines. Bangs quickly completed two long passes and Balboa Park was penalized fifteen yards for slugging on the second pass, leaving the ball on the Balboa Park 10-yard line. The Marines attempted three runs but Balboa Park's defense stopped them for little gain. On fourth down, the ball was handed to Bangs again and he fought through several defenders to score with five minutes left on the clock. Lodell missed the extra point again, leaving the score at 12-6. Balboa Park had five minutes to score a touchdown to tie the game or win with the extra point. Had they scored only the touchdown, it is anyone's guess how the Committee might have handled a tie in the championship game, but it did not matter. Despite a few tense minutes, the Marines stopped Balboa Park and time ran out on the clock with the Marines in possession. Mare Island was victorious and would be the first team to play in back-to-back Rose Bowls.

Mare Island finished the season with a 10-0 record and were among the first college or service teams to record double-digit victories in one season. They had built a new team from scratch and, despite the familiarity of several core players with Lone Star Dietz and his methods, the majority of the team was new to both. Despite the difficulty Great Lakes experienced in molding a team from a collection of individuals, Mare Island thrashed most of its opponents from the start of the season until its end, winning by an average score of 45-3. Though little recognized then or now, Lone Star Dietz's molding of the 1918 Mare Island team stands among the finest coaching performances in that era of American football.

Mare Island's final results for the 1918 regular season are shown in the following table.

1918 Mare Island Marines Regular Season and Playoff Results

Sept. 21	Goat Island/Yerba Buena Sailors	31-0	Grove Street Grounds, Oakland
Sept. 28	Camp Fremont 8th Ammo Train	66-0	Stanford Field, Palo Alto
Nov. 7	Fort Baker	67-0	Fort Baker, San Francisco
Nov. 17	St. Mary's	34-7	Ewing Field, Oakland
Nov. 23	Vancouver Barracks	34-7	Vaughn St. Grounds, Vancouver
Nov. 28	Camp Lewis (13th Division)	16-0	Tacoma Stadium
Nov. 30	Idaho	68-0	Interstate Fair Grounds, Pullman
Dec. 6	Bremerton Naval Yard	89-0	Bremerton, WA
Dec. 14	Mather Field	30-13	California Field, Berkeley
Dec. 25	Balboa Park NTS	12-6	Cycodrome, Vallejo, CA

It was a supremely impressive season for Dietz and the team, but the Balboa Park game left them with a number of injuries, and the third wave of influenza was taking a toll on the Mare Island Marines as their eyes turned south toward Pasadena.

THE DRUMS RUM-TUMMING EVERYWHERE

With the war over, the Tournament of Roses celebration was expected to be the most joyous in its thirty-year history and Pasadena pulled out all stops to make it so. Red, white, and blue bunting was hung from every street lamp and cross wire. The float structures were built and readied to be populated with flowers on New Year's Eve. Silver cups were polished as awards for the winners of the new automotive division of floats, while newspaper reports spotlighted Miss Blanche Farmer for not only decorating her car with red and white roses she had grown in her home garden, but her plan to drive the car in the parade herself!

Following their victory over Purdue on November 30, the Great Lakes team was given a week off from practice, and then turned to preparing for the Rose Bowl. After ten days of practice, they played a tune-up scrimmage on the 16th with the Great Lakes regimental champion, the 7th Regiment team, and boarded the train for Los Angeles on December 20. After arriving, Charlie Bachman, one of their headiest players, went north to San Francisco to scout the Mare Island-Balboa Park game.

McReavy held a spirited practice on December 24 to work out the kinks from the long train ride and acclimate to the warm weather.

This was likely the first time any of the Jackies had been on the West Coast and following practice, the players enjoyed picking oranges from the trees surrounding the practice field. Several did not realize until then that oranges grew on trees. Over the next few days the team held one practice per day, spending parts of each day sightseeing, before returning to football only the last two days before the game.

The Great Lakes team on the movie set for a western at Universal City prior to the Rose Bowl.

Great Lakes, which had suffered injuries to starters throughout the year, came into the Rose Bowl well rested and without nagging injuries. Still, the coaches fiddled with their starting lineup until the day of the game. Unlike today's game with unlimited substitutions, part of coaching strategy in the days of single-platoon football was to decide which player to start when two comparable players differed in their offensive and defensive strengths. At halfback, Dutch Lauer was considered the better blocker on offense, while Harry Eielson was a better pass defender, so McReavy had to decide which player matched up best with Mare Island. On game day, McReavy chose Eielson.

The roster of the Great Lakes starters and substitutes follows. Every starter from the second half of the season was available and all were in tip-top shape.

Player	No.	Position	Weight	College
Dick Reichle	6	LE	180	Illinois
Con Eklund	9	LT	185	Minnesota
Emmett Keefe	1	LG	183	Notre Dame
Charlie Bachman	11	C	180	Notre Dame
Jerry Jones	10	RG	195	Notre Dame
Hugh Blacklock	8	RT	190	Michigan State
George Halas	7	RE	172	Illinois
Paddy' Driscoll	2	QB	154	Northwestern
Harry Eielson	19	LH	170	Northwestern
Andrew Reeves	4	FB	215	Ottawa (KS)
Hal Erickson	3	RH	170	St. Olaf (MN)

Substitutes

Player	No.	Position	Weight	College
Elmer Abrahamson	23	HB	170	Lawrence (WI)
LeRoy Andrews	15	T	210	Pittsburg State (KS)
Chester Barnard	14	E	174	Missouri State
Lester Barnard	12	E	174	Missouri State
Harry Bliss	17	HB	160	Ohio State
Martin Conrad	21	C	200	Alma (MI)
Jimmy Conzelman	18	QB/HB	170	Washington (MO)
Charles Knight	16	C	200	Northwestern
Harold Lauer	5	FB	175	Detroit
Bernard Miller	22	G	200	Bridgeport HS (IL)
Frank Willaman	20	FB	175	Ohio State

Since Raymond MacRae was noted in the lead-in to the 1918 Rose Bowl as being the only practicing physician to start a Rose Bowl game, it is worth mentioning that Con Eklund started at left tackle for Great Lakes after earning his undergraduate dental degree in 1918, and working as a dentist in the Dental Department at Great Lakes.

The Marines left Mare Island the afternoon of the 26th, taking an overnight train to Los Angeles. They arrived a worn and beaten-up team. Coming out of the Balboa Park game, Bangs, Steers, and Shanedling were nursing leg injuries, while Dick and Pat Hanley were hospitalized with influenza. Pat Hanley recovered in time to travel with the team, but did not participate in the first few bowl practices, only to return to practice and start in the Rose Bowl. Dick Hanley, the starting quarterback and kicker, ended his two-week hospital stay on the 30th and traveled to Pasadena to watch the game from the sideline.

Coach Dietz, who believed in working his team hard, did so in the Marines' first practices in Pasadena before letting up two days before the game. Dietz expected that some of those nursing injuries would play only part of the game, so he hoped they could make an impact in whatever time they had available.

By game time, Mare Island's Glover and Shannon also came down with the flu, though Glover started the game anyway. But the Marines were without their starting quarterback and left tackle, and their star halfback, Bangs, was injured and did not start. Shanedling was replaced at left tackle by John Budd. His fellow transfers, League Island's Ed Crosetto and Bremerton's Millard Calhoun, were on the roster as substitutes. The Mare Island starters, substitutes, and those who did not suit up for the game are shown below.

Player	No.	Position	Weight	College
Clarence Zimmerman	9	LE	178	Washington State
John Budd	1	LT	220	Newton HS (NJ)
Carl Lodell	3	LG	175	Oregon State
Jake Risley	5	C	170	Oregon
Mike Moran	11	RG	179	Washington State
Homer Pike	17	RT	180	Gonzaga
Pat Hanley	7	RE	170	Washington State
Bill Steers	15	QB	176	Oregon
John Adams	8	LHB	160	Conway Hall HS (PA)
Lloyd Gillis	19	FB	174	Washington State
Fred Glover	12	RH	174	Washington State

Substitutes

Player	No.	Position	Weight	College
Benton Bangs	2	HB	176	Washington State
Jim Blewett	27	LH	165	California
Leon Bryan	22	E	UNK	Oregon State
Millard Calhoun	4	HB	UNK	Washington State
Ed Crosetto	14	G	UNK	Dubuque
Amor Galloway	24	QB	170	California
Sammy Hern	UNK	HB	170	St. Mary's
Ben Hughes	29	G	175	Williamson (PA)
Alec McGregor	UNK	E	160	Washington State
Bob McGregor	6	B	170	San Bernardino HS (CA)
John 'Hunter' Miles	UNK	C/G	175	Chehalis HS (WA)
Paul 'Dinty' Mohr	30	QB	155	The Dalles HS (OR)
Leo Shannon	16	T	190	Oregon
Hugh 'Al' Stendal	UNK	T	190	None
Burnam Tubbs	21	T	190	Stafford HS (KS)

Sick/Injured

Player	No.	Position	Weight	College
Dick Hanley	NA	QB	175	Washington State
Nate Shanedling	18	LT	190	St. Mary's

Walter Eckersall, the *Chicago Tribune* writer and 1916 and 1918 Rose Bowl referee, was again selected to referee the 1919 game, along with Sam Dolan (Notre Dame) at umpire; Lt. Murray (Camp Fremont) at field judge; and Jack Wells, "Tiny" Leonard, and Lewis Foley at linesmen.

Officials Lt. Murray, Walter Eckersall, and Sam Dolan in a pregame photo. Note the bulbous footballs in the lower right.

The Game

New Year's Day 1919 provided a beautiful day for football with cool temperatures and a slight breeze. The stands held the 22,000 ticketholders, including 10,000 end-zone seats reserved for service men, while 4,000 others found any available nook and cranny from which to watch the game. The Southern California crowd was particularly eager to see the storied Paddy Driscoll, a midwesterner they had read about, but never seen in action. At 154 pounds, the smallest starter on the field, he was easy to spot.

The Jackies wore red jerseys, while the Marines looked menacing in their Navy blue jerseys and black headgear. The Jackies won the toss and chose to defend the goal. Zimmerman kicked off for Mare Island and Hal Erickson was stopped on the return by a hard hit at the 25-yard line. Great Lakes failed to move the ball, so Driscoll punted to John Adams, the fastest man on the Marine team and a first-time starter at halfback. The Marines were similarly unable to move the ball, so Carl Lodell punted to Driscoll, and his winding 22-yard return provided the crowd a glimpse of his game. Punt exchanges followed for a few series with Driscoll gaining field advantage by steadily adding yards on each return of Lodell's long punts. Ten minutes into the game the Jackies had fourth down on the Marines 43-yard line when Driscoll dropped back to attempt a field goal, but a Marine defender penetrated the line causing Driscoll to miss the mark.

On the Marines' first play from the 20-yard line, Glover took a reverse for five yards, fumbling the ball at the end of the run. Blondy Reeves of Great Lakes recovered on the Marine 25-yard line and Driscoll followed that by completing a 20-yard pass to George Halas. The Marines' defense held and Driscoll was forced to attempt another field goal, dropkicking it from 20-yard line to give the Bluejackets a 3-0 lead.

Toward the end of the first quarter, Blewett replaced Adams at left halfback and Ed Crosetto replaced Mike Moran at guard. The new combination of Marines moved the ball to midfield before handing it back to Great Lakes.

With the ball at midfield as the quarter turned and a combination of Erickson and Driscoll runs led to Great Lakes' first rushing first down of the game. Eielson followed the first down with a 20-yard run on a reverse, but the Bluejackets could not move the ball further and the Marines took possession on their own 18-yard line. After another exchange of punts, the Marines got the ball on their own thirty-seven. Gillis ran twice for a total of twelve yards to earn Mare Island's initial first down. While those plays were taking place, a rumble rose from the Mare Island supporters as they saw Benton Bangs warming up on the sideline. Bangs then replaced Blewett at halfback and the Marines used the power game with Bangs making plunge after plunge, driving the ball inside the Great Lakes 10-yard line. Steers inexplicably abandoned the power run game and called four straight passes by Bangs. The Jackies' pass coverage was smothering and all four passes fell incomplete.

The Marines again stuffed the Jackies' offense leading to a punt to the Great Lakes forty. Paul Mohr entered the game at end, replacing Pat Hanley who was sapped by the flu and was done for the day. A few plays later, the Marines attempted a trick play and the Jackies' tackle, Con Eklund, stole the ball as it left Bangs' hands. Eklund rumbled forty yards before being caught from behind by Steers at the Marines' twenty. Driscoll quickly brought Great Lakes into formation and Eielson completed a 17-yard pass, leaving the ball on the three. The next play went to fullback, Blondy Reeves, who drove off-tackle crossing the goal line for the touchdown. Blacklock converted to extend the lead to 10-0.

The Marines received the kick, failed to move the ball, and punted once again. On the Jackies' first play, Reeves fumbled with Glover recovering for Mare Island on the Great Lakes 30-yard line. Bangs quickly threw to Mohr for a 20-yard gain. At the ten and threatening to score near the end of the half, Bangs threw an incomplete pass to Clarence Zimmerman, but the ball rolled over the goal line, resulting in a touchback. (Until 1938, incomplete passes in which the ball crossed the goal line resulted in a touchback.) Since the first half was nearing its end, Driscoll punted to avoid trouble and the Marines ended the half with the ball on their own 47-yard line.

The Marines had threatened twice in the first half and failed to capitalize on either opportunity. Given the injuries that saddled their offense, the Marines could not afford to miss on similar opportunities in the second half against a talented Great Lakes team that was playing well.

The Mare Island Marines attempt to sweep left against Great Lakes.

To ensure the 1919 Rose Bowl halftime activities did not outdo those of the 1918 Rose Bowl, the halftime entertainment once again featured a pushball game. Unfortunately for us, the game reports do not tell us whether the Arcadia Balloon School rose to the occasion to beat the San Pedro Naval Reserves.

The second half started with Great Lakes kicking to Mare Island, who returned the ball to their own 25-yard line. They made a first down running the ball, but Great Lakes defended well on the next two runs and intercepted Bangs' third-down pass at midfield. After Abrahamson lost two yards on a rushing attempt, Driscoll completed a 20-yard pass to Dick Reichle and followed that with a 30-yarder to his other end, George Halas, who dove over the goal line near the right sideline for Great Lakes' second touchdown. The punt-out was caught and Blacklock converted the kick, leaving the score at 17-0 for the Jackies. The Marines were not feeling good about their situation.

Following the kick, the Marines started a comeback with a 23-yard Bangs-to-Mohr pass but were stopped again, leading them to punt, with the ball rolling inside the Great Lakes' ten. Abrahamson punted on first down for Great Lakes and the ball rolled to the Marines' 32-yard line. Looking for something to change the tide of the game, the Marines inserted Amor Galloway for Steers at quarterback and Millard Calhoun in place of Bangs. The new men could not gain a first down and Lodell's punt was blocked with the Jackies recovering on the Marines' 35-yard line. A blowout was in the offing, but Galloway intercepted a Driscoll pass and returned the ball to the Marines' thirty-five. The third quarter ended with Great Lakes in possession on their own 22-yard line.

After a Great Lakes punt and a Galloway return to midfield, Galloway returned to the run game and the Marines again started moving the ball downfield. Despite effective blocking from the line and solid running by its backfield, Galloway abandoned the run game and called up a Blewett pass which was intercepted by Halas inside the ten. Halas scampered down the field headed toward a pick six only to be caught from behind by Blewett at the 3-yard line. For the rest of this life, Halas regretted not diving into the end zone, particularly because the Marines' defense kept Great Lakes out of the end zone the next four plays.

The teams exchanged possessions several more times as a few substitutes finished the game: Frank Willaman, Jimmy Conzelman, Chester Barnard and Lester Barnard came in for Great Lakes, along with Leon Bryan for the Marines. The game ended in a 17-0 Great Lakes victory.

The difference in the game was Great Lakes' ability to mix up their play calling, and having Driscoll, their starting quarterback, available to lead the charge. Mare Island completed only four of seventeen passes for 68 yards with two interceptions being returned for substantial yardage. In the end, the Marines' failure to stick with the run game cost them whatever chance they had to win. George Halas was named the game's Most Valuable Player, though he thought Driscoll earned the award.

The Great Lakes and Mare Island teams were feted at a ball at the Hotel Maryland that evening. Los Angeles and local society members entertained the military poohbahs and team members late into the night. Of course, the Great Lakes boys were far more interested in celebrating that evening, while the Marines recognized their otherwise storied season had closed with disappointment.

The following evening, Great Lakes enjoyed another dance sponsored by a Chicago native where they were joined by motion-picture starlets. Whatever transpired that evening was not covered by the newspapers in the following days. On January 3, Great Lakes left Los Angeles for San Francisco on the same train as the Mare Island team and additional tours and merrymaking ensued in San Francisco for Great Lakes. As a midwestern team that played two games on the East Coast and the Rose Bowl on the West Coast, their long trip back to Chicago made Great Lakes the best travelled team in football history to that time.

THE JACKIES' victory in the 1919 Rose Bowl also brought to a close the brief service Rose Bowl era, a period unlike any other in American football history. Never before or since have service teams played such a dominant role in American sports. Training camp teams were highly rated during WWII as well, but none matched the regular season performance of Great Lakes and Mare Island and their eventual meeting in the Granddaddy of Them All.

The Rose Bowl returned to featuring the best college team from the east against the best of the west in 1920, and that matchup continued until 1944 when WWII travel restrictions resulted in a game between two West Coast teams. Since 1947, the Rose Bowl has featured the best of the Pacific 8, 10, or 12 against the best of the Big Ten, though even that matchup is not guaranteed under the various college championship scenarios of recent years.

After the 1919 game, the war was over, as was the service Rose Bowl era, and the nation quickly began its return to normalcy. With that said, the service football teams of WWI left their mark by proving inaccurate several widely held views regarding post-collegiate football. First, the service football teams showed that "all-star" teams largely comprised of college football players were capable of playing as effective teams rather than as collections of individual stars. Second, they were the first to show that spectators could enjoy high-quality football outside the college environment and align themselves with teams not tied to their alma mater. Since only a small percentage of Americans attended college at the time, the service teams' fan support and press coverage demonstrated there was potential for commercially-successful teams outside the college environment. Third, although men well past college age starred in major league baseball at the time, traditional wisdom held that football was not a game for men beyond their college years. The service teams offered an opportunity for athletes to continue playing a game they loved and clearly dispelled the notion that men could not play football effectively beyond their college years. The service teams undermined each of these views and professional football emerged in the decade following WWI with many of its top players coming from service football teams.

The service Rose Bowl players followed a variety of career paths. Most led lives that were quite ordinary, but others were central to the development of professional football, as well the football tradition in the United States Marine Corp. It is not an exaggeration to say that the NFL would not have developed or, at least, not developed in the manner in which it did, without having been preceded by service football and the men who played those games.

We will cover the story of what became of the service Rose Bowl players in general and their impact on the game of football, but we left the story a while back with two million men in Europe waiting to get back to the States. Let's return to the story of their journey home.

HURRY RIGHT AWAY

At the same moment it was over, over there, it was also over, over here, and the armed services began demobilizing. The training camps morphed into demobilization camps with local commanders keeping only enough troops to manage the demobilization process itself. Regardless of where they had served, the troops received physicals and were discharged unless they had medical conditions requiring resolution. Upon exit, the men were issued a new uniform, allowed to keep their helmets, and were provided back pay and a $60 bonus. They were then marched to the local train station and strongly encouraged to head straight home. Sticking around to gamble, booze it up, and sample the local charms was entirely discouraged. Some, of course, skirted those instructions.

Those returning from Europe spent a week in the camps near the ports and were then sent to the demobilization camp closest to their home, so the divisions were often split apart at their port of disembarkation or at connecting train stations as they crossed the country. Those who were among the first to arrive in their home cities in large numbers were met by welcoming committees and parades. Those ending their journeys in small numbers received less attention. The later returnees from overseas were also more likely to find most jobs filled by those who had not served overseas or who had the good fortune to return home earlier.

All but one of the 1918 Mare Island players were out of the service by mid-March 1919. After being sent home shortly after the Rose Bowl, 80 percent were officially discharged on February 10, 1919. Two players stayed in the reserves for a few years and two others reenlisted at the end of the 1930s, serving during WWII, but none were career Marines.

The Great Lakes team had a similar experience and all were released within a few months of Armistice Day. None of the Great Lakes players stayed in the Navy long term and only two returned to the Navy during WWII.

Sixteen of the twenty-eight players on the 1917 Mare Island team were based in the U.S. on Armistice Day; eleven of those were in officer or flight training at the time. The few that were not in training were discharged in early 1919; those still in training stayed in the Marines for their career or were discharged after completing their training classes. Keith Ambrose was the only player sent outside the country post-Armistice when he was sent to Cuba in February 1919 for a six-month assignment. Ambrose was discharged shortly after returning to the States.

The Waiting Games

The men in Europe had a different experience than their stateside comrades. The troops in France that were not involved in the Army of Occupation had little to do of military value. Beyond continuing to engage the men in monotonuous drills, the Army turned to the YMCA to keep the men entertained. The Y had been involved in service to the military as early as the Civil War and, in France, Pershing gave the YMCA responsibility for enhancing the "amusement and recreation of the troops by means of its usual program of social, physical, educational and religious activities" as well as establishing "exchanges for the American troops in France... operated along the lines of post exchanges whose places they were intended to fill." [22]

The YMCA was everywhere but the frontline, with nearly 13,000

YMCA personnel serving during the war. They were today's U.S.O., Post Office, exchange store, social workers, religious facilitators, and recreation coordinators all wrapped into one. They provided paper, postcards, and stamps; handled 280 million pieces of mail for servicemen; provided entertainment and libraries; and their YMCA huts were used for religious services of all denominations. The Knights of Columbus and similar organizations also served in France, but the YMCA was the dominant provider of these services.

Following the Armistice, the YMCA arranged for troops on leave to spend time in Paris or at various French resorts, and initiated a massive sports program. Beginning in January, every American unit was ordered to organize sporting events for the masses with the best teams and individuals qualifying for further competition. Across all sports, the YMCA sponsored more than 28 million participant events with American football having 75,000 players (745,000 participant events) and 3,745,000 spectators. From January 1 to April 1, 1919, twice as many men saw Army baseball games in the U.S. and Europe as attended major league baseball games the same year.

Football teams were formed at the company and regimental levels, while all-division teams competed in tournaments, and the playoff games garnered up to 25,000 spectators. The top football teams were led by former college stars, including the St. Nazaire team that boasted John Beckett and Eddie Mahan, a three-time All-American halfback from Harvard, both serving with the Headquarters Company of the 13th Marines.

The sports program culminated in America's driving and partici-pating in the Inter-Allied Games, which was akin to an Olympic Games for military personnel, that ran from late June to early July 1919. The Inter-Allied Games included competitors from sixteen nations competing in a dozen traditional sports, as well as martial events such as the hand grenade toss. In basketball, which was played on a limited basis pre-war at YMCA locations across the globe, the U.S. beat France 98-3 in the title game at Pershing Stadium before 12,000 fans. One of the spectators was James Naismith, the inventor of the game, who was in France as a YMCA secretary.

Heading Home

After leaving Belgium, the 91st Division went to their new divisional headquarters in La Ferte-Bernard, France. The regiments then spread out and encamped in towns in a 30-mile radius from headquarters. During the time there, Genl. Pershing reviewed the division. With the 362nd leading the parade, General Pershing remarked on the poor condition of the 91st Division's gear, mentioning that the men who took Gesnes deserved better shoes than they were wearing, not realizing that many wore British shoes received in Belgium while cut off from American supply lines. The 362nd also was visited by Col. John Parker, who was in Paris after recuperating from wounds suffered at Gesnes.

As in Belgium, the division spent much of its time drilling and marching without purpose. Approximately 250 officers and enlisted men were sent to the University of Beaune (AEF University) or other locations to take a variety of three-month college courses. The third wave of influenza struck the division in February with ten percent of the division falling ill. The influenza lasted only two weeks, but twenty-one soldiers died of influenza-induced pneumonia. Their deaths only reinforced the troops' desire to get home.

After more weeks of drilling, the 362nd received orders in late March to entrain for St. Nazaire, where they sat for seven days before sailing home on April 2, 1919. Other units of the 91st Division sailed a week earlier and some a bit later, but the full division was headed home by mid-April, crossing the ocean, and sailing past the Statue of Liberty before disembarking in Hoboken or Brooklyn. After a week's wait, the men departed in groups for camps in California, Wyoming, or their second home, Camp Lewis, where they received their final processing before discharge.

*Among the seized German ships used as a troopship was the S.S.
Vaterland. Renamed the U.S.S. Leviathan, it carried up to 14,000 men
per journey. Coxswain Humphrey Bogart was among its crew in late
1918 and early 1919. Charlie Turner of Camp Lewis returned on the
U.S.S. Leviathan in March 1919.*

The Camp Lewis players who were not with the 91st Division in
Europe trickled back with their various units. Doug McKay sailed
back the second week of January, while A. L. Christensen was the
last service Rose Bowl player to leave France at the end of August
1919.

The men of the 11th and 13th Marines performed a variety of functions supporting the embarkation process in western France. Since
they were among the last to arrive in France and were engaged in
the embarkation process, they stayed in France until the bulk of
American troops were sent home, leaving France in late July 1919.

Taps

After the war, the Army engaged in a substantial effort to consolidate into eight primary cemeteries the war dead from over 2,000
temporary burial locations used during the war. Each of the permanent cemeteries was located near the battlefields on which the men
fell or near the hospitals in Paris or London where they died from
their wounds or disease. The process of disinterring, moving, and
reinterring the bodies was macabre work, largely handled by labor
battalions of African-American troops.

The 321st Quartermaster Labor Battalion digging graves at Fère-en-Tardenois in December 1918. The site is now the Oise-Aisne American Cemetery (Courtesy: Oise-Aisne American Cemetery, American Battle Monuments Commission)

During their odious work, Marine Cpl. Robert H. Wilson's body was found in the Champagne region. He was officially declared killed in action in February 1919. The official declaration of Wilson's demise increased the death toll among service Rose Bowl players to four.

In March 1923, President Warren Harding signed legislation commissioning the American Battle Monuments Commission (ABMC) to construct appropriate monuments at each of the American cemeteries in Europe. Genl. Pershing was deeply involved with the ABMC and leading architects created plans and monuments unique to each location.

Corporal Robert H. Wilson now rests in the Oise-Aisne American Cemetery, Plot C Row 23 Grave 21, about 14 miles from Château-Thierry.

Meuse-Argonne Cemetery shortly after its dedication.

The Meuse-Argonne Cemetery near Romagne-sous-Montfaucon holds the body of Captain Elijah 'Lige' Worsham at Plot C Row 39 Grave 25. Lieutenant Frank "Deke" Gard can be found at Plot B Row 33 Grave 24. Both rest in an area of the Meuse-Argonne battlefield captured by the U.S. Army after the two were killed in action near Gesnes. Lieutenant Ralph "Spec" Hurlburt was buried with them in the Meuse Argonne Cemetery. Prior to the memorials being built, his family chose to have his body repatriated and his remains were transferred to Arlington National Cemetery in 1921, where he now lies in Section 2, Grave 4299.

Among the twenty-two Camp Lewis players that served in Europe, Frank Gard was killed in action, while Bandini Dear, Louis Guisto, and Dixon Kapple were wounded while serving with the 91st. Pete Lenz was also severely wounded while serving with the 1st Division. The toll was higher among the twenty-one 362nd Officers team members that served in France. In addition to Gard and Kapple, who had played for both the Camp Lewis and 362nd teams, the 362nd Officers team saw Elijah Worsham and Ralph Hurlburt killed in action, while nine others were wounded including Howard Angus, William Bell, John Burgard, Ben Dorris, Rhodolph Esmay, Everett May, John McLean, James Montgomery, and Charles Thorpe. In total, thirteen of twenty-one players on the 362nd Officers team that went to France were killed or wounded in action.

FOLLOWING THE WAR, America returned to its isolationist stance. Its world view was confirmed by the decision not to join the League of Nations, primarily due to a League covenant requiring members to help defend other League members threatened by aggression. America chose not to make that commitment.

Given its approach to the world, America quickly shed the large armed forces it built during the war and began its return to normalcy. The American Army that had grown to 4.1 million men by the end of the war was reduced to 111,000 men by 1921. The Marine Corps dropped from 71,000 to 18,000, while the Navy went from more than 500,000 to 120,000 men by 1920.

Of course, since there were fewer Regular Army positions available after the war, the size of the authorized force had implications for those interested in staying in the Army after the war. Many of the available positions were allocated to men trained in armor, aviation, or other advanced skills that did not exist or were limited in number before the war. Similar cutbacks and emphasis on new skills occurred with the Navy and Marines.

As mentioned earlier, none of the 1918 Mare Island or Great Lakes players remained in the service and Everett May of the 362nd Officers team was the only career soldier among those who played for either Camp Lewis team. Rhodolph Esmay, of the 362nd Officers team became Wyoming's Adjutant General shortly after the war and made a career of that position, while others remained in the Reserves or National Guard with six returning to active service during WWII.

The combination of a slightly larger Marine Corps and the loss of senior men during the war meant positions were available for some who joined during the war. Those trained as pilots had greater opportunity to stay in the Corps. Of the twenty-seven Marines on the 1917 Mare Island team that survived the war, seven stayed in the Marines after the war, including John Beckett, Walter Brown, Thomas Cushman, Goodyear Kirkman, Fred Molthen, Stan Ridderhof, and Lawson Sanderson. All seven became commissioned officers with all but John Beckett earning their wings.

Two of those men died while serving in the Marines following World War I, while others served in battle locations ranging from Haiti, to the Dominican Republic, to Pearl Harbor, to Guadalcanal, to Tarawa, to Saipan, to Iwo Jima, to Okinawa, and on to Korea. Remarkably, the twenty-eight men who played on the 1917 Mare Island team entered the Corps as privates, yet five became Marine Corps generals. Three of the 1917 Mare Island players rose to the rank of Brigadier General (one star), another became a Major General (two stars) and the fifth retired as a Lieutenant General (three stars). In addition, Capt. William "Newton" Best, the Mare Island Athletic Director during the 1917 season, also retired as a Brigadier General.

14

TO HAVE HAD SUCH A LAD

With the exception of the eight men that became career soldiers or Marines, the service Rose Bowl players, like the doughboys in general, joined the military for the duration of the war and, once it was over, folded their uniforms, stored them in the attic, and left the military behind. Most joined the newly-founded American Legion and remained in the organization for years afterwards.

Following their release from the armed forces, the men of the service Rose Bowl teams followed several paths based on their stage in life when they entered the services and the experiences they had during their service. The first path was followed by those who kept playing or coaching games. This group included those who had not completed their college eligibility, those who played major league baseball or played in the emerging professional football leagues, and those who turned to coaching. The second path was the most popular. It included men who became butchers, brokers, and envelope makers. These were the men who returned to normalcy; the everyday civilians whose days on the football field and battlefield were over. The final and least trodden path was walked by those who remained in the military.

Each group contributed to American society and their local communities in some form. In fact, one of the striking findings in profiling these men is the number who were civically engaged, whether through elected office or, more often, various fraternal and volunteer organizations. Information on each of 178 service Rose Bowl players, as well as the coaches and administrators, is can be found in individual profiles located in the Appendix.

The College Game

The popularity of college football ballooned in the 1920s. Increased enrollments, expanded newspaper coverage, the introduction of radio coverage, and tremendous increases in the number of automobiles and paved roads resulted in increased interest in and accessibility to the games. Colleges around the country built new stadiums to meet the demand with many stadiums justified, in part, as memorials to the war dead. Twenty-eight of the sixty-four football stadiums used by teams in the five major college football conferences today were built in the 1920s.

Forty-one of the service Rose Bowl players entered or returned to college after leaving the service. Charlie Bachman, who had completed his eligibility, left Great Lakes and was named the football coach at Northwestern University for the 1919 season. His Great Lakes teammates, Harry Eielson and Charles Knight, returned to Evanston and Bachman convinced five other teammates to don the purple, including the Barnard twins, Hal Erickson, Chester Langenstein, and B.H. Miller. Before playing football in 1919, Eielson and Erickson were ruled ineligible and transferred to Washington & Jefferson. The others played only during the 1919 season. The Barnard twins completed their eligibility, while faculty-driven changes and Bachman's departure alienated the others.

Four service Rose Bowl players were team captains during the 1919 season: Paul Dobson (Nebraska), Emzy Lynch (Arizona), Dick Hanley (Washington State), and Nate Shanedling (St. Mary's). Jimmy Conzelman was named All-Missouri Valley as a sophomore at Washington University in St. Louis. He turned pro the next year.

Ken Bartlett, Ward McKinney, Hollis Huntington, and Bill Steers returned to Oregon for the 1919 season and played in the 1920

Rose Bowl. In that process, Hollis Huntington and Ken Bartlett became the first of four men to play every minute of three Rose Bowl games (1917, 1918, and 1920). (Two Stanford players did the same in the 1930s.)

Former service Rose Bowl players on Oregon's 1920 Rose Bowl team included: (Front Row) Ken Bartlett is the third from the left and Ward McKinney is on the far right. (Back row) Hollis Huntington is fourth from left and Bill Steers is next to him on his right. Bill Hayward, who trained Mare Island for the 1918 Rose Bowl, stands on the far right.

Roscoe Minton of Indiana was the only team captain during the 1920 season, while Bill Steers earned All-Pacific Coast honors at quarterback for Oregon and Lloyd Gillis did the same at fullback for Washington State.

Jack "Blondy" Reeves, who scored Great Lakes' first touchdown in the 1919 Rose Bowl, played for Ottawa University in Kansas in 1916 and 1917, but transferred to Emporia State in Kansas after the war. As one of the biggest and most talented running backs in the country, Reeves was the main cog in Emporia's offense. In a game against Washburn on a drizzly day in early November, Reeves took a handoff, ran into the line, and was tackled on the muddy field. Reeves remained on the ground after the play, paralyzed by a spinal injury. He was taken to a nearby hospital, where Phog Allen, the University of Kansas coach and an osteopathic physician, was among those who treated him. Reeves' parents hurried to Emporia, but were slowed by muddy roads and arrived too late, as Blondy Reeves died of his injuries early that Sunday morning.

Harry Bliss and Frank Willaman were teammates at Great Lakes and returned to Ohio State after the war. Willaman was an All-Big Ten fullback in 1919, but was injured much of the 1920 season, during which Ohio State was invited to the 1921 Rose Bowl to face California. Both men played sparingly as Cal dominated in a 28-0 win.

Lawrence Teberg of Great Lakes captained Minnesota in 1921, while Great Lakes' Dutch Lauer (Detroit) and Hal Erickson (Washington & Jefferson), and Mare Island's Mike Moran (Washington State) were named to Walter Camp's Honorable Mention All-American team.

Joe Foley, a backup quarterback on the Great Lakes team, played college football in the 1921 season by following a path that is inconceivable today. Foley played for Blackburn College in Carlinville, Illinois from 1915 to 1917, the first two years as an Academy (high school) student and the third as a college freshman. When he was released from the Navy in 1919, Blackburn named him its Athletic Director and football coach. He returned to student status in 1920 to quarterback and captain the football team. Foley then transferred to Washington & Jefferson for the 1921 season where he was a substitute quarterback, playing in a handful of games and scoring at least one touchdown.

Hal Erickson played for Washington & Jefferson from 1919 through the 1922 season and led W&J during its magical 1921 season. The 1921 W&J team went undefeated with wins over Bucknell, Lehigh, Syracuse, Pitt, and West Virginia, and were invited to the 1922 Rose Bowl to play one of California's Wonder Teams. With a limited budget, W&J traveled to Pasadena with only eleven players, yet they allowed only two first downs, playing Cal to a 0-0 draw. W&J's appearance in the 1922 Rose Bowl game provides a partial answer to the greatest of Rose Bowl trivia questions. That is:

Which four teams have played in the Rose Bowl and do not currently play Division I (FBS or FCS) football?

I have asked this question of hundreds of football fans over the years and no one has answered it correctly, and the vast majority could not name one of the teams. You are fortunate for reaching this point in the book, since you now know the four teams: Mare Island, Camp Lewis, Great Lakes, and Washington & Jefferson. Some argue that a fifth former Rose Bowl participant no longer plays Division I football, but the author feels no need to make light of the Minnesota Golden Gophers' ongoing football plight.

Amor Galloway of the 1918 Mare Island team began the 1922 season playing with his brother, Harold, at USC. However, Amor suffered a vertebrae injury that ended his football career. Harold, meanwhile, split time at quarterback as the team enjoyed a 10-1 season, suffering their only loss to Cal, 12-0. When Cal refused a potential Rose Bowl invitation, USC was selected for the first Rose Bowl game played in the new Rose Bowl Stadium, beating a Hugo Bedzek-led Penn State team, 14-3.

Leo Shannon (Washington State) and Hunter Miles (Washington) completed their eligibility in 1923, and played one another in the Apple Cup. Washington went to the 1924 Rose Bowl, giving Miles a second chance for a Rose Bowl victory over a Navy team. Despite a hard-fought game, Washington could not beat the Midshipmen; they tied them, 14-14.

The last service Rose Bowl player playing college football was John Budd, who had transferred from League Island to Mare Island and started in the 1919 Rose Bowl. He finished his career at Lafayette in 1924. Two years later he was named All-Pro with the Frankford Yellow Jackets.

Service Football

Service football continued through the 1920s and 1930s, but its emphasis was inconsistent from team to team and year to year. Most teams played at the base or ship level. For example, Navy battleships in port played one another and at least one battleship team played and lost to the University of Washington every year from 1922 through 1928.

Mare Island fielded a team in 1919 with Elmer Hall as head coach and John Beckett as his assistant, before Beckett took over head coaching duties in 1920. Similarly, Dutch Molthen coached an informal team at Quantico in 1919.

The best service football was played by regional or national all-star teams. These teams had periods of success despite shifting support from the top brass. The Third Army Corps on the East Coast played competitive schedules in the early 1920s prior to the War Department shifting its remaining football emphasis to Fort Benning.

Marine football was well supported when Maj. Genl. Smedley D. Butler's was Quantico's Commanding General from 1919 to 1924. Butler believed there was recruiting and *esprit de corps* value in a strong football program and tasked several former Mare Island players with building the program. Lawson Sanderson was the player-coach with Walter Brown at quarterback in 1920 and Beckett was Quantico's player-coach from 1921 through 1924, playing alongside Elmer Hall and Lawson Sanderson during those years. Most of their games were against mid-Atlantic colleges, while the 1923 team lost 26-6 to a Michigan team that finished undefeated.

Still, the highlight of their seasons were games against service rivals. Quantico beat the Third Army Corps, coached by Dwight Eisenhower, in 1921 and bested them in 1922 before 60,000 fans, including the Secretary of War, the Secretary of Navy, and over one hundred members of Congress. Interest in the interservice championship was reflected by President Coolidge's 1924 donation of the President's Cup which was awarded annually to the winner of the service championship game in Washington, D.C. The Quantico, and later the All-Marine teams, dominated east coast service play in the 1920s, winning five of seven President's Cups.

The Quantico Marines team was deemphasized in the late 1920s and service football on the east coast petered out. The competition for the President's Cup then shifted to the west coast before dying out entirely several years later.

On the west coast, service football was headlined by the Ninth Army Corps and the Pacific Fleet teams in the 1920s. Both struggled against major college teams, but were competitive with lesser college and athletic club teams. Their season highlight came in the annual Armistice Day game at Tournament Park in Pasadena, before shifting to California Memorial Stadium in Berkeley. Camp Lewis' Everett May and Harry Craig played in the 1921 game. Throughout the period of play, the team rosters included a number of former service academy and other college players with the games attracting big crowds. Over 50,000 attended the 1941 game.

The Marines' football focus on the west coast was in San Diego, where its training function shifted from Mare Island in 1923. The San Diego Marines were the best service football team in the country in the 1930s. Elmer Hall and John Beckett were involved in those teams whenever they were stationed in San Diego. Hall coached the team in the mid-1930s, and led the 1939 and 1940 teams to a combined 20-1 record.

SEPTEMBER	Marines Op.	
10 Santa Barbara Athletic Club .... City Stadium, San Diego, 2:15 P.M.		BRIGADIER GENERAL F. L. BRADMAN
17 Olympic Club .... Kezar Stadium, San Francisco, 2:15 P.M.		Commanding
23 Brigham Young University .... Sports Field, San Diego, 8:00 P.M.		MAJOR K. E. ROCKEY
30 San Diego State College .... Sports Field, San Diego, 8:00 P.M.		Chief of Staff and Supervising Officer of Athletics
OCTOBER		CHIEF Q. M. CLERK J. D. BRADY
7 Arizona State Teachers College ... Sports Field, San Diego, 8:00 P.M.		Adjutant
15 University of Santa Clara .... City Stadium, San Diego, 2:15 P.M.		CAPTAIN J. W. BECKETT
28 La Verne College .... Sports Field, San Diego, 8:00 P.M.		Athletic Officer
NOVEMBER		CAPTAIN E. E. HALL
11 University of California, Los Angeles City Stadium, San Diego, 2:15 P.M.		Head Coach
19 Loyola University of Los Angeles .. City Stadium, San Diego, 2:15 P.M.		Assistant Coaches
26 West Coast Navy .... City Stadium, San Diego, 2:15 P.M.		2nd LIEUTENANTS
		A. SHAPLEY H. C. TSCHIRGI
		P. MORET F. C. THOMPSON
		H. W. BAUER D. F. O'NEILL

A 1933 San Diego Marines football schedule with the facing page showing John Beckett as the base Athletic Officer and Elmer Hall as Head Coach.

Service football restarted on a big scale during WWII with some teams numbering among the best in the land. Randolph Field played in the 1944 Cotton Bowl and four service teams were in the top ten in the final Associated Press ranking for the 1944 season.

Following WWII, the Quantico Marines team returned to the field playing a mix of what are now Division II and III schools, but the program was dropped after the 1972 season, ending a fifty-five year era in which service teams competed on the football field with the nation's colleges.

The Butchers, Brokers, and Envelope Makers

After the war and their college days were over, ninety-three percent of the service Rose Bowl players spent their careers as civilians. Some shifted occupations over the years and their primary careers covered the spectrum of occupations available to the college elite. Since almost all attended college, less than four percent spent their careers as laborers or in the skilled trades.

Thirty percent of the players pursued business careers at various levels of management within emerging corporate America or in small businesses. Leon Bryan of the 1918 Mare Island team raised cattle and owned a butcher shop, there were a number of brokers and other financial industry men, and B.H. Miller of the Great Lakes team owned an envelope manufacturing company.

Just over 15 percent used their college educations to become doctors, dentists, lawyers, and engineers with a number of the engineers involved in the mining sector in the American West. Almost 10 percent of the players returned to the land, spending their lives as farmers, ranchers, and orchardists.

Finally, less than 10 percent became civil servants and most of those were in law enforcement, many as elected county sheriffs.

Across all occupations, these men were overwhelmingly involved in community organizations, particularly the American Legion, which formed in 1919. With the large number of men that served in WWI, the American Legion became an influential political voice at the local, state, and national levels. Candidates sought the veteran vote and the American Legion used that power to serve veterans, capped by their work helping draft the Servicemen's Readjustment Act of 1944, best known for the G.I. Bill, which provided access to higher education to millions of veterans following WWII.

The High School and College Coaches

Almost twenty-five percent of the service Rose Bowl players kept their hands in athletics as professional and college coaches or, more often, as high school teachers and administrators that coached at the secondary level. The high school coaches included a handful who had significant success, including those shown in the following table.

Coach	Service Team	High School Coaching Career
E. J. Abrahamson	Great Lakes	Won state basketball championship in Wisconsin before war.
Hollis Huntington	Mare Island 1918	Won Montana state football title as first-year coach. Won three Oregon state championships in basketball and one in baseball.
Roy Sharp	Camp Lewis	Successful football coach in Oakland. Led American Legion baseball team to national title.
Dick Kapple	Camp Lewis	Won two state basketball titles and six track and field titles in Utah.
Clarence Zimmerman	Mare Island 1918	Won two state basketball titles in Washington.
Lester Barnard	Great Lakes	Head coach at Memphis and Central Michigan. Won numerous Minneapolis city titles.
Jim Blewett	Mare Island 1918	Had 225-70-16 career record and won nine Los Angeles city championships. Mentored Jackie Robinson as backfield coach at UCLA.
Pete Lenz	Camp Lewis	Led Stockton HS Tarzans to conference basketball titles in 24 of 26 seasons. Won four California state championships in basketball and two in swimming.

Nineteen service Rose Bowl players became college head coaches during their careers. (All were football coaches unless noted.) Most notable was Charlie Bachman. Though he never won a conference championship—Michigan State was an independent during his fourteen years there—he made his mark at several schools by beating their intra-state rivals more consistently than his predecessors. He was inducted into the College Football Hall of Fame in 1978.

Dick Hanley had strong teams at the Haskell Institute during the time it was the top football-playing Indian school in the nation. He twice tied for the Big Ten championship at Northwestern and coached the El Toro Flying Marines to winning seasons in 1944 and 1945.

Dick Romney led Utah State's football program for thirty seasons, during which they earned four conference championships. He also won four basketball championships there over twenty-two seasons. The football stadium at Utah State was named in his honor from 1927 to 2015.

The following table shows each player that was a college head coach before or after their years in the service.

Coach	Service Team	Schools
Charles Austin	Camp Lewis	Santa Clara rugby '16, U.S. Olympic rugby '24
Charlie Bachman	Great Lakes	Northwestern '19, Kansas State '20-'27, Florida '28-'32, Michigan State '33-'46, Hillsdale '53
Ed Bailey	Mare Island 1918	Lewis and Clark (OR) '15-'16, '25
Chester Barnard	Great Lakes	Mississippi '24, Kalamazoo '25-'41
Lester Barnard	Great Lakes	Memphis '22, Central Michigan '24-'25
Charles Canup	Mare Island 1918	Billings Polytechnic College football and basketball '14-'15, Gonzaga basketball '22
Jimmy Conzelman	Great Lakes	Washington University in St. Louis '32-'39
Paddy Driscoll	Great Lakes	Marquette '37-'40
Con Eklund	Great Lakes	Augsburg '26-'32
Louis Guisto	Camp Lewis	St. Mary's baseball '32-'55
Dick Hanley	Mare Island 1918	Haskell Institute '22-'26, Northwestern '27-'34
Pat Hanley	Mare Island 1918	Boston University '34-'41
Jerry Jones	Great Lakes	Missouri baseball '22, Columbia College (IA) '32-'33
Emmett Keefe	Great Lakes	St. Viator (IL) '19
T. Everett May	362nd Officers	Clemson baseball '25
L.L. Mendenhall	Great Lakes	Carleton '20, Northern Iowa football and basketball '21-'24, baseball '22-'23
Roscoe Minton	Great Lakes	Indiana baseball '23-'24, Northern Iowa baseball '25
Cliff Mitchell	Mare Island 1917	Nevada '32-'35
Dick Romney	Camp Lewis	Utah State football '19-'48, basketball '19-'41
Bill Steers	Mare Island 1918	California of Pennsylvania football, cross country, basketball '29-'37

The Major Leagues

Paddy Driscoll of Great Lakes played for the Chicago Cubs before the war, while Louis Guisto of Camp Lewis played for the Cleveland Indians before and after the war. George Halas had a short stint with the New York Yankees in 1919, but his former Illinois and Great Lakes teammate, Dick Reichle, had the more memorable major league career due to one swing of the bat. After graduating from Illinois, Reichle spent part of the 1922 season in the minors, before being called up by the Red Sox in September 1922. After a solid training camp in 1923, he was named Boston's starting center fielder and was a spring phenom, having the junior circuit's second-best batting average into mid-June.

Reichle is now best known for his batting in the opening series of the season played in the brand-spanking-new Yankee Stadium. The opening game at Yankee Stadium smashed the major league's single-game attendance record by nearly 30,000 and the crowd saw Babe Ruth swat a four-bagger, the first home run in Yankee Stadium. Two days later, Reichle banged the second homer ever hit in Yankee Stadium. That dinger proved to be Reichle's only major league home run. He broke his leg in spring training in 1924 and never returned to the majors. He did, however, play six games for the Milwaukee Badgers of the NFL in 1923. Thus, three Great Lakes teammates and sons of the State of Illinois—Reichle, Halas, and Driscoll—are the only three men to start in the Rose Bowl, the NFL, and the Major Leagues. That, my friends, is exclusive company.

The NFL

Prior to WWI, baseball was America's pastime and the only professional sport of consequence, other than boxing. Newspaper sports sections from coast-to-coast covered major league baseball. The newspapers in towns outside the major league cities covered the majors with syndicated articles, while also reporting directly on their local minor league baseball teams.

Interest and media coverage for football, on the other hand, was focused on the college game. Although a mishmash of semipro and professional football teams existed before the war, they garnered small crowds and little attention outside their town borders, and their talent pool was similarly local. Few prominent college players played pro football before the war. If they played at all, college alums generally played with local athletic club teams such as the Multnomah Athletic Club and the San Francisco Olympic Club discussed in early chapters.

Things changed after the war. The service football teams of WWI were the first "all-star" football teams with nationally prominent players and coaches, the first to play and consistently beat top college teams, and the first to receive substantial regional and national press coverage. Although much of their popularity stemmed from being military teams in a time of war, they also gained attention due to the high level of football they played and the number of former college stars playing for the service teams. In addition, service football provided millions of service personnel and other fans that were not aligned with a college or university the opportunity to watch and become fans of high-level football. As a result, the service teams planted the seed that post-college football teams could have commercial success. As important, the players themselves recognized the opportunity to play football after college at a level beyond that played by the amateur clubs, while making a few bucks doing so.

In the years immediately after the war, a number of professional football teams were formed in cities of all sizes; most quickly met with failure. Some that survived were sponsored by businesses that saw the teams as advertising assets (e.g., the Green Bay Packers were sponsored by the Acme Packing Company, the Decatur Staleys were sponsored by the Staley Starch Company) or had owners with sufficiently deep pockets to sustain the teams, but even those teams were minor-league in their operations and finances. All professional football teams operated on a shoestring, with players holding jobs at the sponsoring company during the work week or working other outside jobs. Few players earned guaranteed money, earning only a share of the gate, and that money often did not amount to much. Most professional teams had player-coaches run the team to keep expenses as low as possible.

The service Rose Bowl teams, or more accurately the Great Lakes team, was well represented in the early NFL. Six service Rose Bowl players played and coached NFL or AAFC professional teams, twelve others played in the NFL. Each of the service Rose Bowl players that played, but did not coach, in the NFL is listed in the following table.

Player	Service Team	Teams
Benton Bangs	Mare Island 1918	Los Angeles Marauders '25, Los Angeles Buccaneers '26
John Beckett	Mare Island 1917	Buffalo All-Americans '20, Columbus Panhandles '23
Hugh Blacklock	Great Lakes	Decatur Staleys/Chicago Staleys/Chicago Bears '20-'25, Brooklyn Lions '26
Harry Bliss	Great Lakes	Columbus Panhandles '21
Johnny Budd	Mare Island 1918	Frankford Yellow Jackets '26, Pottsville Maroons '27-'28
Marty Conrad	Great Lakes	Toledo Maroons '22-'23, Kenosha Maroons '24, Akron Indians '25
Harry Dastillung	Great Lakes	Cincinnati Celts '21
Mel Doherty	Great Lakes	Cincinnati Celts '21
Jerry Jones	Great Lakes	Decatur Staleys '20, Rock Island Independents '22, Toledo Maroons '23, Cleveland Bulldogs '24
Emmett Keefe	Great Lakes	Chicago Tigers '20, Rock Island Independents '21, '23, Green Bay Packers '22, Milwaukee Badgers '24
Charlie Knight	Great Lakes	Racine/Chicago Cardinals '20-'21
Harold 'Dutch' Lauer	Great Lakes	Rock Island Independents, Green Bay Packers '22, Toledo Maroons, Dayton Triangles '23, Detroit Panthers '25-'26

Most service Rose Bowl players that played in the NFL came from the Great Lakes team, and this occurred for several reasons. First, since the NFL developed in a belt of industrial towns from New York City to the Quad Cities along the Mississippi River, the bulk of professional football players during the 1920s were from that part of the country. The players on the Mare Island and Camp Lewis teams were largely westerners. During a time in which professional football seldom paid the bills, it was financially and otherwise riskier for westerners to move east to play pro football. Second, the westerners lacked the personal connections to the eastern and midwest teams that Great Lakes players gained during their college and service careers. Lacking the same social network, they did not have the same awareness of the early NFL and the connections to former teammates already playing for pay. Third, some of the best players on the western teams found outlets other than the early NFL to continue playing football by playing with the Marines, for Mult-nomah, or other club teams on the West Coast. Fourth, Great Lakes was a massive training base and its 1918 football team had a depth of talent unlike any other team. A number of Great Lakes players who played in the NFL did not start for Great Lakes or started in only one or two games. This speaks to the depth of talent at Great Lakes.

Six service Rose Bowl players became NFL or AAFC head coaches and three—George Halas, Jimmy Conzelman, and Roy Andrews— were among the five winningest NFL coaches in the pre-1933 era. (The NFL was reorganized in 1933 with most franchises having relocated to or been replaced by teams in large cities.) Halas, Conzelman, and Driscoll were also named to the NFL's 1920s All-Decade team. Service Rose Bowl players who became professional head coaches during their careers are shown in the following table.

Coach	Role	Teams
Roy Andrews	Player	St. Louis All-Stars '23
	Player-Coach	Kansas City Blues/Cowboys '24-'26, Cleveland Bulldogs '27, Detroit Wolverines '28
	Coach	New York Giants '29-'30, Chicago Cardinals '31
Jimmy Conzelman	Player	Decatur Staleys '20
	Player-Coach	Rock Island Independents '21-'22, Milwaukee Badgers '23-'24, Providence Steamroller '27-'29,
	Player-Coach-Owner	Detroit Panthers '25-'26
	Coach	St. Louis Gunners '31, Chicago Cardinals '40-'42, '46-'48
Paddy Driscoll	Player	Decatur Staleys '20, Chicago Bears '26-'29
	Player-Coach	Chicago Cardinals '21-'22
	Coach	Chicago Bears '56-'57
Hal Erickson	Player-Coach	Milwaukee Badgers '24
	Player	Milwaukee Badgers '23, Chicago Cardinals '25-'28, Minneapolis Red Jackets '29-'30
George Halas	Player-Coach	Decatur Staleys '20
	Player-Coach-Owner	Chicago Staleys/Bears '20-'29,
	Coach-Owner	Chicago Bears '33-'42, '46-'55, '58-'67
Dick Hanley	Player	Racine Legion '24
	Coach	Chicago Rockets (AAFC) '46

Several service Rose Bowl players influenced the development of the early NFL based on their coaching abilities and their ability as players to attract fans to the gate. The gate impact of players such as Driscoll and Conzelman was significant and they were among the highest paid players for that reason.

Roy Andrews worked as a bank cashier before playing for the St. Louis All-Stars in 1923. He spent the next five years as a player-coach for three NFL teams, before coaching the New York Giants and Chicago Cardinals. He was fired from both roles after apparent player revolts. Entering the 2017 season, Andrews' fifty-one coaching wins ranks him ninety-eighth in NFL history, while he ranks eleventh in win percentage among coaches with at least fifty wins.

John L. "Paddy" Driscoll entered the NFL with George Halas' Decatur Staleys in 1920, but spent the next five years with Halas' crosstown rival, the Chicago Cardinals, acting as the player-coach from 1920-1922. Driscoll was sold to the Bears and played with them from 1926 to 1929, ending a playing career in which he was All-Pro in six of his ten years. (An All-Pro team was not named in two of the other four years). A high school coach during most of his playing days and through the 1936 season, Driscoll had an unsuccessful stint at Marquette University from 1937 to 1940. He returned to the Bears as an assistant and was their head coach in 1956 and 1957, leading them to the championship game in 1956. Though Driscoll was not a top pro coach, he was among the best and most exciting players during the NFL's first decade and his play attracted the paying fans that kept two franchises afloat. Driscoll was inducted into the NFL Hall of Fame in 1965.

Jimmy Conzelman played at WashU during the 1919 season, but his father passed away soon thereafter and, to help support his family, he joined George Halas' Decatur Staleys in 1920. He was playing for the Rock Island Independents in 1921 when, in the midst of a game, the owner fired the team's player-coach and named Conzelman the player-coach at halftime. Conzelman was the player-coach for Milwaukee in 1923 and 1924, before buying the Detroit franchise for $50, a sum that was overpriced then and remains so now. After two years as player-coach-owner in Detroit, one of which he was an All-Pro, Conzelman sold the franchise and became the player-coach for Providence, leading the Steam Rollers to the NFL Championship in 1928 and earning the NFL's Most Outstanding Player Award. He coached at WashU for eight years in the 1930s, and returned to the NFL sidelines as head coach of the Chicago Cardinals from 1940 to 1942 and from 1946 to 1948, winning his second NFL title in 1947. Conzelman then went into the advertising business, but remained a frequent guest speaker at banquets and similar settings. He was considered one of the great storytellers of the sports world; think of him as the Bob Uecker of his day, except Conzelman had talent. Entering the 2017 season, Conzelman's eighty-eight coaching wins ranks him fifty-first in NFL history. He was inducted into the NFL Hall of Fame in 1964.

George Halas played in 12 games with the New York Yankees in 1919, hitting only .091 before being injured. Halas and Driscoll accepted jobs working in South American after the 1919 baseball season, but neither followed that path. Had they done so, things might have turned out differently for the NFL. Instead, Halas took an engineering job in Chicago, which he soon left to coach three sports for the Staley Starch Company, bringing with him several Great Lakes teammates and college friends. Halas was among the twelve attendees at the 1920 meeting in a Hupmobile dealership in Canton at which the AAFC, renamed the NFL in 1921, was founded. When the owner of Staley Starch no longer wanted to support the team in 1921, he offered the team and $5,000 to Halas, recommending Halas move the team to Chicago. His only condition was that the team continue to be called the Staleys for one season. Halas took the offer and moved the team to Chicago and Cubs Park (now Wrigley Field). Despite being in the league's second biggest city, the Bears struggled financially, but Halas made among the biggest decisions in NFL history when he signed Red Grange to a lucrative contract in 1925. Their subsequent barnstorming tour drew large crowds and brought attention to the league.

The Bears' introduction of the T formation in 1930 took Halas to five NFL championship games in the next eleven years, winning three of those games. As important, the T formation formed the basis of almost all offensive football schemes to the present. Halas served thirty-seven months in the Navy during WWII in various roles coordinating recreational and athletic activities. He served twenty months in the Pacific and was awarded a Bronze Star by Admiral Nimitz for his efforts. He won another NFL championship during his first year coaching after the war, but other teams dominated the league in the 1950s and he turned over the coaching duties to Paddy Driscoll for the 1956 and 1957 seasons. Halas returned to the sideline in 1959 and the Bears experienced a resurgence, winning the 1963 title. Halas retired as coach for the fourth and final time after the 1967 season. He remained active with the franchise until his death in 1983.

Halas is reported to have been the first coach to use film to study opponents, the first to have a professional football game broadcast by radio, the first to schedule a professional team barnstorming tour, and a host of other firsts. Halas won six titles and had six losing seasons in forty years as a head coach. He was both the youngest and oldest coach to win an NFL championship and his 324 career coaching wins ranks second in NFL history. By all accounts he was among the most influential figures in the development of the NFL, and despite winning six championships as a coach, his greatest impact on the league came from his strengths as an organizer and promoter of the Bears and the broader league. He was elected to the NFL Hall of Fame as part of its inaugural class in 1963. Even a Packers fan must give the man his due.

The Military

Eleven service Rose Bowl players who did not spend their primary careers in the military returned to active service during WWII. Most that did so remained in the National Guard or the Reserves after WWI, but each found a way to offer their service to the country for a second time. Most took stateside positions that leveraged their civilian administrative skills, enabling younger men to perform duties in the war zones. Others held athletic, conditioning and recreational roles that, even when overseas, were behind the lines, and safe from combat. Exceptions were Pat Hanley, who was in the thick of things early in the Guadalcanal Campaign and later on Saipan, where he was wounded and earned a Bronze Star for bravery. In addition, Henry Shields served on Okinawa during a time of active battle.

Those who returned to the service during the WWII era are shown in the following table.

Player	Service Team	WWII Duties
Howard Angus	362nd Officers	Lt. Col., directed a Lockheed airplane factory in Burbank, CA
Chester Barnard	Great Lakes	Lt. Commander, Athletic Director, Naval Training Station, Dearborn, MI and Naval Air Station Pensacola
Fred Campbell	362nd Officers	1st Lt., Coastal Artillery Corps
George Halas	Great Lakes	Lt. Cmdr., Naval Air Technical Training Center, Norman, OK; Recreation and Welfare Officer, 7th Fleet, Admiralty Islands; Cmdr., Recreation and Athletics, Philippines
Pat Hanley	1918 Mare Island	Lt. Col., Guadalcanal, Saipan. Wounded and earned Bronze Star. Football coach of Maui Marines
Dick Hanley	1918 Mare Island	Major, Lt. Col., two overseas tours
Samuel D. Hays	362nd Officers	Col., commanded Boise Barracks, Camp Adair, and Camp Beale training camps
Charles 'Dick' Kapple	Camp Lewis	Major, Army Air Force, taught math with 36th Army Air Force, Technical School Group
Emzy Lynch	Camp Lewis	Major, commanded POW camps. Two tours with Occupation Army of Japan
George Novinger	Great Lakes	Army Officers training camp
Henry D. Shields	1917 Mare Island	Major, stateside roles and Executive Officer, 1st Motor Transport Battalion on Okinawa
William Steers	1918 Mare Island	Lt. Commander in Navy. 7th Fleet Recreation Director, Admiralty Islands

Beyond those who led civilian lives and served again during WWII, eight others spent their lives as career officers. Seven of those were 1917 Mare Island Marine players and one was from the 362nd Officers team.

Everett May, a 362nd Officer, was discharged from the Army upon his return from France, but he reentered the Army in 1920 and was stationed at Camp Lewis. He then oversaw the ROTC program at Clemson University and served as Clemson's baseball coach in 1925. May was based in Hawaii from 1925 to 1932, before being sent to the Advanced Course at the Infantry School at Fort Benning, where he wrote his primary paper on the operations of his unit in the Meuse-Argonne Offensive. He then worked with the Civilian Conservation Corps until he was assigned as the training officer for the Oregon National Guard in 1934. During WWII, he commanded the Army Band and Musical school before retiring as a Colonel in 1946.

Seven of 1917 Mare Island Marines stayed in the Marines after the war. Lts. Walter Brown and Lawson Sanderson were sent to Port au Prince, Haiti, in July of 1919. The Marines policed Haiti for nineteen years after Woodrow Wilson ordered them there in 1916 to stabilize the country following the assassination of their dictator, President Vilbrun Guillaume Sam. Sam was neither the first nor the last of Haiti's presidents to be assassinated, but he was friendly to the U.S. during a time Germany was challenging the Monroe Doctrine in Haiti and other Caribbean nations. Although the legitimacy of the U.S. actions can be questioned, Sanderson and Brown were there as Marine pilots involved in skirmishes with various Haitian "bandit" groups at a time when aviation had advanced only from the infant to the toddler stage.

Throughout WWI, bombs were dropped from airplanes flying in level flight. While inaccurate by current standards, their accuracy was good enough because the battle lines were well defined and the missions consisted of bombing a general area rather than a specific target. The Marine pilots in Haiti faced a different tactical situation because much of their role involved ground support; that is, using their planes to support Marines fighting on the ground in proximity to the enemy. In that situation, the accuracy of their strafing and bombing was critical because they needed to hit the bandits, not their fellow Marines. To meet the new need, Lawson Sanderson developed a new tactic, or at least, improved upon and was the first to consistently apply a new tactic. In simple terms, he rigged up a mechanism in which bombs, placed inside dirt-filled mail pouches, were released as he dove his plane toward the target. Dropping the bombs while diving reduced the distance between his plane and the target, and simplified the parabolic arc as the bomb fell. The tactic proved far more accurate than level-flight methods and, based on his success, Sanderson became known worldwide as the "father of dive bombing." Dive bombing was a key aerial tactic in WWII, particularly in the naval-air battles in the Pacific.

Brown and Sanderson's friend and teammate Fred "Dutch" Molthen graduated from flight training with them in January 1919 and then was transferred to Quantico, where he spent part of his time with aviation squadrons, completing the Officers Training Camp in late 1919. On June 25, 1920, Molthen readied a modified DH-4 he was to pilot with two other Marine officers aboard for a flight to Savannah, Georgia. They took off uneventfully and rose to 500 feet, at which point the plane caught fire. Molthen maintained control of the aircraft and descended to 100 feet when the DH-4 burst into flames and crashed, killing all three men. Molthen's body was returned to Butte, Montana, where he now lies under a veteran's headstone.

Walter Brown, the star quarterback of the 1918 Rose Bowl team, was in training as a Marine pilot when the war ended. He finished his training and went to Haiti in January 1919 with Lawson Sanderson. After returning to the States, he completed the Officer Training Camp in July 1920. Brown participated in the Pulitzer Trophy race on Thanksgiving Day in 1920, indicating he was among the Marines' best flyers. In January 1921, Brown took command of Flight F of the 3rd Air Squadron at Quantico.

During the same period, Army Genl. Billy Mitchell returned from Europe convinced that air power would soon become the equal of land and sea power, an idea rejected by most others in the U.S. military. Mitchell's political maneuvering allowed him to conduct a proof of concept in which Army bombers attempted to sink two obsolete battleships that were otherwise headed to the scrapyard. The Navy hierarchy did not consider aerial bombing of ships feasible either, but planned their own tests targeting surplus vessels in Chesapeake Bay. On a practice run for the Navy tests, Walter Brown took off from Quantico on June 9, 1921, commanding his squadron of six DH-4Bs. Having completed their mission, the six planes turned back to their airfield. As they closed on Quantico, they encountered fog, so each pilot became responsible for finding his way home. The other five planes landed safely, but Brown's flight path led him into worse fog. Brown attempted a sharp right-hand turn to find better visibility, but the sharp turn put Brown's plane into a tail spin resulting in the plane crashing one mile off the beach, buried in mud. Brown was killed in the crash. His mechanic, flying with him, survived to recount the events of the flight.

Like his friend, Fred Molthen, Brown's family chose to bring his body home and he is buried beneath a veteran's headstone in Milton-Freewater, Oregon. Following his death, the Marine flying field at Quantico was named in his honor. Although the flying field became obsolete and was replaced in the 1930s, the original location remains named in his honor and is the site of today's Marine Officer Candidate School.

Brown's good friend, Lawson H. M. Sanderson, remained active in air racing and became the "world's fastest man" when he set a world record by flying his plane 259 miles per hour in October 1923. Several weeks later he won the Pulitzer Trophy and won other air races through the mid-1930s. During the 1920s and 1930s, Sanderson also returned to the Dominican Republic for a three-year tour and commanded an air squadron in Nicaragua where he won the Distinguished Flying Cross for twice flying replacement wings strapped underneath his plane's wings to another pilot whose plane was damaged in action.

At the outbreak of WWII, Col. Sanderson was the Operations Officer of the 1st Marine Aircraft Wing. Following the Navy's victories at the Battle of the Coral Sea and the Battle of Midway, U.S. forces in the Pacific landed at Guadalcanal in early August 1942. The 1st Marine Air Wing became operational at Guadalcanal's Henderson Field less than two weeks later with Sanderson as its Operations Officer. The Marines struggled until February 1943 to keep Henderson Field open and take the island, but the Guadalcanal Campaign became one of the key victories of the war. Later in the war he commanded the 4th Marine Air Wing and was the Commander, Shore-Based Air Forces in the Marshall-Gilbert Islands area. In that role, then Brig. Genl. Sanderson accepted the Japanese surrender of Wake Island on September 4, 1945, 1,362 days after it fell in December 1941. He commanded the 1st Marine Air Wing in China in 1946 and retired from the Marines in 1949.

The Marines' Attack Squadron of the Year Award remains named in his honor.

Stanley Ridderhof earned his wings following the war and served two years on Guam in the early 1920s where he helped direct the building of the first airfield on the island. He was stationed in Nicaragua from 1928 to 1930. While there, he earned the Navy Cross and the Nicaraguan Medal of Merit for leading a raid on a major rebel supply depot. Stationed on Oahu in 1941, Ridderhof birdied the first hole at the Oahu Country Club the first Sunday morning in December, when his match was interrupted by Japanese planes attacking Pearl Harbor. He hurried to Pearl Harbor and spent the next three days directing efforts in his golf attire. He returned to the continental U.S. in July 1942 and spent the rest of WWII stateside, rising to Chief of Staff of Marine Air Forces on the West Coast. He earned the Legion of Merit and the Distinguished Flying Cross during the war.

After leaving the Marines, Ridderhof completed the requirements for the undergraduate degree he interrupted to join the Marines in 1917, became an executive with a military contractor, and was president of the Southern California Golf Association.

Tom Cushman was commissioned a 2nd Lt. in October 1918 after completing ground training and was retained in a staff role at MIT before completing flight training in July 1919. After the war, Cushman rose through a succession of command and staff assignments, interspersed with further training, and tours on Guam, the Dominican Republic, and Nicaragua.

As the nation was mobilizing prior to WWII, the Marines began developing what is now the Marine Air Station Cherry Hill in North Carolina. Cushman was its commanding officer during the development and initial operation until September 1943 when he became Chief of Staff to the commanding officer of the Marine Air Wings in the Pacific. After the U.S. took Saipan, Guam, and Tinian in the Marianas Islands in July and August of 1944, American forces built airfields on Saipan and Tinian for the B-29s that executed the strategic and atomic bombing campaigns against Japan. In November 1944, Cushman took command of the Marine Air Wings defending the Marianas and he remained in command there until

April 1945. He was awarded the Bronze Star and Legion of Merit for his efforts.

After WWII, he held high-level commands on both coasts and with the onset of the Korean War, Cushman was named the Assistant Wing Commander and then, Commander, of the 1st Marine Air Wing in Korea. In his final role with the Marines, he was Assistant Commander, Fleet Marine Force, Pacific, and was promoted to Lt. General at retirement.

After returning from France in 1919, Elmer Hall spent much of the 1920s and 1930s in staff roles, often personnel related. During that time, he was instrumental in the development of the Marines' football programs at Quantico and in San Diego, coaching through the 1930s when he was not stationed overseas. He had two tours in Nicaragua and one in Shanghai, and also commanded Marine detachments aboard Navy warships. Hall was the commander of the 2nd Engineers Battalion at Pearl Harbor in December 1941 and received the Navy Commendation Medal for his leadership during the attack. He was named commander of the 8th Marine Regiment and led his unit on the beach at Tarawa, for which he was awarded the Legion of Merit. After Tarawa, Hall returned to the U.S. and held staff roles until his retirement in 1946. Hall Field, the football stadium at the Marine Recruit Depot San Diego, was named in his honor in 1960.

Which brings us, finally, to John Beckett. Beckett returned from France in July 1919. He is considered an NFL alum for playing two games for the Buffalo All-Americans in 1920 and one game for the Columbus Panhandlers in 1922. Beckett was instrumental in the development of the Marine Corps football program as the player-coach of the Mare Island Marines in 1920, the Quantico Marines from 1921-1924, and the San Diego Marines in 1925. He was an assistant coach at the Naval Academy from 1926 to 1928, before commanding the Marine detachment in Beijing from 1929 to 1931. He returned to the States and again coached the San Diego Marines in 1931 and 1932.

Prior to the start of WWII, Beckett had roles overseeing Marine basic training and spent the early part of WWII assigned to the Officer Candidate School at Quantico. By April 1944, he was deployed in a staff role with the 5th Marines and landed on Iwo Jima two days before the iconic flag raising on Mt. Surabachi. After the war ended, Beckett had a homecoming as the commandant of the Marine Barracks at Mare Island from 1946 until his retirement in 1949.

The Final Whistle

Seventy-one of the service Rose Bowl players lived into the 1970s, twenty-one were still going as the 1980s began, and four witnessed the start of the 1990s. William Hutchinson, of the 362nd Officers team, survived the attack on Gesnes and was the longest living of the service Rose Bowl team members, passing away well into his 97th year, while Frank Shoemaker, who was on Mare Island's roster for the 1919 Rose Bowl, was the last living service Rose Bowl player when he passed away in 1995 having just celebrated his 96th birthday.

During their lives, the service Rose Bowl players fought in the war to end all wars, only to learn they had not succeeded in that task. They saw the beginning of powered flight, yet many lived to see man's footprints on the moon. They witnessed the consumerization of radio, television, and computers, and they saw massive social changes ranging from women getting the right to vote, to Prohibition and its repeal, and on to the Civil Rights movement.

At the time they played, the Granddaddy of Them All was little more than an infant, but the service Rose Bowl teams helped keep alive the tradition of playing on New Year's Day in Pasadena, playing in the Rose Bowl before the Rose Bowl was built, before professional football was truly professional, and before fighting for a country that was not yet a military power. All of that changed in time, and these men were in the midst of it all at the beginning.

The service Rose Bowl players and their exploits are largely forgotten today, but perhaps this book helps to further the appreciation for these men and their time, as well as its impact on us 100 years on.

EPILOGUE

Having accounted for each of the service Rose Bowl players, we return to John Beckett's article published on the eve of the fiftieth anniversary of the 1918 Rose Bowl in which Beckett wrote:

> "Most of us on both teams that day knew we were scheduled to go overseas within a matter of weeks (nearly half the 32 players were to die in action in World Wars I or II); so this was the last battle we would fight in the name of sport."[1]

It is certain that most of the soldiers and Marines on the field during the 1918 Rose Bowl thought they would be sent to Europe to fight in the coming months. They were, after all, in the military and had completed their basic training at a time America was sending its sons into a conflict that had already claimed five million lives with another fifteen million wounded by New Year's Day 1918. Moreover, given the Allies' expectation that the war would last well into 1919 or 1920, every man in the service at the time expected that they, and many of their comrades, might be added to the casualty numbers in the coming years. That was the reality they faced.

So, while the potential for the loss of life existed and John Beckett surely mourned the loss of his teammates and all others who died in the service, his statement is inconsistent with the reality of what happened to the men of the 1918 Rose Bowl teams. Of the thirty-two men that played in the 1918 Rose Bowl, Frank Gard, who substituted into the game at right end for Camp Lewis, was the only one to die in action. None of the other players that saw action in Europe, the Caribbean, WWII or other conflicts were killed in action.

Similarly, of the forty players that dressed for the Rose Bowl, Gard was the only player to die in action. Two others, Brown and Molthen, died in flying accidents while in the service. Even counting the two Camp Lewis players who cannot be accounted for, we fall far short of nearly half the players dying in action. The same applies if we look at all the players on the team rosters during the 1918 season. Doing so adds Robert Wilson as a player who died in action, but we must add 33 other players to the roster totals, including five more who are unaccounted for. The most conservative calculation still falls far short of nearly half. Finally, if we add the 362nd Officers team to the mix, Worsham and Hurlburt were killed in action, but nineteen others were not and one more player is unaccounted for.

The following table summarizes the number of deaths in action, deaths in the service, and those who are unaccounted for among the members of the 1918 Rose Bowl teams.

	Played in 1918 Rose Bowl	Rose Bowl Roster	Season Roster	Season Roster, incl. 362nd
Mare Island				
Total	12	17	28	28
Died in Action	0	0	1	1
Died in Service	1	2	2	2
Unaccounted For	0	0	0	0
Camp Lewis				
Total	18	23	45	45
Died in Action	1	1	1	1
Died in Service	0	0	0	0
Unaccounted For	0	2	7	7
362nd Officers*				
Total	NA	NA	NA	22
Died in Action	NA	NA	NA	2
Died in Service	NA	NA	NA	0
Unaccounted For	NA	NA	NA	1
Total	30	40	73	95
Died in Action	1	1	2	4
Died in Service	1	2	2	2
Unaccounted For	0	2	7	8

* Four who played for both Camp Lewis and the 362nd Officers are counted with Camp Lewis.

Regardless of how you count the numbers, and even if we assume that all the players who are unaccounted for died in the service, the death rate falls far short of that stated by Beckett.

Since the numbers do not bear out Beckett's statement, we are left to speculate on why Beckett might have made the statement in his article. First, it is worth remembering that the statement was made in a syndicated newspaper article written by Beckett fifty years after the fact. It was not a slip of the tongue or an error in quotation by a nameless reporter. The words were Beckett's own and would have been reviewed and edited more than once. Beckett also opens the article by saying, "Time has eroded many subsequent and perhaps more important milestones in my life, but somehow I can recall everything I saw, smelled, touched, tasted and heard on New Year's Day in 1918…" [1] Beckett clearly does not claim a lack of memory from those days.

Perhaps Beckett was focused on his Mare Island teammates and the three Mare Island players that died in the service, but Wilson was the only one that died in action and he was not on the Rose Bowl roster. In addition, Brown and Molthen, his good friends, died in training accidents while in the Marines, but neither "died in action," [1] a term with specific meaning to a highly-respected, career Marine officer. Beckett was also likely aware that the 91st Division incurred significant losses during its time at Meuse-Argonne and in Flanders, but the losses among the Camp Lewis football players do not support his claim either.

Beckett made two other statements in his article that seem intended for dramatic affect and are incorrect. First, he tells the reader that Mare Island entered the game "unbeaten, un-tied and unscored-upon" [1] and later adds that Camp Lewis' "Romney and McKay led a drive that ended in the first points scored on us that season." [1] Although the Camp Lewis scored the first touchdown given up by Mare Island that season, Mare Island was scored on early in the season when the San Francisco Athletic Club kicked a field goal in their game with Mare Island on October 11, 1917. Every football player knows the difference between "unscored-upon" and giving up three points by a field goal.

Second, Beckett's article is titled "The Game that Saved the Rose Bowl" and his third paragraph starts with the following:

> "Two weeks before this historic Rose Bowl game was played, George Creel, the White House press chief, went to President Wilson and laid the Rose Bowl quandary on his desk. Wilson consulted his cabinet, then consented –on December 23– to an inter-service game between ourselves and a formidable Army eleven team from Camp Lewis." [1]

Once again, part of this story is true, but other parts are not. The Tournament of Roses did seek and receive Wilson's approval to move forward with their celebration, but they received Wilson's approval on November 24, not December 23. Mare Island was invited to the Rose Bowl the same day–November 24– and USAAS received its invitation on November 29. USAAS then declined the invitation and Camp Lewis gained its invitation on December 8. Moreover, Beckett and his teammates arrived in Pasadena on December 23, 1917 after sailing for two days and the Camp Lewis team arrived a day later after a three-day train ride. Neither team would have made that trip without proper clearance. While one cannot begrudge Beckett for failing to recall some details and dates fifty years after the event, Beckett's comment about the approval coming on a specific date, shortly before the game was played, can only be seen as a dramatic ploy.

Despite questioning Beckett's memory or motives from a rational perspective, much of memory is not rational. Memory has emotional components and memories are imperfectly categorized by each individual. Time, dates, and numbers compress and expand for anyone recalling the past. Perhaps some of these effects were at work and Beckett, lacking access to the internet to easily check some of these facts, wrote his article based on his impressions of the facts.

That said, Beckett's claims regarding Mare Island being unscored-upon and his recollection of the timing of Wilson's approval are simply wrong. The number of 1918 Rose Bowl players who were killed in action is exaggerated regardless of how one counts the numbers. In telling this story we can set the record straight regarding Beckett's claim, while also acknowledging that the number of American men who died in action in WWI was horrendous given the short time American troops were in battle. The memories of the men who died in battle, along with those who fought but did not die while facing a determined enemy, should not be forgotten. Their willingness to put their lives on the line is sufficient and humbling to anyone looking back one hundred years later.

I do not know why Beckett made his claim, but his misstatement does not matter in the end. The ultimate issue is not the math, it's the men. The real story is about the men that fought in WWI and those that followed in later generations that showed a willingness to train for and enter battle despite their fears. Their willingness to face those odds deserves our respect whether they faced those odds one hundred years ago or will do so tomorrow.

APPENDIX A: PROFILES

The Profiles includes key information for each player. Newspaper articles were among the key information sources for identifying which players were on the rosters, the details of the games, and many elements of the players' military and civilian careers. The newspapers articles often have errors, so every effort was made to use multiple sources to document the lives of the players and the games they played. Judgment was applied when the sources conflicted and some errors in judgment were likely made along the way.

Beyond newspaper articles, other sources included:

- Census records indicating their family structure, places of birth, residence, and death, as well as their occupations
- Military records such as WWI draft registration forms, "Old Man's" draft registration forms completed during WWII, and applications for veterans' headstones, if completed. Veterans from California, Utah, Ohio, and Pennsylvania often have state-level records useful in tracking their movements within the military. Troopship passenger/embarkation lists for those traveling to or from

France were useful for those in Army, and a handful of Marines.

- Unit histories commonly published by alumni of those units following WWI. Campaign and unit histories published by the military and related commissions were also used extensively
- Other information came from college yearbooks, alumni directories, fraternity publications, and the like
- Newspaper obituaries, state death indices, and Social Security Claim records related to their passing

Summary biographical information and a limited number of citations are provided for each player, coach, and athletic official. The citations focus on their time immediately before, during, and after their military service and team membership.

Some players were identified as having been on the teams, but insufficient information was found to profile them. Generally, the players that have not been accounted for were identified as being on one of the teams in one or two sources those sources provide minimal information to identify them (e.g., last name only or last name and initials only. The information that has been found for these players is included below.

The information for each player follows the following format:

Surname, First and Middle Names

Birth: Date of birth | | Death: Date of death | | Football team and seasons played | | Participation in 1917 or 1918 service football season | | WWI: Military rank/rating and unit during the WWI era | | Military rank/rating and unit post WWI as appropriate

The high schools, colleges, and other amateur teams they played for are listed where known, along with the seasons/years during which they played rather than academic years. All information is limited by the level of detail available in game reports, military records, and other sources, in addition to my ability to locate and confirm relevant information.

APPENDIX B: CAMP LEWIS / 91ST DIVISION

The roster for the Camp Lewis team is based on newspaper articles covering individual games, pre-Rose Bowl articles listing the soldiers that trained for and/or traveled to Pasadena, and articles published in the days leading up to the 1918 Rose Bowl. Key sources listing multiple players follow.

'How Camp Lewis Sizes Up,' *Los Angeles Times*, December 27, 1917.

'All-Star Eleven Ready for New Year's Day Struggle in South,' *Over The Top (Camp Lewis)*, December 29, 1917.

'Camp Lewis Has Strong Grid Eleven to Battle the Marines New Years Day,' *Salt Lake City Tribune*, December 30, 1917.

'Camp Lewis has a Big Line and a Light but Fast Set of Backs,' *Los Angeles Times*, December 31, 1917.

Austin, Charles Allphin

Born: June 6, 1892 || Died: March 15, 1980 || Stanford '14-'15 || Practiced with the team prior to the Rose Bowl || WWI: Pvt., 2nd Lt., Air Service, Gerstner Field

Austin played rugby and baseball for Stanford, becoming Santa Clara's rugby coach in 1916. He was coaching there at the time he was drafted. After the war, Austin was involved in automotive sales and was the coach of the 1924 U.S. Olympic Rugby team that won a gold medal in Paris. He also coached high school rugby in the 1930s while working for Ford Motor Company.

'"S" Men of Past Nearly All in U.S. Service,' *Daily Palo Alto,* January 18, 1918.

'Athletics is Big Feature of Camps,' *Great Falls Tribune,* March 6, 1918.

Austin, C.A. 'Report of Coach of Rugby Team' in Thompson, Robert M. *Report on VIII Olympiad, Paris, France, 1924.* New York: American Olympic Association, 1924.

Bartlett, William Kenneth

Born: October 23, 1896 || Died: December 12, 1946 || Football: Oregon '14-'16, '19 || Started for 316ᵗʰ Sanitary Train against 91ˢᵗ Division, then started all remaining games for Camp Lewis || WWI: AEF 361ˢᵗ Ambulance Co, 316ᵗʰ Sanitary Train

Ken Bartlett played every minute of the 1917, 1918, and 1920 Rose Bowls for Oregon and Camp Lewis. He set the American junior record in the discus before placing fifth in the event at the 1920 Olympic Games in Antwerp. Bartlett coached Oregon's freshmen football team in 1920 and played football for the Multnomah Athletic Club during the early 1920s. He later became involved in insurance, investments, and the importing business in San Francisco.

'Oregon Football Supports Sing Praises of Heads,' *Oregon Daily Journal (Portland),* December 8, 1918.

'Oregon is Ready for Grid Work,' *Oregon Daily Journal (Portland),* September 14, 1919.

'Oregon's Discus Ace Will Face Husky Finn,' *Evening Journal (Wilmington, DE),* August 10, 1920.

Bynon, Allan Alfred

Born: February 29, 1896 || Died: May 4, 1946 || Willamette '16 || Substituted in two games || WWI: AEF 2ⁿᵈ Lt., promoted to 1ˢᵗ Lt. and Captain while serving in the Quartermaster Corps in Tours, France

A track and football athlete at Willamette, Bynon passed the Oregon bar exam before enlisting. He was practicing for the Rose Bowl when he received orders to ship to Europe. Bynon was the first service Rose Bowl player to reach France, returned to the States for a brief time, and went back to France in March 1918. After the war, Bynon was a lawyer in private practice, then spent four years as an Assistant U.S. Attorney. He was in the Oregon state legislature from 1928 to 1936 and later served as a legal adviser to Oregon's governor.

'Star Athletes of Northwest Enlist,' *Sunday Oregonian*, May 27, 1917.

'Miss Florence Hofer and Lieutenant Allan Bynon Marry – more,' *Statesman Journal*, December 11, 1917.

'Captain Bynon Home From San Francisco on Liberty,' *Statesman Journal (Salem)*, May 2, 1919.

Christensen / Christy, Anker Lawrence

Born: April 20, 1890 | | Died: June 3, 1974 | | Montana '15-'16, '19 | | Started all but one game at guard, including the 1918 Rose Bowl | | WWI: AEF. Shipped to France in March 1918 with Quartermaster Corps, General Repair Unit. Promoted to Captain

Christensen graduated from Montana State in mechanical engineering in 1920. He changed his surname to Christy in early 1920s and spent much of his career with Pure Oil Company. The company named the "world's most advanced" tugboat in his honor. He became President of the Missouri Valley Terminals in 1960.

'Montana Athletes Show in Line-Up of Soldier Teams,' *Great Falls Tribune*, January 2, 1918.

'Most Modern Tow-Boat Ducks Under Bridges,' *Star Tribune (Minneapolis)*, August 18, 1941.

Cook, Samuel "Sam"

Born: December 23, 1889 | | Died: June 20, 1980 | | Oregon '13-'14, Montana '15 | | Started for 316th Sanitary Train against 91st Division, then started 3 games for Camp Lewis, including the 1918 Rose Bowl | | WWI: AEF. 316th Sanitary Train, 364th Field Hospital

Sam Cook was an assistant football coach at Montana in 1916. After the war, he was a civil engineer in general practice and then held several highway-engineering roles.

'Sam Cook Assistant Coach,' *Eugene Guard*, November 14, 1916.

'Football Stars are after Commissions,' *Oregon Daily Journal (Portland)*, January 13, 1918.

Craig, Harry John

Born: November 30, 1894 || Died: January 29, 1933 || Wyoming '13-'16 || Started all but one game at fullback, including 1918 Rose Bowl || WWI: 2nd Lt. with 361st, G, H, and HQ. Cos.; Promoted to 1st Lt for gallantry. Promoted to Captain in France

Craig became a high school teacher and coach and played for the first professional basketball team on the West Coast (Arleta Athletic Club of Portland).

'Officers' Team Plays U. of W.,' *Tacoma Times*, January 31, 1918.

'War Service of the University of Wyoming." *University of Wyoming Bulletin*, December 1918,

'Multnomah Beats Army Boys, 14-7,' Oregon Daily Journal (Portland), November 20, 1921.

Damkroger, Ernest Leapart

Born: June 6, 1894 || Died: June 6, 1984 || Springfield College'15-'16 || Started at guard versus 316th Sanitary Train and Oregon State Freshman. On roster for Mare Island game || WWI: AEF 2nd Lt., 361st. 361st Athletic Officer at Camp Lewis. Coordinated supplies during Meuse-Argonne

Damkroger served as the athletic officer for the 361st Infantry while playing on the Camp Lewis team. He spent most of his career on Maui and is frequently mentioned, though not admiringly, in Julie Checkoway's *The Three-Year Swim Club*, which chronicles the path of Japanese-Americans youths on Maui as they progress from swimming in a sugar-plantation ditch to national and Olympic prominence. He was the USO Director on Maui during WWII. One of his sons, Ernest, was killed in action in Italy during WWII. He retired in 1951 and returned to his home in Santa Cruz, California where he was active in the Kiwanis, Goodwill, and Boy's Club.

'Betrothal of Miss Firestein and Lieut. Damkroger,' *Santa Cruz Evening News,* December 7, 1917.

'Camp All-Stars Win,' *Sunday Oregonian,* November 4, 1917.

Checkoway, Julie. *The Three-Year Swim Club, Untold Story of Maui's Sugar Ditch Kids and Their Quest for Olympic Glory.* New York: Grand Central Publishing, 2015.

Dear, Bandini

Born: July 27, 1889 || Died: January 14, 1970 || Alhambra HS || No record of playing during the regular season, but was on the 1918 Rose Bowl roster || WWI: AEF. Stable Sgt., 364th MG Co., Wounded by shrapnel at Meuse-Argonne

Following the war, Bandini returned to San Marino, California, to manage the family farm and later became an oil broker.

'Stir Athletes with Hit Iron,' *Los Angeles Times,* December 8, 1907.

'Sergt. Bandini Wounded in Action,' *Los Angeles Herald,* October 31, 1918.

Dee, Emmet Lawrence "Skimmett"

Born: May 10, 1896 || Died: June 2, 1952 || Butte HS '14-15, Montana State '19 || No record of playing during the regular season, but substituted at right end in the 1918 Rose Bowl || WWI: Pvt., 166th Depot Brig., Batt. 19, 75 Co. while at Camp Lewis

A high school teammate of Fred Molthen (1918 Mare Island), they won the 1915 Montana and Intermountain championships. Dee played at Montana State for one year, and coached high school and semipro football over the years. He spent his career in insurance sales and management.

'Sport Comment,' *Great Falls Tribune,* December 9, 1914.

'Montana State Loses Well Played Contest to Utah Aggies' Team,' *Great Falls Tribune,* October 26, 1919.

'Two Montana Men to Play in Rose Bowl,' *Great Falls Tribune,* December 24, 1943.

Frolich, A. T.

Born: Unknown || Died: Unknown || Unknown school || Traveled with the team to the 1918 Rose Bowl, but did not play in the game || WWI: Pvt., 347th Field Artillery

Insufficient information found to identify this player.

'Camp Team Gets Daily Practise,' *Tacoma Times,* December 13, 1917.

Gard, Frank Jacob "Deacon" or "Deke"

Born: March 27, 1892 || Died: September 29, 1918 || Stanford Rugby '11-'14 || Started at left end in the 362nd Officers' games and for Camp Lewis against Multnomah. Substituted in two other games, including the 1918 Rose Bowl || WWI: AEF. 1st Lt., 362nd, M Co.; Killed in action during the attack on Gesnes in the Meuse-Argonne

Gard captained Stanford's Rugby team in 1914, lettered in track as a half-miler, and graduated with a degree in Chemistry. He captained the American rugby team in their games against Australia in 1912 and New Zealand in 1913.

'Camp Lewis Athlete Killed in Fighting,' *Sunday Oregonian,* December 1, 1918.

'Honor Roll,' *Stanford Illustrated Review,* Palo Alto: The Alumni Association of Leland Stanford Junior University. Vol. 20, Issue 7, 1919.

McCrery, Nigel. *Into Touch, Rugby Internationals Killed in the Great War.* South Yorkshire, United Kingdom: Pen & Sword Military, 2014.

Gougar, Edward Eugene

Born: June 11, 1891 || Died: November 11, 1954 || None || On travel roster for the 1918 Rose Bowl || Pre-WWI: Four years as an ordinary seaman in the U.S. Navy, serving aboard the U.S.S. Vermont in 1910 || WWI: 316th Engineers, D Co.

Gougar worked as a machinist prior to joining the Army. After the war he joined the Los Angeles Fire Department and was credited with rushing into a burning building to save a crippled woman. He also was the trainer for the LAFD football team in 1928 that beat the New York FD, 59-0, before 37,000 fans at the Polo Grounds.

'Fighting Footballers From Camp Lewis, Ready For The Marines,' *San Francisco Chronicle*, December 30, 1917.

'Police Man and Dog Save Lives,' *Los Angeles Times*, May 13, 1927.

'Firemen Entrain Tonight,' *Los Angeles Times*, October 11, 1928.

Green, Harry Melvin

Born: September 4, 1894 || Died: June 27, 1977 || Utah State '12-'14 || Started against Mare Island at right guard and substituted in five other games, including the 1918 Rose Bowl || WWI: Sgt., 362nd, G Co.; 2nd Lt.

Harry Green farmed and did mechanical work before going to Camp Lewis. He entered the ROTC program in 1918 and was sent to Camp Bowie for further training and did not go to France. After the war, he worked as a mechanical engineer, before spending most of his career involved in tire sales and sales management.

'Utah Agricultural College Football Squad of 1913,' *Salt Lake Tribune*, December 21, 1913.

'Marine Eleven to Meet Soldiers,' *Ogden Standard*, November 10, 1917.

'Football Stars are after Commissions,' *Oregon Daily Journal (Portland)*, January 13, 1918.

Guisto, Louis Joseph

Born: January 16, 1895 || Died: October 15, 1989 || St. Mary's (CA) '12-'15 || Did not appear in a game for Camp Lewis, but was touted in newspaper reports as being likely to play in the Mare Island and Multnomah AC games. He also played baseball for Camp Lewis || WWI: AEF Sgt., 363rd, H Co.; Wounded in the thigh and gassed at Meuse-Argonne

Guisto played for the Cleveland Indians in 1916 and 1917, and rejoined the Indians for the 1921, 1922, and 1923 seasons, but had difficulty breathing in Cleveland's climate and was sent back to the minors. After his playing career, he managed minor league teams for three years (1929-1931) and then took over the program at St.

Mary's, which he coached as late as 1955. He also was an assistant football coach at St. Mary's and ran the student commissary for years. St. Mary's named its baseball stadium for him in 1928. It remains named in his honor today.

'Guisto is Called Equal of Lajoie,' *Fort Wayne News*, March 22, 1917.

'Guisto in Football Squad at Camp Lewis,' *Oakland Tribune*, November 14, 1917.

'Louis Guisto is Home from the War,' *San Francisco Chronicle*, April 24. 1919.

Hastings, (Unknown)

Born: Unknown | | Died: Unknown | | Unknown school | | Traveled with the team to the 1918 Rose Bowl, but did not play in the game | | WWI: Unknown rank

Insufficient information found to identify this player.

Camp Team Gets Daily Practise, *The Tacoma Times*, December 13, 1917.

'All-Star Eleven Ready for New Year's Day Struggle in South,' *Over The Top (Camp Lewis)*, December 29, 1917. (Not sourced from newspapers.com.)

Holden, William Forrest

Born: December 1, 1891 | | Died: September 29, 1974 | | Oregon '11-'13, Multnomah AC '14-'16, 19 | | Started for the 316ᵗʰ Sanitary Train versus the 91ˢᵗ Division and substituted for Camp Lewis against Mare Island | | WWI: Sgt., 316ᵗʰ Sanitary Train; Lt., Motor Transport Corps

William Holden was involved in the automotive business before the war. That experience led him to being transferred to the Motor Transport Corps in Detroit until his discharge in January 1919. He played football for the Multnomah AC from 1919 to 1923. During that time, he opened an "automotive hotel" in Portland with 400 cars available for sale, repair shops, and elevators to move the cars in the multi-story building. The business appears to have failed. He became a merchant seaman and was in the insurance business in

Shanghai at the start of Sino-Japanese hostilities. Information on his later life has not been located.

'Field Hospital Unit Leaves City Tonight for American Lake,' *Oregon Daily Journal (Portland), July 15, 1917.*

'Oregon Furnishing Stars for Football Team at Camp Lewis,' *Oregon Daily Journal (Portland),* October 21, 1917.

'Bill Holden is Home,' *Morning Register (Eugene),* July 19, 1919.

Hollywood, Walter Parks

Born: January 6, 1894 || Died: October 1, 1967 || Santa Monica HS '12; USC Law || No record of playing during the regular season, but was on the 1918 Rose Bowl roster || WWI: Pvt., 364th, H Co.; then Cpl., 316th Engineers. Transferred to the Air Service Signal Corps at Kelly Field, Dallas, then to Payne Field, Mississippi where he was promoted to Sgt.

Hollywood worked as the Los Angeles agent for International Correspondence Courses before the war. He became a carpenter and then was involved in advertising sales in the early days of radio broadcasting. He worked in real estate development in the Los Angeles area during the late 1920s and returned to carpentry and construction work for the remainder of his career.

'One Pasadenan on Team from Camp Lewis: W. P. Hollywood Gets Free Trip Home for Xmas with Relatives,' *Pasadena Star News,* December 26, 1917.

'Large Owners Bear Cost,' *Los Angeles Times,* February 12, 1928.

'Fifteen Million Dollars to be Spent in 1928 Subdivision Development,' *Van Nuys News,* February 10, 1928.

Hunter, Frederick Preston "Jumbo"

Born: November 12, 1886 || Died: May 29, 1962 in Mexico City || Washington State '08-'10 (captain '10), Camp Lewis '18 || Started two games, substituted in two others on the line, and was on the 1918 Rose Bowl roster || WWI: Sgt., 362nd, L Co.; Entered ROTC and was commissioned as 2nd Lt.

Hunter was the captain of the Washington State football team in 1910. Prior to Camp Lewis, he worked in mining and was a fraternity inspector. He stayed at Camp Lewis for the duration of the war, helping train the 13th Division. Green was married soon after his discharge, but his wife died of influenza in 1920. He worked in the mining industry and eventually moved to Mexico.

'Many Pullmanites Fraternize at Butte,' *Pullman Herald,* February 2, 1917.

'Staters to Meet Fast Army Team,' *Pullman Herald,* October 5, 1917.

Hughes, Ed R., 'Sport Talk,' *San Francisco Chronicle,* January 15, 1918.

Huntley, Floyd Jerry "Peck"

Born: September 16, 1890 || Died: February 17, 1959 || Oregon State '09-'10, '13-'14 || Huntley started at end in the regular-season Mare Island game, but there are no records indicating he played in other games || WWI: AEF. Sgt., 346th Field Artillery, HQ Co.

Huntley worked as a commercial fisherman before the war. He was the Sheriff of Curry County, Oregon from 1920 to 1928, operated a drug store, and ended his career as a laborer for a concrete firm. He was named to Oregon State's All-Time Football team in the 1940s or 1950s.

'Butte Lad Plays on Marine Eleven,' *Butte Daily Post,* November 10, 1917.

'211 Successful in Training Camp,' *Oregon Daily Journal (Portland),* April 26, 1918.

'Oklahoman Boosts Oregon Hunting,' *Oregon Daily Journal (Portland),* October 19, 1920.

Kapple, Charles Dixon "Dick"

Born: March 1, 1892 || Died: August 17, 1949 || Utah State '13, '15-'16 || Played on 362nd Officers and Camp Lewis teams. Started at QB for both teams in most games. Substituted at QB in the 1918 Rose Bowl || WWI: AEF. 1st Lt., 362nd, F Co.; Hospitalized after being gassed at Meuse-Argonne || WWII: Rejoined Army prior to WWII, transferred to the Army Air Force, taught math for the 36th Army Air Force, Technical School Group. Major at retirement.

Dick Kapple became a high school teacher and coach in Utah, winning two state basketball championships and reaching the finals three other times. He also coached six state track championship teams. Following a heart attack while in the Army Air Corps in 1944, he returned to high school teaching.

'Cowboys Trim Watson's Team in Logan Game,' *Salt Lake City Tribune*, October 22, 1916.

'Utah Boys Star in Football,' *Ogden Standard*, November 26, 1917.

'Famous Aggie Star Wins Decoration for Valor,' *Salt Lake City Tribune*, April 17, 1919.

Keck, Walter McHewell

Born: July 16, 1890 | | Died: April 17, 1980 | | Oregon State '09-'11, Multnomah '12-'15 | | Substituted in three games for Camp Lewis; practiced with team prior to the Rose Bowl, but did not travel to Rosa\e Bowl | | WWI: AEF. 1ˢᵗ Lt., 362ⁿᵈ, F Co. | | Post WWI: Oregon National Guard during WWII

Keck captained the Multnomah Athletic Club football team in 1913 and 1914. He operated several retail stores during his career. Keck and his wife were active in VFW fundraising during WWII.

'Keck's Punting is Key to Clubmen,' *Oregon Daily Journal (Portland)*, December 28, 1911.

'Tacoma Gets Game,' *Morning Oregonian*, November 27, 1917.

'Captain Ackley Back With Cross,' *Oregon Daily Journal (Portland)*, April 3, 1919.

Lane, Charles David "Truck"

Born: November 17, 1892 | | Died: March 27, 1948 | | California '17 | | Started at right guard versus Multnomah and was on 1918 Rose Bowl roster | | WWI: Acting Sgt., 364ᵗʰ Artillery; As a 2ⁿᵈ Lt., he transferred to Fort Sill, Oklahoma

Truck Lane worked as a gold miner after the war, and then was an insurance agent in Long Beach for several decades.

'Stars Coming Back,' *San Francisco Chronicle*, October 16, 1917.

'Truck Lane Shines in Multnomah Defeat,' *Oakland Tribune,* November 17, 1917.

'Athlete Makes Good in 'Foreign Legion',' *Oregon Daily Journal (Portland),* November 28, 1918.

Lentz, Harry Brewer

Born: June 6, 1891 || Died: December 8, 1977 || Occidental '13-'15, UC-Santa Barbara baseball '16 || Substituted at quarterback versus 316th Sanitary Train || WWI: Pvt., engineering unit at Camp Lewis, transferred to 41st Division, 116th Engineers, transferred to 1st Division, C Co. in France. Severely wounded

Lenz starred at quarterback for three years at Occidental before transferring to UC-Santa Barbara for his senior year. He was teaching industrial arts and physical education at Stockton High School when he was drafted and sent to Camp Lewis. Lenz was one of 500 men transferred from Camp Lewis to the 41st Division, 116th Engineers and shipped to France in November 1917. Upon arrival, the 41st Division became a replacement division and Lenz was transferred to the 1st Division. He was severely wounded and returned to the U.S. in October 1918. By 1919, he was teaching at Stockton High School where his basketball teams won 24 conference titles in 26 years and won four state titles. He also coached the swimming team to two state titles. He was a referee for major college football games in California for several decades.

Note: A newspaper box score shows a player named "Lentz" substituted at quarterback for the 91st versus the 316th. Although Harry Brewer Lenz has not been independently confirmed as that player, he was at Camp Lewis at the time and as a former star college QB, is believed to be the player mentioned in the article.

'Huns and Tigers Trying to Justify Themselves,' *Los Angeles Times,* November 19, 1915.

'Californians in the Casualties,' *Santa Cruz Evening News,* November 7, 1918.

'Prep Sports: Tarzans Were Powerhouse,' *Record,* September 30, 2015. Accessed November 2, 2017.

http://www.recordnet.com/article/20150930/sports/150939961

Luis, Franklin Alfred

Born: February 19, 1891 || Died: August 19,1965 || Stanford, Arizona '12-'15 || Substitute QB versus Multnomah AC and Fort Stevens || WWI: AEF, Pvt., then Cpl., 316th Engineers. Became member of 316th Engineers Band in Europe

F.A. Luis and Emzy Lynch played for Arizona in 1915 when they played Occidental, quarterbacked by Pete Lenz, their Camp Lewis teammate. Occidental beat Arizona in that game, but Arizona fought valiantly in the defeat prompting a *Los Angeles Times* reporter to write, "The Arizona men showed the fight of wild cats." The description caught on and Arizona's athletic teams have since been known as the Wildcats. Fluent in Chinese, Luis planned to move to Shanghai after graduating with a mining engineering degree, but it is not clear whether he did so. Luis worked in engineering after the war, and then took over the family farm in Alisal, California, where he appears to have spent the rest of his life.

Alma Moter to Send Children All Over Globe, *Arizona Daily Star*, May 25, 1915.

Little, George C. *History of the 316th Engineers, A Record of Military Operations from August 1917 to April 1919.* 316th Engineers. U.S. Army Heritage and Education Center, Carlisle, PA.

'Arizona Album,' *Tucson Daly Citizen*, February 7, 1973.

Lynch, Emzy Harvey

Born: November 13, 1895 || Died: July 4,1979 || Arizona '14-'16, '19 (Capt.) || Started three games on offensive line and substituted in three others. Was on the 1918 Rose Bowl roster || WWI: AEF Lt., 347th Field Artillery. Was part of the Army of Occupation of Germany || WWII: Remained in the Army Reserves for decades and served in domestic roles during WWII, along with two tours in Japan after the war, where he is reported to have served as an aide to General Douglas MacArthur.

Emzy Lynch was Arizona's captain in 1919 and was All-Southwestern for the third time, before being named the captain Arizona's all-time team later in the 1920s. He coached at Northern Arizona, but spent most of his career in government services. His son was killed in action in the Pacific during WWII. Lynch held a series of court-related and civil-service roles after WWII.

'Phoenix Society to Miss Mrs. E. H. Lynch,' *Arizona Republic*, October 5, 1919.

'E.H. "Swede" Lynch Made Athletic Coach at Flagstaff School,' *Arizona Republic*, August 25, 1927.

'They Fought Like Wildcats Centennial (1914-2014): Emzy Lynch family member recalls peculiar prediction by great uncle,' *AllSports Tucson.com*, August 24, 2014. Accessed November 2, 2017.

http://allsportstucson.com/2014/08/10/they-fought-like-wildcats-centennial-1914-2014-emzy-lynch-family-member-recalls-peculiar-prediction-by-great-uncle/

MacRae, Raymond D.

Born: February 10, 1888 || Died: September 15, 1966 || Willamette '10-12, Multnomah '13-'14 || MacRae started at end the second half of the season, including the 1918 Rose Bowl || WWI: 1st Lt., 316ᵗʰ Sanitary

MacRae captained Willamette's football team in 1912 before going to medical school and was a railroad doctor before entering the military. He stayed at Camp Lewis during the war and published an article in the January 1919 *Journal of the American Medical Association* based on his work there. After the war, MacRae stayed the Tacoma area where he was a radiologist at several hospitals, the Burlington Northern Railroad, and McNeil Island Prison.

'M'Rae Captain,' *Tacoma Times*, December 12, 1911.

'Pick Camp Lewis Team for Trip,' *Los Angeles Times*, December 21, 1917.

Jackson, William D., M.D., *History of Radiology in Pierce County. Accessed* November 2, 2017.

http://bearboat.net/PierceCountyRadiology/111007PierceCounty RadiologyHistoryV2

Maguire, Alfred Leo

Born: February 18, 1892 || Died: July 7, 1964 || California '12'-15 || Substituted in three games during regular season || WWI: 2ⁿᵈ Lt., Was transferred to Washington, D.C. in unknown role

Alfred Maguire returned to Los Angeles after the war and was involved in insurance and dairy sales.

'California's Football Prospects are Bright,' *Los Angeles Herald,* September 18, 1916.

'All-Cantonment Team to Start Season Saturday,' *Tacoma Times,* October 24, 1917.

'War Service Record.' The California Alumni Fortnightly, October 1918.

McKay, Douglas Cameron

Born: August 21, 1894 || Died: May 28, 1949 || North Dakota '13-'16 || Started every game for Camp Lewis, generally at left halfback || WWI: AEF. Sgt., Sgt. Maj., Graduated from the third ROTC at Camp Lewis and was commissioned in France as a 2ⁿᵈ Lt. Was with 59ᵗʰ Coastal Artillery at St. Mihiel and Meuse-Argonne.

McKay was a mining engineer in Utah before the war and returned there afterward. In 1939, McKay and his family moved to the Philippines where he was the General Manager of the Mindanao Mother Load Mines in Surigao. They were in the Philippines when the Japanese invaded. McKay, his wife, and daughter escaped to the hills and were eventually rescued and taken by submarine to Australia. Their son, Robert, was interned, spending the last nine months of the war in Manila's infamous Bilibid Prison. The McKays went back to the Philippines in 1947, but returned to the U.S. soon after due to McKay's poor health.

'Camp Lewis Coach and Two Soldiers Gridiron Stars,' *Oregon Daily Journal (Portland),* November 4, 1917.

'Officers Training Camp', *Great Falls Tribune,* May 1, 1918.

'McKays Are Safe In Philippines,' *Reno Gazette-Journal,* December 25, 1943.

McKinney, Ward Frank

Born: September 17, 1894 || Died: January 16, 1945 || Oregon '16, '19 || Played for the 316ᵗʰ Sanitary Train versus 91ˢᵗ Division, then started one game and substituted in two others at end for Camp Lewis, including the 1918 Rose Bowl || WWI: AEF. Sgt., 316th Sanitary Train

Ward McKinney played on Oregon's 1917 and 1920 Rose Bowl teams. He operated a cigar store in the Hotel Olympic in Salem, Oregon for many years.

'Ambulance Corps Has Football Team,' *Eugene Daily Guard,* September 13, 1917.

'Veterans of 316ᵗʰ Sanitary Train to be Given Welcome,' *Oregon Daily Journal (Portland),* May 7, 1919.

'Former Webfoot Gridder Passes,' *Daily Capital Journal (Salem),* January 18, 1945.

McLoughlin / McLaughlin, (Unknown)

Born: Unknown || Died: Unknown || Unknown school || Substituted at right tackle against the 316ᵗʰ Sanitary Train || WWI: Unknown rank

Insufficient information found to identify this player.

'Army Elevens Tie,' *Sunday Oregonian,* October 28, 1917.

Millard, L.C.

Born: Unknown || Died: Unknown || Unknown school || Mentioned in article as practicing with team before the Rose Bowl, but did not travel to the 1918 Rose Bowl || Pvt., 166ᵗʰ Depot Brigade || WWI: Unknown rank

Insufficient information found to identify this player.

'Camp Team Gets Daily Practise,' *Tacoma Times,* December 13, 1917.

Monteith, Thomas Orville

Born: January 26, 1896 || Died: May 28, 1955 || Oregon '14-'16 || Played for the 316ᵗʰ Sanitary Train versus 91ˢᵗ Division, then started two games and substituted in four others, primarily at fullback, including the 1918 Rose Bowl || WWI: AEF. Pvt., 316ᵗʰ Sanitary Train, Sgt., 316ᵗʰ Sanitary Train

Monteith played on Oregon's 1917 Rose Bowl team and was

working in a cannery in Alaska when America entered the war. Monteith became an osteopathic surgeon and practiced in Springfield, Massachusetts.

'Oregon Spirit Does the Trick,' *Morning Register (Eugene)*, November 21, 1915.

'Oregon Physicians Reach New York on Way Home,' *Oregon Daily Journal (Portland)*, April 21, 1919.

'1916 'Greats' Now Business Men', *Old Oregon*, University of Oregon Alumni Association, October 1941.

Olsen, O.C.

Born: Unknown | | Died: Unknown | | Unknown school | | Mentioned in article as practicing with team before the Rose Bowl, but did not travel with the 1918 Rose Bowl | | WWI: Unknown rank

Insufficient information found to identify this player.

'Camp Team Gets Daily Practise,' *Tacoma Times*, December 13, 1917.

Patterson, "Pat"

Born: Unknown | | Died: Unknown | | Unknown school | | Substituted at right halfback versus Multnomah | | WWI: Unknown rank

Sources indicate Patterson was from Minnesota and was living in Ogden, Utah, in the 1930s, but this information has been insufficient to identify this player.

'Marine Eleven to Battle with Soldiers' Team,' *Oregon Daily Journal (Portland)*, November 9, 1917.

'Utahns Played in Rose Bowl Game,' *Ogden Standard-Examiner*, December 27, 1934.

'Fighting Footballers from Camp Lewis, Ready for Marines', *San Francisco Chronicle*, December 30, 1917.

Quill, Carl John "Jack" or "C. J."

Born: May 3, 1891 | | Died: November 5, 1968 | | None | | Started for 316ᵗʰ Sanitary Train versus 91ˢᵗ Division and substituted into the Fort Stevens game. He was injured during practice in Pasadena and did not suit up for the 1918 Rose Bowl || WWI: Pvt., 316th Sanitary Train. Accepted into ROTC, but does not appear to have completed the class.

Quill was an engineer with the Tacoma Railway and Power Company and a top amateur baseball player before the war. Quill returned to TR&P after the war before joining and becoming an executive with North Coast Transportation Co., which was consolidated into the Greyhound network. He was also the President of the Tacoma Tigers minor league baseball organization.

'With the Amateurs', *Tacoma Times.* March 17, 1917.

'What has Become of the Old-Fashioned Football Star Who Had to Do Up His Hair at Nights?,' *Tacoma Times,* October 29, 1917.

'Moleskins Abandoned for Uniforms of O.D,' *Tacoma Times,* January 7, 1918.

Rheinschild, George William

Born: September 4, 1888 || Died: August 23, 1943 || Loyola Marymount '07-'09, Georgetown '11-'12 || Did not play in any games for Camp Lewis, but practiced with the team prior to the 1918 Rose Bowl || WWI: Pvt., 364th, D Co. Discharged for medical reasons in January 1918

Rheinschild played three years at Loyola Marymount and two years at Georgetown. While at Georgetown, he started in its 1912 game against Carlisle and Jim Thorpe, but was then declared ineligible for accepting money from fellow students. He worked as a fireman for a pipeline company before the war. Afterward, he worked as a carpenter, a fruit salesman, and in highway maintenance.

'Saints Strong in Utility Men,' *Los Angeles Herald,* September 26, 1908.

'Virginia had Ban put on G.U. Star, it is Said,' *Washington Post,* November 11, 1912.

'Camp Team Gets Daily Practise,' *Tacoma Times,* December 13, 1917.

Romney, Ernest Lowell "Dick"

Born: February 12, 1895 || Died: February 5, 1969 || Utah State '14-'16

|| *Romney started at right halfback throughout the season, including the 1918 Rose Bowl* || *WWI: Cpl., 166th Depot Brig., Batt. 10, Co. 38; Entered ROTC at Camp Lewis and was commissioned a 2nd Lt. before being sent to Camp Zachary Taylor as part of the 7th Regiment Field Artillery Replacement Depot*

Dick Romney lettered in football, basketball, baseball, and track at Utah State, and started on the 1916 AAU National Champion basketball team, before becoming a teacher. He was discharged in early 1919 and within months became head football, basketball, and track coach at Utah State. He remained the basketball coach until 1941 and the football coach until 1949, making Halls of Fame in both sports. He finished his career as the commissioner of the Mountain States Conference, the forerunner of the Western Athletic Conference. Utah State's football stadium was named in his honor until 2015.

'Romney Elected Basketball Pilot,' *Daily Utah Chronicle*, April 27, 1916.

'Utah Gridders Star on Camp Lewis Team,' *Salt Lake City Tribune*, December 9, 1917.

'Dick Romney Dies of Heart Attack,' *Ogden Standard-Examiner*, February 6, 1969.

Rowland, Raymond Holliday "Ray"

Born: June 3, 1892 || *Died: January 28, 1959* || *Willamette '10-'13* || *Started the Oregon State Freshmen game at fullback and substituted in three others at quarterback. He was not on the 1918 Rose Bowl roster* || *WWI: 2nd Lt., 1st Lt.*

Rowland was a practicing attorney in Astoria, Oregon, before volunteering for the first ROTC program at the Presidio. After the war, he worked as a laborer and foreman in steel mills in Cleveland and Massillon, Ohio. He later worked at or owned a tavern in Massillon, was arrested for operating slot machines, and had several alcohol-related arrests over the last fifteen years of his life.

'Galaxy of Willamette Football Stars,' *Statesman Journal (Salem)*, November 28, 1912.

'Camp All-Stars Win,' *Sunday Oregonian,* November 4, 1917.

'Slot Machines Seized at Club,' *Evening Independent (Massillon, OH),* August 18, 1943

Russell, William Alexander

Born: December 14, 1893 || Died: December 22, 1927 || California '13-'16 || Played for the 362ⁿᵈ Officers and Camp teams, starting at center in every game other than against the Chemawa Indian School. He was the team captain and started in the 1918 Rose Bowl || WWI: 2ⁿᵈ Lt., 362ⁿᵈ, MG Co., 1ˢᵗ Lt.

Russell played rugby for Cal until they reinstated football his junior and senior seasons, and was All-Pacific Coast as a senior. He worked as a civil engineer in the bridge industry, was married and had three children, but little else is known about his activities during and after the war.

'Opening American Football Game Saturday,' *San Francisco Chronicle,* September 12, 1916.

'Entire West Is Watching Big Grid Game Here,' *Tacoma Times, November 10, 1917.*

Sewell, Edward Granville

Born: September 13, 1899 || Died: April 22, 1954 || California '16, '19 || Played for the 362ⁿᵈ Officers and Camp Lewis teams. He started for the 362ⁿᵈ Officers versus Fort Flagler and substituted for Camp Lewis versus the University of Washington Naval Training Station. He was not on the 1918 Rose Bowl roster || Pre-WWI: AEF U.S. Navy, 4 years, Yeoman || WWI: 2ⁿᵈ Lt., 362ⁿᵈ, H Co.; In action at Meuse-Argonne and Lys-Scheldt

Edward Sewell returned to Cal for the 1919 season where he started several games. He had a long career as a high school teacher in the Los Angeles area and coached football and track.

'Straight Football Wins Over the Aerial Attack,' *Oakland Tribune,* November 11, 1916.

'Fighting Footballers From Camp Lewis, Ready For The Marines,' *San Francisco Chronicle,* December 30, 1917.

'Athletics at San Rafael High,' *San Anselmo Herald,* September 4, 1925.

Sharp, LeRoy Bassett "Roy"

Born: September 24, 1894 | | Died: August 5, 1977 | | California '14-'16 | | Started one game at left halfback for Camp Lewis and played in two other games as a substitute before starting the 1918 Rose Bowl at quarterback | | WWI: Pvt., 364th; 2nd Lt., 13th Balloon

Roy Sharp returned to the family farm after the war, but shortly thereafter started teaching and coaching in California, primarily in the Oakland public schools. He also coached an American Legion junior baseball team to the national championship in the 1930s.

'Great Football Speedster Has Earned Own Way Through Grammar, High School, College,' *Reno Gazette-Journal,* December 7, 1916.

'Grid Stars at U.S. Camp,' *Seattle Star,* October 12, 1917.

'Roster of Officers of the 13th Balloon Company,' 2nd Army, November 30, 1918, Accessed November 2, 2017.

https://www.fold3.com/image/19901817

'Ex-U.C. Grid Star to Coach Fremont High,' *Oakland Tribune,* August 9, 1925.

Snyder, William Carroll

Born: July 21, 1892 | | Died: March 4, 1934 | | Oregon '14-'16 | | Played for the 316th Sanitary Train versus 91st Division and started the rest for the season for Camp Lewis at left guard, including the 1918 Rose Bowl | | WWI: Pvt. 316th Sanitary; Passed the artillery officers' exam and was commissioned as a Lt. at Camp Taylor; Transferred to Camp Jackson

Snyder played for Oregon in the 1917 Rose Bowl and was named to Walter Camp's All-American third team. Snyder worked in technical and engineering-related sales before entering a home for disabled veterans in 1933.

'Three Members of the Famous 1916 Oregon Football Team,' *Sunday Oregonian,* December 2, 1917.

'Lieut. Snyder is Ill with Pneumonia,' *Oregon Daily Journal (Portland)*, October 2, 1918.

'Wartime Romance Ends with Armistice Wedding,' *Albany Evening Herald*, November 21, 1921.

Taylor, (Unknown)

Born: Unknown || Died: Unknown || Unknown school || Mentioned in article as practicing with team before the Rose Bowl, but did not travel to the 1918 Rose Bowl || WWI: Pvt., 166ᵗʰ Depot Brigade

Insufficient information found to identify this player.

'Camp Team Gets Daily Practise,' *Tacoma Times*, December 13, 1917.

Turner, Charles E. "Charlie"

Born: May 29, 1893 || Died: April 30, 1946 || Texas '13-'15 || Started at left end through most of the season, including the 1918 Rose Bowl || Pre-WWI: Pvt., Texas 2ⁿᵈ Infantry || WWI: Commissioned a 2ⁿᵈ Lt. in the artillery section at the Presidio, was sent from Camp Lewis to Camp Jackson for additional training. Joined the 91ˢᵗ Division's 347ᵗʰ Field while in France and spent time in the Army of Occupation in Germany

Turner was a star in football and wrestling at Texas and played for the 2ⁿᵈ Texas Infantry before the war. After his discharge, he worked in New York and Chicago as an electrical engineer and electrician. He was unemployed by 1940, but other details of his later life are unknown.

'Texas and Sewanee and Clash Here on Saturday, *Houston Post*, October 31, 1915.

'Marine Eleven to Meet Soldiers,' *Ogden Standard*, November 10, 1917.

Roster of the 347th Field Artillery, A.E.F., 1918-1919. San Francisco: H.S. Crocker. 1919. U.S. Army Heritage and Education Center, Carlisle, PA.

Warner, (Unknown)

Born: Unknown | | Died: Unknown | | Unknown school | | Substituted at right end versus the 316th Sanitary Train | | WWI: Unknown rank

Insufficient information found to identify this player.

'Army Elevens Tie,' *Sunday Oregonian*, October 28, 1917.

Coaches and Administrators

Cook, Trevanion George "Van"

Born: March 10, 1871 | | Died: September 15, 1945 | | No college | | WWI: Captain, Athletic Director for Camp Lewis for both the 91st and 13th Divisions; then Director of Athletics, General Staff of the Army

Cook came to Camp Lewis after working twenty-one years as an athletic director including ten years at the New Your State School for the Deaf and Dumb, eight years at a Portland high school, two years with the Wallace, Idaho schools, and one year in Butte (MT) High School. A civilian, Cook was appointed a Captain when the Commission on Camp Activities gave commissions to a number of camp athletic directors to allow them to go with their division to France. After the war, he spent two years at Director of Athletics on the General Staff of the Army in Washington, D. C. He then returned to Washington and held various athletic director roles with community organizations and schools.

'Cook to Teach Soldiers,' *Statesman Journal*, August 29, 1917.

Henderson, Alice Palmer. *The Ninety-First, The First at Camp Lewis.* Tacoma, WA: John C. Barr, 1918.

'Athletic Course Will Be Given at Reed This Month,' *Oregon Daily Journal (Portland)*, February 4, 1921.

Kienholz, Edgar Harrison

Born: May 18, 1889 | | Died: March 27, 1948 | | Washington State '10-12 | | Assistant Athletic Director | | WWI: Pvt., Sgt.

Kienholz played halfback for Washington State, earning a master's degree in 1915, and was an assistant coach for their 1916 Rose Bowl team. He was the athletic instructor and coach at Long Beach (CA) High School when drafted. He returned to Long Beach after the war before being named the coach of all sports at Santa Clara. He moved to Occidental in 1928 and then to Cal Tech. He later became the principal at Glendale (CA) High School.

Henderson, Alice Palmer. *The Ninety-First, The First at Camp Lewis.* Tacoma, WA: John C. Barr, 1918.

'From the Fellows in the Service to the Fellows in the Service, Letter from Sgt, E. H. Kienholz,' *Powwow*, Washington States University, June 1918.

'Oxy Preps for Cal,' *Los Angeles Times*, November 6, 1930.

Pipal, Joseph A.

Born: January 18, 1874 || Died: August 10, 1955 || Beloit ex'05, Chicago, Yale, Harvard || Consulting Coach || WWI: Consulting coach for Camp Lewis leading up the 1918 Rose Bowl

Pipal was born in Bohemia, then part of the Austro-Hungarian Empire. He attended Beloit College, but did not graduate before leaving for Doane (1902). He subsequently studied at Chicago under Amos Alonzo Stagg, at Harvard and Yale. Pipal coached at Dickinson (1907) and South Dakota (1910) before taking the helm at Occidental from 1911 to 1915. He coached Oregon State in 1916 and 1917, before becoming the athletic director for Camp Kearney. Sent to France he coached the U.S. track team in the Inter-Allied Games before the YMCA sent him to coach the Czech team in the 1920 Olympic Games. He also coached the Czech track team in the 1932 Olympic Games in Los Angeles. He was Occidental, coaching football from 1921 to 1923, before concentrating on track until his retirement in 1946.

'Pipal to Aid Camp Lewis,' *Los Angeles Times*, December 14, 1917.

'Coach Who Devised Lateral Pass is Dead,' *St. Louis Post-Dispatch*, August 12, 1955.

Stanton, William Lewis "Fox"

Born: May 20, 1874 || Died: November 28, 1946 || Drexel '92, Pennington Seminary '94-'96 || Head Football Coach, Camp Lewis || Pre-WWI: Pvt., Cpl. 3rd New Jersey Volunteer Infantry during Spanish-American War || WWI: 1st Lt., F Co., 316th Ammunition Train

Stanton was the captain of the Drexel football team in 1892 and played for Pennington Seminary from 1894-1896, captaining the team his senior year. He joined the 3rd New Jersey Volunteer Infantry during Spanish-American War, but his unit remained stateside. He then coached several Eastern prep schools before taking over at Pomona from 1908 to 1915, winning four conference titles. He coached Occidental to a conference title in 1916 and took on the role for Camp Lewis in 1917. Stanton served in France with the 91st Division's 316th Supply Train. He returned to Occidental for the 1919 and 1920 seasons before moving to Cal Tech where he coached from 1921 to 1941.

Stanton, William L., *General Index to Compiled Service Records of Volunteer Soldiers Who Served During the War with Spain.* Accessed November 2, 2017.

https://www.fold3.com/image/1/309317347

'"Fox" Stanton Resigns,' *Cal Tech Alumni Review,* California Institute of Technology, 1941.

APPENDIX C: 362ND REGIMENT OFFICERS

The roster for the 362nd Officers team includes those listed on the roster or included in the team picture in the game program for the Washington State game. Most officers were also verified using the 362nd Division's unit history. Others were added based on mentions in newspaper articles during the season.

Souvenir Football Program, Officers, 362nd Inf., vs. Washington State College, October 13, 1917. *Access*ed November 2, 2017. http://content.libraries.wsu.edu/utils/getfile/collection/wsu_fb/id /366/filename/339.pdf.

'Officers Tie Dietz,' *Sunday Oregonian*, October 14, 1917.

Meldrum, T. Ben and Axel A. Madsen. *A History of the 362nd Infantry Regiment*. Ogden & Salt Lake. A. L. Scoville Press. 1920.

Frank Gard, Dick Kapple, Bill Russell, and Edward Sewell played for the 362nd Officers and Camp Lewis teams. Their profiles are included with the Camp Lewis team.

Angus, Howard Weldon

Born: September 13, 1890 || Died: abt. February 9, 1956 || Occidental '10 || Started at left halfback versus Fort Flagler || WWI: AEF. 2nd Lt., D Co., 362nd; Promoted to 1st Lt., D Co. following the attack on Gesnes and promoted to Captain, D Co. later at Meuse-Argonne. Wounded and gassed, he rejoined the company for the Lys-Scheldt Offensive | | WWII: Lt. Col assigned to direct a Lockheed airplane factory in Burbank, California

Graduated from Occidental in 1913 and USC Law in 1916, while also working as a sportswriter for the *Los Angeles Times* from 1914 until he volunteered. Angus stayed in the Army until 1925 and then embarked on a career in advertising with RCA and NBC. After his return to duty in WWII, Angus became the Executive Vice President of the Air Power League, an industry group supporting the expansion of airports across the country.

'Football at Occidental,' *Los Angeles Times,* October 15, 1910.

'Camp Lewis Men Find Life of Soldier is Not All Drilling,' *Los Angeles Times,* November 25, 1917.

'Captain Howard Angus Back,' *Los Angeles Times,* May 8, 1919.

'Former 'Times' Sportswriter Dies,' *Los Angeles Times,* February 15, 1956.

Bell, William Morris

Born: November 29, 1895 | | Died: July 15, 1990 | | HS '16, Cal '20-'22 | | Played in the game versus the enlisted men, then started at left halfback versus Washington State and fullback versus Fort Flagler | | Pre-WWI: Served on Mexican border with the 7ᵗʰ Infantry of the California National Guard prior to WWI | | WWI: AEF. Sgt. 7ᵗʰ Inf. CA NG, 2ⁿᵈ Lt., 362ⁿᵈ, D Co., wounded while with 362ⁿᵈ, returned to U.S. as 1ˢᵗ Lt., 309ᵗʰ Infantry

After graduating from California, he joined Pacific Bell and was transferred to New York Bell, spending most of his career in Olean, New York. He was active in many community organizations.

'Big Squad Reports at Redlands High,' *Los Angeles Times,* September 22, 1916.

'West's Division Off to the Front,' *Los Angeles Times,* October 2, 1918.

'Hot Shots By Williams,' *Los Angeles Times,* March 1, 1922.

Burgard, John Clark

Born: March 21, 1891 || Died: May 31, 1962 || Oregon '16 || Substituted at guard against Washington State || WWI: AEF 1st Lt., 362nd, HQ Co., H Co., Awarded the Distinguished Service Cross for actions in Meuse-Argonne. Wounded twice in Belgium

Burgard was the Oregon baseball team student manager for three years. Burgard lived in California and Oregon after the war and helped manage the family insurance and investment business.

'Men in Many Lines Win Commissions,' *Sunday Oregonian*, August 19, 1917.

'Lieutenant Burgard Formerly with 91st is Back Again,' *Oregon Daily Journal (Portland)*, January 16, 1919.

'U.S. Gives Cross For Heroism to Californians,' *San Francisco Chronicle*, June 14, 1919.

Campbell, Frederick Lorne

Born: June 18, 1894 || Died: April 15, 1975 || Unknown || Played versus the enlisted men, substituted at guard against Washington State, and started at left tackle versus Fort Flagler || WWI: AEF 2nd Lt., 362nd, L Co., 1st Lt., 4th Division, 59th Infantry Regiment, L Co. || WWII: 1st Lt., Coastal Artillery Corps

Campbell was raised in Virginia, but worked for Bethlehem Steel before and after the war, and was working for them in Los Angeles when he volunteered. Campbell went to France with the 362nd, but transferred into the 4th Division's 59th Infantry Regiment while overseas. After the war, he worked for Bethlehem Steel for several years in Cuba and otherwise worked for them in Indiana throughout his career.

'Mr. and Mrs. Campbell and Son Have Returned,' *Winston-Salem Journal*, July 17, 1918.

Crary, George Egleston

Born: September 7, 1894 || Died: November 7, 1959 || Stanford Rugby '13-'14, LAAC Football '15 || Substituted in the line against Washington State || WWI: AEF 2nd Lt., 362nd, K Co.

Crary was a teammate of Frank Gard on Stanford's rugby team

prior to the war. After the war, he entered the investment business and held positions with E.F. Hutton and BankAmerica.

'Stanford Beats Barbs, 18-0,' *San Francisco Chronicle*, October 5, 1913.

'Billetted in a French Village,' *Los Angeles Times*, October 10, 1918.

'Soldiers Glad They are Back,' *San Bernardino County Sun*, May 3, 1919.

Dorris, Benjamin Fultz

Born: February 9, 1890 || Died: May 3, 1983 || Oregon '15 – no sports || Substituted at end against Washington State || WWI: AEF. 2nd Lt., 362nd, E Co.; H Co. Wounded in Belgium and awarded the Belgian Croix de Guerre

Dorris was president of his senior class at Oregon and involved in organized sports, but was not a varsity athlete. Following the war, he grew filberts and other nuts on his orchard in Oregon, was heavily involved in the American Legion as well as state politics, and was Oregon's Game Commissioner for a number of years.

'Salem Boy to Edit It,' Statesman Journal (Salem), May 2, 1913.

'Portland's Sons Make Most Wonderful War Record,' *Sunday Oregonian, July 20, 1919.*

'Lieutenant Dorris Badly Wounded, Home,' *Morning Register,* April 1, 1919.

Duerr, Arthur Christian

Born: March 6, 1895 || Died: August 4, 1976 || Culver Military '14, USC '16 - no sports || Played in the game versus the enlisted men, then started at right end against Washington State and Fort Flagler || WWI: AEF. 2nd Lt., 362nd, B Co., Promoted to 1st Lt. in France; Returned with the 101st Military Police Battalion

Attended Culver Military Academy in Indiana, is reported to have played football at the University of Chicago, and attended USC as a freshman in the 1916-17 academic year. After returning from France, he worked in real estate in Pasadena, then moved to Tulsa and was an oil broker and wildcatter the rest of his career.

'Little Fellow is Honored,' *Indianapolis Star,* December 18, 1913.

'Local Football Stars with U.S. in N.W.,' *San Francisco Chronicle,* October 13, 1917.

'Billetted in a French Village,' *Los Angeles Times,* October 10, 1918.

'Oil Men Here,' *El Paso Evening Post,* November 14, 1927.

Esmay, Rhodolph Leslie

Born: May 15, 1898 || Died: November 13, 1965 || Unknown || Played versus the enlisted men and substituted in the backfield versus Washington State || Pre-WWI: 2nd Wyoming National Guard || WWI: AEF. 2nd Lt., 362nd], I Co., Sent to France in June 1918 with 91st Division Advanced Party. Wounded in Europe

Esmay was a member of Wyoming's National Guard before the war. On his return, he worked for a short time as a civil engineer and was named the Adjutant General of Wyoming's National Guard, a position he held for thirty-five years. He was also the state Selective Service Commissioner from WWII into the Vietnam era.

'Officers Named from Students in Training,' *Oregon Daily Journal (Portland),* August 14, 1917.

Meldrum, T. Ben and Axel A. Madsen. *A History of the 362nd Infantry Regiment.* Ogden & Salt Lake. A. L. Scoville Press. 1920.

'Wyoming Draft Head Dies of Heart Attack,' *Idaho Free Press,* November 13, 1965.

Evans, Harry Llewellyn

Born: March 1, 1888 || Died: March 31, 1961 || Harvard '07 – no sports || Substituted at quarterback versus Washington State || WWI: AEF. 1st Lt., 362nd, A Co. AEF. Earned a regimental citation.

Prior to and after WWI, Evans spent his career in the family shipping and steamship business in San Francisco. His son, Harry L. Evans, Jr., a Marine lieutenant, was killed in action on Okinawa during WWII.

Harvard University Directory, Compiled by a Committee of the Harvard Alumni Association. Cambridge: Harvard University Press. 1913.

'Harry L. Evans Succumbs,' *Daily Independent Journal (San Rafael, CA),* June 14, 1961.

Hays, Samuel Dent "Jack"

Born: April 8, 1894 || Died: September 22, 1972 || Idaho '13-'16 || Started at guard versus Washington State || WWI: 2ⁿᵈ Lt. 362nd, promoted to 1ˢᵗ Lt. and remained at Camp Lewis during the war || WWII: Col., Commanded Boise Barracks, Camp Adair and Camp Beale training camps

Hays was Idaho's football captain in 1916, lettered three years in tennis, and completed an undergraduate degree in law. After the war, he remained in Idaho's National Guard and was a lawyer in private practice. He became a school superintendent and then held state government roles related to unemployment compensation and employed services. He was a real estate agent late in his career.

'Hayes is Idahos Captain,' *Morning Oregonian,* December 5, 1915.

'Portland Soldiers at American Lake Given Promotions,' *Oregon Daily Journal (Portland),* June 28, 1918.

'Col. G.H. McCoy to Leave Camp Adair; Col. Hays is Due,' *Corvallis Gazette-Times,* September 24, 1943.

Heilig, Vernon Vincent

Born: May 24, 1893 || Died: February 1, 1973 || Unknown || Substituted at end versus Washington State || Pre-WWI: Pvt., Idaho National Guard || WWI: 2ⁿᵈ Lt., 362ⁿᵈ, 361ˢᵗ Supply Co. He remained at Camp Lewis during the war

Heilig was a bookkeeper at a bank before the war. After the war, he held bookkeeping and accounting jobs with the state government and a lumber mill.

'At Camp Lewis,' *Great Falls Tribune,* September 13, 1918.

Hurlburt, Ralph Jay "Spec"

Born: October 2, 1888 || Died: September 29, 1918 || Michigan '09-'10, Multnomah AC '12-'13 || Practiced with 362ⁿᵈ before a temporary transfer to Ft. Sill || WWI: AEF. 2ⁿᵈ Lt., 362ⁿᵈ, K Co. Killed in action during attack on Gesnes in Meuse-Argonne

Hurlburt was a reserve player on Michigan's 1909 and 1910 football teams. Although Hurlburt did not play in the game, he was a member of the 1909 Michigan team that was the first to play Minnesota for the Little Brown Jug. After graduating from Michigan with an undergraduate law degree in 1912, Hurlburt practiced law in Portland and coached high school football from 1912 to 1915. He was captain of the 1912 Multnomah football team, an assistant coach in 1915, and head coach in 1916.

'Speck Hurlburt Will Coach P.A.,' *Oregon Daily Journal (Portland)*, June 23, 1912.

'Pigskin Artist to Kick Windbag Today,' *Oregon Daily Journal (Portland)*, August 29, 1915.

'Portlanders Write Eye Witness Accounts of Action,' *Oregon Daily Journal (Portland)*, December 1, 1918.

'Coast Stars Die on Battlefields,' *Washington Times*, December 8, 1918.

Hutchinson, William Nelson Lindsay

Born: December 7, 1892 || Died: May 19, 1989 || Stanford '15 || Hutchinson was a reserve halfback in the Washington State game || WWI: AEF. 1ˢᵗ Lt., 362ⁿᵈ, H Co.

Hutchinson grew up on a farm in Palo Alto. He played rugby as a freshman and lettered in tennis his freshman and sophomore years at Stanford. Hutchinson was involved in coordinating the attack on Gesnes in the Meuse-Argonne and securing the position after the village was taken. After his discharge, Hutchinson became a walnut grower and later was a politically active member of the American Fruit Growers Cooperative.

'Santa Clara Ties with Stanford,' *San Francisco Call*, September 28, 1911.

'Veterans of Racquet Beaten at Stanford,' *San Francisco Call*, January 25, 1913.

Hutchinson, William N.L. *Report of Operations of 362nd Infantry during the Offensive, 26th to 29th September (both dates inclusive)*, December 1, 1918. Granger, Farley E. File, 91st Division World

War I Veterans Survey, U.S. Army Heritage and Education Center, Carlisle, PA

'Angelenos Named to Farm Group,' *Los Angeles Times,* April 12, 1944.

May, Thomas Everett

Born: March 5, 1888 || Died: April 5, 1965 || Oregon State '11-'13 || Started at right tackle in Washington State game || WWI: AEF. 2nd Lt.; Capt., I Co.; Slightly wounded in eye by shrapnel at Meuse-Argonne

May captained the Oregon State football team in 1911, while also starting on a Pacific Coast Conference basketball championship team. He was an assistant football and basketball coach there from 1914 to 1916. May was discharged from the Army upon his return from France, worked for a short time in life insurance, but reentered the Army in 1920 and was stationed at Camp Lewis. He then oversaw the ROTC program at Clemson University and was Clemson's baseball coach in 1925. May was based in Hawaii from 1925 to 1932, before being sent to the Advanced Course at the Infantry School at Fort Benning, where he wrote his primary paper on the operations of his unit (362d, I Co.) at Meuse-Argonne. After that, he was on duty with the Civilian Conservation Corps until he was assigned as the training officer for the Oregon National Guard in 1934. During WWII, he commanded the Army Band and musical school. He retired as a Colonel in 1946 and lived in Carmel, CA.

'Tie Predicted in State Title Game,' *Morning Oregonian,* November 20, 1914.

'Camp Lewis Soldiers Thanks Corvallisites,' *Corvallis Gazette-Times,* December 6, 1917.

'Yes, This is an Army Man and His Bald Head,' *Sunday Oregonian,* October 6, 1918.

'Everett May is Captain,' *Sunday Oregonian,* December 15, 1918.

'Bayonets, Boogie-Woogie, All in Day's Work for Army Band,' *Independent Record (Helena, MT),* December 26, 1942.

McLean, John Reginald

Born: January 5, 1892 || Died: March 11, 1929 || McGill '10-12, '14 || Played versus the enlisted men, started at fullback against Washington State, and at halfback versus Fort Flagler || Pre-WWI: 1ˢᵗ Arizona Infantry National Guard || WWI: AEF. 1ˢᵗ Lt., 362ⁿᵈ, L Co., Sent to Ft. Still for several months to study fortifications. Sent to France in June 1918 with 91ˢᵗ Division Advanced Party. Wounded on September 29, 1918 at Gesnes

Canadian-born, McLean studied at McGill University in Montreal and was a mining engineer in Arizona before the war. His whereabouts after the war are not known until he became engaged to Kathleen Burke. Burke was nationally known as an "Angel of France" for her work as a nurse in France and met McLean while caring for him in France. After the war, she married Frederick Forrest Peabody, a multimillionaire and President of the firm that sold Arrow collars and shirts. Peabody died in 1927. McLean and Burke were married in February 1929. Following their wedding, they took a short trip prior to their planned honeymoon. McLean was killed in a car accident while returning from the trip, less than two weeks after their wedding.

'Eleven Arizonans on Day's List of Casualties Abroad,' *Copper Era and Morenci News,* December 27, 1918.

McGill University, *McGill Honour Roll, 1914-1918,* Montreal: McGill University, 1926.

'Extensive Honeymoon Planned,' *Los Angeles Times,* March 6, 1929.

'Colonel Died to Save Wife,' *Arizona Daily Star,* March 24, 1929.

Middlestate, Carl Goad

Born: August 30, 1891 || Died: June 1, 1953 || Unknown || Substituted as a lineman versus Washington State || Pre-WWI: Cpl., Washington 2ⁿᵈ Infantry, L Co. during deployment to Mexican border, then 1ˢᵗ Sgt. || WWI: 2ⁿᵈ Lt., 362ⁿᵈ, C Co.: Remained at Camp Lewis as 1ˢᵗ Lt., 13ᵗʰ Division, 44ᵗʰ Infantry, I Co.

Middlestate was a chauffeur in Denver and a porter in Seattle before the war. He was also in the Washington National Guard and was deployed to the Mexican border before attending the first ROTC at the Presidio. Following the war, Middlestate held various sales positions in Seattle and Portland

Washington National Guard, The Official History of the Washington National Guard, Volume 5 of Washington National Guard in World War I. Washington: Office of the Adjutant General

'At Camp Lewis,' *Great Falls Tribune,* September 13, 1918.

Montgomery, James Richard

Born: October 7, 1879 || Died: February 4, 1957 || None || At age 38, substituted at tackle versus Washington State || Pre-WWI: Montgomery served with the 1ˢᵗ Texas Volunteers during the Spanish-American War and was wounded in 1899 while with the 33ʳᵈ U.S. Volunteers in the Philippines. Promoted to corporal, he also served in China during the Boxer Rebellion before leaving the Army in 1906 || WWI: Pvt., Cpl. 33ʳᵈ Vols., Capt., 362ⁿᵈ, B Co.; Wounded twice in France and promoted to Major for valor

Montgomery was a newspaper reporter in El Paso when he volunteered. His commissioning as a Captain was due in part to his being one of the rare ROTC men with combat experience. After his discharge, Montgomery became the Chief of Police in El Paso. He left El Paso after several years and had no known occupation after that.

'Reported Insurgent Garrison Did Not Materialize, - Additional Casualties,' *Evening Star (Washington, D.C.),* December 4, 1900.

'Camp Lewis Boys of the Finest,' *Oxnard Courier,* September 29, 1917.

'Speakers Will Urge Buying of Liberty Bonds,' *El Paso Herald,* April 24, 1919.

Morse, Jr., Wellslake Demarest

Born: February 22, 1894 || Died: February 26, 1984 || Cincinnati '13-'16 || Started at right guard versus Washington State || WWI: 2ⁿᵈ Lt., 362ⁿᵈ, I Co.; Promoted to 1ˢᵗ Lt. in August. Returned to US in July 1919 with a casual unit from Beaune/AEF University in France

Morse played football at the University of Cincinnati from 1913 to 1916. He was among the last of the 362ⁿᵈ men to leave France since he either taught or took classes at the AEF University in Beaune, France. After his discharge, Morse returned to Pasadena and was in the real estate business for more than fifty years.

University of Cincinnati, *1917 The Cincinnatian*, Cincinnati: Students of the University of Cincinnati.

'Portland Soldiers at American Lake Given Promotions,' *Oregon Daily Journal (Portland)*, June 28, 1918.

O'Brien, Thomas J.

Born: Unknown || Died: Unknown || Notre Dame College || Substituted in backfield versus Washington State || WWI: 2nd Lt., I Co., 362nd

Insufficient information found to identify this player.

Thorpe, Charles Alfred

Born: February 1, 1886 || Died: March 29, 1934 || Stanford '06-'09 || Played versus the enlisted men, started at left guard versus Washington State, and at right tackle against Fort Flagler || WWI: AEF. Capt., 362nd, I Co., Wounded with four bullets in leg during the first few hours of Meuse-Argonne

Thorpe played football as a freshman at Stanford and three years of rugby after Stanford dropped football. He was in the investment business when he volunteered for the Army. Following his discharge, he returned to the brokerage business and was selected to open a new office in San Francisco. Thorpe did not fully recover from his war wounds and passed away in 1934.

'Strong Varsities are Selected for the Annual Rugby Game To-Morrow,' *San Francisco Chronicle*, November 12, 1909.

'Society,' *Los Angeles Times*, October 21, 1917.

'Yellow Streak Costly to Ten,' *Los Angeles Times*, January 7, 1919.

'Rites Arranged for C.A. Thorpe,' *Los Angeles Times*, April 1, 1934.

Tuller, Walter Kimble

Born: October 6, 1886 || Died: September 27, 1939 || Cal '07 captain || Started at right guard against Fort Flagler || WWI: AEF. Maj., 362nd; 348th Machine Gun Battalion, Sent to France in June 1918 with 91st Division Advanced Party. Graduated from the Staff Officers and Training School in France

Tuller was captain of Cal's 1907 rugby team and crew as well, while earning an undergraduate degree in law. He became an authority on constitutional law prior to enlisting. After the war, Tuller was a delegate to the convention that led to the creation of the American Legion and became an executive with the organization. In addition to his law practice, he was active in civic affairs in the Los Angeles.

'University Athletes Admitted to the Bar,' *Oakland Tribune*, April 30, 1908.

'S.F. to Have Four Delegates at Caucus,' *San Francisco Chronicle*, May 6, 1919.

Clark, R. D., *91ˢᵗ Division National Army Camp Lewis*, Seattle: Clark Co. 1917.

'Tuller Funeral Will Be Held Today,' *Los Angeles Times*, September 29, 1929.

Worsham, Elijah W. "Lige"

Born: December 14, 1886 || Died: September 29, 1918 || Purdue '04 || Played versus the enlisted men and started at left tackle against Washington State || Pre-WWI: Sgt., 3rd Oregon Infantry Machine Gun unit on Mexican border || WWI: Capt., 362ⁿᵈ, K. Co., then 362ⁿᵈ Machine Gun Co. Killed in action during the attack on Gesnes. Posthumously awarded the Distinguished Service Cross

Worsham played running back at Purdue in 1904, managed a coal mine in Indiana, and coached high school football. He then worked in sales in Seattle before venturing off to the Yukon Territory. He made his way to Oregon where was a salesman for the Golden Egg macaroni brand. His Oregon National Guard experience qualified him for the ROTC at the Presidio and he was commissioned a Captain. Worsham became engaged to Corona Ghirardelli of San Francisco in 1917. At Camp Lewis and in France, Worsham was considered a friendly but strong leader of his troops.

'Squad of Gridiron Players From Which Coach Cutts Will Select a Team to Represent Purdue University During Season of 1904,' *Indiana News*, October 5, 1904.

'Football Game Ends in Row,' *Indianapolis Star*, November 30, 1906.

'Coming Events,' *La Grande Observer*, April 30, 1917.

'"War" Engagement of San Francisco,' *Honolulu Star-Bulletin,* September 15, 1917.

'Dr. Worsham Died Sunday,' *Evansville Press,* September 30, 1918.

'Capt. Worsham, Evansville, Killed in Action in France,' *Indianapolis Star,* November 9, 1918.

'D.S.C. Given Posthumously to 'Lige' W. Worsham,' *Oregon Daily Journal (Portland, OR),* August 4, 1919.

APPENDIX D: 1917 MARE ISLAND MARINES

Twenty-eight Marines were identified as having practiced or played with the 1917 Mare Island Marines. Newspaper and magazine articles helped identify players, but the key source of information for the 1917 Marine team were Marine muster rolls. The muster rolls for November and December 1917 showed that every football player at Mare Island was moved into specific units (e.g., the 35th Co. or 117th Co.) and indicated which Marines were on furlough with the team for its trips to the Northwest and the Rose Bowl. Conversely, the muster rolls show other Marines, known to be on the team early in the season, that were not on furlough pattern, indicating they did not travel with the team on one or both of those trips. The muster rolls also identify eight Marines who were on the team early in the season and were transferred to other locations prior to the 1918 Rose Bowl.

'Marines Are Husky,' *Sunday Oregonian*, September 16, 1917.

'Marines Have Grid Stars,' *Seattle Star*, October 17, 1917.

'Marine Eleven Composed of Huskies in the Line and Backfield,' *Los Angeles Times*, December 31, 1917.

Ambrose, Keith Kapp

Born: October 22, 1888 || Died: May 8, 1968 || Montana '06-'07 || Substituted in one game and started three, including the 1918 Rose Bowl || WWI: Pvt., Cpl., Sgt., Commissioned as 2ⁿᵈ Lt. and sent to Cuba in February 1919, returning in July 1919

Before the war, Amrose played at Montana and moved to Klamath Falls, Oregon, becoming the Fire Chief. After his discharge, he returned to Klamath Falls and was the Fire Chief, Police Chief, or both, retiring in 1948.

'Montana School of Mines Goes Down to Defeat in Hard-Fought Battle with State University,' *Anaconda Standard*, October 26, 1907.

'Keith Ambrose on the Gridiron,' *Evening Herald (Klamath Falls, OR)*, September 10, 1917.

'Keith Ambrose, Kicker,' *Evening Herald (Klamath Falls, OR)*, June 6, 1940.

Bailey, Edward Flint "Red"

Born: February 25, 1891 || Died: June 13, 1974 || Oregon '09 -'12, Multnomah '13-'14|| Started every game at right tackle, including the 1918 Rose Bowl || WWI: Pvt., Cpl., Sgt., Commissioned as 2ⁿᵈ Lt. in February 1919, he was court martialled one month later, but it was overturned and he was discharged in August 1919

Bailey was an All-Northwest tackle for Oregon from 1910 to 1912, earning a law degree. As a practicing lawyer, he also was head football coach at Albany College in 1915 and 1916, where his team beat the Oregon freshmen despite Albany having only 31 men in the school. After his discharge, he returned to Oregon and practiced law, coaching at Albany College again in 1925. He was elected to the Oregon State House of Representatives in 1923, the State Senate in 1927, and was the Democratic nominee for governor in 1930. He specialized in real estate law through much of his career.

'Oregon Men Who Play Saturday,' *Oregon Daily Journal (Portland, OR)*, November 16, 1911.

'Bailey to Coach Albany College,' *Eugene Guard*, August 30, 1915.

"'Fat' Bailey Going to Officers' Camp,' *Oregon Daily Journal (Portland, OR)*, August 20, 1918.

'Ed Bailey Here,' *Albany Daily Democrat, August 26, 1919.*

'Home Rule Charter to Attorney's Life of Service,' *Eugene Register-Guard,* October 7, 1962.

Beckett, John Wesley

Born: January 12, 1893 || Died: July 26, 1981 || Oregon '13 -'16; AEF Marines '19, Mare Island '19-'20, Quantico '21-'24 || Player-coach and captain of the 1917 Mare Island team, Beckett started every game at left tackle, including the 1918 Rose Bowl || WWI: AEF Pvt., Cpl., Sgt., Commissioned as 2nd Lt. and promoted to 1st Lt., 13th Regiment. In France from October 1918 to July 1919 || WWII: Held roles with the Officer Candidate School at Quantico. By April 1944, he was in a staff role with the 5th Marines and was on Iwo Jima two days before the iconic flag raising on Mt. Surabachi. Retired as Brig. Genl.

Beckett was an All-American at Oregon and was captain of the 1917 Rose Bowl team. Following WWI, he was instrumental in the development of the Marine Corps football programs as the player-coach for the Mare Island Marines in 1920, the Quantico Marines from 1921-1924, and the San Diego Marines in 1925. He then was an assistant coach at the Naval Academy from 1926 to 1928 before commanding the Marine detachment in Beijing from 1929 to 1931. He returned to the States and again coached the San Diego Marines in 1931 and 1932. He also played two games for the professional Buffalo All-Americans in 1920 and one game for the Columbus Panhandlers in 1922.

Beckett spent the latter part of the 1930s commanding the Marine detachment on the *U.S.S. Houston*, attending senior schooling, and at the Puget Sound Naval Base. Prior to the start of WWII, Beckett had roles overseeing basic training and then moved to the 5th Marines. After WWII, Beckett commanded the Marine Barracks at Mare Island from 1946 until his retirement in 1949.

'Beckett, of Oregon on Third All-American,' *Morning Register (Eugene),* December 28, 1916.

'John Beckett King for Day,' *Los Angeles Times,* January 3, 1918.

'John Beckett Play Football 'Over There',' *Morning Register,* March 13, 1919.

'Marine Offense is Terrific with Great Goettge Leader in Assault,' *Tennessean*, October 5, 1924.

'High Climber,' *Eugene Guard*, May 7, 1944.

'Col. John Beckett, Marine Hero, Retires,' *Oakland Tribune*, May 29, 1949.

Brown, Walter Vernon "Jap"

Born: February 6, 1895 || Died: June 19, 1921 || Wisconsin Frosh '14, WSU '16, Quantico '19-'20 || Started every game at quarterback, including the 1918 Rose Bowl || WWI: Cpl., Gy. Sgt., Commissioned as a 2ⁿᵈ Lt., Marine Aviation in January 1919. In Haiti by April 1919

Prior to joining the Marines, Brown played freshman football at Wisconsin in 1914, transferred to Washington State and was part-time starter in 1916. During the war, he completed pilot training and was stationed in Haiti, and completing the Officer Training Camp in July 1920. Brown participated in the Pulitzer Trophy Race on Thanksgiving Day in 1920, indicating he was among the Marines' best flyers. During a training flight on June 9, 1921 Brown commanded a squadron of six DH-4Bs for a practice bombing run. On their return to base, the flight encountered fog and Brown was killed when his plane crashed off the beach near Quantico. Following his death, the Marine flying field at Quantico was named in his honor. Although the flying field became obsolete and was replaced in the 1930s, the original location remains named in his honor and is the current site of the Marines' Officer Candidate School.

'Washington State is Trounced by Oregon Aggie Team, 13-0,' *Oregon Daily Journal (Portland, OR)*, October 15, 1916.

'Mare Island Marines Roll Up 27-0 Score on Oregon's Varsity,' *Oregon Daily Journal (Portland, OR)*, November 4, 1917.

'Marine Air Man Spins to Death at Beach,' *Washington Times*, June 9, 1921.

Buss, William Kenneth,

Born: May 31, 1892 || Died: August 23, 1955 || Nebraska '10, '11 – no sports || Mentioned as team member in newspaper articles early in the season

|| *WWI: AEF. Pvt., Cpl., promoted to Cpl. and Sgt. in France. Missing in action and hospitalized for psychoneurosis (shell shock) during Battle of Soissons. Purple Heart*

Buss worked for a glass company before enlisting. Transferred from Mare Island in October 1918, and was in France by April 1918. Following the war, Buss worked in sales and was a hotel clerk.

Maxwell, William J. *The Catalogue of the Phi Delta Theta Fraternity,* 1918. Oxford, OH: Phi Delta Theta Fraternity. 1918.

Addenda Roll AEF, 1 January 1918 to 31 July 1919, Volume One A-K, Accessed November 2, 2017.

https://www.ancestry.com/interactive/1089/T977_146-0089

'Hotel Holdup Nets $145,' *Nebraska State Journal,* November 26, 1934.

Cocks, Jr., James

Born: September 23, 1887 || Died: May 1, 1963 || Redlands AC Boxing || Substituted at guard in second Cal game || WWI: Pvt. Special duty as carpenter at Mare Island. Discharged February 1919, then reenlisted for two years in October 1920

Cox was a carpenter and amateur boxer before the war and returned to carpentry following his discharge.

'S.F. Club Plans Good Series of Bouts,' *San Francisco Call,* June 12, 1912.

'Prizefighter $10,000 Richer,' *Santa Cruz Evening News (CA),* August 2, 1928.

Coshow, John Milton,

Born: June 12, 1893 || Died: November 2, 1942 || Oregon Frosh '12, Oregon BB '14, Multnomah '16 || WWI: Pvt., Cpl., Transferred to Quantico, then Newport Torpedo Station in Rhode Island. Promoted to Sgt.

Coshow taught at a high school and attended Oregon's law school before the war. After the war, he worked as a farm laborer and ultimately worked as an agent for Bureau of Reclamation.

'Oregon Freshies Defeat Eugene 10-0,' *Oregon Daily Journal (Portland, OR)*, October 6, 1912.

'Mrs. Coshow Has Two Sons In Service,' *Hood River Glacier*, October 11, 1917.

Craig, Gerald Allen

Born: March 22, 1892 || Died: March 1, 1968 || USC '15, '16 || Started at right halfback in the first Cal game and substituted in the second. Transferred to Puget Sound in October 1917, then to OTC at Quantico and on to France in September 1918 || WWI: AEF. Pvt., Cpl., 2nd Lt., 11th Regt., 1st Lt.

Craig played football and was on the track and field team at USC before the war. After his discharge, he worked in automotive parts and the telephone business. In 1933, he was sentenced to one year in prison for plotting to have his wife killed. After his release, he owned a retail nursery until his death.

'Bears Praise Trojan Eleven,' *Los Angeles Times*, October 27, 1915.

'Craig Now Wants to be a Speedster,' *Los Angeles Time*, January 18, 1916.

'Craig Receives Jail Sentence,' *Los Angeles Times*, April 7, 1933.

Cushman, Thomas Jackson

Born: June 27, 1895 || Died: July 15, 1972 || Washington '14, '16 football, '14, '16-'17 crew || Cushman started four games at center early in the season before being injured, but was on the 1918 Rose Bowl roster || WWI: Pvt., Cpl., 2nd Lt. in Marine Flying Corps || WWII: Maj., Brig. Genl. Commanding Marine Air Station, Cherry Hill, then Air Defenses in Marianas || Korean War: Commander, First Air Wing, Korea. Retired as Lt. Genl.

Cushman played football and was captain of the 1917 crew team at Washington. After the war, Cushman rose through a succession of command and staff assignments, interspersed with further training, and had tours in Guam, the Dominican Republic, and Nicaragua.

Cushman was the commanding officer during the development and initial operation of Marine Air Station Cherry Hill in North

Carolina until September 1943, when he became chief of staff to the commanding officer of the Marine Air Wings in the Pacific. After the U.S. took Saipan, Guam, and Tinian in the Marianas Islands in July and August of 1944, the American forces built airfields on Saipan and Tinian for the B-29s that executed the strategic and atomic bombing campaign against Japan. In November 1944, Cushman took command of the Marine Air Wings defending the Marianas and he remained in command there until April 1945. He was awarded the Bronze Star and Legion of Merit for his efforts.

After WWII, he held high-level commands on either coast and with the onset of the Korean War, Cushman was named the Assistant Wing Commander and then, Commander, of the First Marine Air Wing in Korea. In his final role with the Marines, he was Assistant Commander, Fleet Marine Force, Pacific and he was promoted to Lt. General at retirement.

'Cushman Must Pay Alimony to His Girl-Wife,' *Seattle Star,* May 6, 1915.

'Crew Activities Get Underway at University of Washington; Captain Cushman Recovering,' *Seattle Star,* January 10, 1917.

'Air Duels Feature Races,' *Los Angeles Times,* August 31, 1928.

'Cherry Point Head,' *Greenville News (SC),* June 1, 1945.

'Marine Corps Makes Air Command Shift,' *Fresno Bee Republican,* January 14, 1953.

Gardner, Clinton Perry "Mark"

Born: November 25, 1895 || April 10, 1973 || Utah '14-'15 || Substituted in several games at running back || WWI: AEF Pvt., Cpl., Sgt., 1ˢᵗ Marine Aviation Force

Clinton Gardner lettered in football at Utah in 1914 and 1915. During the war, he served with the First Marine Aviation Force near Dunkirk, which acted as the Day Wing of the Navy's Northern Bomber Group. Following the war, he was a mining engineer as well as a consulting engineer in highway construction, and worked in Brazil with Pan American Airlines.

'Utah University Makes Awards,' *Ogden Standard,* December 11, 1915.

'Marine-Oregon Interest is High,' *Morning Oregonian,* November 2, 1917.

'Utah Men Who Have Joined Various Branches of the U.S. Fighting Forces,' *Salt Lake Tribune, August 25, 1918.*

Gardner, Darrell

Born: August 12, 1893 || Died: April 16, 1963 || Utah '13-'15 || Started most games at right halfback, including the 1918 Rose Bowl || WWI: AEF. Pvt., Cpl., Sgt. and possible pilot, 1ˢᵗ Marine Aviation Force

Darrell Gardner was named to the All-Rocky Mountain Conference team in 1913 through 1915. During the war, he served with the First Marine Aviation Force near Dunkirk, which acted as the Day Wing of the Navy's Northern Bomber Group. After being discharged, he was an assistant football coach at Jordan High School in Utah. He then began his career as a mining engineer, rising to become the general manager of a large mine in Arizona.

'Utah University Makes Awards,' *Ogden Standard,* December 11, 1915.

'Former Marines Unite in Oregon,' *Herald and News (Klamath Falls),* May 28, 1945.

'Darrel Gardner Rites to be Held in Superior,' *Arizona Republic,* April 15, 1963.

Hall, Elmer Edwards

Born: April 4, 1890 || Died: September 9, 1958 || Oregon '10- '13, AEF Base Section #2 Spring '19, Mare Island Marines '19, Quantico Marines '21, '23 || Started every game at guard, including the 1918 Rose Bowl || WWI: AEF. 2ⁿᵈ Lt., 13ᵗʰ Regt. || WWII: Commander, 8th Marines. Retired as Brig. Genl.

Elmer Hall spent much of 1920s and 1930s in staff roles, often related to personnel. During that time, he was instrumental in the development of the Marines' football programs at Quantico and San Diego. He was Quantico's head coach in 1929 and 1930, and was San Diego's head coach in 1926, 1933, 1939, and 1940. He had two tours in Nicaragua, one in Shanghai, China, and command Marine detachments aboard Navy warships. Hall was the commander of the 2nd Engineers Battalion at Pearl Harbor in December 1941 and received the Navy Commendation Medal for his leadership during the attack. He was named commander of the 8th Marine Regiment and led his unit on the beach at Tarawa, for which he was awarded the Legion of Merit. After Tarawa, Hall returned to the U.S. and held staff roles until his retirement in 1946. Hall Field, the football stadium at the Marine Recruit Depot San Diego, was named in his honor in 1960.

'Oregon Men Who Play Saturday,' *Oregon Daily Journal (Portland, OR)*, November 16, 1911.

'Seven Oregon Men Will Train for Commission,' *Eugene Guard*, April 15, 1918.

'Lieut. Grayson Tells of Oregon Boys in Marines,' *Oregon Daily Journal (Portland, OR), January 27, 1919.*

'Navy Set for Contest with Marine Outfit,' *Los Angeles Times*, December 1, 1933.

'Behind the Line,' *Los Angeles Times*, May 30, 1942.

Hobson, Cloy St. Claire

Born: February 4, 1893 || Died: January 24, 1972 || Nebraska '12-'16 - no sports || Started every game at right end, including 1918 Rose Bowl. Hospitalized for three months due to leg injury suffered in the Rose Bowl || WWI: Pvt., Cpl., Sgt., promoted to Gunnery Sgt. while in aviation training

Hobson does not appear to have played football in college, but graduated Phi Beta Kappa from Nebraska with a teaching certificate in 1916, becoming a high school principal that fall. After his discharge, Hobson was a teacher, principal, and superintendent of schools in Kansas and Illinois for several decades. During that time, he earned his master's and Ph.D. from the University of Chicago and joined the faculty at the University of Kansas in the 1950s where he headed the Department of Curriculum.

'Scholarship Honors Announced Thursday,' *Lincoln Journal Star,* Mya 23, 1916.

'Vallejo News,' *San Francisco Chronicle,* January 14, 1918.

'Dr. Hobson to Replace R.C. Carter,' *Fairbanks Daily News-Miner,* August 7, 1963.

Huntington, Hollis Wilson

Born: September 20, 1895 || Died: June 3, 1969 || Oregon '16, '18, '19 || Started every game at fullback, including the 1918 Rose Bowl || WWI: Pvt., Cpl., Sgt.

Huntington played in the 1917 Rose Bowl for Oregon. Following his release, he returned to Oregon and played in the 1920 Rose Bowl, setting a record for playing all sixty minutes of three Rose Bowl games. He won a state title in his first of year coaching high school football in Montana in 1920, followed by coaching football, basketball, and baseball at North Salem High School where his basketball team played in seven state championship games, winning three, and his baseball team won one state title. He then left teaching to open a men's clothing shop.

'Athletic Interest Centers in Football,' *Hood River Glacier,* October 26, 1911.

'All Star Team of Coast is Chosen by Coach Huntington,' *Eugene Guard,* December 2, 1919.

'Sport Sparks,' *Statesman Journal,* December 21, 1941.

Kirkman, Goodyear Wycherly

Born: April 8, 1896 || Died: Unknown || California '15 – no sports || Traveled with team on trip to Northwest, but not Rose Bowl || WWI: Pvt., Cpl., Gt. Sgt., 2nd Lt. Marine Aviation

Goodyear Kirkman was a student at Cal (and Oregon) before enlisting. He became a Marine aviator, was hospitalized in 1919 for burns on his face and neck, presumably resulting from activities in the service, and served in Nicaragua. In 1924, he was court martialed for drunkenness and conduct unbecoming an officer, a charge for which he was acquitted in January 1925. He was hospitalized again in August 1925 and was mustered out due to "incapacity resulting from an incident of the service." He later lived in New York and San Francisco, but little else is known of his post-military life.

In case you were wondering, Goodyear Kirkman is the fourth cousin twice removed of Charles Goodyear, the inventor of vulcanized rubber.

'An Echo of the Kirkman Affair,' *Kansas City Times*, June 16, 1910.

'Oregon Stars Leave, Enlisted in Marines,' *Eugene Guard*, May 14, 1917.

'Marine Corps Exam,' *Portsmouth Herald (NH)*, February 19, 1925.

MacMillan, Donald George

Born: November 5, 1890 || Died: June 4, 1968 || Yosemite Club '09-'13, Expositions '15, Nationals '20 || Substituted at fullback in the first game against California. Transferred to Quantico on October 15, 1917 || WWI: AEF. Pvt., transferred to Quantico, then to Galveston and promoted to Cpl.; Promoted to Sgt. and sent to France with 13th Marines. Court martialed in April 1919 for being AWOL. Demoted to Pvt.

MacMillan worked as an electrician for Pacific Telephone and Telegraph, and played football for the Yosemite Club, the Expositions, and other Bay Area clubs. After the war, he attended Cal-Davis, ran a hotel, was a fruit buyer, and ran a fruit stand.

'Century Eleven Easily Defeats Yosemite Team,' *Oakland Tribune*, December 20, 1909.

'All-Star Marines from Mare Island to Meet Trojans,' *Southern California Trojan*, November 20, 1917.

'War Veteran to Wed Local Belle,' *San Francisco Chronicle*, November 28, 1920.

McGregor, John Maurice

Born: March 24, 1894 || Died: April 14, 1956 || Washington State '15-'16 || Mentioned in newspaper reports as being on the team, but did not appear in a game and transferred out in October || WWI: AEF. Pvt., transferred to Quantico in October 1917 and was in Cuba from November 1917 to

May 1918. Entered ROTC and commissioned as 2ⁿᵈ Lt. in August 1918. Sent to France with 13ᵗʰ Marines. Discharged August 1919

McGregor was a member of Washington State's 1916 Rose Bowl team, but did not travel to the Rose Bowl. After his discharge, he returned to the family's farm/ranch and became the secretary of the family corporation.

'Varsity-Alumni Game Saturday,' *Pullman Herald*, October 8, 1916.

'Marine Promotions Due, *Washington Post*, December 8, 1918.

Miszewski / Maze, Arelius Harry

Born: September 20, 1895 | | Died: August 4, 1957 | | Minnesota Frosh '16 | | Substituted at left guard in first game versus Cal and started the second Cal game at right end. Transferred / discharged in December 1917 | | WWI: Pvt., Cpl., C Co.,

Miszewski played freshman football at Minnesota in 1916. He enlisted in Marines, but was discharged to enter the US. Army Medical Corps, which sent him to continue his dental education at Minnesota. He changed his surname to Maze by 1920 and practiced dentistry in Winona, Minnesota, where he was active in a range of civic, dental, and athletic organizations.

University of Minnesota. *The Annual Register of the Year, 1917-1918.* Minneapolis: University of Minnesota, 1917.

Bolek, Rev. Francis. *Who's Who in Polish America,* New York: Harbinger House, 1943.

Mitchell, Clifford L. "Brick"

Born: July 10, 1894 | | Died: October 21, 1963 | | Oregon '15-'16 | | Started every game for Mare Island other than the 1918 Rose Bowl (due to injury). Then was all but two plays in Rose Bowl due to injury to Hobson | | WWI: Pvt., Cpl., Gunnery Sgt.

Mitchell was named Second Team All-American by Walter Camp following the 1916 season and was the only non-Oregonian on Oregon's 1917 Rose Bowl team. After the war, he was an assistant football coach at Stanford and Cal, before becoming head coach at Nevada from 1932 through 1935. He then moved to the high school ranks. In the early 1960s Mitchell owned an olive orchard and was noted in the newspaper for having a trained monkey pick olives from the treetops.

'Oregon Team is Off for South,' *Statesman Journal,* December 26, 1916.

'Walter Camp Names Five Oregon Stars,' *Oregon Daily Journal (Portland),* January 13, 1918.

'Mitchell is Given Coach Contract at Nevada U.,' *Reno Gazette-Journal, November 11, 1933.*

'Monkey to pick olives in tree tops,' *Mason City Globe Gazette,* May 9, 1962.

Molthen, Frederick Theodore "Dutch"

Born: April 4, 1896 || Died: June 25, 1920 || Montana '16, Quantico '19 || Started five and substituted in one game at left halfback, but did not play in 1918 Rose Bowl due to injury || WWI: Pvt., Cpl., Sgt., Gy. Sgt., Entered MIT ground school and was commissioned 2nd Lt. || Post–WWI: Killed in flying accident at Parris Island, SC in 1920

Molthen was a multisport star in high school, winning the Intermountain high school football championship and placing first in a national high school track meet. He remained in the Marines after earning his wings and coached the Quantico Marines football team in 1919. Molthen was killed while piloting a plane in June 25, 1920 at Parris Island.

'Falls Players on All-State,' *Great Falls Tribune,* January 16, 1916.

'Prep Stars of Nation in Stagg Meet Today,' *Chicago Tribune,* June 10, 1916.

'Marines Meet Lewis Eleven,' *Daily Missoulian,* December 16, 1917.

'Three Aviators Dead in Airplane Accident at Parris Island,' *Times Dispatch (Richmond, VA),* June 26, 1920.

Parker, John Merrel "Merrill" or "Mel"

Born: October 29, 1893 || Died: December 12, 1978 || North Carolina '13-'15 || Substituted at left end in the first Cal game, played versus SFOC, and substituted at fullback versus Oregon. On Rose Bowl roster, but did not play | | WWI: AEF, Pvt., Cpl., Gy Sgt., 1ˢᵗ Marine Aviation, Northern Bombing Group

Parker played three years at North Carolina. was on the track team for two years, and was President of the campus YMCA. After graduating, he was an assistant football coach and worked at the YMCA at the Colorado School of Mines. After the war, he coached high school football for one year, coached North Carolina's freshman team in 1920, and then earned his medical degree at Washington University in St. Louis in 1924. He spent his career practicing in Rochester, New York, as a pediatrician and was involved in the early treatment of cystic fibrosis.

'Parker Out of Game,' *Charlotte Observer,* November 21, 1915.

'Untitled note,' *Daily Tar Heel,* December 8, 1917.

'Dr. John Parker, pediatrician,' *Democrat and Chronicle (Rochester, NY),* December 13, 1978.

Purdy, Irving Breward

Born: August 18, 1892 | | Died: November 3, 1972 | | Minnesota Frosh '15 | | Substituted into both Cal games at right tackle. On the 1918 Rose Bowl roster | | WWI: AEF Pvt., Cpl., Sgt., Commissioned as a 1ˢᵗ Lt. in September 1918 and sent to France with the 11ᵗʰ Marines

Purdy played freshman football at Minnesota in 1915 while studying civil engineering. After returning from France, he completed his studies and was a founding member of the engineering fraternity at Minnesota. He spent more than ten years in California and then moved to the New York City area where he spent the rest of his career. He was issued a patent in 1953 for an anti-skid device for automotive wheels.

University of Minnesota. The *Annual Register, 1913-1914,* Minneapolis: University of Minnesota, 1915.

'The Times-Democrat Newsy Page of Pictures,' *Muskogee Times-Democrat,* November 3, 1917.

Minnesota Chapter Theta Xi Installed, *Star Tribune (Minneapolis),* April 18, 1920.

Ridderhof, Stanley Emanuel

Born: June 23, 1896 || Died: December 13, 1962 || Occidental '16 || Started at guard in every game, including the 1918 Rose Bowl || WWI: Pvt., Cpl., Sgt., 2ⁿᵈ Lt. || WWII: Col., serving at Pearl Harbor and then in stateside roles. Retired as Brig. Genl.

Ridderhof played end for Occidental before the war. He earned his wings following the war and served two years in Guam in the early 1920s where he helped direct the building of the first airfield on the island. He was stationed in in Nicaragua from 1928 to 1930. While there, he earned the Navy Cross and the Nicaraguan Medal of Merit for leading a raid on a major rebel supply depot. Stationed on Oahu in 1941, Ridderhof started a round of golf one Sunday morning, birdying the first hole, when the match was interrupted by the Japanese attack on Pearl Harbor. He returned to the mainland in July 1942, and spent the rest of WWII stateside, rising to Chief of Staff (second in command) of Marine Air forces on the West Coast. He earned the Legion of Merit and the Distinguished Flying Cross during the war. After leaving the Marines, Ridderhof completed the requirements for the undergraduate degree he interrupted to join the Marines in 1917, became an executive with a military contractor, and was president of the Southern California Golf Association.

'Dobie's Strength Will be Test Today at Oregon,' *Oakland Tribune*, October 28, 1916.

'30,000 Persons See New Year Football Game at Pasadena, *Eugene Guard*, January 1, 1918.

'Minneapolis Man Given War Medal,' *Star-Tribune, Minneapolis*, December 8, 1929.

'Col. Ridderhof Gets New Post,' *Los Angeles Times*, October 9, 1943.

'General Back in Class After Lakewood Fling,' *Los Angeles Times*, January 23, 1951.

Sanderson, Lawson Harry McPherson "Sandy" or "Woody"

Born: June 22, 1895 || Died: June 11, 1979 || Montana 14-16, Quan-

tico '20-'23 || *Substituted at right halfback and started three others at left halfback, including the 1918 Rose Bowl* || *WWI: Pvt., Cpl., Entered ground training, earned his wings and was commissioned as a 2ⁿᵈ Lt. in January 1919; Sent to the Dominican Republic in July 1919 as 1ˢᵗ Lt, 52ⁿᵈ Co.* || *WWII: Col., Ops. Officer of 3ʳᵈ Air Wing, Guadalcanal. Commander, 4ᵗʰ Air Wing. Retired as Maj. Genl.*

Sanderson attended the University of Washington and University of Montana, where he was active in football, basketball, baseball, and track. After WWI, Sanderson led the development of dive bombing while in the Dominican Republic. He became the 'world's fastest man' when he flew his plane 259 miles per hour in October 1923, then the highest speed ever achieved by man. Several weeks later he won the Pulitzer Trophy and would win other air races through the mid-1930s. During the 1920s and 1930s, Sanderson returned to the Dominican Republic for a three-year tour and commanded an air squadron in Nicaragua where he won the Distinguished Flying Cross.

Sanderson was the Operations Officer of the First Marine Aircraft Wing at Guadalcanal. Later in the war he commanded the 4ᵗʰ Marine Air Wing and was the Commander, Shore-Based Air Forces in the Marshall-Gilbert Islands area. In that role, then Brig. Genl. Sanderson accepted the Japanese surrender of Wake Island on September 4, 1945, 1,362 days after it fell to the Japanese in December 1941. He commanded the 1ˢᵗ Marine Air Wing in China in 1946 and retired from the Marines in 1949. The Marines' Attack Squadron of the Year Award is named in his honor.

'Montana Scores on Washington,' *Great Falls Tribune*, November 7, 1915.

'Marine Football Team in Training in Eugene,' *Morning Register (Eugene, OR)*, November 6, 1917.

'Navy Aviator Flies 259 Miles an Hour', *Minneapolis Star*, September 21, 1923.

'May be in Limelight at Stadium,' *Baltimore Sun*, December 3, 1924.

'American Flag Again Flies on Wake Island,' *Tribune (Seymour, IN)*, September 5, 1945.

Shields, Henry Donald

Born: April 29, 1895 || Died: December 20, 1971 || Michigan '14-'16 - no sports || Mentioned in early newspaper reports but did not play in a game || WWI: Pvt., Cpl., transferred to Newport, RI, Completed ROTC and commissions 2ⁿᵈ Lt.; Sent to Dominican Republic for one year, promoted to 1ˢᵗ Lt, 52ⁿᵈ Co, 3ʳᵈ Marines || WWII: Capt. in stateside posts. Promoted to Major, serving as Executive Officer of the 1ˢᵗ Motor Transport Battalion on on Okinawa. Retired as Lt. Col. in the Reserves in 1956

Shields attended Michigan before the war. After his discharge, he returned to the family farm in Lewiston, Illinois. He worked in sales in Oregon in the 1930s before rejoining the Marines during WWII serving stateside and on Okinawa.

'Illinois Club,' *1916 Michiganensian,* Ann Arbor: University of Michigan Senior Class of 1916. 1915.

'Marines Have Grid Stars,' *Seattle Star,* October 17, 1917.

'Past Commander Club Names New Leaders in Meet,' *Medford Mail Tribune,* June 27, 1934.

Teberg, Lawrence Earl

Born: May 13, 1896 || Died: June 7, 1991 || Minnesota '16, '20-'21 || Substituted at center in one game and started the last three games, including the 1918 Rose Bowl || WWI: Pvt., Cpl., Sgt., Completed ROTC and commissioned 2ⁿᵈ Lt. in January 1919

Lawrence Teberg played on Minnesota's 1916 team, returned to Minnesota for the 1920 season, and captained the 1921 squad while earning 3ʳᵈ team All-Big Ten honors. He stayed in the Minneapolis area, spending his career in construction and maintenance management.

'Coyotes No Match for Minnesotans,' *Argus-Leader (Sioux Falls, SD),* October 23, 1916.

'Sea Soldiers to Begin Hard Training Again,' *San Francisco Chronicle,* December 6, 1917.

'He Says Gophers Will Beat Hawkeyes,' *Star Tribune (Minneapolis),* November 3, 1921.

Wilson, Robert Harold

Born: December 18, 1892 || Died: July 18, 1918 || Michigan '14-'17 - no sports) || Substitute tackle in first Cal game. Transferred to Quantico in November 1917 || WWI: Pvt., Sent to France in February 1918, promoted to Cpl., 6th Regt. 84th Co. Initially listed as missing in action at the Battle of Soissons. Later declared killed in action July 18, 1918. Awarded French Croix de Guerre

Born in Ohio, Wilson's family moved to Los Angeles, but he studied liberal arts and law, and was a member of Delta Chi at Michigan from 1914 to 1917. He was the first member of a service Rose Bowl team to be killed in action.

'Delta Chi,' *1917 The Michiganensian*, Ann Arbor: University of Michigan Senior Class of 1917. 1917.

'That Liberty Shall Not Perish From the Earth,' *San Bernardino Sun*, February 23, 1919.

'Michigan Men Who Have Received the Croix de Guerre and Other Military Honors,' *Michigan Alumnus*, (May 1919), Ann Arbor: The Alumni Association of the University of Michigan Publishers.

Zuver, George W.

Born: February 22, 1895 || Died: April 2, 1972 || Minnesota '14-'16 (no sports) || Early season press reports indicate he was with the team, but he did not play in a game || WWI: Pvt., Cpl., Transferred to Guam by April 1918 and promoted to Sgt., then to Mare Island and Norfolk, Virginia; Sent to Quantico and ROTC, commissioned as 2nd Lt. in June 1919, then moved to reserves

Zuver attended Minnesota from 1914 to 1916 and is reported to have played independent football before enlisting. He worked in sales and branch management during the 1920s, before moving to Pennsylvania and getting involved in the construction business.

'Marines Have Grid Stars,' *Seattle Star*, October 17, 1917.

'Home Folks to Meet Marines at Seaports,' *Star-Tribune (Minneapolis)*, July 13, 1919.

Coaches and Administrators

Best, William "Newton"

Born: August 14, 1887 || Died: March 3, 1978 || Columbia '11 || Athletic Director || Pre-WWI: 1ˢᵗ Lt., Marine Section, 7ᵗʰ California Naval Militia || WWI: Capt., Mare Island Athletic Officer in 1917 and first part of 1918 season || WWII: Col., Quartermaster, Quantico, then 6ᵗʰ Marine Service Battalion, Okinawa, then 2ⁿᵈ Marines, China. Awarded Legion of Merit.

Best joined the California Naval Militia in May 1916. The unit was absorbed into the Marine Corps in April 1917 and he was assigned to Mare Island, commanding the Supply Detachment and acting as Post Athletic Officer. He was transferred to Quantico in September 1918 and the 14ᵗʰ Marines. In the interwar years, he had a number of Quartermaster assignments, and spent a number of years in Haiti, Nicaragua and China. During WWII, he led quartermaster efforts at Quantico, then did the same with the 6ᵗʰ Marines at Okinawa, for which he was awarded the Legion of Merit. Best led the advance party into China in October 1945 to coordinate activities and supplies. Best was promoted to Brig. Genl. upon retirement.

'Fraternity Dance,' *Los Angeles Evening Herald*, December 26, 1916.

Works Progress Administration. *History of the California Naval Militia, 1ˢᵗ Company, Marine Corps (36ᵗʰ Company, U.S. Marine Corps), 1917.* 1940.

'Lieut. Best is Again, Marines' Athletic Chief,' *Oakland Tribune*, August 9, 1917.

U.S. Marine Corps. *The United States Marines in North China, 1945-1949.* Washington, D.C.: Historical Branch, Reprinted 1968.

Bedzek, Hugo

Born: April 1, 1884 || Died: September 19, 1952 || Chicago '04-'05 || Consulting coach in week prior to regular-season Camp Lewis game. Head Coach for 1918 Rose Bowl || WWI: Civilian

Born near Prague, Bohemia (now the Czech Republic), Bedzek emigrated to America at age six and grew up on the south side of Chicago. His high school did not have a football team, so he played with the Morgan Park Athletic Club, an amateur team that morphed into the Racine Cardinals, the Chicago Cardinals, the St.

Louis Cardinals, and the Arizona Cardinals. He then played in the backfield at the University of Chicago under Amos Alonzo Stagg.

After Bedzek graduated, he became the coach at Oregon for one year before returning to Chicago as an assistant, and then was head coach at Arkansas. Bedzek returned to Oregon in 1913 to coach football, basketball, and baseball, taking them to the 1917 Rose Bowl. He also scouted for the Pittsburgh Pirates and in the middle of the Pirates' 1917 season, was hired as their manager, and he kept that job through the 1919 season while continuing to coach Oregon. He coached Penn State from 1919 to 1930, including a trip to the 1923 Rose Bowl. During the 1924 season, he was a consulting coach with the Quantico Marines, flown there and back by Lawson Sanderson each Sunday. He also coached the NFL's Cleveland Rams in 1937, and Delaware Valley in 1949. Bedzek was elected to the College Football Hall of Fame in 1954.

'Early Baseball Practice Starts,' *Eugene Guard,* February 21, 1914.

'Bedzek's Eleven Wins Coast Football Game; Coach Journeys East, *Pittsburgh Daily Post,* January 2, 1918.

'Bedzek on Wings,' *Harrisburg Telegraph,* November 4, 1924.

'Hugo Bedzek, Spin Play Inventor, Dies of Heart Attack,' *Tribune (Coshocton, OH),* September 20, 1952.

APPENDIX E: GREAT LAKES NAVAL TRAINING STATION

Great Lakes published several lists of selected players trying out for the team in August and September 1918. Among those trying out for the team, 103 sailors were invited to participate in the team's practice on September 5, 1919. Other players arrived at Great Lakes or joined the team after September 5, 1918, including 26 of the 47 players considered to be part of the roster. Ultimately, the team was cut down to approximately 60 players and additional players were cut as the season unfolded.

For our purposes, players are considered part of the Great Lakes roster if they played in a game, are known to have traveled to an away game, or appear in the team picture taken late in the season. The roster count for Great Lakes includes forty-six men. Players known to have played for Great Lakes' second team that do are not meet the criteria above are listed, but not profiled, in the Great Lakes profile section of the Appendix.

Key information sources for identifying players are below.

'St. Louis Team May Play Here,' *Great Lakes Bulletin,* October 31, 1918. Accessed November 2, 2017.

http://idnc.library.illinois.edu/cgi-bin/illinois?a=d&d=GLB19181031.1.7

'Order,' *Great Lakes Bulletin*, September 5, 1918. Accessed November 2, 2017.

http://idnc.library.illinois.edu/cgi-bin/illinois?a=d&d=GLB19180905.1.4

'All Have Been Through Mill,' *Los Angeles Times*, December 31, 1918.

'Station Machine Which Won Coast-To-Coast Gridiron Championship,' *Great Lakes Recruit*, January 1919.

Buzzell, Francis, *The Great Lakes Naval Station, A History*, Boston, Small, Maynard and Company, 1919.

Abrahamson, Elmer Julius

Born: August 13, 1891 || Died: September 28, 1978 || Lawrence '11-'14 || Abrahamson started at left halfback in two games and substituted into three others, including the 1919 Rose Bowl || WWI: Machinist's Mate

Abrahamson played football and competed in track at Lawrence. Following his graduation, he became a high school teacher and coached the school's basketball team to the 1916 state championship in Wisconsin. After the war, he was a long-time teacher, coach, and athletic director in Oshkosh, Wisconsin.

'Will Play Football,' *Oshkosh Northwestern*, September 17, 1919.

'Football Began with Ripon Defy,' *Post-Crescent (Appleton, WI)*, April 30, 1932.

'Chaff 'N Chatter', Post-Crescent (Appleton, WI), November 8, 1937.

Andrews, LeRoy B. "Roy" or "Bull"

Born: June 27, 1896 || Died: July 1978 || Pittsburg State '15-'17 || Substituted into the Notre Dame and Purdue games at left tackle and was on the roster for the 1919 Rose Bowl || WWI: Seaman

After being discharged, Andrews returned to Kansas and became a bank teller. His helped form the Kansas City Blues that morphed into the NFL's St. Louis All-Stars in 1923. He spent the next five years as a player coach, and three more year as a full-time coach.

Andrews is still ranked in top 100 for NFL coaching wins with 51, and is 11th in winning percentage among coaches with at least 50 wins. After the NFL, he moved to Texas and worked in life insurance sales.

'Former Normal Man Star at Naval Station,' *Sun (Pittsburg, KS),* August 16, 1918.

'L.B. Andrews to Play Football,' *Sun (Pittsburg, KS),* November 15, 1918.

'Andrews Resigns as Coach of Cardinals,' *Green Bay Press-Gazette,* October 5, 1931.

Bachman, Jr., Charles Smith

Born: December 1, 1892 || Died: December 14, 1985 || Notre Dame '14-'16 || Started six games in the line, including the 1919 Rose Bowl || WWI: Chief Boatswain's Mate, promoted to Ensign

Bachman was a 1916 Walter Camp 2nd Team All-American and also was a hurdler and thrower at Notre Dame prior to enlisting. After the war, he was the head football coach at Northwestern, Kansas State, Florida, Michigan State, and Hillsdale. His twenty-six years as a head coach earned him a spot in the College Football Hall of Fame.

'Former Notre Dame Grid Star Takes Place in Navy,' *Indianapolis News,* January 14, 1918.

'Purple to Command Respect of All 'Big Ten' Elevens,' *Chicago Daily Tribune,* September 19, 1919.

'Football Gives Bachman 2 Big Moments; Great Lakes Figures in Both,' *Detroit Free Press,* March 11, 1947.

Barnard, Chester Smith

Born: October 25, 1894 || Died: October 16, 1952 || Missouri State '14-17, Northwestern '19 || Substituted into the Purdue game at left end and was on the 1919 Rose Bowl roster || WWI: Seaman 1c || WWII: Lt. Commander, athletic director at Naval Training Station in Dearborn, Michigan. Transferred to Naval Air Station Pensacola.

Chester earned eleven letters in football, basketball, and track and field at Missouri State prior to the war. After Great Lakes, he played football and basketball for Northwestern in 1919. He became an assistant at Missouri State, head coach as Ole Miss, and a long-term coach at Kalamazoo. After the war, he was an assistant coach at Missouri State and Missouri School of Mines. Chester faced his brother, Lester, as coaches in 1922 when Chester was an assistant as Missouri State and Lester was the head coach at Memphis.

'Barnard Chosen Normal Captain,' *Springfield Missouri Republican,* December 9, 1915.

'Twin Footballers Get Even Break on Football Honors,' *Indianapolis News,* October 24, 1918.

'Chester Barnard Leaves Local College,' *Springfield Leader,* July 6, 1924.

'Lieut. Chester Arthur U.S. Naval Training Instructor,' *Rolla Herald,* July 30, 1942.

Barnard, Lester Smith

Born: October 25, 1894 | | Died: June 1, 1985 | | Missouri State '13-16, Northwestern '19 | | Substituted into three games, including the 1919 Rose Bowl | | WWI: Seaman 1c

Like Chester, Lester was a multisport athlete at Missouri State and played football at Northwestern in 1919. He coached high school football in Oklahoma, before becoming the head football coach at Memphis in 1922 and their basketball coach from 1922 to 1925. He was head football coach and football coach at Central Michigan for two years before moving to coach Minneapolis South High School to a shipload of city and state titles through 1957. The football field at Minneapolis South was named after him and he was inducted into the Minnesota High School Coaches Hall of Fame.

'Drury and Normal Rooters Holding 'Pep' Gathering,' *Springfield Missouri Republican,* November 29, 1916.

'Barnard Twins are Star Ends,' *Scranton Republican,* November 1, 1919.

'Central Normal Regains Parker,' *Detroit Free Press,* June 22, 1926.

'South Pays Tribute to Barnard,' *Star Tribune (Minneapolis, MN),* December 14, 1937.

Blacklock, Hugh McNeal "Chief"

Born: January 1, 1893 || Died: May 21, 1954 || Michigan State '13-'15, Grand Rapids Ramonas '16, Great Lakes '17 || Started at right tackle in every game other than versus Notre Dame || WWI: Boatswain's Mate 2c

Blacklock played football for Great Lakes in 1917 and 1918 and was named to Walter Camp's All-American second team in 1917 and the All Service first team in 1918. He played hockey for Great Lakes as well. After the war, he worked as a furniture upholsterer and deputy sheriff, and played seven years in the NFL, primarily with the Decatur/Chicago Staleys and the Chicago Bears. He later became the long-time Sheriff in Kent County, Michigan.

'Michigan Aggies' Star Tackle,' *Fort Wayne Daily News,* November 6, 1915.

'Sailors Strong in Hockey As in Other Sport, *Detroit Free Press,* February 10, 1918.

'Sheriff, Ex-Athlete Hugh Blacklock Dies,' *Battle Creek Enquirer,* May 21, 1954.

Bliss, Harry William

Born: August 26, 1897 || Died: January 1, 1976 || Ohio State '19-'20 || Substituted in Notre Dame and Purdue games, on roster for the 1919 Rose Bowl || WWI: Seaman

Harry Bliss played football for Ohio State in 1919 and 1920, including the 1921 Rose Bowl. After graduating, he played for the Columbus Panhandles of the AFCA in 1921, and was an assistant coach at New Mexico for ten years. He worked for the Works Progress Administration during the Depression and then for the IRS.

'Gobs Hit Stride in Third Quarter and Bowl Over Purdue Eleven, 27-0,' *Great Lakes Bulletin,* December 1, 1918.

'Ohio State University Models Team After Old Gridiron Stars; Chick Harley Helps,' *New Castle Herald (PA),* October 20, 1920.

'Lobo Football Squad Banqueted and Praised by University; Big Season Predicted for Next Year,' *Albuquerque Journal,* December 18, 1928.

Byers, William McKinley "Mac"

Born: March 3, 1897 || Died: August 26, 1967 || Iowa State Frosh '17, Iowa State '20, Drake track '21 || Substitute QB in Purdue game and on 1919 Rose Bowl roster || WWI: Seaman

Byers was Iowa's 220- and 440-yard dash champion while in high school and played freshmen football at Iowa State before joining the Navy. He started at quarterback for Iowa State in 1920, but transferred to Drake to run track. Byers coached a club football team in the mid-1920s. He worked as an engineer for the county highway department before becoming the Deputy Sheriff in Polk County, Iowa, later working in security for Goodyear Tire and Rubber.

'Freshmen Material Good,' *Des Moines Register,* November 29, 1917.

'Paine Gives Ames Good Shaking Up,' *Des Moines Register,* October 8, 1920.

'Sheriff Overtuff's Key Men,' *Des Moines Register,* December 20, 1938.

Chapeck, Addison Travis

Born: April 4, 1894 || Died: August 29, 1942 || Lane Tech (IL) '13, Illinois Freshman '17 || Traveled to Iowa and Pitt, substituted at QB versus Illinois, and started at QB for Second Team versus North Central || WWI: Unknown rank

Chapeck was an All-Cook County (Chicago area) quarterback in 1913 and placed third in the 880-yard run in the Illinois state track meet in 1914. He attended Knox College as a sub-freshman in 1915 and is reported to have played freshman football at Illinois in 1917. Before and after the war, Chapeck worked in advertising and publication sales in the Chicago area.

'County Elevens Develop Stars,' *Chicago Tribune,* December 8, 1913.

'Illini Falls Before Attack of Great Lakes Bluejackets, 7-0,' *Chicago Tribune,* October 13, 1918.

Collins, John Richard "J. R."

Born: September 11, 1898 || Died: February 5, 1941 || Baylor '17 || Started at left tackle versus Rutgers, played in both second team games, and appears team picture taken late in the season || WWI: Seaman 2c

J. R. Collins' brother, Francis, played guard for Baylor's varsity before and after the war, while J. R. may have played only freshman football. After the war, he worked for Studebaker in South Bend, Indiana, lived in South America for several years, and then lived in New York City, traveling internationally as part of an investment and/or energy concern.

'Bears Crush Trinity, Tigers by Big Score of 55 to 0 Saturday,' *Lariat (Waco, Texas)*, October 18, 1917.

'Baylor Boys at the Great Lakes Station,' *Waco News-Tribune, June 30, 1918.*

'Great Lakes Gobs Outplay Crack Rutgers Eleven and Pile Up On-Sided Score,' *Democrat and Chronicle (Rochester, NY)*, November 17, 1918.

'In The Air,' *Waco News-Times*, December 18, 1928.

Combs, John Perry

Born: February 7, 1897 || Died: January 1, 1948 || Threlkeld Select School (HS) || Combs appears in the Great Lakes team picture taken late in the season, but did not play in any games || WWI: Fireman 2c

Combs returned to Kentucky after his discharge where he farmed and was a Deputy Sheriff, Sheriff, and County Clerk.

'Gobs Hit Stride in Third Quarter and Bowl Over Purdue Eleven, 27-0,' *Great Lakes Bulletin*, December 1, 1918.

'With the Legionnaire,' *Courier-Journal (Louisville, KY)*, November 24, 1919.

'Jessamine Ex-Sheriff, John P. Combs, Dies,' *Courier-Journal (Louisville, KY)*, January 13, 1948.

Conrad, Martin Henry "Marty"

Born: November 30, 1895 || Died: July 1, 1942: Kalamazoo '14-'16 ||

Started four games and substituted in two others at center, on 1919 Rose Bowl roster | | *WWI: Hospital Apprentice*

Conrad played football and baseball at Kalamazoo and was a high school principal and coach before joining the Navy. After the war, he taught and coached at three high schools while playing in the NFL on weekends from 1922 to 1925. He later became an attorney.

'Rosy Outlook at Kalamazoo,' *Detroit Free Press*, September 26, 1916.

'Increasing Work for Football Squad,' *Great Lakes Bulletin*, September 20, 1918.

'Colts Select Grid Mentor,' *Detroit Free Press*, June 1, 1923.

Conzelman, James Gleason "Jimmy"

Born: March 6, 1898 | | *Died: July 31, 1970* | | *Washington University in St. Louis '16, '19* | | *Started at quarterback versus Illinois and Northwestern and substituted in several games, including the 1919 Rose Bowl* | | *WWI: Pharmacist's Mate 3c*

Jimmy Conzelman played freshman football and basketball at Washington University in 1916, but like many young men of the day with medical and dental interests, Conzelman was accepted into the American Ambulance Field Service. He applied for a passport in June 1917 and was scheduled to sail on the *S.S. La Tourraine* for France, but he changed his mind and enlisted in the Navy as a Pharmacists' Mate 3c and became part of the 1917 Great Lakes football team.

After the war, he returned to WashU for the 1919 season, becoming an All-Missouri Valley quarterback. His father passed away soon thereafter and, to help support his family, he joined George Halas's Decatur Staleys in 1920. He played for the Rock Island Independents in 1921 when, in the midst of a game, the owner fired the team's player-coach and named Conzelman the new player-coach at halftime. Conzelman was the player-coach for Milwaukee in 1923 and 1924 and was the coach-owner of the Detroit Panthers from 1925-1926 and was named All-Pro, Conzelman sold the franchise and became the player-coach for Providence, leading the Steam Rollers to the NFL Championship in 1928 and earning the NFL's Most Outstanding Player Award. He coached at WashU for eight years in the 1930s, and then returned to the NFL sidelines as head coach of the Chicago Cardinals from 1940 to 1942 and from 1946 to 1948, winning division titles in 1947 and 1948, and his second NFL title in 1947.

Entering the 2017 season, Conzelman's eighty-eight coaching wins ranks him fifty-first in NFL history. He was inducted into the NFL Hall of Fame in 1964.

'Conzelman Quits Washington; Will Enter St. Louis U.,' *St. Louis Post-Dispatch*, December 22, 1916.

'Sid Keener's Column,' *St. Louis Star and Times*, December 28, 1935.

'Conference Official Picks Conzelman as All-Valley Captain,' *St. Louis Star and Times*, November 29, 1919.

'Sid Keener's Column,' *St. Louis Star and Times*, January 18, 1940.

'How to Take a Biscuit Apart and Put It Back Just Like It Was,' *Sports Illustrated*, September 18, 1961. Accessed November 2, 2017.

http://www.si.com/vault/1961/09/18/617180/how-to-take-a-biscuit-apart-and-put-it-back-just-like-it-was

Jimmy Conzelman, National Football League Hall of Fame Profile. Accessed November 2, 2017. http://www.profootballhof.com/players/jimmy-conzelman/

Dastillung, Harry

Born: April 2, 1897 | | Died: November 30, 1982 | | Northside Club '17 | | Started at right tackle versus Notre Dame and substituted versus Purdue | | WWI: Carpenters Mate 2c

Dastillung played minor league baseball in 1921 with Martinsburg of the Blue Ridge League and Tarboro of the Virginia League. He also played for the Cincinnati Celts of the NFL in 1920 and 1921. Dastillung worked as a carpenter and home builder. (Note: Eight different spellings of Harry Dastillung's surname were identified during the research, so his profile may contain some inaccuracies).

'Great Lakes Team – It's Record,' *Los Angeles Times*, December 15, 1918.

'Jim Thorpe Hurt, Bulldogs Beaten; Buffalo is Winner,' *Pittsburgh Daily Post*, October 24, 1921.

'Malones Will Put Pro Grid Eleven in Field,' *Pittsburgh Press*, August 21, 1921.

Dobson, Paul Arthur

Born: April 1, 1897 || Died: April 1, 1978 || Nebraska '16-'19 || Substituted versus Iowa and started against Illinois at fullback, transferred to aviation ground school at MIT, was discharged and played in the last two games of Nebraska's 1918 season || WWI: Aviation cadet

Dobson played for Nebraska's Missouri Valley Conference championship team in 1917 and was captain of the 1919 team. After graduating, Dobson moved to California and became an orchardist and rancher, He became President of a Grape Growers Association and later spent ten years as President of the Diamond Walnuts organization. In 1970, President Johnson nominated him to the Farm Credit Bureau and he became its President in 1970.

'Nebraska Loses to Notre Dame,' *Lincoln Star*, December 1, 1916.

'Dodson, Great Lakes Star, Wings Way to Flying Corps,' *Chicago Daily Tribune*, October 15, 1918.

'Dobson is Elected Cornhusker Captain,' *St. Louis Star and Times*, January 11, 1919.

'Exeter Man Heads Farm Credit for U.S.,' *Fresno Bee*, April 19, 1970.

Doherty, John Lawrence "Mel"

Born: April 21, 1896 || Died: July 17, 1942 || Marietta '19 || Doherty substituted in the Iowa game and appears in the Great Lakes team picture taken late in the season || WWI: Seaman 2c, Seaman

John "Mel" Doherty was a difficult guy to track down since his surname was commonly misspelled, and he used a mix of nicknames and his formal name. In the end, name changes seem fitting for him. In 1919, Doherty played football for Marietta College in Ohio and then played for the NFL's Cincinnati Celts, including at least one game playing against an aging Jim Thorpe Doherty coached football at Xavier University in Cincinnati as well, but made his mark as one of the top bandleaders in Ohio. During that time, one of Doherty's sons was the dancing partner of a young woman named Doris Kappelhoff. One evening, two of Doherty's sons were in a car with Doris when they tried to beat a train at a railroad crossing. The train clipped the car, flipping it over, and Doris Kappelhoff suffered leg injuries that ended her dancing career. Resilient, she focused on using her voice rather than her legs. You likely know her by her stage name, Doris Day.

'Great Lakes Defeats Iowa in Hard Fought Game By 10-0 Score,' *St. Louis Post–Dispatch*, September 29, 1918.

'18 Get Letters,' *Akron Beacon Journal*, December 15, 1919.

'Celts-Flyers Battle Today,' *Star Press (Muncie, IN)*, October 16, 1920.

'Funeral Set,' *News-Journal (Mansfield, OH)*, July 18, 1942.

Driscoll, John Leo "Paddy"

Born: January 11, 1896 || Died: June 29, 1968 || Northwestern '14-'16, Chicago Cubs '17, Hammond Clabbys '17 || Substituted at left halfback versus Iowa, started the next two games at left halfback, and started the rest to the season at quarterback || WWI: Chief Yeoman, Ensign

Driscoll played for Northwestern, the Chicago Cubs, and the Hammond Clabbys before Great Lakes. After his discharge, he played minor league baseball and football for the Hammond Pros. In 1920, he signed as the player-coach for the Racine /Chicago Cardinals, playing for them through 1925, before being sold to the Chicago Bears, where he played for four seasons. He was a six-time All-Pro. Driscoll began coaching high school football, basketball, and baseball while playing in the NFL and was the football coach at Marquette for three years starting in 1937. He rejoined the Bears and remained with them until his death, including two years as their head coach in 1956 and 1957. Driscoll was elected to the NFL Hall of Fame in 1965.

'Driscoll is Power in the Gridiron World,' *Sunday Oregonian*, December 2, 1918.

'Driscoll Released From Navy,' *Chicago Daily Tribune*, March 12, 1919.

'In the Wake of the News,' *Chicago Tribune*, September 2, 1966.

"Paddy" Driscoll, National Football League Hall of Fame Profile. Accessed November 2, 2017.

http://www.profootballhof.com/players/john-paddy-driscoll/

Eielson, Harry Albert "Dizzy"

Born: November 10, 1896 || Died: May 8, 1983 || Northwestern Frosh '17, NW BB & T&F '19; Washington & Jefferson '19-'20 || Substituted in one game and started four others, including the 1919 Rose Bowl || WWI: Seaman

Eielson played freshmen football at Northwestern before Great Lakes and returned there, setting the school pole vault record, but encountered eligibility issues and transferred to Washington & Jefferson, playing football there for two years. He returned to the family lumber business in Springfield, Illinois, before becoming the Sangamon County Sheriff and Mayor of Springfield. Eielson won the national doubles handball championship in 1950.

'Freak Tackle At Annapolis Puzzles Officials,' *Chicago Tribune*, November 25, 1918.

'Bachman Welcomes Flock of Gridders for Practice,' *Chicago Tribune*, September 16, 1919.

'Dull Gridiron Games Extinct Affairs Now,' *Indianapolis News*, December 27, 1919.

'Springfield to Enter Float in 'Roses' Parade,' *Freeport Journal-Standard (Freeport, IL),* November 11, 1949.

Eklund, Conrad Lawrence "Con"

Born: February 19, 1894 || Died: March 18, 1953 || Macalaster '14, Minnesota '16-'17 || Started four of the last five games at left tackle, including the 1919 Rose Bowl || WWI: Dental Department

Eklund was named All-Big Ten for Minnesota in 1916 and 1917, lettered in basketball twice, and graduated with his undergraduate dental degree before heading to Great Lakes. After the war, he practiced dentistry in Minneapolis, coached youth basketball for a number of years, and was the head football coach at Augsburg from 1925 to 1932.

'Gopher at Strength in Two Regulars,' *Minnesota Star*, September 25, 1917.

'Use Conference Timber,' *Oshkosh Northwestern*, November 6, 1918.

'The Coaches Await Start of State College Grid Season,' *Minneapolis Star Tribune*, September 13, 1931.

'Gopher Great Passes,' *Minneapolis Star*, March 19, 1953.

Erickson, Harold Alexander "Swede"

Born: March 10, 1898 || Died: January 27, 1963 || St. Olaf '16 (no FB), Great Lakes '17, Northwestern'19 (ineligible), Washington & Jefferson '19-'22 || Substituted at halfback in the Iowa game and started every other game, including the 1919 Rose Bowl || WWI: Pharmacist's Mate

Hal Erickson first played football at Great Lakes in 1917 and 1918, while also playing basketball. Following the war, he made a quick stop at Northwestern before transferring to Washington & Jefferson where he started four years and led the team to the 1922 Rose Bowl. He ran track for W&J as well. Erickson played for the Milwaukee Badgers '23'-'24 (player-coach in '24), the Chicago Cardinals '25-'28, and the Minneapolis Red Jackets '29-'30. He was an assistant coach at DePauw in 1923. He also played in a barnstorming game with Jimmy Conzelman in 1922, and toured with Red Grange and the Chicago Bears on the famous barnstorming team during the winter of 1925-26. During that tour he played in 19 games over 66 days after playing 14 NFL games in 1925. Following his football career, Erickson worked as a radio inspector and then entered the life insurance business, ending his career as the President of Security National Life Insurance.

'Sensational Backfield Talent at Great Lakes,' *Des Moines Tribune*, September 25, 1918.

Henderson, Gloomy Gus. 'Erickson is the Individual Star of the Annual Classic, Is of All-American Caliber,' *Los Angeles Times*, January 3, 1922.

'Bears Load Up New Stars for South Invasion,' *Minneapolis Star,* December 21, 1925.

'Rose Bowlers are Scattered,' *Daily Notes (Cannonsburg, PA)*, May 2, 1946.

'City's Erickson Played in Two Rose Bowls, Never Lost,' *Minneapolis Star*, December 21, 1960.

Foley, Joseph Algernon "Jack"

Born: March 19, 1898 | | Died: February 11, 1971 | | Blackburn '17, 20, Washington & Jefferson '21 | | Substituted at quarterback in the Iowa game and on the roster for the Notre Dame game | | WWI: Ensign

Foley attended Blackburn Academy and College in Carlinville, Illinois where he played for Blackburn from 1915 to 1917, the first two years as an Academy student and the third as a college freshman before heading to Great Lakes in 1918. After his released from the Navy in 1919, he was named Blackburn's Athletic Director and football coach. He returned to student status in 1920 to quarterback and captain the football team. (He was a star basketball and baseball player as well.) He then transferred to Washington & Jefferson for the 1921 season where he was a substitute quarterback, playing in a handful of games and scoring at least one touchdown. After graduating from W&J, he entered Harvard Law School, but appears not to have graduated, and spent most his career teaching math at the high school and college levels.

'Our Football Season,' *Blackburnian*, Blackburn College, December 1917.

'New Director,' *Decatur Daily Review (IL)*, September 17, 1919.

'Blackburn Trims the Normal Varsity,' *Pantagraph (Bloomington, IL)*, October 4, 1920.

'W.&J. Will Graduate Few Stars,' *Pittsburgh Press,* June 4, 1922.

Griffith, Bartholomew Joseph "Bert"

Born: March 3, 1896 | | Died: May 5, 1973 | | Christian Brothers (HS) | | On the roster through most of the season, the only confirmed playing time came as a substitute right guard in the 1919 Rose Bowl | | WWI: Coxswain

Griffith was a top amateur baseball player in the St. Louis area and did not play football prior to arriving at Great Lakes. He was the acting company commander over the sixty men on the team, leading them through military drills and the like. He played minor league baseball after the war before breaking into the big leagues with the Brooklyn Robins in 1922 and 1923, and handful of games with the Washington Senators in 1924. He was among fourteen major leaguers sent on a barnstorming tour to Japan in the winter of 1922-1923. He later owned a café in Los Angeles.

'Bert Griffith is Latest St. Louis Boy on Navy Team,' *St. Louis Star and Times*, September 15, 1918.

'Griffith an All- Around Star,' *St. Louis Post-Dispatch*, April 2, 1919.

'Blues Make Deal with Washington,' *Indianapolis News*, July 18, 1924.

Halas, George Stanley

Born: February 2, 1895 || Died: October 31, 1983 || Illinois '14-17 || Started every game at right end, including the 1919 Rose Bowl for which he was the MVP || WWI: Chief Carpenter's Mate, Ensign || WWII: Lt. Commander, Commander of recreational and athletic activities. Awarded Bronze Star for his services

Halas played football, basketball, and baseball at Illinois and at Great Lakes. He was the 1919 Rose Bowl MVP. Halas played in twelve games with the New York Yankees in 1919. In 1919, Halas left his engineering job to coach three sports for the Staley Starch Company of Decatur, Illinois and was among the twelve attendees at the 1920 meeting in a Hupmobile dealership in Canton during with the AAFC, renamed the NFL in 1921, was founded. Halas took ownership of the Staleys in 1920, moving them to Chicago, and renamed them the Bears in 1921.

He coached the Bears for forty seasons, winning six NFL championships. His 324 career coaching wins ranks second in NFL history. Despite his success as a coach, his greatest impact on the league came from his strengths as an organizer and promoter of the Bears and the broader league. He was elected to the NFL Hall of Fame as part of its inaugural class in 1963.

'Great Lakes Provides Two Players for Yanks,' *Washington Times*, December 14, 1918.

'Ensigns Driscoll and Halas Signed by South America,' *Great Lakes Bulletin*, February 11, 1919.

'George Halas Out of Navy; To Become Bear Observer,' *Cincinnati Enquirer*, November 14, 1945.

George Halas, National Football League Hall of Fame Profile. Accessed November 2, 2017. http://www.profootballhof.com/players/george-halas/

Davis, Jeff. *Papa Bear: The Life and Legacy of George Halas.* New York: McGraw-Hill. 2005.

Hyde, Merrill James

Born: January 13, 1895 || Died: November 23, 1970 || Alma '14-'15 || Substituted at fullback versus Notre Dame and on the roster for the cancelled Pitt game, but is not known to have played in other games || WWI: Seaman

Hyde lettered in football, baseball, and track and field at Alma, and was working in the crop insurance business prior to Great Lakes. After the war, he spent his career in fire insurance administration and management.

'Alma Expect to Win Final,' *Detroit Free Press*, November 13, 1915.

'Hyde Showing Form,' *Indianapolis Star*, November 12, 1918.

'Ex-Addison Man Dies,' *Hillsdale Daily News*, December 5, 1970.

Ivy, Hyrle Archibald "Red"

Born: May 12, 1896 || Died: May 17, 1976 || Salina HS (KS), Kansas '20, '22 || Listed on the roster for the cancelled Pitt game and is in the team picture taken late in the season, but is not known to have played in any games || WWI: Musician

Ivy played football for Kansas in 1920 (playing under Phog Allen) and 1922, taking off from school in 1921 work at his hometown YMCA when his father passed away. Ivy started at center for Kansas in 1922 when they lost to Army, 13-0. He went on to become a long-time teach and coach at North Side High School in Ft. Wayne, Indiana.

'Football Squad Off for Bronx Today,' *Great Lakes Bulletin*, November 14, 1918.

'K.U. Prospects Only Fair for Winning Eleven,' *Wichita Daily Eagle*, September 24, 1920.

'Army 13 K.U. 0, Jayhawk Stock Climbs in East,' *Kansas City Kansas*, October 8, 1922.

Jones, Jerald Joseph "Jerry"

Born: October 9, 1896 | | Died: May 24, 1938 | | Notre Dame '14-'15, Dubuque '16 | | Started at guard in every game except versus Purdue. Started the 1919 Rose Bowl | | WWI: Coxswain

Jones earned letters in football, baseball, and track and field at Notre Dame, though he did not receive his baseball and track letters in 1916 after being barred from further competition for playing as a ringer in a semipro baseball game. Jones finished his college career at Dubuque. After Great Lakes, Jones played with the Hammond Pros in 1919 prior to joining Halas with the Decatur Staleys in 1920, after which he played three more years in the NFL. During that time, he also owned and managed the Sepulpa, Oklahoma baseball team in the Southwestern League, was an assistant football and head baseball coach at Missouri, an assistant football coach at Xavier from 1923 to 1929, and coached at Columbia College (IA) from 1931 to 1934 and was head coach in 1932 and 1933. During the 1930s, he coached the Tulsa Oilers in two failed southern professional football leagues.

'Notre Dame Drops Stars For Playing on 'Pro' Team,' *Chicago Tribune*, June 4, 1916

'Purdue Meets the Great Lakes Team,' *New Castle Herald*, November 20, 1918.

'Jerry Jones, Missouri Coach,' *Fort Scott Daily Tribune*, August 23, 1921.

'Jones Funeral Rites Tomorrow,' *Sepulpa Herald (Creek County, OK)*, June 28, 1938.

Keefe, Emmett

Born: April 28, 1893 || Died: September 11, 1965 || Notre Dame '12-'15 || Team captain, he started at guard in every game, including the 1919 Rose Bowl || WWI: Fireman 1c

Keefe was Knute Rockne's teammate and Notre Dame's football captain during in a career that included Notre Dame's legendary victory over Army in 1913. After completing his ND career, he was the head coach at St. Viator (IL) in 1917. After leaving Great Lakes, he played four years in the NFL and followed that with a long career as an engineer in R&D at the Pullman Company in Chicago.

'Keefe New Coach at St. Viator's,' *Decatur Daily Review*, September 28, 1917.

'Keefe Expected to be Real Star for Great Lakes,' *Los Angeles Herald*, December 30, 1918.

'Kraehe Signs 4 Football Stars for 'Pro' Eleven,' *St. Louis Post-Dispatch*, July 25, 1923.

'Emmett Keefe,' *Journal and Courier (Lafayette, IN)*, September 14, 1965.

Knight, Charles E. "Charlie"

Born: October 1, 1899 || Died: February 17, 1979 || Northwestern Frosh '17, Northwestern '19 || Started at center against Purdue and substituted in three other games, including the 1919 Rose Bowl || WWI: Seaman

Charles Knight played for Northwestern during the 1919 season and remained a student there in 1920, but played the professional Chicago Cardinals in 1920 and 1921. He then ran a soda-dispensing company in the Chicago area before popping up in Fort Lauderdale, where he owned one of its major hotels and was heavily involved in civic affairs.

'Three in Scrap for Center Job on Purple Team,' *Chicago Tribune*, September 21, 1919.

'Cardinals Takes On Rock Island at Normal Park,' *Chicago Tribune*, October 16, 1921.

'Charles E. Knight City Commission Advertisement,' *Ft. Lauderdale News*, April 6, 1957.

Langenstein, Chester Gift

Born: November 29, 1898 || Died: May 26, 1954 || Freeport HS (IL), Northwestern '19 || Started at left tackle versus Iowa, substituted in two games, and was on the roster for the 1919 Rose Bowl || WWI: Musician

Langenstein started for the Illinois high school basketball championship team as a sophomore. After Great Lakes, he played football and basketball at Northwestern for one year and coached high school teams in Illinois and Hawaii during the 1920s. Langenstein then moved to California where became a barber and appeared as a musician on radio programs.

'Freeport Basketball Squad – Northern Champions,' *Decatur Herald*, March 11, 1915.

'Langenstein Joins Navy,' *Belvidere Daily Republican (Belvidere, IL),* April 23, 1918.

'Badgers Inquire Status of 4 Purple Players, Report,' *Chicago Daily News*, October 7, 1919.

'Honolulu Lads Play in Their Bare Feet,' *Alta Vista Journal (KS)*, December 23, 1920.

Lauer, Harold Sebastian "Dutch"

Born: January 8, 1898 || Died: August 9, 1978 || Detroit '17, '19-'21 || Started at fullback against Navy and Purdue, and substituted in two other games. Was on the 1919 Rose Bowl roster || WWI: Seaman 2c

Lauer lettered in football at the University of Detroit before joining Great Lakes. He returned there after his discharge, was named All-Western and Honorable Mention All-American at fullback in 1921, leaving as Detroit's all-time leading scorer. He played four years in the NFL, including two seasons with his hometown Detroit Panthers. He was an assistant coach at Detroit in 1924. After his playing days, Lauer was an insurance agent and an auto parts importer.

'U. of D. Gridders Pick Fitzgerald to Pilot Eleven,' *Detroit Free Press,* December 5, 1917.

'Statistics on the Rival Football Teams Today At Annapolis,' *Baltimore Sun,* November 23, 1918.

'Ranks with Best Fullbacks in the West,' *Detroit Free Press,* November 28, 1921.

'W&J Wins Intersectional Game from University of Detroit,' *Detroit Free Press,* December 4, 1921.

'Line Plunging of Packers Wins, 7-0,' *Post-Crescent (Appleton, WI),* November 29, 1926.

McCauley, G. (George) Kent

Born: May 30, 1895 || Died: August 29, 1951 || Geneva 15-16, Great Lakes '17, Denver '19-'21 || Played on the 1917 Great Lakes team. In 1918, he substituted at fullback versus Purdue || WWI: Chief Yeoman

McCauley played football at Geneva College. After his discharge, he returned to Colorado and played for the University of Denver. He became a teacher and coach, but spent most of his career as the superintendent of schools in several Colorado school districts.

'Collegians are Beaten Badly,' *New Castle Herald (PA),* November 15, 1915.

'Great Lakes Eleven Comes From Behind, Beating Iowa, 23-14,' *Chicago Tribune,* November 4, 1917.

'Wyoming Cowboys Hold University of Denver to Tie,' *Arizona Republic,* October 20, 1921.

McClellan, William Oswald

Born: May 9, 1897 || Died: April 15, 1973 || Parkersburg (WV) HS '15 || Started at quarterback versus Iowa and substituted at left halfback versus Purdue || WWI: Chief Yeoman

McLellan was the Assistant Physical Director of the Army and Navy YMCA at Newport News, before transferring to a YMCA in Elyria, Ohio. After his release, he returned to Elyria and became the General Secretary of the YMCA. He was a frequent high school football referee. Following one game during which he made some close calls, the losing team's fans attacked McClellan, severely beating him before the police intervened. Despite the experience, McClellan continued refereeing for at least fourteen more years. Later in his career, McClellan was the secretary-treasurer for the Elyria Board of Education and held state roles in the Rotary and American Legion.

'C.H.S. Boys Named on All-Stars Team,' *Charleston Daily Mail (WV)*, November 29, 1915.

'A Former Newporter,' *Newport Mercury*, June 1, 1917.

'Jackies Win At Iowa City' *Topeka Daily Capital*, September 29, 1918.

'Athletics are Stopped,' *Cincinnati Enquirer*, November 18, 1924.

Mendenhall, Leland Lester "L.L."

Born: January 6, 1892 || Died: October 4, 1970 || Drake '13, Iowa '15-'17 || Started at left halfback versus Iowa and substituted versus Illinois. Qualified for aviation training, transferred to Dunwoody Institute, and played two games for them || WWI: Aviation cadet

Mendenhall played football and ran track for Drake and Iowa before the war. He also wrestled at Iowa. After his release, he taught and coached for one year at an Iowa high school, then coached at Carleton College for one year, before being named the head coach and Athletic Director at Northern Iowa. Mendenhall was the Athletic Director and head of the Physical Education department at UNI from 1921 to 1960. He was inducted into UNI's Hall of Fame in 1985.

'How Iowa and Grinnell Look,' *Des Moines Register*, October 15, 1916.

'Navy Loses Mendenhall,' *Des Moines Register*, October 13, 1918.

'L. L. Mendenhall,' *University of Northern Iowa Press Release*, October 6, 1970. Accessed November 2, 2017.

https://www.library.uni.edu/collections/special-collections/biographical-sketches/l-l-mendenhall

Miller, Bernard Howard (born Howard Bernard)

Born: January 28, 1898 | | Died: February 17, 1967 | | Bridgewater HS (IA), Northwestern '19 | | Started at right guard versus Purdue and was on the 1919 Rose Bowl roster | | WWI: Seaman

B. H. Miller, joined Charlie Bachman at Northwestern, played during the 1919 season, but did not play again after taking on the role of sophomore class president. By the late 1920s, he had life licked at the part owner of an envelope manufacturing company in Chicago. He remained affiliated with Northwestern for years, helping fund the McGaw Hall Sports Center, where Northwestern basketball plays its games today.

'Great Lakes Sailors Easily Defeat Purdue,' *Star Tribune (Minneapolis)*, December 1, 1918.

'Purple Grid Men to Name Captain Early Next Week,' *Chicago Daily Tribune*, September 20, 1919.

'Badgers Inquire Status of 4 Purple Players, Report,' *Chicago Tribune*, October 17, 1919.

'Three Employees Purchase Heco Envelope Company,' *Chicago Tribune*, March 30, 1929.

Minton, Roscoe "Cow"

Born: December 24, 1995 | | Died: July 3, 1968 | | Indiana Frosh '16, Indiana '17, '19-'20 | | Started the first three games at left end, then qualified for aviation training, transferred to Dunwoody Institute, and played two games for them | | WWI: Landsman Quartermaster, Seaman 2c, Aviation cadet

Minton played at Indiana before and after Great Lakes, captained the Indiana football team in 1920, and played baseball the following spring. He was Indiana's head baseball coach in 1923 and 1924, was an assistant football coach at Centenary, was hired by his Great Lakes teammate, L.L. Mendenhall, at Northern Iowa as the head baseball coach and football assistant. Minton then moved on to a successful career as a high school coach in Fort Worth, Texas. His brother, Sherman, was a U.S. Senator and Associate Justice of the U.S. Supreme Court.

'Former Crimson Star Becomes Aviation Pilot,' *Indianapolis News*, October 11, 1918.

'Roscoe Minton Chosen Captain of Indiana,' *Courier-Journal (Louisville, KY)*, October 8, 1920.

'Pedagogs Sign New Ball Coach,' *Des Moines Register*, June 22, 1924.

Moxley, Auben Edwin

Born: October 20, 1892 || Died: December 27, 1949 || Bethel (KY) '14, '19 || Traveled with team to the Iowa game as a backup center || WWI: Landsman

Before the war, Moxley played football at Bethel College (KY) while studying to become a preacher and spent one year as a cook in the Kentucky National Guard. He spent most of the 1918 season playing on the Great Lakes First Regiment team. After the war, he tried his hand at preaching, assisted a stunt pilot, and sold cars and vacuum cleaners. He also was involved in starting a paint company and earned two patents during the 1940s.

'Salem,' *Crittenden Record-Press (KY)*, July 26, 1917.

'First Regiment Cops Stubborn Grid Go,' *Great Lakes Bulletin*, October 19, 1918.

'Bethel College Smothers Ogden,' *Courier-Journal (Louisville, KY)*, November 4, 1919.

'Moon Journeyer Here, Planning Death Stunts in Plane Over Sea,' *Asbury Park Press*, June 6, 1922.

United States Patent and Trademark Office, *Inspirator for Gas Burner*, Patent #US002388930. Accessed November 2, 2017.

http://pdfpiw.uspto.gov/.piw?PageNum=0&docid=02388930

Nevins, Zenas Arthur

Born: March 29, 1895 || Died: September 14, 1978 || Baker (KS) '15-'17, '19 || Member of Great Lakes' second team || WWI: Seaman

Nevins earned four letters each in football, basketball, baseball, and track and field at Baker. After graduating, he coached high school football and basketball in Kansas and Mississippi. Nevins then worked in sales for Maytag and an implement dealer, while also serving nine years as the Mayor of Dodge City, four years in the

Kansas House of Representatives, and as chairman of the Democratic Party in Kansas. Nevins was also a candidate for Lt. Governor of Kansas in 1962 and was a long-time volunteer with the Salvation Army.

'No Game in Sight for First Team,' *Great Lakes Bulletin*, November 1, 1918.

'Baker-O.U. Teams Well Matched,' *Ottawa Herald*, November 26, 1919.

'Z. Arthur Nevins,' *Garden City Telegram*, August 3, 1962.

Novinger, George John

Born: February 15, 1898 || Died: September 4, 1975 || Kirksville HS (MO), Missouri '19-'20, Truman State '22 || Traveled with team to the Iowa game as a backup guard || WWI: Unknown rank || WWII: Entered Army Officers Training program

Novinger worked on the family farm before entering the Navy and played with the team early in the season. After discharge, he was among Missouri's top freshman in 1919 and played with the varsity in 1920 before transferring to Truman State, where he played in 1922. Novinger coached football, basketball, and track at Fergus County High School (MT) and was twice elected head of the Montana Athletic Officials organization. He entered Army officers training during WWII. After WWII, he settled in California working as a clerk for the post office and YMCA.

'Order,' *Great Lakes Bulletin*, September 5, 1918. Accessed November 2, 2017.

http://idnc.library.illinois.edu/cgi-bin/illinois?a=d&d=GLB19180905.1.4

'Missouri Wins by Dropkick Margin,' *Des Moines Register*, November 7, 1920.

'Iowa Wesleyan Loses to Kirksville,' *Des Moines Register*, October 6, 1923.

'Will Go to Utah,' *Great Falls Tribune*, November 13, 1942.

Paulsen, C. L. "Whitey"

Born: Unknown || Died: Unknown || Kansas Normal || Substituted at left tackle in Iowa game, started In backfield in second team games, and appears in team picture taken late in the season || WWI: Landsman Electrician Radio

Insufficient information found to identify this player.

'Great Lakes Takes Off with 22 Players,' *Chicago Tribune*, September 28, 1918.

'Great Lakes Seconds Find It Easy in Defeating Cornell Eleven, 33-3,' *Great Lakes Bulletin*, November 4, 1918.

'Station Machine Which Won Coast-To-Coast Gridiron Championship,' *Great Lakes Recruit*, January 1919.

Reeves, Andrew J. "Jack" or "Blondy"

Born: May 11, 1896 || Died: November 7, 1920 || Ottawa (KS) '16-'17, Emporia (KS) '20 || Started two games at fullback, including the 1919 Rose Bowl, and substituted in four other games || WWI: Landsman Electrician Radio

Reeves lettered in football, basketball, and baseball at Ottawa before the war. He became Great Lakes' starting fullback after Willaman was injured and scored the first touchdown in the 1919 Rose Bowl. After his release, he coached at his hometown high school and then transferred to Emporia where he played football in 1920. Reeves died of injuries suffered in a football game that season.

'Reeves Will be in O.U.,' *Ottawa Herald*, August 18, 1917.

'Great Lakes Eleven Humbles Sanford's Great Machine,' *Brooklyn Daily Eagle*, November 17, 1918.

'Reeves, Normal Fullback, Dies of Broken Neck,' *Wichita Daily Eagle*, November 8, 1920.

'Mother Speeding to Deathbed of Son is Too Late,' *Wichita Daily Eagle*, November 8, 1920.

Reichle, Richard Wendell

Born: November 23, 1894 || Died: June 13, 1967 || Illinois '16, '19, '21 || Substituted at left end the first three games of the season and started the remaining games at end, including the 1919 Rose Bowl || WWI: Seaman

Reichle played football and baseball at Illinois before and after Great Lakes. After graduating, he spent part of the 1922 season in the minors and was called up by the Red Sox in September 1922. He is best known today for swatting the second home run ever hit in Yankee Stadium. Reichle broke his leg in spring training in 1924 and never returned to the majors, but he played six games for the Milwaukee Badgers of the NFL in the 1923 season. After his athletic career, he was in the investment and insurance business in St. Louis.

'Great Lakes Team Beat Rutgers, 54-14 – Driscoll is Star,' *Chicago Tribune*, November 17, 1918.

'Iowa Team is Too Strong for Illinois,' *Iowa City Press-Citizen*, October 17, 1921.

'Ruth Again a Hero,' *Fitchburg Sentinel (MA)*, April 21, 1923.

'Sports Snap Shots,' *Nevada State Journal*, November 17, 1923.

'Dick Reichle: More Than One for the Book,' *St. Louis Post-Dispatch*, January 26, 1964.

Richards, Vernon R. "Verne"

Born: January 7, 1897 || Died: April 26, 1973 || Alma '14-'17 || Included in team picture taken late in the season, but did not appear in any games || WWI: Musician

Richards played on Alma's 1914 team that suffered a 56-0 loss to Notre Dame, but Richards scored a touchdown in their 14-7 victory over Michigan State that season. He was All-MIAA in football in '15, '16, '17 and captain of Alma's '16-'17 basketball team prior to entering Great Lakes. Richards earned his D.D.S. from Michigan in 1924, while also assisting Alma's football team in 1922. He practiced dentistry in the Detroit area throughout his career and was inducted into Alma's Hall of Fame in 1971.

'Alma Gridders Win Over M.A.C. Eleven,' *Lansing State Journal*, October 8, 1917.

'Station Machine Which Won Coast-To-Coast Gridiron Championship,' *Great Lakes Recruit*, January 1919.

'A Death Wish for Alma Mater,' *Sports Illustrated, September 25, 1967.* Accessed November 2, 2017.

https://www.si.com/vault/1967/09/25/609675/a-death-wish-for-alma-mater

Swanekamp, Frederick William

Born: April 16, 1896 || Died: September 25, 1971 || Superior HS (WI) || Included in team picture taken late in the season, but did not appear in any games || WWI: Unknown

Swanekamp was the foreman of a telephone switchboard installation crew when he was drafted. After his discharge, he returned to work at Western Electric and held a variety of supervisory roles the company over his 44-year career.

'Men Enlist in Pittsburgh to Save Nation in War,' *Pittsburgh Post-Gazette,* July 20, 1918.

'Station Machine Which Won Coast-To-Coast Gridiron Championship,' *Great Lakes Recruit,* January 1919.

'Hawthorn Employees Who Have Returned from the Military and been Reinstated Since the Last Issue of the News,' *Western Electric News,* April 1919.

Welsh, Harry Ellsworth,

Born: December 11, 1900 || Died: May 23, 1979 || Toledo Scott HS || In team picture taken late in the season || WWI: Unknown rank

Welsh grew up in Toledo and moved to the Los Angeles area after the war. He held a range of sales and management positions with Southern California Edison and other utilities. He was actively involved in the Red Cross, USO, and Orange County Chamber of Commerce during the 1930s and 1940s.

'Order,' *Great Lakes Bulletin,* September 5, 1918, p. 5

'Station Machine Which Won Coast-To-Coast Gridiron Championship,' *Great Lakes Recruit,* January 1919.

Buzzell, Francis, *The Great Lakes Naval Station, A History,* Boston, Small, Maynard and Company, 1919.

'Welsh Heads USO Campaign,' *Santa Ana Register*, April 17, 1942.

Willaman, Frank Reeves

Born: August 16, 1897 || Died: February 9, 1926 || Ohio State '16-'17, '19-'20 || Started first four games of the season at fullback, was injured, and did not play again until he substituted into the 1919 Rose Bowl || WWI: Landsman Electrician Radio

Willaman played at Ohio State before and after the war, earning All-Big Ten honors at fullback in 1919. He was injured much of his senior year, but appeared in the 1921 Rose Bowl for the Buckeyes. Willaman also threw the discus for Ohio State. After graduating, he an assistant football and track coach at Iowa State under his brother, and was then promoted to the Director of Intramural Athletics. Willaman died in 1926 after a three-day bout with pneumonia.

'Great Lakes Football "Beef Trust",' *Pittsburgh Press*, September 29, 1918.

'Grid Stars in Last Game for Ohio State at Pasadena,' *Ohio State University Monthly*, January 1921.

'Famous Salem Athlete Dies at Ames, Iowa,' *Evening Review (East Liverpool, OH)*, February 10, 1926.

Williams, Roy Wesley,

Born: November 30, 1888 || Died: December 10, 1971 || Emporia State '16 || Substituted at right end versus Iowa and appeared in the team picture taken late in the season || WWI: Musician 2c, Ensign

Williams played football at Emporia State and was named All-Kansas in 1916, in addition to being on the track team. After Great Lakes, he was a teacher and football coach at several high schools and in 1922 was named the Director of Athletics for the Oklahoma City schools. He later worked for the Boy Scouts and Chevrolet.

'Oklahoma Schools Busy at Football,' *Wichita Beacon*, September 18, 1916.

'Naperville Team Defeated 21-0 by Seconds,' Great Lakes Bulletin, November 11, 1918.

'Roy Williams Direct Play at Oklahoma City,' *Emporia Gazette*, September 9, 1922.

Second Team Players Not Considered Part of Team Roster

Brown, (Unknown) || Listed on Port team roster on October 30, 1918

Dorgan, J. W. || St. Mary's || Cut from team on October 29, 1918

Jones, M. W. || Cut from team on October 29, 1918

Kiley, H. K. or H. T. || Blue City || Cut from team on October 29, 1918

McCarthy, W. || Listed on Starboard team roster on October 30, 1918

McConley, (Unknown) || Listed on Starboard team roster on October 30, 1918

McGrath, J. E. || Listed on Port team roster on October 30, 1918

McQuillen, (Unknown) || Listed on Port team roster on October 30, 1918

Mosser, J. W. || Penn State || Listed on Port team roster on October 30, 1918

Murphy, Mike || Notre Dame || Listed on Port team roster on October 30, 1918

Nichol, A. G. || Cut from team on October 29, 1918

Orschel / Oerschel, Fred H. || Cut from team on October 29, 1918

Sadenwasser / Sadenwesser, (Unknown) || Listed on Port team roster on October 30, 1918

Sayles, H. E. || Listed on Port team roster on October 30, 1918

Schultz, (Unknown) || Listed on Starboard team roster on October 30, 1918

Thomas, Jack || Listed on Port team roster on October 30, 1918. Great Lakes heavyweight boxing and shot put champion.

Coaches and Administrators

Kaufman, M.D., John B.

Born: July 30, 1890 || Died: March 15, 1950 ||Richmond '98, Pennsylvania (Medical School) || Athletic Director and Recreation Officer || WWI: Lt. Commander, Commander, Captain

A Virginia native, Kaufman played quarterback for Richmond in 1898 before attending medical school at Penn. He joined the Naval Medical Corp in 1906 in roles aboard ship and at base hospitals. Kaufman revised the Navy's primary training manual for hospital corpsmen in 1917 and oversaw the Hospital Corps training program at Great Lakes, while also commanding the Seventh Regiment (Hospital Corps), and supervising all athletic and recreational activities. Great Lakes developed the finest training camp athletic program under his watch and he is credited with discovering Jack Benny when Benny, a Great Lakes recruit, performed at a show. Kaufman planned to retire from the Navy in the early 1940s and was stationed at Pearl Harbor at the time of the Japanese attack. As a result, he remained in the Navy until 1947.

'Athletic Officer Will Leave Station,' *Great Lakes Bulletin,* November 14, 1918.

'Jackies Receive Athletic Course,' *Lansing State Journal,* November 22, 1918.

Hull, Charles. 'John B. Kaufman, Navy Doctor,' *San Diego Union,* September 16, 1965, pp. 19, xx, 1 of 2

Hacala, Mark T, 'There Were Many Heroes: Hospital Corpsmen in World War I,' *Navy Medicine,* July-August 1997, pp. 22-27

McReavy, Clarence James "C.J."

Born: July 30, 1890 || Died: March 15, 1950 || Whitworth '08-'09, Naval Academy '10-'13 || Assistant, then Head Coach || WWI: Lt., served aboard U.S.S. Potter early in war, then assigned to Great Lakes as head of Officer Material School || WWII: Commander

McReavy played two years of football at Whitworth College before accepting an appointment to the Naval Academy, where he played football and basketball. He lettered three years in each sport and captained the basketball team one year. He served aboard the U.S.S. Connecticut in 1915 and was one the *U.S.S. Potter* early in the war when it sailed in European waters. Assigned to Great Lakes, he ran the Officer Material School (training for would-be ensigns) and was the assistant and then head coach of the football team, leading them to a victory in the 1919 Rose Bowl. After the war, he returned to sea duty and was the coach of the Navy's West Coast football team in 1923. He left the Navy in 1926 and worked as a realtor. He returned to the Navy as a Commander during WWII.

'Tacoman Helped Navy Win,' *Alaska Citizen*, December 2, 1912.

'Sailors' Coach Has a Record,' *Los Angeles Times*, December 31, 1918.

'Pacific Fleet Team Will Meet Olympics,' *Oakland Tribune*, October 31, 1923.

Moffett, William Adger

Born: October 31, 1869 | | Died: April 4, 1933 | | Naval Academy '90 | | Pre-WWI: Aboard U.S.S. Charleston during Spanish-American War; Awarded Congressional Medal of Honor in 1915 while captaining U.S.S. Chester near Veracruz, Mexico | | WWI: Commander, Great Lakes Naval Station | | Post-WWI: Rear Admiral. Led the Navy's Bureau of Aeronautics from its inception in 1921 until his death in the crash of the dirigible, U.S.S. Akron

Moffett graduated from the Naval Academy in 1890. He served in the Pacific during the Spanish-American War and was awarded the Congressional Medal of Honor for his actions off Veracruz, Mexico in 1914. Later that year he took command of the new Great Lakes Naval Training Station. After the war, he commanded the *U.S.S. Mississippi* and became a proponent of integrating aviation into fleet operations. He led the Navy's Bureau of Aeronautics from its inception in 1921 until his death in the crash of the dirigible, *U.S.S. Akron*. Under his watch, the Navy's first three purpose-built aircraft carriers were launched and designs for key engines and aircraft were initiated. Despite his support for lighter-than-air ships, he is widely regarded as the "father of naval aviation."

"Gob' is Favorite Name with American Sailors,' *Jackson Daily News (MS)*, September 26, 1918.

'Captain Moffett New Director of Naval Aviation,' *Arizona Republic*, January 1, 1921.

Trimble, William F. *Admiral William A. Moffett: Architect of Naval Aviation.* Annapolis, MD: Naval Institute Press, 1994. iBook

Olcott, Herman P. ,

Born: January 1, 1879 || Died: November 3, 1929 || Yale '97-'00 || Head coach during training and first three games || WWI: Civilian

Olcott studied law at Yale, playing freshman and three years of varsity football, earning All-American honors his senior year. After graduating from Yale, Olcott was the head football coach at North Carolina for two years. He then became a partner in a New York law firm while also serving a six-year stint as head coach at NYU. During this time, he assisted Yale and Navy in periodic sessions. He moved on to coach Kansas from 1915 to 1917 before Walter Camp appointed him the athletic director at Great Lakes. Olcott coached Great Lakes for the first three games of the 1918 season, before being replaced by Lt. McReavy. Although positioned to the public that Olcott would remain involved, his role diminished and he did not travel with the team to the 1919 Rose Bowl. Olcott was freshman athletic director at Yale from 1919 to 1921 before becoming athletic director at nearby Choate School, leaving there due to ill health in 1926.

'Gobs Refused to Take Civilian Coach Seriously,' *St. Louis Star and Times*, November 5, 1918.

'H.P. 'Bo' Olcott, Yale Football Star, Dies at 49,' *Evening News (Pittsburgh, PA)*, November 5, 1929.

APPENDIX F: 1918 MARE ISLAND MARINES

The 1918 Mare Island team members were identified through three sources: 1) a newspaper article previewing the Goat Island game listing 31 Marines who suited up for the game, 2) miscellaneous newspaper articles identifying players who joined the Marines or were transferred to Mare Island after the first game, and 3) the Marine muster rolls for November and December of 1918 showing that every football player at Mare Island was moved into a specific unit (e.g., the Supply Depot or Recruit Depot). The muster rolls verify other sources and tease out which Marines were part of the team's three-week swing through the Northwest in November and December of 1918 versus those who traveled to Pasadena for the 1919 Rose Bowl.

The roster count for the 1918 Mare Island team includes 37 Marines. Several men who played for Mare Island during the 1918 season were at Mare Island during the 1917 season, but no documentation has been found indicating that any of them were involved with the team during the 1917 season.

'Marines Will Have Another Strong Team,' *San Francisco Chronicle*, September 15, 1918.

'Weatherman Runs True to Form with Dark Skies Early in the Morning,' *Oakland Tribune*, September 21, 1918.

'Marine Eleven is Here,' *Los Angeles Times*, December 28, 1918.

'Devil Dogs Are Husky,' *Los Angeles Times*, December 31, 1918.

Adams, John Q. "Babe"

Born: Unknown || Died: Unknown || Conway Hall (HS) or Dickinson (PA) || On roster for Goat Island, played halfback versus Camp Fremont, and started the 1919 Rose Bowl at left halfback || WWI: Pvt. Enlisted April 5, 1918, Discharged February 10, 1919

Information has not been found beyond Adams' time at Mare Island.

'Marines Will Have Another Strong Team,' *San Francisco Chronicle*, September 15, 1918.

'Marines May be Short-Enders in the Betting,' *San Francisco Chronicle*, December 29, 1918.

'Marines Take 17 to 0 Defeat After Great Fight, Teams Evenly Matched,' *Oakland Tribune*, January 2, 1919.

Bangs, Benton Maxwell "Biff"

Born: September 5, 1893 || Died: June 7, 1970 || Idaho State Normal - Albion '13, WSU '14-'17 || Started the last eight games of the season at left halfback, including the 1919 Rose Bowl || WWI: Pvt.

Bangs attended Albion Normal in Idaho before joining Washington State and helping them to the 1916 Rose Bowl. He was the captain, an All-Pacific Coast player, and was named to Walter Camp's All-America Top 75 in 1917. After graduation, he worked as a county agricultural agent while working on his master's degree. After the war, he managed and owned orchards. He also played for the Los Angeles Marauders in 1925 and the Los Angeles Buccaneers in 1926, and was an assistant coach at Wyoming in 1925 under Lone Star Dietz, He became a county commissioner and was a delegate to the 1956 Republican National Convention. Bangs attended the 50th anniversary of the 1916 Rose Bowl.

'W.S.C. Fans Joyful,' *Morning Register (Eugene, OR)*, September 20, 1914.

'Benton Bangs to be W.S.C. Captain,' *Eugene Guard*, January 5, 1916.

'"Bing" Bangs to Play on Marines at Mare Island,' Post Intelligencer (Seattle), November 30, 1918.

'Nixon's Lead Large, Delegation Poll Shows,' *Democrat and Chronicle (Rochester, NY)*, August 21, 1956.

Blewett, James Joseph

Born: November 15, 1898 || Died: October 16, 1982 || California Frosh '17, '19 || Started five games at right half and substituted in three other games, including the 1919 Rose Bowl || WWI: Pvt.

Blewett was the 1916 California high school shot put champion and a star on the Los Angeles Manual Arts football team. He starred on Cal's freshman football team in 1917, during which his brother and teammate, George Blewett, broke his leg and died when bone fragments entered his blood stream. Following the war, Blewett's career at Cal was hampered by injuries so he turned to high school coaching, where we led his alma mater, Manual Arts, to nine Los Angeles city championships. Midway through the string of high school titles, he was the backfield coach at UCLA where he mentored Jackie Robinson who broke the color barrier in major league baseball with the Brooklyn Dodgers. He ended his 36-year coaching career with a 225-70-16 record.

'California Freshmen Actually Died From Leg Broken in Football Game,' *Oregon Daily Journal (Portland, OR)*, October 14, 1917.

'James Blewett to Re-Enter California,' *Los Angeles Herald*, August 14, 1919.

'Just Due for UCLA's Jim Blewett', *Classic UCLA Bruins Rediscovered*, February 7, 2015. Accessed November 2, 2017.

https://lvironpigs.wordpress.com/2015/02/07/just-due-for-uclas-jim-blewett/

Bridewell, Robert "Earl"

Born: July 23, 1890 || Died: November 2, 1970 || Brazil HS (IN)

'07-'08 | | Listed on roster for the Goat Island Sailors game, but did not appear in any games | | WWI: Pvt.

Bridewell grew up in Phoenix, but attended high school in Indiana and was working as a locomotive fireman in Spokane when he enlisted. Post war, he worked for a railroad, as a salesman, and then spent most of his career working in the hydroelectric industry.

'First Practice,' *Brazil Daily Times (IN),* September 9, 1908.

Bryan, Leon Horan

Born: March 9, 1898 | | Died: December 14, 1974 | | Oregon State '15-'16 (no FB) | | Started two games at left guard and substituted in three others, including the 1919 Rose Bowl | | WWI: Pvt.

Bryan was orphaned as a child and grew up with his aunt and uncle. He attended Oregon State, but did not play football. After the war, he was in the cattle business and owned a butcher shop for more than 40 years in Yreka, California.

'Pledges Made to O.A.C. Fraternities,' *Oregon Daily Journal (Portland, OR),* October 1, 1916.

'Marine Footballers Granted Furlough,' *San Francisco Chronicle,* January 11, 1919.

'Anniversary is Observed,' *Medford Mail Tribune,* December 9, 1963.

Budd, John Walter

Born: January 14, 1899 | | Died: December 26, 1963 | | League Island '17-'18, Lafayette '20-'21, '23-'24 | | Played the full season with the League Island Marines, transferred to Mare Island and started the 1919 Rose Bowl | | WWI: Pvt., Cpl., Sgt.

Budd played the 1917 and 1918 seasons with the League Island Marines in Philadelphia and was named to Walter Camp's All-Service First Team, before transferring to Mare Island to play in the 1919 Rose Bowl. Budd was the last service Rose Bowl player in college football while playing for Lafayette in 1920 and 1921, taking a year off for academic reasons, and returning for the 1923 and 1924 seasons. By then, he was a veritable monster, tipping the scales at 240 pounds while remaining the fastest man on the team. Most important, he helped Lafayette beat Lehigh the four years he played. Budd then won an NFL championship and was All-Pro with the Frankford Yellow Jackets, before playing two more years with the Pottsville Maroons. After pro football, Budd worked in the steel mills in Bethlehem, Pennsylvania.

'Here's Eddie Mahan's Crack Eleven from League Island, Pa.,' *Washington Herald*, November 18, 1917.

'Local Marines in Game Today,' *Evening Public Ledger (Philadelphia, PA)*, January 1, 1919.

'Six Lafayette Men to Play Last Game Saturday,' *Wilkes-Barre Times Leader*, November 18, 1924.

'Johnny's Pair of Goals Beats Giants,' *Philadelphia Inquirer*, October 17, 1926,

Calhoun, Millard R.

Born: April 13, 1890 || Died: April 11, 1963 || Kent HS (WA) '10, Washington State basketball '08, Bremerton '18 || Played the full 1918 season for Bremerton before transferring to Mare Island and substituting at left halfback in the 1919 Rose Bowl || WWI· Pvt., Cpl.

Following high school, Calhoun worked in area sawmills before attending Washington State and lettering in basketball in 1908. He was working as a pipefitter's assistant when he enlisted in December 1917, was trained at Mare Island, and transferred to Puget Sound / Bremerton in March 1918, where he played football. Following Bremerton's game against Mare Island, he transferred back to Mare Island for the Rose Bowl. He was named to Walter Camp's 1918 All-Service Honorable Mention Team for his play at Bremerton. After the war, Calhoun served as a Deputy Sheriff and Sheriff of Columbia County, Washington, for several decades.

'W.S.C. Wins From Idaho,' *Pullman Herald*, February 1, 1908.

'Marines are Back from Hard Trip Badly Battered,' *San Francisco Chronicle*, December 10, 1918.

'Football,' *Oregon Daily Journal (Portland, OR)*, January 10, 1919.

Canup, Charles Emmet

Born: February 26, 1889 || Died: October 19, 1967 || DePauw football and track '11-'13 || On roster for Goat Island Sailors game, but did not appear in any games. Camp Lewis basketball coach '18 || WWI: Pvt., Cpl., transferred to Quantico for ROTC in January 1919, discharged partway through

Canup lettered in football and track at DePauw. He was a high school teacher and basketball coach in Indiana in 1914, was on the faculty and was the football and basketball coach at Billings Polytechnic College in 1915 and 1916, and was at Fergus County (MT) High School in 1917. He was Mare Island's basketball coach in December 1918 and Gonzaga's basketball coach during the 1921-1922 season. He then spent several decades teaching English at Lewis and Clark High School in Spokane.

'Chicago Next for Indiana,' *Indianapolis News*, September 29, 1913.

'Fergus County High School Loses Physical Instructor,' *Great Falls Tribune*, June 16, 1918.

'A Full Hand of Marine Basketers,' *Oakland Tribune*, December 25, 1918.

'News in Colville,' *Colville Examiner (WA)*, January 14, 1922.

Conkey, Glen Byron

Born: December 18, 1896 || Died: May 13, 1966 || La Grande (WA) '15, HS Culver Military '16 || On roster for Goat Island Sailors game, but did not appear in any games || WWI: Pvt.

Conkey was among the top high school sprinters in Washington before transferring to Culver Military Institute in Indiana. Following the war, he graduated from Washington and spent his career in credit and insurance positions.

'Conkey Will Enter Culver,' *La Grande Observer*, September 16, 1916.

'Local Men on the Marine Eleven,' *La Grande Evening Observer*, August 20, 1918.

Crosetto, Edward Francis

Born: February 6, 1897 || Died: abt. July 19, 1964 || St. Bonaventure '16, Dubuque '17, League Island '18 || Played 1918 season for League

Island before transferring to Mare Island and substituting at right guard in the 1919 Rose Bowl | | WWI: Pvt.

Crosetto played football for St. Bonaventure and Dubuque before enlisting and playing the 1918 seasons with League Island in Philadelphia He transferred with John Budd just prior to the 1919 Rose Bowl. After the war, Crosetto worked as a highway engineer and then worked in sales and engineering roles in the road material industry.

'Geneva is Beaten,' *Pittsburgh Daily Post*, October 8, 1916.

The Key 1919, Dubuque College. Accessed November 2, 2017. https://archive.org/details/key19191919unse

'Local Marines in Game Today,' *Evening Public Ledger (Philadelphia, PA)*, January 1, 1919.

Galloway, Amor S.

Born: April 25, 1899 | | Died: April 1987 | | LA Manual Arts HS '16-'17, DePauw '19, USC '21-'22 | | Started at quarterback versus Camp Fremont and Balboa Park, substituted in four other games at halfback and quarterback, including the 1919 Rose Bowl | | WWI: Pvt.

Galloway starred with Jim Blewett for Los Angeles Manual Arts in the fall of 1917, entered USC Law in the spring of 1918, and then enlisted in the Marines. After the war, he played for one year at DePauw before returning to USC. A spinal injury ended his football career in 1922. Galloway then managed an orchard, worked in sales, and moved to Calgary where he lived for thirty years.

'Marine Eleven is Here,' *Los Angeles Times*, December 28, 1918.

'Great Gridiron Twins to Come Saturday, DePauw's Pair of "Galloping Galloways",' *Courier-Journal (Louisville, KY)*, November 18, 1919.

'Record Trojan Turnout,' *Los Angeles Times*, September 16, 1921.

Gillis, Lloyd Adrian

Born: December 21, 1897 | | Died: May 25, 1942 | | WSU '16-'17, '19-'20 | | Started six games and substituted in two others, primarily at fullback. Started the 1919 Rose Bowl at fullback | | WWI: Pvt.

Gillis played two years of football at Washington State before and after the war, and was name All-Pacific Coast his last two years. After graduating, he returned to the family farm. His death-bed wish was for his friends to buy war bonds in lieu of flowers for his funeral.

Cronin, R. A. 'Marines Beat Vancouver Team by 39-0 Score,' *Oregon Daily Journal (Portland, OR)*, November 24, 1918.

'Best Fullbacks on Coast to Meet Saturday, Power of Oregon Aggies to Oppose Gillis,' *Oregon Daily Journal (Portland, OR)*, November 19, 1919.

'Three Veteran State College Players Win Coveted Recognition on All-Star Team,' *Pullman Herald*, December 3, 1920.

Associated Press. 'Instead of Flowers,' *Decatur Herald*, May 31, 1942.

Glover, Frederick Lewis

Born: July 21, 1896 || Died: October 17, 1935 || WSU '16–'17 || Substituted in two games and started six others, primarily at halfback, including the 1919 Rose Bowl || WWI: Pvt.

Glover was on the football, basketball, and track teams at Washington State before enlisting. After the war, he worked as a logging contractor for a period and then moved to Los Angeles, joining the Los Angeles Police Department in 1923. He was an assistant probation officer at the time of his death.

'Bangs, Halfback, Out of O.A.C. Game,' *Pullman Herald*, November 9, 1917.

'Fred Glover Joins Mare Island Marines,' *Pullman Herald*, August 23, 1918.

'Officer Dies in Lengthy Illness,' *Los Angeles Times*, October 19, 1935.

Hanley, LeRoy Bernard "Pat"

Born: August 21, 1896 || Died: July 20, 1966 || WSU '16–'17, '19–'20 || Started every game at right end other than Balboa Park, including the 1919 Rose Bowl || WWI: Pvt. || Post-WWI: 1ˢᵗ. Lt., Kansas National Guard || WWII: Lt. Col. In action at Guadalcanal and Saipan. Bronze Star. Wounded. Football coach of Maui Marines

Pat Hanley played football at Washington State for two years before and after the war, and was named All-Pacific Coast in 1919. He also started at third base for Washington State's baseball team. He was an assistant coach under his brother at Haskell and Northwestern, and then was head coach Boston University for eight years before rejoining the Marines. He spent some of his time during WWII in coaching roles, including winning the Central Pacific championship with the Maui Marines, but saw action on Guadalcanal and, as a Lt. Colonel, was among the first Marine officers on the beach at Saipan, where he was wounded and awarded the Bronze Star for putting out a fire on a truck loaded with explosives. He was involved in insurance sales after WWII.

The Delta. Indianapolis: The Sigma Nu Fraternity. October 1918.

'Who's Who With Cougars,' *Morning Oregonian*, November 7, 1919.

'Ex-Boston U Coach Hits Saipan Beach,' *Marine Corps Chevron (San Diego)*, July 22, 1944.

Hanley, Richard Edgar "Dick"

Born: November 19, 1895 || Died: December 16, 1970 || WSU '15-'17, 19 || Started at quarterback in seven games, but did not play versus Balboa Park or in the 1919 Rose Bowl due to influenza || WWI: Pvt. || WWII: Major, Lt. Col. including two overseas tours

Hanley played football for three years at Washington State, playing in the 1916 Rose Bowl, before joining the Marines. After being discharged, Dick Hanley was the head coach at the Haskell Institute for Indians in Kansas (1922-1926) and played in 1924 with the NFL's Racine Legion. He later took over at Northwestern (1927-1934), winning two Big Ten championships. During WWII, he led the development of a new physical training program for the Marine Corps, was in charge of combat conditioning for Marine aviation on the West Coast, and coached the El Toro Marines, a top service football team. After the war, he coached the Chicago Rockets of the All-America Football Conference, before returning to insurance sales. Bangs attended the 50th anniversary of the 1916 Rose Bowl.

'Football Title Will be Played for Wednesday,' *Oregon Daily Journal (Portland, OR)*, December 29, 1918.

'Cougars Win from Montana Eleven,' *Pullman Herald*, December 5, 1919.

'East Meets West in Bay City Battle Today,' *Los Angeles Times*, January 1, 1935.

'Dick Hanley Dies, Ex-N.U. Football Coach,' *Chicago Tribune*, December 17, 1970.

Hern, Samuel Burnett

Born: February 15, 1895 | | Died: July 17, 1978 | | Sacramento baseball (PCL) '14, Sacramento AC Rugby '14, Mare Island baseball '18 | | Started at quarterback versus St. Mary's and Bremerton | | WWI: Pvt., Cpl.

Hern played semipro and minor league baseball, as well as club rugby before the war, and played baseball for Mare Island during the spring of 1918. After the war, he primarily worked in the title insurance business, and helped manage baseball leagues, ultimately becoming the president of the semipro California League.

'School Lad Stars in Defeating the Oaks,' San Francisco Chronicle, June 27, 1914.

'Marines are Beaten 4 to 2 by Letterman,' *Oakland Tribune*, September 3, 1918.

'St. Mary's Football Snowed Under by Marines from Mare Island,' *Oakland Tribune*, November 17, 1918.

'State Loop Opens Season Tomorrow,' *Oakland Tribune*, April 2, 1938.

Hughes, Benjamin B.

Born: March 10, 1898 | | Died: May 20, 1928 | | Williamson College '15-'16 | | On roster versus Goat Island and furlough pattern indicates he traveled with the team throughout the season, including the 1919 Rose Bowl | | WWI: Pvt., Cpl.

Hughes married in Washington in 1925, but no other information was been found on his post-service life.

'Weatherman Runs True to Form with Dark Skies Early in the Morning,' *Oakland Tribune*, September 21, 1918.

'Devil Dogs Are Husky,' *Los Angeles Times*, December 31, 1918.

Lodell, Carl Allen

Born: November 16, 1896 || Died: December 10, 1955 || Oregon State '16-'17, 19 || Started all but two games at left guard, including the 1919 Rose Bowl || WWI: Pvt.

Lodell played for Oregon State for two seasons before the war and one season after the war. He then coached high school football for two years before becoming the graduate manager / athletic director at Oregon State from 1922 to 1937. He coached track at OSU in 1937. He later worked in insurance sales and was president of the Oregon AAU.

'Washington State is Victorious Over the Oregon Aggie Eleven,' *Oregon Sunday Journal*, November 11, 1917.

'Sailors Have Tough form in Marine Team,' *Quad-City Times (Davenport, IA)*, December 31, 1918.

'Oregon "Aggies" Beat Washington State by 6-0,' *San Francisco Chronicle*, November 23, 1919.

'Carl Lodell to Coach Track at Oregon State,' *Post-Register (Idaho Falls, ID)*, March2, 1937.

May, George Louis

Born: April 4, 1898 || Died: September 8, 1992 || Wisconsin basketball '16, Montana basketball '17 || On roster for the Goat Island Sailors game || WWI: Pvt.

May played high school basketball for Stevensville High School in Montana, played freshman basketball at Wisconsin during the 1916-1917 season, and played at Montana the next season. While he was on the Mare Island football team early in the season, he formed and captained Mare Island's basketball by November 1918. May ultimately become part owner of department store operated by his wife's family and was active in the running horse shows in Missoula.

'Stevensville Athlete is Star at Wisconsin,' *Daily Missoulian*, March 25, 1917.

'Marines Will Have Another Strong Team,' *San Francisco Chronicle*, September 15, 1918.

'Weatherman Runs True to Form with Dark Skies Early in the Morning,' *Oakland Tribune*, September 21, 1918.

'A Full Hand of Marine Basketers,' *Oakland Tribune*, December 25, 1918.

McGregor, Alexander Taylor

Born: September 16, 1897 | | Died: January 19, 1945 | | WSU '16 | | On roster versus Goat Island, subbed into the St. Mary's game, and furlough pattern indicates he traveled with the team throughout the season, including the 1919 Rose Bowl | | WWI: Pvt.

Alec McGregor played at Washington State before. After his discharge, he raised sheep in Washtucna, Washington.

'W.S.C. Trounces Idaho Team,' *Morning Register (Eugene, OR)*, November 5, 1916.

'St. Mary's Football Snowed Under by Marines from Mare Island,' *Oakland Tribune*, November 17, 1918.

McGregor, Robert Stewart

Born: February 20, 1898 | | Died: February 7, 1934 | | San Bernardino HS (CA) | | On roster versus Goat Island, started the Balboa Park game at full-back, and furlough pattern indicates he traveled with the team throughout the season, including the 1919 Rose Bowl | | WWI: Pvt., Cpl.

Robert McGregor was raised in Highland, California, and moved to Sacramento to work as a shipping clerk for the Southern Pacific Railroad. Following the war, he worked in San Francisco and then returned to the San Fernando area where he founded a trucking company and then worked as a truck mechanic. He died in Petaluma, California in 1934 when he was crushed by a truck he was working on.

'Personals,' *San Bernardino Sun*, November 16, 1917.

'Marines Smash Balboans,' *Los Angeles Times*, December 26, 1918.

'Highland,' *San Bernardino Sun*, December 31, 1918.

'Coroner Conducted Six Inquests,' *Petaluma Argus-Carrier*, April 2, 1934.

Miles, John Hunter

Born: August 28, 1898 || Died: January 25, 1986 || Chehalis HS (WA) '17, Washington '20-'23 || Furlough pattern indicates he traveled with the team during the second half of the season, including the 1919 Rose Bowl || WWI: Pvt.

Miles was a high school baseball star and joined the Marines shortly after graduating. After the war, he played baseball and football at the University of Washington and was a member of the 1924 Rose Bowl team. He also toured Japan with Washington's baseball team. After graduating, he was in the bonds and securities business before moving to Taylor, Texas, where he became a pecan grower and worked in banking. He was a delegate to the 1944 Republican National Convention.

'Athlete Gets Discharge,' *Oregon Daily Journal (Portland, OR)*, February 17, 1919.

'Washington Team to Start Tour in August,' *Oregon Daily Journal (Portland, OR)*, June 12, 1921.

'Data on Today's Game,' *San Bernardino County Sun*, January 1, 1924.

'Pecan Growers Organize,' *Taylor Daily Press (TX)*, March 30, 1933.

Mohr, Paul Wallace "Dinty"

Born: April 8, 1894 || Died: December 21, 1972 || The Dalles HS (OR) '11 || Substituted into four games. Two at quarterback and the other two at right end, including the 1919 Rose Bowl || WWI: Pvt., Cpl. Sgt.

Mohr played football at The Dalles High School in Oregon where he was a teammate of Hollis Huntington of the 1917 Mare Island Marines. He was working in The Dalles as a machine operator when he enlisted in July 1917. After the war, he sold cars in Eugene and then sold heavy machinery in San Francisco. He attended the 50th anniversary of 1917 Rose Bowl.

'Hood River's Team Plays Tomorrow,' *Hood River Glacier*, October 19, 1911.

'Football Title Will be Played for Wednesday,' *Oregon Daily Journal (Portland, OR)*, December 29, 1918.

'Lane Auto Company to Sell Used Cars on Certified Plan,' *Eugene Guard*, November 25, 1925.

'Want a Rebuilt Concrete Mixer?,' *Oakland Tribune*, December 16, 1942.

'Happy Reunion,' *Independent Star-News (Pasadena, CA)*, December 28, 1968.

Moore, Earl Hugh

Born: August 27, 1899 | | Died: January 16, 1967 | | None | | On roster versus Goat Island, substituted into the Vancouver Barracks game at halfback, and traveled with the team throughout the season, including the 1919 Rose Bowl | | WWI: Pvt.

Moore grew up in Minneapolis and enlisted in May 1917. After his discharge, Moore owned a ranch in Orange County, California and then worked as a police officer, becoming Chief of Police in Santa Ana.

'Army Team Routed By Marines, 39-0,' *Sunday Oregonian*, November 24, 1918.

'Officers Elected by Peace Officers,' *Santa Ana Register*, March 5, 1942.

Moran, Michael Leo,

Born: November 7, 1896 | | Died: June 29, 1951 | | Gonzaga '15-'16, WSU Frosh '17, WSU '19-'21 | | Started at right guard in every game other than Bremerton, including the 1919 Rose Bowl | | WWI: Pvt.

Moran played at Gonzaga before transferring to Washington State before enlisting. After the war, he returned to Washington State, lettered in 1920 and 1921, and was named an Honorable Mention All-American by Walter Camp in 1921. He then played for the Multnomah Athletic Club. He entered the sporting goods business and was a high school and college referee before perishing in an apartment fire in 1951.

'Two Washington College Stars Now with Mare Island Football Team,' *Oakland Tribune*, September 15, 1918.

'Four Cougars Draw Honorable Mention,' *Pullman Herald*, December 23, 1919.

'Mike Moran Dies in Oswego Fire,' *Bend Bulletin*, Jun 29, 1951.

Pearson, Elmer Alvin

Born: July 9, 1896 | | Died: September 14, 1978 | | None | | Played in the Camp Fremont game and traveled with the team throughout the season, including the 1919 Rose Bowl | | WWI: Pvt.

Pearson grew up in Santa Clara, California. He spent most of his career as a laborer in the oil industry in Long Beach and later worked as a carpenter.

'Santa Clara's Service Men Have Reception,' *Oakland Tribune*, March 11, 1919.

'Paradise Found: A Well-Run Park,' *Los Angeles Times*, June 8, 1975.

Pike, Homer B. "Roscoe

Born: April 30, 1897 | | Died: September 14, 1978 | | Gonzaga '15-'16 | | Started every game at right tackle other than versus Bremerton, including the 1919 Rose Bowl | | WWI: Pvt.

Following the war, Pike played for the Keel Club in Los Angeles in 1919 and was a player coached for the San Francisco Athletic Club in 1920 and 1921. He spent most of his career as a driller in the oil industry in Long Beach.

'Catholics Win From Idaho U.,' *Statesman Journal (Salem, OR)*, October 15, 1915.

'Mare Island Plays Barracks Men Today,' *Morning Oregonian*, November 23, 1918.

'Olympic Club Signs California and Stanford Stars for Game,' *San Francisco Chronicle*, November 23, 1920.

Risley, Jacob Swayne "Jake"

Born: July 31, 1893 | | Died: June 27, 1948 | | Oregon '14-'16 | | Team

*captain who started at center in very game, including the 1919 Rose Bowl | |
WWI: Private*

Risley was and All-Northwest player for Oregon in 1915 and 1916,
and played in the 1917 RB. He also played basketball for Oregon in
1916 and 1917. Following his discharge, Risley worked in the automotive business, sold machine tools, and then became a road
contractor.

'Coach Bedzek Thinks He is Lost, *Los Angeles Times,* December
24, 1916.

'Famous Marines Will Play with Fort Baker Today,' *San Francisco
Chronicle,* November 2, 1918.

'Mountain to be Leveled in Big Dynamite Blast, *Statesman Journal
(Salem, OR),* July 26, 1931.

Shanedling, Nate

*Born: April 21, 1897 | | Died: June 10, 1958 | | St. Mary's '17, '19 | |
Started six games at left tackle and substituted into another. Injuries kept him out
of the 1919 Rose Bowl | | WWI: Pvt.*

Shanedling played for St. Mary's in 1917 and was the captain of the
St. Mary's football team in 1919. He then played and managed
minor league baseball on the Pacific Coast and in the Midwest.
After his baseball career, Shanedling joined his brothers as
publishers of *The Argonaut,* a San Francisco-based political magazine, and several trade publications. Shanedling was also active in
War Bond fundraising activities during WWII.

'These are St. Mary's Boys Who Play A.C.,' *San Francisco Chronicle,*
November 10, 1917.

'Teufelhunden to Throw Strong Fire at Winged M,' *Oregon Daily
Journal (Portland, OR),* November 17, 1918.

'Sports,' *Decatur Herald,* April 15, 1923.

'Brother of C.S. Shanedling Dies,' *Santa Cruz Evening News,*
September 4, 1929.

Shannon, Leo M.

Born: May 4, 1898 || Died: April 15, 1979 || WSU Frosh '21, WSU '22-'23 || Started five games at tackle and substituted into two other games. || WWI: Pvt., Cpl.

Shannon enlisted in the Marines in November 1917. After his release, Shannon entered Washington State in 1921 and played two more years before opening a business that supplied boxes and packaging material to the fruit-packing business.

'Local Men to be with Grid Team,' *Oregon Daily Journal (Portland, OR)*, August 1, 1918.

'La Grande Squad is Shaping Up Better,' *Daily East Oregonian*, October 1, 1920.

'Cougars Give Cal A Surprise,' *Salt Lake Telegram*, October 28, 1923.

Shoemaker, Jr., Frank Marion

Born: March 1, 1899 || Died: February 5, 1995 || East Denver HS '15-'17, Colorado College '20 || On roster versus Goat Island and traveled with the team throughout the season, including the 1919 Rose Bowl || WWI: Pvt.

Shoemaker enlisted in the Marines two days after graduating from high school. Following his discharge, he coached high school football in Ellis, Kansas, then entered Colorado College and was named 2nd team All-Rocky Mountain in 1920. He then worked as a chauffeur and drove a cab before managing the bus station for the next several decades in Greeley, Colorado. Shoemaker was the last surviving service Rose Bowl player when he passed away in 1995.

'Marines Will Have Another Strong Team,' *San Francisco Chronicle*, September 15, 1918.

'Two Utah Stars Awarded Places,' *Ogden Standard-Examiner*, December 1, 1920.

'Who's Who in Local Business Circles,' *Greeley Daily Tribune*, February 21, 1930.

Steers, William Henry "Bill"

Born: April 13, 1897 || Died: December 20, 1957 || Oregon '16 '17, '19-20 || Started eight games at halfback and fullback and started the 1919

Rose Bowl at quarterback || WWI: Pvt. || WWII: Lt. Commander, US Navy. Recreation Director, 7th Fleet, in the Admiralty Islands

Steers was the consensus All-Pacific Coast Conference in 1917 and 1919, and made Walter Camp's All-American Third Team in 1919. And played in the 1920 Rose Bowl. He began the 1920 season as a high school coach, but left early in the season for his final year of play at Oregon. He played for the Multnomah Athletic Club in 1921 and 1922. Steers then earned in master's degree at Columbia and became the coach at California of Pennsylvania from 1929 to 1937. Steers became as assistant football coach at Columbia while earning his Ph.D., and then was a Lt. Commander in the Navy during WWII, serving as the 7th Fleet Recreation Director in the Admiralty Islands. After WWI, he became head of the Department of Physical Education at the University of Miami.

'California Coaches Say There is No Chance,' *Morning Register (Eugene, OR),* November 16, 1917.

'Bill Steers, U.S.M.C. Stops on Way South,' *Eugene Guard*, January 31, 1919.

'Every Member of Eleven is an Oregonian,' *Oakland Tribune*, December 31, 1919.

'William Steers Athletic Coach at California,' *Daily Courier (Connellsville, PA),* August 29, 1929.

'30,000 Yanks at a Time Disport at Island Resort,' *Chicago Daily Tribune,* January 1, 1945.

Stendal, Hugh Alvin "Al"

Born: August 2, 1892 || Died: November 22, 1942 || None || Started the Camp Lewis game at left guard and substituted into the St. Mary's and Vancouver Barracks games. || WWI: Pvt.

Stendal was working as a grocery clerk when he enlisted in the Marines within a week of America declaring war. He spent August 1917 to August 1918 stationed at the Tiburon coaling station in San Francisco Bay before returning to Mare Island. After his discharge, he worked as a grocery clerk, sold radio advertising, real estate, and cars, and worked at the Kaiser Shipyard in Vancouver, WA.

'Army Team Routed By Marines, 39-0,' *Sunday Oregonian*, November 24, 1918.

'Marines Footballers Granted Furlough,' *San Francisco Chronicle*, January 11, 1919.

'Ex-Marine Will Take Chance on Jaunt to Paris,' *Eugene Guard*, July 14, 1927.

Tescher, Lionel Jay

Born: June 7, 1899 | | Died: October 30, 1960 | | Unknown | | Listed on roster for the Goat Island, but did not travel with the team on the Northwestern or Rose Bowl trips | | WWI: Pvt.

After the war, Tescher attended college in Denver and then moved to Southern California where he sold cars, became a sales manager, and owned a motor replacement business in the 1940s before returning to selling cars.

'Weatherman Runs True to Form with Dark Skies Early in the Morning,' *Oakland Tribune*, September 21, 1918.

'Lionel Tescher,' *Press Democrat (Santa Rosa, CA)*, November 1, 1960.

Tubbs, Burnam Alonzo

Born: May 11, 1892 | | Died: June 9, 1975 | | Stafford HS (KS) '13 | | Listed on roster for Goat Island, substituted at tackle versus Vancouver Barracks and his furlough pattern indicates he traveled with the team throughout the season, including the 1919 Rose Bowl | | WWI: Pvt.

Tubbs played football and basketball at Stafford High School in Kansas. He was teaching and farming in Kansas when he enlisted. After the war, he entered the auto sales business, ultimately owning a Chevrolet dealership in Arkansas City, KS.

'Hutchinson and Stafford Highs Battle to a Tie,' *Hutchinson News (KS)*, October 7, 1912.

'Army Team Routed By Marines, 39-0,' *Sunday Oregonian*, November 24, 1918.

'Tubbs,' Catholic Advance (Wichita, KS), June 12, 1975.

Wilson, Elmer August

Born: February 16, 1897 | | Died: October 26, 1970 | | Unknown | | Listed on roster for Goat Island game and traveled with team on Northwestern trip, but did not travel to the 1919 Rose Bowl | | WWI: Pvt.

Wilson worked in fuel sales for twenty years after his discharge and worked for a shipbuilder during WWII.

'Weatherman Runs True to Form with Dark Skies Early in the Morning,' *Oakland Tribune*, September 21, 1918.

Zimmerman, Clarence Arthur

Born: August 13, 1896 | | Died: June 21, 1975 | | Washington State '14-'17 | | Zimmerman started every game at left end, including the 1919 Rose Bowl | | WWI: Pvt.

Zimmerman played at Washington State from 1914 to 1917, played in the 1916 Rose Bowl, earned All-Northwest honors in 1915 and 1917, and was the captain of the 1917 team. After his discharge, he coached the Washington State freshmen in 1919 and then began a career as a high school teacher, coach, principal and superintendent of schools. Zimmerman attended the 50th anniversary of the 1916 Rose Bowl.

'Zimmerman to Captain 1917 Football Team,' *Pullman Herald*, December 15, 1917.

'Two Football Stars Want to Join Marines,' *San Francisco Chronicle*, August 21, 1918.

'Prominent Alumni,' *Evergreen, State College of Washington*, March 19, 1927.

'Rivals in 2nd Rose Bowl Meet Again,' *Chicago Tribune*, January 2, 1956.

'Zimmerman No Ordinary Athlete,' *Hilltopics, Washington State University*, October 1975.

Coaches and Administrators

Coovert, Lynn Baker

Born: March 9, 1889 | | Died: October 21, 1944 | | Athletic Director | |

Pre-WWI; First Sgt., Lt. Marine section of Oregon Naval Militia | | WWI: 2ⁿᵈ Lt., 1ˢᵗ Lt., Captain

Coovert passed the Oregon bar exam in 1911 and practiced law until WWI. He helped organize the Marine section of the Oregon Naval Reserve in 1915, becoming its First Sergeant. He was promoted to Lieutenant days before America entered the war. When the Oregon Naval Militia was federalized, he was stationed at Puget Sound Naval Yard, then completed officer training at Quantico before being promoted and sent to Mare Island. After the war, Coovert practiced law in Portland and was accused of filing false veterans' loan applications. He was a salesman for a Portland loan company in 1925 and was selling concrete machinery in Boston in 1930, but no further information is available.

'Coovert is Naval Militia Lieutenant,' *Oregon Daily Journal (Portland, OR)*, April 2, 1917.

Two Sisters Dead of Influenza, *Oregon Daily Journal (Portland, OR)*, November 8, 1918.

'Two Cubes Got Dietz in "Dutch",' *Oregon Daily Journal (Portland, OR)*, February 16, 1919.

'Nine Applications Made,' *Bend Bulletin*, February 21, 1923.

Dietz, William Henry "Lone Star"

Born: August 17, 1884 | | Died: July 20, 1964 | | Friends '04, Carlisle '09-'11 | | Head Coach | | WWI: Civilian

Although his origins remain controversial, Dietz claimed he was born of a white father and Native American mother, though he was raised by his father and white "stepmother," and learned his true identity as a young adult. He became immersed in Native American culture, attending Carlisle Indian School and playing football for and coaching with Pop Warner. As a first-year head coach, his Washington State team won the 1916 Rose Bowl. Dietz was tried in 1919 for draft dodging based on his Native American heritage being questioned. He later coached at Purdue, Louisiana Tech, Wyoming, and Albright. He also coached the Boston Redskins in 1933 and 1934. He was inducted into the College Football Hall of Fame in 2012.

'Lone Star Dietz, Coach of the Marines' Football Team,' *San Francisco Chronicle*, October 6, 1918.

Waggoner, Linda M., '*On Trial, The Washington R*dskins Wily Mascot,*' Lone Star Dietz,' *Montana Magazine of Western History,* Spring 2003.

Benjey, Tom. *Keep A-Goin', The Life of Lone Star Dietz,* Carlisle, PA: Tuxedo Press, 2006.

Riner, Clarence Chrisman "C.C."

Born: December 11, 1887 || Died: May 28, 1960 || Naval Academy ex '08 || WWI: Capt., Major, Mare Island Post Adjutant

Riner was a fourth year at the Naval Academy in 1907 when he was recommended for expulsion and subsequently resigned. (He missed getting back to his ship due to certain interactions with "chorus girls.") By 1909, as a 2nd Lt. in the Marines, he was reviewed by the retirement board, but was allowed to remain in the Marines. His subsequent hospitalization for venereal disease offers a hint at the reason for his review. He was then assigned to Panama and the Philippines, before returning to the States in October 1917. Assigned to Mare Island, he was promoted to Major and named the post Adjutant, assisting the commander in administrative functions. Riner was a key character witness for Lone Star Dietz during his 1919 trial for draft dodging. He served in the Dominican Republic after the war, before leaving the Marines. He later worked in insurance sales and engineering.

'Army and Navy Gossip,' *Washington Post*, October 31, 1909.

'Life of an United States Marine While in Training,' *Daily Deadwood Pioneer-Times (deadwood, SD)*, August 9, 1918.

'Major Clinton, Now Lieutenant-Colonel,' *Oakland Tribune*, September 13, 1918.

'Marine Officers Say Dietz Not Guilty,' *Pullman Herald*, February 21, 1919.

BIBLIOGRAPHY AND CITATIONS

The bibliography is organized first by the major topics that cross chapter boundaries and then by subheading within each chapter. The sources listed by major topic are not cited repeatedly in the bibliography. To assist those interested in references for individual players, most bibliographic information for players and coaches is cited in the Profile sections of the Appendix rather than in the Bibliography.

Regarding newspaper citations:

- Unless otherwise noted, all newspaper articles were accessed through newspapers.com.
- Articles from the *Great Lakes Bulletin* were accessed at: https://digital.library.illinois.edu/collections/8d40fbd0-84bc-0133-a845-0050569601ca-0
- A handful of newspaper articles were clippings for which the original publisher is unknown. For these, the university or other archive sources are noted.
- While the articles were first accessed at various times in the research process, access to all articles was verified between November 1 and 2, 2017. The access dates for newspaper

articles are not listed repeatedly in the Bibliography and Profiles sections.

World War I

American Battle Monuments Commission. *American Armies and Battlefields in Europe, A History, Guide, and Reference Book.* Washington, D.C.: U.S. Government Printing Office, 1938.

Keene, Jennifer D. *The United States and The First World War.* London and New York: Routledge Taylor and Francis Group, 2014. iBook

Kennedy, David M., *Over Here, The First World War and American Society.* Oxford University Press. 2004.

U.S. Army in WWI

The United States Army in the World War, 1917-1919, Organization of the American Expeditionary Forces, Vol. I. Washington, D.C.: Center of Military History, United States Army, 1988.

91st Division

Burton, Harold H. *600 Days' Service, A History of the 361st Infantry Regiment of the United States Army.* Portland: James, Kern & Abbot, 1921.

Calkins, John Umberto. *History of the 347th Machine Gun Battalion.* Oakland, CA: Horwinski Company, 1919.

Henderson, Alice Palmer. *The Ninety-First, The First at Camp Lewis.* Tacoma, WA: John C. Barr, 1918.

Hubbell, Irving D. *The Book of Company C, 316th Field Signal Battalion.* San Francisco: Ingrim-Rutledge, 1919.

Little, George C. *History of the 316th Engineers, A Record of Military Operations from August 1917 to April 1919.* 316th Engineers, 1919.

Meldrum, T. Ben and Axel A. Madsen. *A History of the 362nd Infantry Regiment.* Ogden & Salt Lake. A. L. Scoville Press. 1920.

Sumner, Maj. Lee, *The 362nd Infantry in the First Phase of the Meuse-*

Argonne Offensive, September 26-29. Student Paper, Advance Course, Infantry School, Fort Benning, GA.

The Story of the 91st Division. San Francisco: 91st Division Publication Committee, 1919.

Tibbals, Mirton L. and Melvin T. Solve. *Nine Month Overseas, Being the History of "H" Company.* 361st Infantry, 91st Division, 1919.

Wilson, Bryant and Lamar Tooze. *With the 364th Infantry in America, France, and Belgium.* New York, The Knickerbocker Press, 1919.

War Department Annual Reports, 1919, Volume I, Part 3, Report of the Surgeon General. Washington: Government Printing Office, 1920.

U.S. Marine Corps in WWI

McClellan, Maj. Edwin N. *The United States Marine Corps in the World War.* Washington, D.C.: Historical Branch, United States Marine Corps, 1920.

Simmons, Brig. Genl. Edward H. and Col. Joseph H. Alexander. *Through The Wheat, The U.S. Marines in World War I.* Annapolis: Naval Institute Press, 2008. iBook

U.S. Navy in WWI

Gleaves, Vice Adm. Albert. *A History of the Transport Service, Adventures and Experiences of United States Transports and Cruisers in the World War.* New York: George H. Doran Company, 1921.

Spector, Ronald H. *At War At Sea, Sailors and Naval Combat in the Twentieth Century.* New York: Viking Penguin, 2001.

Preface

[1] Beckett, John W. The Game That Saved the Rose Bowl, *Salt Lake City Tribune*, December 30, 1967.

Hibner, John Charles. *The Rose Bowl, 1902-1929, A Game-by-Game History of Collegiate Football's Foremost Event, from Its Advent Through Its Golden Era.* Jefferson, NC: McFarland and Company. 1993.

Gems, Gerald R. 'For Pride, Profit, and Patriarchy; Football and the Incorporation of American Cultural Values,' American Sports History Series, No. 16, Lanham, MD: Scarecrow Press, 2000.

'Spotlight, Bellotti Ducks BCS Controversy,' *Los Angeles Times*, January 4, 2002.

Flynn, Daniel J. *The War on Football, Saving America's Game*. Washington, D.C.: Regnery Publishing, 2013.

Gems, Gerald R. and Linda J. Borish, and Getrude Pfister. *Sports In America, From Colonization to Globalization, 2ⁿᵈ Edition*. Champaign, IL: Human Kinetics, 2017.

Introduction

De Camp, James, *'Crowd of Twenty Five Thousand Sees Marines Whip Army Eleven'*, Los Angeles Times, January 2, 1918.

Chapter 1: From The Towns And The Tanks

The World They Lived In

United States Census Bureau. *History, Urban and Rural Area*. Accessed November 2, 2017.

https://www.census.gov/history/www/programs/geography/urban_and_rural_areas.html

United States Census Bureau. *Population of the 100 Largest Urban Places: 1910*. Accessed November 2, 2017.

https://www.census.gov/population/www/documentation/twps0027/tab14.txt

'Tallest Building In The World Title Holders Through History,' *World of Architecture*, Accessed November 2, 2017.

http://www.worldofarchi.com/2013/01/tallest-building-in-world-tittle.html

Bakke, Gretchen. *The Grid, The Fraying Wires Between Americans and Our Energy Future*. New York: Bloomsbury, 2016.

Moore, Stephen and Julian L. Simon. *It's Getting Better All The Time, 100 Greatest Trends of the Last 100 Years*. Washington, D.C.: CATO Institute, 2000.

'Emzy Lynch,' *Arizona Republic*, July 6, 1979.

The Rules of the Game

Davis, Parke H. *Football, The American Intercollegiate Game*. New York: Charles Scribner's Son. 1911.

Des Jardins, Julie. *Walter Camp, Football and the Modern Man*. New York: Oxford University Press. 2015. iBook

Herget, James E., *American Football, How the Game Evolved*, CreateSpace Independent Publishing Platform, 2013.

Nelson, David M. *Anatomy of a Game: Football, the Rules, and the Men Who Played the Game*, University of Delaware Press, 1994.

Revsine, Dave. *The Opening Kickoff, The Tumultuous Birth of A Football Nation*, Guilford, CT: Lyons Press, 2014. iBook

Warner, Glenn S. *Football for Players and Coaches*, Carlisle, PA, 1912.

Football in Context

Goldfield, Edwin D. (ed.). *Statistical Abstract of the United States*. Department of Commerce, Washington, D.C.: Government Printing Office. 1955.

Snyder, Thomas D. (ed.). *120 Years of American Education, A Statistical Portrait*. U.S. Department of Education. National Center for Education Statistics. 1993.

Thwing, Charles Franklin. *The American Colleges and Universities in the Great War, 1914-1919*. New York: Macmillan. 1920.

The 1917 Chinook of Washington State College, Pullman: Junior Class of the Year 1916. 1917.

'Thirty-Five "W" Men in Uniform', *Seattle Daily Times*, December 16, 1917.

The Development of the Rose Bowl

Hibner, *The Rose Bowl*.

Samuelson, Rube. *The Rose Bowl Game, A Revealing History of Football's Annual Classic*. New York: Doubleday. 1951.

'Chicago's Eleven,' *San Francisco Call*. December 24, 1894.

'Post Season Football Game,' *Pittsburgh Press*, December 29, 1901.

'New Year's Football,' *Los Angeles Times*, November 2, 1902.

'Wisconsin to Come,' *Los Angeles Times*, November 26, 1902.

'Pasadena Brevities,' *Los Angeles Times*, December 1, 1902.

'Michigan and Stanford Match,' *San Bernardino Sun*, November 4, 1905.

'Season Almost Ended,' *Los Angeles Times*, December 4, 1903.

'Stanford Declines to Play,' *Los Angeles Herald*, November 17, 1905.

'Eleven May Go West,' Evening Statesman (Walla Walla, WA), November 10, 1908.

'Famous Wright Brothers May Give Demonstration,' *Los Angeles Herald*, December 8, 1908.

'Yost Machine at Tournament,' *Los Angeles Times*. November 3, 1909.

'May Bring Wolverines,' *Los Angeles Times*, November 3, 1915.

'Brown University and Pullman are to Meet,' *San Francisco Chronicle*, November 18, 1915.

Chapter 2: The Yanks Are Coming

America Enters the Great War

Beamish, Richard J. and Francis A. March. *America's Part in the World War, A History of the Full Greatness of our Country's Achievements*. New York: The John C. Winston Co., 1919.

Cameron, Rebecca Hancock. *Training to Fly: Military Flight Training, 1907-1945*. Air Force History and Museums Program, 1999.

Preparing the Army

Brief Histories of Divisions, U.S. Army, 1917-1918. Washington, D.C.: U.S. Army General Staff, War Plans Division, 1921.

Coffman, Edward M. *The War To End All Wars, The American Military Experience in World War I.* New York: Oxford University Press, 1968. iBook

Lengel, Edward G. *To Conquer Hell, The Meuse-Argonne, 1918, The Epic Battle that Ended the First War.* New York: Henry Holt and Company, LLC, 2008. iBook

Spickelmier, Maj. Roger K. *Training of the American Soldier During World War I and World War II.* (Thesis for Master of Military Art and Science, Army Command and General Staff College, Fort Leavenworth, 1987).

Official Bulletin, U.S. Committee on Public Information, August 25, 1917.

The United States Army in the World War, 1917-1919, Organization of the American Expeditionary Forces, Vol. I. Washington, D.C.: Center of Military History, United States Army, 1988.

Preparing the Marines

McClellan, *The United States Marine Corps in the World War.*

MCB Quantico - A Brief History of the Marine Corps Base and the Marine Corps Development and Education Command. Quantico: Marine Corps Development and Education Command, 1976.

Condon, Maj. Genl. John P. *U.S. Marine Corps Aviation.* Washington, D.C., Deputy Chief of Naval Operations (Air Warfare) and the Commander, Air Systems Command, 1987.

Fuller, Capt. Steve M. and Graham A. Cosmas. *Marines in the Dominican Republic, 1916-1924.* Washington, D.C.: U.S. Marine Corps, History and Museums Division, 1974.

Preparing the Navy

Fry, Lt. Henry J., ed. *The War Record of the U.S.S. Henderson.* Brooklyn: Eagle Press, 1919.

Gleaves, Vice Adm. Albert. *A History of the Transport Service, Adventures*

and Experiences of United States Transports and Cruisers in the World War.
New York: George H. Doran Company, 1921.

World War I Era Naval Aviation Stations. Accessed November 2, 2017.

https://bluejacket.com/usn-usmc_avi_ww1_air_fields.html

Sitz, Capt. H. W., *A History of U.S. Naval Aviation, Technical Note No. 18, Series of 1930.* Washington, D.C.: U.S. Government Printing Office, 1930.

Athletics in America

Des Jardins, *Football and the Modern Man.*

Watson, Nick J. and Weir, Stuart and Friend, Stephen. 'The Development of Muscular Christianity in Victorian Britain and beyond, ' *Journal of Religion and Society*, 7, 2005.

Athletics in the Camps

'Athletics Help Morale of Uncle Sam's Fighting Men, Help to Keep Soldiers Fit,' *Pittsburgh Press,* October 27, 1918.

[2] 'Athletics Real Backbone of Good Soldiers, Says Edwards,' *New York Sun,* October 26, 1918.

[3] Camp, Walter. 'Football of 1891.' *Outing*, November 1891.

Des Jardins, *Football and the Modern Man.*

[4] 'Military Leaders Say Sports Makes the Army,' *Los Angeles Times,* December 29, 1917.

Summary of World War Work of the American Y.M.C.A., The International Committee of the Young Men's Christian Association, 1920.

Chapter 3: Every Son of Liberty

Nelson, *Anatomy of a Game.*

The 1917 Mare Island Team

McClellan, *The United States Marine Corps in the World War.*

'War Time Growth of Mare Island,' *Recruiter's Bulletin*, April 1919.

'Bruin Fodder Devoured by Marine Team,' *San Francisco Chronicle*, September 16, 1917.

'California Varsity is Given 27-0 Beating by Marines, Blewetts Star for Freshmen,' *Oakland Tribune*, September 16, 1917.

'California Varsity Given Another Beating by Marines,' *Oakland Tribune*, September 30, 1917.

'Marines Once More Repeat on California,' *San Francisco Chronicle*, September 30, 1917.

'Mare Island Beats California, Score: 26-0,' *Recruiters' Bulletin*, November 1917.

'Marines Beat Olympics,' *Oakland Tribune*, October 15, 1917.

'Marines Beat Olympic Club on Gridiron,' *San Francisco Chronicle*, October 15, 1917.

'Football Stars on Marine Corps Team,' *Recruiters' Bulletin*, November 1917.

'Base-Ball!' *Memphis Daily Appeal*, May 9, 1882.

'Mr. Brown is Bright Star on the Field,' *San Francisco Chronicle*, October 22, 1917.

'Marines Win Tough Fight From Saints', *Oakland Tribune*, October 22, 1917.

[5] 'Bedzek Sees No Chance of Winning,' *Sunday Oregonian*, October 7, 1917.

'Oregon May Play Marines', *Sunday Oregonian*, October 7, 1917.

'Crack Oregon Team to Battle Oregon U. Here Next Saturday,' *Oregon Daily Journal*, October 28, 1917.

[6] 'Marines Here for Game with Oregon,' *Morning Oregonian*, November 3, 1917.

[7] Richardson, James J. 'Marines' Machine Wins From Oregon,' *Sunday Oregonian*, November 4, 1917.

'Mare Island Marines Roll Up 27-0 Score on Oregon's Varsity,' *Oregon Daily Journal*, November 4, 1917.

The Camp Lewis Team

Meldrum, *A History of the 362nd Infantry Regiment*.

Henderson, *The Ninety-First, The First at Camp Lewis*.

'Men Who are Helping to Train and Bring Recreation to Men at Camp,' *Spokesman Review (Spokane, WA)*, December 2, 1917.

Stanton, William L., General Index to Compiled Service Records of Volunteer Soldiers Who Served During the War with Spain. Accessed November 2, 2017.

https://www.fold3.com/image/1/309317347

'Football Part of Training at Camp Lewis These Days,' *Santa Ana Register*, October 3, 1917.

'Conference Teams Will Open Season,' *Morning Oregonian*, October 13, 1917.

'Washington State Meets Army Eleven', *Eugene Guard*, October 13, 1917.

Souvenir Football Program, Officers, 362nd Inf., vs. Washington State College, October 13, 1917. Accessed November 25, 2017.

http://content.libraries.wsu.edu/utils/getfile/collection/wsu_fb/id/366/filename/339.pdf.

'Officers Tie Dietz', *The Sunday Oregonian*, October 14, 1917.

'It's No Easy Job to Select Army Eleven,' *Tacoma Times*, October 17, 1917.

'Officers' Eleven Barely Able to Hold W.S.C. to Tie Game,' *Pullman Herald*, October 19, 1917.

'Army Elevens Tie,' *Sunday Oregonian*, October 28, 1917.

'Camp All-Stars Win', *Sunday Oregonian*, November 4, 1917.

Chapter 4: The Old Red-White-And-Blue

'Everett May is of Belief Army Will Lose Game,' *Oregon Daily Journal,* November 4, 1917.

'Marines Football Men Guests Here,' *Eugene Guard,* November 5, 1917.

'Marine Football Team in Training in Eugene,' *Morning Register (Eugene, OR),* November 6, 1917.

'Army Team Grinds,' *Morning Oregonian,* November 8, 1917.

'Rooters Rally While Players Practice Hard,' *Seattle Daily Times,* November 8, 1917. (Not sourced from newspapers.com.)

'Marines Defeat Army Team, 13-0,' *Sunday Oregonian,* November 11, 1917.

'Marines from Mare Island Defeat Sammies,' *Statesman Journal,* November 10, 1917.

Finishing the Regular Season

'Trojans Will Tackle Marines November 24,' *Los Angeles Times,* November 14, 1917.

'Camp Lewis Wins,' *Sunday Oregonian,* November 18, 1917.

'Club Boys Lose Army Game, 10-3,' *Oregon Daily Journal,* November 18, 1917.

'Indians Play at Camp Lewis,' *Statesman Journal,* November 21, 1917.

'No Thanksgiving Day Game in Tacoma Stadium,' *Tacoma Times,* November 21, 1917.

'Soldiers Defeat Reds', *Sunday Oregonian,* November 25, 1917.

'Marines Down U.S.C. 34-9,' *Los Angeles Times,* November 25, 1917.

'McKay Leads Army to Easy Victory Over Indian Team,' *Seattle Daily Times,* November 26, 1917. (Not sourced from newspapers.com.)

'Rain Will Not Interfere with Army-Navy Game,' *Tacoma Times,* November 29, 1917.

'Camp Lewis is Victor,' *Morning Oregonian*, November 29, 1917.

'Army Winner Over Jackies,' *Seattle Star*, November 30, 1917.

'Camp Lewis Plays Last Game,' *Tacoma Times*, December 6, 1917.

'Camp Lewis Boys Give Enemy a Trimming,' *San Francisco Chronicle*, December 9, 1917.

The 1918 Rose Bowl Selection Process

Daye, John. *Encyclopedia of Armed Forces Football: The Complete History of the Glory Years*. Haworth, NJ: St, Johann Press. 2014.

'West to Meet East in Gridiron Battle,' *Honolulu Advertiser*, September 26, 1917.

'Refuse Offer to Play at Pasadena,' *Los Angeles Times*, November 1, 1917.

'Trip to California for USAAC Eleven,' *Allentown Leader*, November 8, 1917.

'Marines Will Play,' *Daily Oregonian*, November 24, 1917.

'Sanctions Show,' *Oakland Tribune*, November 25, 1917.

'Coast Teams May Meet Jan. 1, Pasadena May Not Invite East,' *Oregon Daily Journal*, November 27, 1917.

'Allentown Ambulance Corps Team to Play on Coast New Year's Day,' *Pittsburgh Daily Post*, November 29, 1917.

[8] '4,000 Children to Participate,' *San Bernardino County Sun*, November 29, 1917.

'Georgetown Drives Back USAACS and Gains a 27-0 Victory on Muddy Field,' *Washington Post*, November 30, 1917.

'91st Team Is Believed Fit for Pasadena,' *San Francisco Chronicle*, December 1, 1917.

'Grant Goes Over Top For Custer,' *Chicago Daily Tribune*, December 2, 1917.

'Rose Tournament Football Date Still in Doubt,' *Los Angeles Times*, December 2, 1917.

'Teams Picked for Rose Fete,' *Los Angeles Times,* December 9, 1917.

'Camp Lewis to Play Marines New Year's Day,' *Oregon Daily Journal,* December 9, 1917.

[9] 'Tournament of Roses Tomorrow,' *Los Angeles Times,* December 31, 1917.

Chapter 5: Take It On The Run

'Tournament of Roses Theme is Patriotism,' *Santa Ana Register,* November 30, 1917.

'Tournament of Roses Tomorrow,' *Los Angeles Times,* December 31, 1917.

'Myriads of Nation's Emblems Add Color To Pasadena's Fete,' *Los Angeles Times,* January 2, 1918.

'War Flavor the Predominant Feature in Parade,' *San Bernardino Sun,* January 2, 1918.

Preparing for the Game

'Camp Team Gets Daily Practise,' *Tacoma Times,* December 13, 1917.

'Camp Lewis Sending a Real Team to Pasadena,' *Los Angeles Times,* December 16, 1917.

'Camp Lewis Team on Way Tonight,' *Tacoma Times,* December 21, 1917.

'Teams Speed for Pasadena,' *Los Angeles Times,* December 23, 1917.

'How Camp Lewis Sizes Up,' *Los Angeles Times,* December 27, 1917.

'91st Division Football Squad Off to Meet Marines,' *Over The Top (Camp Lewis, WA),* December 29, 1917. (Not sourced from newspapers.com.)

'Army and Navy Team Work Out in Pasadena,' *Morning Register (Eugene),* December 30, 1917.

'Dope On the Marines,' *Los Angeles Times,* December 31, 1917.

'How Camp Lewis Sizes Up,' *Los Angeles Times*, December 31, 1917.

'Mare Island Squad is Favored by Dopesters,' *Los Angeles Times*, December 31, 1917.

The Game

'Marines Win From Camp Lewis, 19-7,' *Oregonian*, January 2, 1918.

'Crowd of Twenty Five Thousand Sees Marines Whip Army Eleven,' *Los Angeles Times*, January 2, 1918.

[10] Richardson, James J. 'Marines Win From Camp Lewis, 19-7,' *Oregonian*, January 2, 1918.

'Marines Retain Title of Coast Champs,' *Oregon Daily Journal*, January 2, 1918.

'Marines Undisputed Coast Champions of Gridiron,' *Oakland Tribune*, January 2, 1918.

'Pasadena Game Play By Play,' *Los Angeles Times*, January 2, 1918.

'Injury List of Yesterday's Game,' *Los Angeles Times*, January 2, 1918.

Chapter 6: We're Coming Over

American Troops Over There

Gleaves, *History of the Transport Service*.

McClellan, *The United States Marine Corps in the World War*.

German Spring Offensive

Kennedy, *The First World War and American Society*.

McClellan, *The United States Marine Corps in the World War*.

Château-Thierry and Belleau Wood

[11] Simmons, Brig. Genl. Edward H. and Col. Joseph H. Alexander. *Through The Wheat, The U.S. Marines in World War I*. Annapolis: Naval Institute Press, 2008. iBook

Battle of Soissons

History of the Sixth Regiment, United States Marines. Tientsin, China, The Tientsin Press, Ltd. 1928.

Wilson, Robert H. in United States Marine Corps Muster Rolls. Accessed on November 2, 2017.

http://search.ancestry.com/cgi-bin/sse.dll?
db=marine_muster&gss=sfs28_ms_db&new=1&rank=1&msT=1&
gsfn=Robert%20H.&gsfn_x=1&gsln=Wilson&gsln_x=1&msidd=9
&msidm=6&msidy=1917&MSAV=1&uidh=5m5

'*Michigan Men Who Have Received the Croix de Guerre and Other Military Honors,*' Michigan Alumnus, May 1919. Ann Arbor: The Alumni Association of the University of Michigan Publishers.

Buss, William K. in United States Marine Corps Muster Rolls. Accessed on November 2, 2017.

http://search.ancestry.com/cgi-bin/sse.dll?
_phsrc=dKH64&_phstart=successSource&usePUBJs=true&db=ma
rine_muster&gss=angs-
d&new=1&rank=1&msT=1&gsfn=William%20K.&gsfn_x=1&gsln
=Buss&gsln_x=1&MSAV=1&uidh=5m5&gl=&gst=

Getting Over There

'City Opens Arms to Yanks; Cheering Crowds Express Welcome to Visiting Troops,' *Winnipeg Tribune,* June 25, 1918.

Simmons, *Through The Wheat.*

The Story of the 91st Division.

Meldrum, T. Ben and Axel A. Madsen. *A History of the 362nd Infantry Regiment.*

Facts and Fancies of 363rd Field Hospital Co. 316th Sanitary Train, 91st Division, U.S.A., 1917-1919, 1919.

'Assistant Navy Secretary Overseas,' *Oxnard Courier,* July 21, 1918.

'(Witness Weeps) – The Tragedy of Allan O. Monson,' *ba-ckground,* July 25, 2014. Accessed November 2, 2017. *http://ba-kground.com/witness-weeps-tragedy-alvin-o-monson/*

St. Mihiel

Meldrum, *A History of the 362nd Infantry Regiment.*

Chapter 7: Send The Word To Beware

College Enrollments and the Students' Army Training Corps

Aydelotte, Frank. *Final Report of the War Issues Course of the Students' Army Training Corps.* Washington: War Department, 1919.

Students' Army Training Corps Regulations, 1918, Special Regulations No. 103. Washington, D.C.: Government Printing Office, 1918.

Thwing, *The American Colleges and Universities in the Great War.*

'Colleges to Train Pupils for Service in Armed Forces,' *Pittsburgh Press,* July 28, 1918.

[12] 'Restrictions on Intercollegiate Athletics,' *Brooklyn Daily Eagle,* September 15, 1918.

'Big Eastern Colleges Hold Up Grid Sport Awaiting War Department Order,' *Akron Evening Times,* September 23, 1918.

Eckersall, Walter. 'New Order Will Cause Big Games to be Cancelled,' *Chicago Daily Tribune,* September 30, 1918.

[13] 'Rules to Guide Football Teams are Made Known,' *Lima News (OH), October 4, 1918.*

The Influenza Pandemic

Barry, John M. *The Great Influenza, The Epic Story of the Greatest Plague in History.* New York: Penguin Books, 2004.

Byerly, Carol R. '*The U.S. Military and the Influenza Pandemic of 1918–1919.*' Public Health Reports 125, (Supplement 3), 2010.

Byerly, Carol R. *Fever of War: The Influenza Epidemic in the U.S. Army in World War I.* New York University Press, 2005. iBook

The Great Lakes Team

Buzzell, Francis, *The Great Lakes Naval Station, A History,* Boston: Small, Maynard and Company, 1919.

Gogan, Roger S. *By Air, Ground & Sea.* Kenosha, WI: Great Lakes Publishing, 2013.

'Grid Call Made at Great Lakes,' *Lansing State Journal*, August 12, 1918.

'Great Lakes Gridders Face Stiff Program,' *Times Herald (Port Huron, MI)*, August 21, 1918.

'Gridiron Stars Galore in Great Lakes Squad,' *Indianapolis News*, August 24, 1918.

'1,700 Bandsmen at Great Lakes,' *Wichita Beacon*, October 4, 1918.

'Football Men to Sleep and Eat Together,' *Great Lakes Bulletin*, September 21, 1918.

'George Kent McCauley Biographical Data,' *FamilySearch.org*. Accessed November 2, 2017.

https://familysearch.org/photos/artifacts/4483711

The 1918 Mare Island Team

Benjey, Tom. *Keep A-Goin', The Life of Lone Star Dietz,* Carlisle, PA: Tuxedo Press, 2006.

[14] 'Zimmerman No Ordinary Athlete,' *Hilltopics*, Washington State University, October 1975.

'Marine Football Team of Mare Island is After the Championship of America,' *Oakland Tribune*, October 6, 1918.

'Lone Star Dietz, Coach of the Marines' Football Team,' *San Francisco Chronicle*, October 6, 1918.

'Thousands Expected to be On Hand for Opening Game of Football Season,' *Oakland Tribunes*, September 17, 1918.

'American Style of Playing Develops the Best Kind of Fighters', *Oakland Tribune*, September 19, 1918.

'Parade, Bands and Yells Will Feature in Game,' *Oakland Tribune*, September 20, 1918.

'Weatherman Runs True to Form with Dark Skies Early in the Morning,' *Oakland Tribune*, September 21, 1917.

Hauser, Herbert. 'Superior Team Work is Best Answer to Shutout Which Sailors Suffered,' *Oakland Tribune*, September 22, 1918.

Wilcox, Barbara, '"Fremont, The Flirt",' Unearthing Stanford's World War I Battleground,' *Sandstone & Tile*, Stanford Historical Society, Spring-Summer 2013.

'Marines Will Play Fremont Football Team,' *San Francisco Chronicle*, September 26, 1918.

'Marines Have Easy Time at Camp Fremont,' *Oakland Tribune*, September 28, 1918.

'Prospects for Football Not Bright,' *San Francisco Chronicle*, September 29, 1918.

'St. Mary's is Stronger for the Gridiron Game,' *San Francisco Chronicle*, October 3, 1918.

Snyder, Capt. Thomas L., MC, USNR (Ret.), 'The Great Flu Crisis at Mare Island Navy Yard, and Vallejo, California' *Navy Medicine*, September-October 2003.

'77 Jackies Perish,' *Logansport Pharos-Tribune (IN)*, September 26, 1918.

'No Flu at the Navy-Buckeye Game Today,' *Daily Times (Davenport, IA)*, September 28, 1918.

Henger, George Y. '22 Players Will Make Trip to Iowa City,' *Great Lakes Bulletin*, September 26, 1918.

Eckersall, Walter. 'Great Lakes Team Downs Iowa in Football Opening, 10-0,' *Chicago Tribune*, September 29, 1918.

Doyle, Francis J. 'Station Gridiron Eleven Opens Season with Win Over Iowa,' *Great Lakes Bulletin*, September 30, 1918.

Chapter 8: And We Won't Come Back

[15] Pershing, John J. *My Experiences in the World War, Volume II*, Pickle Partners Publishing, 2013.

Ayres, L.P. *The War with Germany. A Statistical Summary.* Washington: Government Printing Office, 1919.

The Meuse-Argonne Offensive

91ˢᵗ Division Summary of Operations in the World War, American Battle Monuments Commission, United States Government Printing Office. 1944.

Dykes, George P. *10 Years Ago with the 362nd Infantry, Compiled from Extracts of Orders, Memos and Diaries.* Granger, Farley E. File, 91st Division World War I Veterans Survey, U.S. Army Heritage and Education Center, Carlisle, PA.

Granger, Farley E. U.S. Army Field Message Book. Granger, Farley E. File, 91st Division World War I Veterans Survey, U.S. Army Heritage and Education Center, Carlisle, PA.

Hutchinson, William N.L. *Report of Operations of 362nd Infantry during the Offensive, 26th to 29th September (both dates inclusive).* December 1, 1918. Granger, Farley E. File, 91st Division World War I Veterans Survey, U.S. Army Heritage and Education Center, Carlisle, PA.

Lengel, *The Meuse-Argonne.*

May, Capt. Thomas E. *Operations of Company I, 362nd Infantry, 91st Division, in the Meuse-Argonne Offensive, September 26-October 3, 1918,* (Student paper, The Infantry School, Fort Benning, GA, 1933.

[16] McDonald, J.B. and Parker John H. *Letter Exchange, February 1919.* Granger, Farley E. File, 91st Division World War I Veterans Survey, U.S. Army Heritage and Education Center, Carlisle, PA.

Officers Killed, Gassed, Wounded in Action, HQ, 362ⁿᵈ. Granger, Farley E. File, 91st Division World War I Veterans Survey, U.S. Army Heritage and Education Center, Carlisle, PA.

Palmer, Frederick. *Our Greatest Battle, The Meuse-Argonne.* New York: Dodd, Mead and Company, 1921.

Parker, John H., Report of Operations of the 362nd Infantry during the Offensive, 25th to 29th September. Granger, Farley E. File, 91st Division World War I Veterans Survey, U.S. Army Heritage and Education Center, Carlisle, PA.

Rubin, Richard. *The Last of the Doughboys: The Forgotten Generation and*

Their Forgotten World War. New York: First Mariner Books. 2013. iBook

The Fifty-Ninth - It Came From Brooklyn, *Liaison, The Courier of the Big Gun Corps*, June 7, 1919.

Woodcock, Maj. Bryan L. *The 91st Infantry in World War I, Analysis of an AEF Division's Efforts to Achieve Battlefield Success.* (Thesis, Fort Leavenworth, KS), 2013.

[17] *United States v. Alvin O. Monson*, U.S. Circuit Court of Appeals, 9th District, No. 8237, gov.uscourts.ca9.08237.b.01

Yockleson, Mitchell. *Forty-Seven Days: How Pershing's Warriors Came of Age to Defeat the Germans in World War I*. New York: NAL Caliber. 2016.

[18] Blatt, Heiman. *Sons of Men, Evansville's War Record*, Abe P. Madison, 1920.

'Angelenos Capture Hun Battery,' *Los Angeles Times*, November 3, 1917.

'Captain Howard Angus Back,' *Los Angeles Times*, May 8, 1919.

Death of Worsham Real Loss to 91st, Unknown newspaper, 91st Division World War I Veterans Survey, Worsham, Elijah W. File, U.S. Army Heritage and Education Center, Carlisle, PA.

[19] 'Honor Roll,' *The Stanford Illustrated Review*, Palo Alto: The Alumni Association of Leland Stanford Junior University, 1919.

The Battle of Blanc Mont Ridge

Addenda Roll AEF, 1 January 1918 to 31 July 1919, Volume One A-K. U.S. Marine Corps, Accessed November 2, 2017. https://www.ancestry.com/interactive/1089/T977_146-0089?pid=1890361&backurl=http://

Camp Lewis Players Elsewhere in France

'Boys Sorry They Didn't Get Crack at Germans,' *Oregon Daily Journal*, February 3, 1919.

The Mare Island Marines in the War

United States Marine Corps. *A Brief History of the 9th Marines*, Washington, D.C: USMC, Revised 1967.

Van Wyen, Adrian O., *Naval Aviation in WWI*, Washington D.C.: Chief of Naval Operations, 1969.

White, Maj. Taylor P. *U.S. Marine Corps Operations in Nicaragua from 1927 to 1933*, (Thesis for Master of Military Studies, Marine Corps University. Quantico, VA), 2011.

Santelli, James S. *A Brief History of the 7th Marines*. Washington, D.C.: History and Museums Division, Headquarters, U.S. Marines Corps, 1980.

Chapter 9: Show Your Grit

'East Vs. West When Great Lakes Meets Pitt Saturday,' *Chicago Tribune*, October 1, 1918.

'Pitt Squad Cut, Warner Picks Men,' *Pittsburgh Post-Gazette*, October 3, 1918.

'Have Won 28 Games in a Row,' *Pittsburgh Press*, October 4, 1918.

'Disappointed in Having Game Cancelled,' *Great Lakes Bulletin*, October 7, 1918.

'Great Lakes Proves No Match for Pittsburgh in Practice Skirmish,' *Washington Times*, November 2, 1918.

'Football Teams Loses Two Regulars,' *Great Lakes Bulletin*, October 11, 1918.

'Great Lakes Defeats Illini,' *Decatur Herald*, October 13, 1918.

'Great Lakes is Victor over Illinois in Hard-Fought Game, 7-0,' *St. Louis Post-Dispatch*, October 13, 1918.

Yenger, George H. 'Illinois Holds Great Lakes Eleven to 7 to 0 Victory at Urbana,' *Great Lakes Bulletin*, October 12, 1918.

'Stagg Gridders Take Oath For Service Today,' *Chicago Tribune*, October 1, 1918.

'Half Dozen Regulars Will Tank Maroons,' *Indianapolis News*, October 15, 1918.

'Dobson is Lost to Great Lakes Eleven,' *Great Lakes Bulletin*, October 15, 1918.

'Chicago is Passing Up Grid Clash,' *Oregon Daily Journal*, October 18, 1918.

Eckersall, Walter. 'Purple-Great Lakes Game Treat for Gridiron Fans Today,' *Chicago Daily Tribune*, October 26, 1918.

Eckersall, Walter. 'Purple and Great Lakes Elevens Battle to Scoreless Tie,' *Chicago Daily Tribune*, October 27, 1918.

Young, Fred H. 'Northwestern and Great Lakes Battle to a Scoreless Tie,' *Great Lakes Bulletin*, October 28, 1918.

'Darkness Bothers Aggies Practice,' *Lansing State Journal*, October 29, 1918.

'Lieut. M'Reavy Named Head Coach,' *Great Lakes Bulletin*, October 29, 1918.

'Billikens Decline to go to Chicago,' *St. Louis Post-Dispatch*, October 31, 1918.

'Great Lakes Shifts Lineup,' *Chicago Daily Tribune*, November 5, 1918.

'Contest is Assured,' *Indianapolis Star*, November 8, 1918.

'Notre Dame Holds Great Lakes Team to 7-7 Score,' *South Bend News-Times*, November 10, 1918.

'Notre Dame 11 Battles Gobs to 7-7 Contest,' *Indianapolis Star*, November 10, 1918.

'Great Lakes and Notre Dame Battle to 7-7 Tie Saturday,' *Great Lakes Bulletin*, November 11, 1918.

'Marine Football Team of Mare Island is After the Championship of America,' *Oakland Tribune*, October 6, 1918.

'Orders Given for Oakland Grippe Fight,' *Oakland Tribune*, October 11, 1918.

'Marines Game Off Till Nov.,' *Oregon Daily Journal,* October 8, 1918.

'Influenza Spreading Over Entire Nation,' *San Francisco Chronicle,* October 17, 1918.

'Football Get Its Hard Jolts This Season,' *Oakland Tribune,* October 23, 1918.

'Emergency Measure Hits All Persons,' *San Francisco Chronicle,* October 25, 1918.

'Health Chief Urges Full Precautions,' *San Francisco Chronicle,* October 26, 1918.

'Famous Marines Will Play with Fort Baker Today,' *San Francisco Chronicle,* November 2, 1918.

'Marines Pile Up Big Score at Fort Baker,' *San Francisco Chronicle,* November 3, 1918.

'Captain of Marines Gives 'Bear' Talk,' *Morning Oregonian,* November 5, 1918.

'Vancouver Will Clash with Reds,' *Oregon Daily Journal,* November 7, 1918.

'Season Longer for Teams in Coast Games,' *Salt Lake Herald-Republican,* November 18, 1918.

Chapter 10: Show The Hun

'J.C. Burgard is Wounded,' *Morning Oregonian,* November 16, 1918.

'Lieut. Dorris is Witness to Fall of His Comrades,' *Oregon Daily Journal,* December 20, 1918.

'Lieutenant Burgard Formerly with 91st is Back Again,' *Oregon Daily Journal,* January 16, 1919.

'Ben Dorris Safe in United States,' *Eugene Guard,* February 9, 1919.

'Twice Wounded 'U' Grad Here Visiting,' *Eugene Guard,* February 11, 1919.

Piper, Edgar B. *Somewhere Near The War.* Portland: The Morning Oregonian, 1919.

'Jaw Shot Off But Dorris Didn't Know', *Corvallis Gazette-Times,* April 18, 1919.

'Sergt. Bandini Wounded in Action,' *Los Angeles Herald,* October 31, 1918. Accessed November 2, 2017.

http://cdnc.ucr.edu/cgi-bin/cdnc?a=d&d=LAH19181031.2.241

HQ, 362nd, Officers Killed, Gassed, Wounded in Action.

Armistice and Demobilization

Sparrow, John C., *History of Personnel Demobilization in the United States Army.* Washington, D.C.: Department of the Army, 1952.

'Paul Dobson Has Returned,' *Lincoln Evening Journal,* November 25, 1918.

'Cornhuskers of 1918,' *Daily Nebraskan,* November 28, 1918.

'Pikers Rank with Big Ten Leaders, Figure Indicate,' *St. Louis Post-Dispatch,* December 9, 1918.

Chapter 11: It's Over, Over There

'Great Lakes to Meet Rutgers at Ebbets Field in Brooklyn', *Great Lakes Bulletin,* November 12, 1918.

'Colored Star to Play at Ebbets Field,' *Brooklyn Daily Eagle,* November 12, 1918.

'Great Lakes Goes East,' *Oshkosh Daily Northwestern,* November 13, 1918.

'Great Lakes Team has Many Stars', *Central New Jersey Home News (New Brunswick, NJ),* November 15, 1918.

'Great Lakes Eleven Humbles Sanford's Great Machine,' *Brooklyn Daily Eagle,* November 17, 1918.

'Fall of Rutgers Biggest Surprise in Many Seasons,' *Evening Public Ledger (Philadelphia),* November 18, 1918.

'All Minds on Driscoll,' *Baltimore Sun*, November 18, 1918.

'All Eyes on Annapolis Game Saturday,' *Great Lakes Bulletin*, November 19, 1918.

'New Team Will Face Annapolis Eleven,' *Great Lakes Bulletin*, November 20, 1918.

'Football Gives Bachman 2 Big Moments; Great Lakes Figures in Both,' *Detroit Free Press*, March 11, 1947.

[20] Hibner, *The Rose Bowl, 1902-1929.*

'Missed Field Goal and Fumble Result in Academy's Defeat,' *Capital (Annapolis)*, November 25, 1918.

'Navy Believes Season Championship Will Be Decided by Saturday's Game,' *Washington Times*, November 20, 1918.

'Statistics on the Rival Football Teams Today At Annapolis,' *Baltimore Sun*, November 23, 1918.

'Great Lakes Triumphs in Spectacular Clash Over Navy Team, 7-6,' *Washington Times*, November 24, 1918.

'Freak Tackle At Annapolis Puzzles Officials,' *Chicago Tribune*, November 25, 1918.

'Eielson Sprints 103 Yards for Touchdown,' *Great Lakes Bulletin*, November 25, 1918.

'Bonehead Play of Football is Made by Middy,' *Muncie Evening Press*, November 25, 1918.

'Referee Tells Real Story of Midshipmen Saunders' Queer Tackle In Great Lakes Battle,' *Democrat and Chronicle (Rochester, NY)*, December 1, 1918.

'1954 Cotton Bowl: Dicky Maegle – Tommy Lewis Tackle Play,' Accessed November 2, 2017.

https://www.youtube.com/watch?v=eSteCSinjTs

'Move Purdue to Evanston Gridiron', *Great Lakes Bulletin*, November 30, 1918.

'Great Lakes Guns Reduce Purdue; Score 27-0,' *Chicago Sunday Tribune*, December 1, 1918.

'Gobs Hit Stride in Third Quarter and Bowl Over Purdue Eleven, 27-0,' *Great Lakes Bulletin*, December 2, 1918.

Mare Island Returns to Action

'Zimmerman No Ordinary Athlete,' *Hilltopics*, Washington State University, October 1975.

'Bangs is County Farmer,' *Oregon Daily Journal*, December 26, 1917.

'Bangs Joins Marines,' *Vancouver Daily World*, October 31, 1918.

'Marines Defeat St. Mary's, 34-7,' *San Francisco Chronicle*, November 17, 1918.

'St. Mary's Football Snowed Under by Marines from Mare Island,' *Oakland Tribune*, November 17, 1918.

'Two Sisters Dead of Influenza,' *Oregon Daily Journal*, November 8, 1918.

'Multnomah Goes Full Speed Ahead in Work for Aggie Thursday', *Oregon Daily Journal*, November 25, 1918.

'Marines Will Meet Vancouver Saturday at Vaughn Street Park,' *Oregon Daily Journal*, November 22, 1918.

'Army Team Routed By Marines, 39-0,' *Sunday Oregonian*, November 24, 1918.

Cronin, R. A. 'Marines Beat Vancouver Team by 39-0 Score,' *Oregon Daily Journal*, November 24, 1918.

'Marines Making Ready,' *Morning Oregonian*, November 25, 1918.

'"Devil Dogs' to Meet Army Eleven Today,' *Morning Oregonian*, November 28, 1918.

'Doughboys of Sea Win 16-0 Fight,' *Oregon Daily Journal*, November 29, 1918.

'Camp Lewis Beaten by Marines, 16-0,' *Morning Oregonian*, November 29, 1918.

'Idaho is Bewildered by Marine's Speed,' *Sunday Oregonian,* December 1, 1918.

'Marines Romp Off with Navy by 89-0,' *Oregon Daily Journal,* December 7, 1918.

'Marines Have Walkover with Camp Perry Eleven,' *Morning Register (Eugene, OR),* December 7, 1918.

'Injuries and Glory Cover Mare Island Team,' *Oakland Tribune,* December 10, 1918.

1919 Rose Bowl Selection Process

'Marines Play Aviators Here,' *San Francisco Chronicle,* November 12, 1918.

'Football Tourney to Decide Team to Tackle Great Lakes,' *Oakland Tribune,* November 26, 1918.

'Undefeated Teams Play,' *Los Angeles Times,* November 26, 1918.

'Solve This Grid Puzzle,' *Los Angeles Times,* December 3, 1918.

'Biography, General James Harold Doolittle,' Accessed November 2, 2017. *http://www.15thaf.org/BIOs/Doolittle.htm*

'Play Tie Contest,' *Sun Bernardino Sun,* December 8, 1918.

'Injuries and Glory Cover Marine Team,' *Oakland Tribune,* December 10, 1918.

'Marines Have Good Material in Their Backfield,' *San Francisco Chronicle, December 12, 1918.*

[21] Hughes, Ed. R. 'Sea Soldiers Going to Game in High Style,' *San Francisco Chronicle,* December 14, 1918.

'Rockwell is Loser Balboa,' *San Bernardino Sun,* December 15, 1918.

'Balboa Whips Rockwell,' *Los Angeles Times,* December 15, 1918.

'Flyers Make Game Finish, But Lose Out,' *Oakland Tribune,* December 15, 1918.

'Mare Islanders Winners Over Mather,' *San Bernardino County Sun,* December 15, 1918.

'Marines Wallop Mather,' *Los Angeles Times*, December 15, 1918.

'Marines Win From Aviators, 30-13,' *Sunday Oregonian*, December 15, 1918.

'Three Elevens in the Running,' *Los Angeles Times*, December 15, 1918.

'Balboa Would Play Marines,' *Los Angeles Time*, December 16, 1918.

'Funny Mixup in North,' *Los Angeles Times*, December 20, 1918.

'Marines Forced to Meet Balboa Park,' *Morning Oregonian*, December 21, 1918.

'Marines Decline to Meet Balboa Squad,' *Sunday Oregonian*, December 22, 1918.

'Marines Seek Boost in Ante,' *Los Angeles Times*, December 23, 1918.

'Balboa Tars Full of Fight,' *Los Angeles Times*, December 25, 1918.

'Marines Play Balboa Park Today,' *San Francisco Chronicle*, December 25, 1918.

'Balboa Trimmed by Marines' Eleven,' *Morning Oregonian*, December 26, 1918.

'Marines Just Manage to Win From Sailors,' *San Francisco Chronicle*, December 26, 1918.

'Marines Prove Championship Their Property,' *Statesman Journal*, December 26, 1918.

'Marines Smash Balboans,' *Los Angeles Times*, December 26, 1918.

'Marines Have Close Call,' *Morning Oregonian*, December 27, 1918.

'Local Marines in Game Today', *Evening Public Ledger (Philadelphia, PA)*, January 1, 1919.

Chapter 12: The Drums Rum-Tumming

'Station Squad is Granted Rest This Week,' *Great Lakes Bulletin*, December 3, 1918.

'Strong Station Eleven Blanks Seventh Regiment Team, 26 to 0,' *Great Lakes Bulletin,* December 17, 1918.

'Great Lakes on Last Practice,' *Chicago Daily Tribune,* December 18, 1918.

'Great Lakes Grid Players Spend Xmas on Drill Field,' *Chicago Daily Tribune,* December 26, 1918.

'Picking of Officials is Last Detail of Pasadena Game,' *Los Angeles Times,* December 27, 1918.

'Marine Eleven is Here,' *Los Angeles Times,* December 28, 1918.

'Stage Set for Rose Fete,' *Los Angeles Times,* December 29, 1918.

'Marines Bring in Three Eastern Stars for Game,' *Great Lakes Bulletin,* December 31, 1918.

'Odds on Betting in Favor Great Lakes,' *Nevada State Journal,* December 31, 1918.

'Devil Dogs Are Husky,' *Los Angeles Times,* December 31, 1918.

'All Have Been Through Mill,' *Los Angeles Times,* December 31, 1918.

'Lakes Gridders and Coast Team Ready to Fight,' *Chicago Tribune,* January 1, 1919.

The Game

'Ball Is Climax to Festivities,' *Los Angeles Times,* January 2, 1919.

Eckersall, Walter. 'Attacks in Air Reduce Marines of Mare Island,' *Chicago Tribune, January 2, 1919.*

'Game is Far More Even than the Score Shows; Marines Fought,' *San Francisco Chronicle,* January 2, 1919.

'Great Lakes Is A Winner Over Marines in Football,' *San Bernardino County Sun,* January 2, 1919.

'Great Lakes Wins From Mare Island,' *Morning Oregonian,* January 2, 1919.

'Gobs The Best Machinc,' *Los Angeles Times,* January 2, 1919.

'How The Battle Was Fought,' *Los Angeles Times,* January 2, 1919.

'Mighty Tars Crush The Marines,' *Los Angeles Times,* January 2, 1919.

'Half of Mare Island Team on Bench with Flu New Year's Day,' *Eugene Guard,* January 4, 1919.

'Out-of-Town Society,' *Los Angeles Times* January 5, 1919.

'Gridiron Champs Go on Brief Leaves,' *Great Lakes Bulletin,* January 10, 1919.

Eckersall, Walter. 'The Great Lakes Trip as Told by "Eckie" Himself,' *Great Lakes Recruit,* March 1919.

Sparrow, John C. *History of Personnel Demobilization in the United States Army.* Washington D.C.: Department of the Army, 1952.

Thompson, Garry L. *Army Downsizing Following Work War I, World War II, Vietnam, and a Comparison to Recent Army Downsizing,* (Master's Thesis, Fort Leavenworth), 2002.

Chapter 13: Hurry Right Away

The Waiting Games

[20] *Summary of World War Work of the American Y.M.C.A.,* The International Committee of the Young Man's Christian Association, 1920.

Terret, Thierry. *The Military "Olympics" of 1919.* Journal of Olympic History, Vol. 14, No. 2, August 2006.

Heading Home

Enderlin, Dean A. *Corporal George J. Enderlin in World War.* Accessed November 2, 2017.

http://www.deanenderlin.com/family/stories/CPL-GJE-WWI.pdf

HQ, 362nd, Officers Killed, Gassed, Wounded in Action.

Taps

American Battle Monuments Commission. *American Armies and Battlefields in Europe.*

Wilson, Robert H. burial location. Accessed November 2, 2017.

https://www.abmc.gov/node/501744

Worsham, Elijah W. burial location. Accessed November 2, 2017.

https://www.abmc.gov/node/331045

Gard, Frank J. burial location. Accessed November 2, 2017. https://www.abmc.gov/node/328817

Hurlburt, Ralph J. burial location. Accessed November 2, 2017.

https://www.findagrave.com/cgi-bin/fg.cgi?
page=gr&GSln=hurlburt&GSfn=ralph&GSbyrel=all&GSdyrel=all
&GSob=n&GRid=57192275&df=all&

Chapter 14: To Have Had Such A Lad

The College Game

Schmidt, Raymond. *Shaping College Football, The Transformation of an American Sport, 1919-1930.* Syracuse University Press, 2007.

The Military

MCB Quantico - A Brief History of the Marine Corps Base and the Marine Corps Development and Education Command. Quantico, VA: Marine Corps Development and Education Command, 1976.

Daugherty III, Leo J., *Pioneers of Amphibious Warfare, 1898-1945, Profiles of Fourteen American Military Strategists.* Jefferson, NC: McFarland and Company, Inc., 2009.

Sparrow, *History of Personnel Demobilization in the United States Army.*

Thompson, *Army Downsizing Following Work War I, World War II, Vietnam.*

ILLUSTRATIONS

Most illustrations are period postcards from the author's personal collection. Citations are not provided for the postcards.

The maps were created for this book by Phillip E. Brown. Most are adaptations of maps found in: American Battle Monuments Commission. *American Armies and Battlefields in Europe, A History, Guide, and Reference Book.* Washington, D.C.: U.S. Government Printing Office, 1938. Phillip E. Brown also created the *91ˢᵗ Division in Meuse-Argonne Offensive* map. The map is adapted from the Zone of Action, 91ˢᵗ Division, Meuse-Argonne map found in: Sumner, Maj. Lee, *The 362nd Infantry in the First Phase of the Meuse-Argonne Offensive, September 26-29.* (Student Paper, Advance Course, Infantry School, Fort Benning, GA.)

The tables showing team schedules, rosters, and post-WWI athletic and military service information were created by MJ Brown. The information in the tables is consolidated from many sources that contain conflicting information. The information shown is based on the author's judgment. All significant information sources are listed in the Bibliography or the Profiles section.

Squatting quarterback: Mahan, Edward, *How To Play The Backfield*, Pamphlet. Compliments of The Draper-Maynard Co., c. 1918.

Pop Warner football play diagrams: Warner, Glenn S., *Football for Players and Coaches*, Carlisle, PA, 1912.

1923 Rose Bowl ticket stub: Author's personal collection.

Western shore of Mare Island and the Marine Barracks. Courtesy: Mare Island Museum, Vallejo, CA.

1917 Mare Island team picture: 'Football Stars on Marine Corps Team,' *Recruiters' Bulletin*, November 1917.

Football program cover and 362nd Officers team picture: Souvenir Football Program, Officers, 362nd Inf., vs. Washington State College, October 13, 1917. Courtesy: Manuscripts, Archives, and Special Collections, Washington State University.

Camp Lewis team practice or scrimmage. Courtesy: Walter P. Hollywood family.

Camp Lewis team picture: Originally published by Goodrich New Bureau. 'Fighting Footballers from Camp Lewis, Ready for Marines', *San Francisco Chronicle*, December 30, 1917. Courtesy: U.S. Army, Lewis Army Museum, Joint Base Lewis-McChord

1918 Rose Bowl game action shot: Tournament of Roses

Influenza Deaths by Day chart was created using figures from: *Officers and Enlisted Men of the United States Naval Service Who Died During the World War*. Washington, D. C.: Bureau of Navigation of the Navy Department, 1920. Accessed on November 2, 2017. http://www.naval-history.net/WW1NavyUS-CasualtiesChrono1918-09Sep1.htm

Mare Island-Goat Island ticket: Author's personal collection

Mare Island versus Camp Fremont game: Wasco County Pioneer Association and Columbia Gorge Discovery Center.

U.S. Army Field Message, September 29, 1918, 5:35 P.M.: Capt. Farley E. Granger's Field Message Book: Capt. Farley E. Granger Field Message Book: 91st Division World War I Veterans Survey, United States Army Heritage and Education Center, Carlisle, PA.

Great Lakes football team, Harry Eielson in football uniform, and

Great Lakes practicing field goals: '*Station Machine Which Won Coast-To-Coast Gridiron Championship*,' *Great Lakes Recruit*, January 1919.

1918 Mare Island Marines composite. Courtesy: Manuscripts, Archives, and Special Collections, Washington State University.

Rockwell Field-Balboa Park game program cover: Author's personal collection.

Great Lakes team visiting movie set, 1919 Rose Bowl officials, and 1919 Rose Bowl game images: 'The Great Lakes Trip as Told by "Eckie" Himself,' *Great Lakes Recruit*. March 1919.

321st Quartermaster Labor Battalion digging graves at Fère-en-Tardenois in December 1918. Courtesy: Oise-Aisne American Cemetery, American Battle Monuments Commission.

1933 San Diego Marines football schedule: Author's personal collection.

INDEX

The pages numbers in the Index are based on the print version of the book. Those reading the book in electronic format can use the search function to find key words.

(v1.1)

FIELDS OF FRIENDLY STRIFE

The Doughboys and Sailors of the WWI Rose Bowls

Set in the context of the evolving game of football and America's mobilization for WWI, *Fields of Friendly Strife* tells the story of the players and teams from the military training camps of WWI that played in the 1918 and 1919 Rose Bowls. We follow the Camp Lewis and Mare Island teams through the 1917 season, culminating in the 1918 Rose Bowl, before the players complete their training and ship to Europe, seeing action at Belleau Wood, the Meuse-Argonne, and in Flanders. Back home, a new set of servicemen train for war while playing in the 1918 season, which is upended by the federalization of America's colleges and the Spanish Flu. By season's end, teams from the Great Lakes and Mare Island training camps battle in the 1919 Rose Bowl, completing one of the most remarkable periods in the history of American football. *Fields of Friendly Strife* follows these men after the war, tracing their impact on the game of football—including the development of the NFL—as well as America's military.

+ + +

TIMOTHY P. BROWN is the author of *Fields of Friendly Strife* and its companion blog, www.fieldsoffriendlystrife.com. Combining 25 years of research experience with the insight of a former college football coach, Tim artfully blends the familiar and the strange to provide insight into the evolution of football, the Rose Bowl, and the American experience during the WWI era. Deeply researched, *Fields of Friendly Strife* is a fun and informative read for fans of military and football history.

Empty nesters, Tim and his wife, Carolyn, live in southeast Michigan, where she lets him collect Rose Bowl memorabilia.

Cover design: Robin Locke Monda

Top cover photo:
Two American soldiers run towards a bunker. H. D. Girdwood, United States Library of Congress Prints and Photographs division.

Background photo:
Laura Lefurgey-Smith/Unsplash.com

Camp Lewis team photo:
U.S. Army, Lewis Army Museum, Joint-Base Lewis-McChord

Author photo: MJ Brown

ISBN 978-0-9995723-2-0

90000

9 780999 572320

SPINE

FIELDS OF FRIENDLY STRIFE

TIMOTHY P. BROWN

FRONT COVER

FIELDS OF FRIENDLY STRIFE

The Doughboys and Sailors of the WWI Rose Bowls

TIMOTHY P. BROWN

www.ingramcontent.com/pod-product-compliance
Lightning Source LLC
Chambersburg PA
CBHW070917150426
42812CB00047B/851